Th[illegible] [illegible] Gentiles

St Paul and the Church of the Gentiles

St Paul and the Church of the Gentiles

BY

WILFRED L. KNOX

CAMBRIDGE

at the University Press

MCMLXI

PUBLISHED BY
THE SYNDICS OF THE CAMBRIDGE UNIVERSITY PRESS
Bentley House, 200 Euston Road, London, N.W. 1
American Branch: 32 East 57th Street, New York 22, N.Y.

First published 1939
Reprinted 1961

First printed in Great Britain at the University Press, Cambridge
Reprinted by offset-lithography by Bradford and Dickens, London, W.C. 1

PRAESIDI SOCIIS ET SCHOLARIBUS
COLLEGII SANCTAE ET
INDIVIDUAE TRINITATIS
IN ACADEMIA OXONIENSI:
NEC NON
CUSTODI SOCIIS ET SCHOLARIBUS
AULAE MARIAE DE VALENTIA
IN ACADEMIA CANTABRIGIENSI:
DOMUUM VENERABILIUM
QUARUM ALTERA NUTRIVIT ALTERA ADSCIVIT

CONTENTS

PREFACE

ST PAUL's letters are an attempt to express in terms of the theology of his day an ultimate fact of his experience. He was "in Christ" or Christ was "in him". The fact of his experience may have been no more than an illusion; but for him it was a matter of immediate certainty. It followed from this that nothing else mattered: even the venerable form of Semitic religion out of which the Pharisees were laboriously constructing an edifice of ethical monotheism was by comparison with this merely a service of weak and beggarly elements. It also followed that the truth could be expressed in any terms which served to bring home to others the truth which had been revealed to him.

His writings, which are the earliest attempt to formulate a system of Christian theology, can only be understood if they are interpreted in the light of the conventional language of Hellenistic theology in which he expounded them to the Greek-speaking world. Otherwise the meaning they were intended to convey will be lost; we shall instead read into them a preconceived system of our own. On the other hand, the study of his language may seem to relegate his writings to the general level of the thought and religion of the world of his day, and so fail to do justice to the titanic force of his personal religion. I am acutely conscious that I have failed to do justice to the difference in quality between primitive Christianity, as it finds expression in St Paul, and the creeds and cults of his contemporaries. But it is impossible to do justice to the full intensity of his knowledge of God in Christ Jesus; his own Epistles convey the fullness of his faith more adequately than any paraphrase can hope to do. But it is only in relation to the world of thought in which he lived and preached that we can understand his Epistles.

Professor E. R. Goodenough's *By Light, Light* did not come into my hands until this book had almost reached its final shape. It will be obvious to anyone who has read his work and passes from it to the present book that we differ entirely as to the whole meaning of Philo's work and view of life. I am quite clear that his attempt to read a "Light-mystery" religion into Philo's writings entirely misconceives the whole aim of Philo's work. He writes of the "passionate desire of the Hellenistic man to experience emotionally the concepts he has learned from Greek rationalism". The opposite seems to me to be the case; the passionate desire of the Hellenistic man, in so far as he cared for these things, was to find a philosophic basis which would justify him in continuing to practise the form of religion which attracted him or which he had inherited. Chrysippus had shown how this could be done: but often the "passionate desire" was little more than a mild interest in such things. Philo's object was to justify Judaism in terms of contemporary thought, and to read into it as much of the conventional theology of the Hellenistic world as he could drag in by hook or by crook. His desire was partly due to the need of countering anti-Semitic propaganda; but it was enhanced by the fact that Judaism was far more of a missionary religion than most contemporary cults. The fact that Philo in the closing sections of *De Mund. Op.* 61 (170 *seqq.*, M. 1. 41) summarises the value of a cosmogony which is based on the *Timaeus* and Posidonius in terms of purely conventional Judaism which ignores alike the Logos and the divine pattern, seems a decisive proof that he did not really care about it; in the same way his "powers" are merely the Stoic manifestations of the one God in the figures of pagan religion; if rabbinical Judaism accepted them so easily as "attributes" of God, there was no reason why Philo should not do the same (cf. below, p. 50, for the origin of the idea). I am happy to find myself entirely in agreement with Professor A. D. Nock's review in *Gnomon* 13. 3. 156 *seqq.* (March 1937) on this point. I have refrained from detailed controversy, which would extend this book to an unconscionable length.

My thanks are due to Mr H. M. Loewe, Reader in Rabbinics in the University of Cambridge, for his assistance in the study of the Hebrew language and the literature of Judaism; my debt to him is so large that I shall not attempt to express it. Naturally I am alone responsible for any inferences I may have drawn from that literature. To Professor A. D. Nock of Harvard University I owe my deepest thanks for his unfailing kindness in helping me, whether in conversation or by correspondence. The references in the index to his published works represent a very small fraction of what I have learnt from him. I can only hope that he will forgive me if at any point I have put forward as my own suggestions which I have borrowed from him without remembering that I have borrowed them.

It was my privilege to attend the late Professor Burkitt's Seminar during the last year of his life; to sit at the feet of so great a teacher even for so short a time was an education in itself. Since then his work has been continued by Professor Dodd; to him and to the members of the Seminar my thanks are due for all I have learnt from them.

WILFRED L. KNOX

November 1938

ABBREVIATIONS, ETC.

Ap. and Ps. *Apocrypha and Pseudepigrapha of the Old Testament*, ed. Charles.

Apocr. N.T. *The Apocryphal New Testament*, translated by M. R. James.

Conversion. *Conversion*, by A. D. Nock.

Dox. Gr. *Doxographi Graeci*, ed. H. Diels.

E.R.E. Hastings' *Encyclopædia of Religion and Ethics.*

G.J.V. *Geschichte des jüdischen Volkes im Zeitalter Jesu Christ*, by E. Schürer.

H.z.N.T. *Handbuch zum Neuen Testament*, ed. H. Lietzmann.

J.T.S. *Journal of Theological Studies.*

Judaism. *Judaism*, by G. Foot Moore.

Kyrios. *Kyrios als Gottesname*, by Graf W. von Baudissin.

Orpheus. *Orpheus and Greek Religion*, by W. K. C. Guthrie.

Papp. Mag. Gr. *Papyri Magicae Graecae*, ed. Preisendanz.

Rel. Or. *Les Religions Orientales dans le Paganisme Romain*, by F. Cumont (4th ed. 1929).

Str.-B. *Kommentar zum Neuen Testament aus Talmud und Midrash*, by H. L. Strack and P. Billerbeck.

T.W.z.N.T. *Theologische Wörterbuch zum Neuen Testament*, ed. G. Kittel.

Urspr. u. Anf. *Ursprung und Anfänge des Christenthums*, by E. Meyer.

v. Arn. *Stoicorum Veterum Fragmenta*, ed. Hans von Arnim.

Voc. Gr. N.T. *Vocabulary of the Greek New Testament*, by Moulton and Milligan.

References to Philo are given with initials (or abbreviations) of the titles in Cohn-Wendland's edition; the number of the paragraph is given after the titles, followed in brackets by the number of the section in Cohn-Wendland and the volume and page of Mangey's text.

References to Josephus are given by the book, chapter and paragraph of the conventional text, followed by the number of the section in Niese.

References to Origen are taken from the edition of Lommatzsch.

References to Mandean documents are given from Lidzbarski's translation, the number of the chapter or section being followed by the page and line of his version.

In a few passages I have referred to my earlier book *St Paul and the Church of Jerusalem*, described as *Jerusalem*.

CHAPTER I

THE FAILURE OF ESCHATOLOGY

THE meeting between Paul and the philosophers of Athens on the Areopagus revealed the limitations of the apocalyptic version of Christianity which he had been content to accept from the Church of Palestine. The meeting was apparently an accident,[1] the result of Paul's inability to keep silence in a city of such intense and misguided piety, and the publicity which the arrival of a new variety of teaching attracted in a city so given over to curiosity. Paul's speech began with the commonplaces by which Hellenistic Judaism sought to establish the unity of God; they were acceptable enough, for they were largely borrowed from conventional philosophy, though they were scarcely novel or interesting.[2] But these commonplaces were quite inconsistent with the belief that the world could come to an end. An end of the world presented no difficulty to the followers of Epicurus; the world was the result of a fortuitous concourse of atoms, and there was no reason why the atoms should not at any moment fly asunder.[3] But to the godless believers in atoms the rest of Paul's speech was merely a borrowing of fragments of the absurd theistic philosophies which they had long since rejected.

Stoics went further than other schools of philosophy in the direction of admitting the possibility of an end of the world. According to the strict view of the Stoa the world was governed by a divine principle of intelligent fire, permeating the whole, and passing by degrees from its nature of fire into the other elements of the cosmos. In immense periods of time it must return again to its nature of pure fire. Thus at

[1] Acts 17. 16 *seqq.* seems to imply that Paul had no intention of preaching there. Meyer's suggestion (*Urspr. u. Anf.* 3. 90) that he had any serious intention of conquering the Greek world for Christianity is hardly probable; he was not really concerned with philosophy. The "affliction" of 1 Thess. 3. 7 may of course refer to his failure at Athens; but it may refer to some unknown incident. It is not easy to reconcile Meyer's view here with the statement (3. 309 n. 2): "Athens, as is well known, from Sulla to Hadrian was quite unimportant (*lag ganz darnieder*) and was only of consideration as a place of study for strangers, especially Romans."

[2] For the speech cf. Jos. *c. Ap.* 2. 22 (190), the prologue to *Or. Sib.* (Fr. 1. 1–9, *Ap. and Ps.* 2. 377), Wisd. 13. 3 *seqq.*, Philo, *De Spec. Legg.* 1 (*De Sacr.*), 3 (271, M. 2. 253), *ib.* (*De Mon.*) 1 (16 *seqq.*, M. 2. 214), *De Virt.* (*De Poen.*), 2 (183, M. 2. 406), *De Sacr. Ab. et Cain*, 18 (67, M. 1. 175), *De Conf. Ling.* 27 (136, M. 1. 425). For the quotation from Aratus cf. pp. 26 and 90.

[3] *Placita* 2. 4. 6 and 10 (*Dox. Gr.* 331).

the end of recurring periods all things returned to a state of incandescence and the process then began once more.[1] The soul of man, being a spark of that divine fire, might indeed retain its conscious existence until the next of these conflagrations; survival beyond that date was impossible, while it was uncertain whether that measure of survival was proper to man as such or only to the wise.[2] Later developments of Stoicism allowed a larger measure of transcendence to God, recognising that the divine fire or reason was concentrated as a dominant element in the firmament;[3] they were therefore able to allow a greater transcendence to the principle of reason in man, which beside being diffused through the whole body was also particularly concentrated as a dominant element in the heart (which was regarded by most Stoics as the seat of reason rather than the head). This tradition allowed both for the real transcendence of God and for the immortality of the soul; but came no nearer to believing in the possibility of an end of the world. Panaetius had even expressed doubts as to the return of all things to the state of fire at the suitable periods of time.[4]

But the Stoicism of Paul's age had no doubts on this point. It was faced with the task of reconciling philosophy and religion with science in the form of astrology. To those acquainted with the teachings of astrology there could be no question of the end of the world. The end of each Great Year must witness the return of the stars to their original positions at the first moment of creation, and this for the Stoics simply meant that all things must return to their original state of fire; science had proved that Panaetius' doubts were unfounded. From this state the world must proceed to an exact repetition of all the events of every preceding cycle; whatever the length of each cycle of the Great Year might be, there could be no doubt that it must witness a precisely identical procession of the heavenly bodies through their courses, and therefore a precise repetition of the events of all its predecessors. The fate of man throughout all the ages must be an infinite

[1] For the strictly physicist view as laid down by Heraclitus (Diog. Laert. 9. 8) and carried on by the earlier Stoa cf. Diog. Laert. 7. 142 and 156; *Placita* 1. 7. 33 (*Dox. Gr.* 305).

[2] Diog. Laert. 7. 157 for the difference between Cleanthes and Chrysippus on this point; *Placita* 4. 7. 3 (*Dox. Gr.* 393).

[3] Diog. Laert. 7. 147 and 159; Ar. Did. *Epit.* 29. 7 (*Dox. Gr.* 465) and *Placita* 4. 4. 4 (*ib.* 390). Cf. Cicero, *De Nat. Deor.* 2. 11. 29 *seqq.* Bevan (*Stoics and Sceptics* 43) traces the doctrine back to Zeno. It certainly is true that the later Stoics made this distinction, but it seems doubtful how far Zeno allowed this measure of transcendence to God and how far he was forced at times to use it by the difficulty of expressing a pantheistic system in language drawn from a tradition of theistic religion.

[4] Cicero, *De Nat. Deor.* 2. 46. 118; cf. 2. 33. 85; Diog. Laert. 7. 142.

series of identical details.[1] The Stoics, though they might be falsely charged with believing in the end of the world in virtue of their doctrine of periodical returns to the original state of fire,[2] were less able than any other school of philosophy to believe in its final termination. Even if the latest development of Stoicism had forsaken the strict demands of its own logic so far as to allow for some real measure of immortality to the best and wisest of mankind, the privilege was normally reserved for a select few.[3] Thus the conception of a general resurrection at the end of the world was ridiculous and impious; it is possible that some of the audience were sufficiently familiar with Oriental beliefs to know that something of the kind was to be found in the religion of Persia; Paul's Gospel may have seemed a variation of that contemptible and barbarous religion, as indeed it was in so far as Judaism was indebted to Zoroastrianism for a large measure of its eschatology.[4] The final verse of his speech as recorded in the Acts (17. 31) could only arouse the ridicule of the philosophers of Athens.

There had indeed been a period, nearly a century before Paul addressed the Areopagus, when apocalyptic hopes had been widely entertained in the Hellenistic world. They may indeed, like the hopes of Judaism, have drawn their ultimate inspiration from the religions of Babylonia and Persia. But they had been amalgamated with beliefs of an entirely different character and drawn from sources whose contact with the East, if any such existed, lay far back in history. The belief in successions of world-ages lay behind Heraclitus and Hesiod; the latter's conception had become part of the permanent stock of Greek culture, while the former's series of world-ages beginning and ending in fire would appear to have been necessitated by the fact that the other elements had already been adopted by his predecessors.[5]

[1] For these cycles cf. Ar. Did. *Epit.* 37 *ap.* Eus. *Pr. Ev.* 15. 9. 1 (*Dox. Gr.* 469); Philo, *De Aet. Mund.* 3 (8, M. 2. 489); Chrysippus *ap.* Lact. *Div. Inst.* 7. 23; Philo, *De Cher.* 32 (114, M. 1. 159) (here Philo has incorporated a fragment implying reincarnation in successive world-periods, a view which he certainly does not hold); Orig. *c. Cels.* 5. 20.

[2] Philo, *De Aet. Mund. loc. cit.* and *passim.* I find it difficult to believe, in spite of Cumont, that Philo could really commit himself so completely not merely to abandoning belief in the end of the world, but actually to polemising against it. Cf. Diels, *Dox. Gr.* intr. p. 107.[1] The interest of the author in Judaism can be paralleled from Hecataeus *ap.* Diod. Sic. 40. 3 and Varro *ap.* Aug. *De Consens. Evang.* 1. 30 (xxii); see also below, pp. 45 *seqq.*

[3] See below, p. 75.

[4] For the Iranian influence on the origin and development of the eschatology of the O.T. cf. Bousset, *Rel. des Judenthums* 578 *seqq.*; Meyer, *Urspr. u. Anf.* 2. 58 *seqq.* For the general Greek opinion of Persian religion see Note I.

[5] Water by Thales and air by Anaximenes. Earth could not be used for the purpose, since this would have involved a relapse into mere mythology, cf. Wilamowitz-Möllendorff, *Glaube der Hellenen* 1. 204.

Its adoption by the Stoics gave it an enormously increased importance; but by 50 B.C. it was tending to be syncretised with one which was in nature and origin entirely different. In the *Timaeus*, the bible of Hellenistic cosmogony, Plato held that at long intervals, as a result of planetary disturbances, cosmic catastrophes are fated to occur on a vast scale.[1] Elsewhere we learn that these catastrophes are the not unnatural effect of the reversing of the courses of the heavenly bodies.[2] The source of the scheme appears to be Plato's imagination assisted by the statement of Hecataeus that the Egyptian priests had preserved records of four such changes in the past 11,340 years.[3] The belief had many advantages; it harmonised with the old belief in a series of world-ages[4] and with the remains of the older Minoan civilisations, which could hardly be fitted into the scheme of classical mythology and history; it also explained how barbarians in Egypt and elsewhere appeared to possess a civilisation more ancient than Hellas.

The scheme was even more attractive to exponents of Eastern religions who could claim an older and truer account of one such cosmic catastrophe, the great deluge. When Berossus came from Babylon and introduced the history and astrology of his countrymen to the Greeks, he was entirely ready to accept the probability of a cosmic conflagration to counterbalance the historical deluge, though he corrected the astronomical conceptions of Plato and the Egyptians; the deluge had occurred when all the planets stood in line in the sign of Capricorn, the conflagration would occur when they reached a similar position in Cancer.[5] His influence led the later Stoics to modify their original belief in periodical conflagrations of a strictly physical character by the inclusion of deluges; in any case the influence of the *Timaeus* in the Alexandrine period might have produced the same effect without his assistance.[6] After all there was no reason why the period furthest from the conflagration should not be marked by an

[1] *Timaeus* 22d. For the Great Year see 39d.

[2] *Politicus* 269a *seqq.* How far Plato was influenced by Babylonian astrology is a matter on which I offer no opinion.

[3] *Ap.* Herodotus 2. 142.

[4] For the Hesiodic scheme (*Works and Days* 109 *seqq.*) as an attempt to fit the old beliefs as to the souls of the dead into the Homeric view of the Gods and of history cf. Rohde, *Psyche* 67 *seqq.* (Eng. tr. 1925). Reitzenstein and Schäder, *Studien zum Antiken Syncretismus* 57 *seqq.*, find an Iranian origin for Hesiod.

[5] Seneca *N.Q.* 3. 29. 1. Cf. Censorinus (*De Die Nat.* 18. 11), where the "winter" of the Great Year is marked by a deluge, its "summer" by a conflagration. It appears that there is no evidence of the latter doctrine in the Babylonian sources (Clemen, *Religionsgeschichtliche Erklärung des N.T.* 147; cf. Bousset, *Rel. des Judenthums* 573): the Jewish parallels suggest that he invented it in order to win acceptance in philosophical circles.

[6] Cf. Seneca, *loc. cit.* and Dio Chrys. 36. 42 *seqq.* (v. Arn. 2. 178).

excess of water. The latest development of Stoic philosophy of the first century B.C. even abandoned the supposedly Babylonian scheme so far as to dissociate the periods of world-catastrophes from the Great Year, leaving the Great Year to be inaugurated by some other suitable event of a portentous character both in heaven and earth.[1] The belief in this form had the advantage of avoiding the destruction of all mankind at the end of each world-period: the individual could hope to survive into the new era.[2]

The cosmogony of Judaism was a variant of the Babylonian, and Hellenistic Judaism was quite as ready as Berossus to adapt it to the Platonic view of world-catastrophes. The end of the world, an awkward legacy from the tradition of the Scriptures, could easily be reduced to insignificance or omitted entirely.[3] This had been found necessary long before Paul excited the ridicule of the Areopagus. On the other hand, world-catastrophes could be employed to enhance the credit of Moses. Not only had he recorded the true story of the deluge, in which he was confirmed by many heathen writers;[4] he had also recorded a great conflagration. If any one doubted this story he could easily be convinced by a visit to the Dead Sea, where the traces of that disaster were plainly visible.[5] Further, the story confirmed the modernity of Greek history and so enhanced the prestige and antiquity of Moses.[6] It could even be claimed that the wise man who had

[1] In Cicero, *De Rep.* 6. 21. 23 and 22. 24 (*Somn. Scip.*), while we have cosmic catastrophes at fixed periods, as in the *Timaeus*, the end of the Great Year is marked by portentous events in heaven and earth (the last Great Year was marked by the eclipse at the death of Romulus); it is not marked, at any rate necessarily, by a cosmic catastrophe. Presumably this is Posidonius. Cf. p. 93.

[2] Seneca however, following Berossus, believes in catastrophes by flood and fire which annihilate mankind (*loc. cit.* 5).

[3] Note the insignificance of the judgment of the world in the Wisdom of Solomon. Philo ignores it or positively controverts it, if he is the author of the *De Aet. Mund.* (see above, p. 3, n. 2).

[4] Philo, *De Vit. Moys.* 2. 10 (53 *seqq.*, M. 2. 142), with the technical Stoic term παλιγγενεσία; cf. *De Aet. Mund.* 3 (9, M. 2. 489); Wisd. 10. 4. For the remains of the ark cf. Jos. *Antt.* 1. 3. 6 (93) following Berossus; another proof of the truth of the Bible seems to be implied in Philo's statement that Noah means "righteous" (*Leg. Alleg.* 3. 24 (77, M. 1. 102)); there seems no excuse for this, since Gen. 6. 9 does not imply that the name means "righteous". But Sydyk, the Phoenician deity of Sanchuniathon *ap.* Philo of Byblus (Eus. *Pr. Ev.* 1. 10. 10), means "righteous"; he is also the father of the Dioscuri, Cabeiri, Corybants and Samothracians (*sic*), who were the inventors of ships. I suspect that Philo has incorporated a tradition of Judaism which explained that Sydyk and his sons were a Gentile perversion of the true story of Noah and his sons in the ark.

[5] Philo, *De Vit. Moys. loc. cit.* 56; Wisd. 10. 7; Jos. *B.J.* 4. 8. 4 (484). For the two catastrophes by water and fire, cf. *Ad. et Ev.* 50 (*Ap. and Ps.* 2. 152; cf. Wells' note *ad loc.*). Celsus treats the Jewish-Christian last judgment as a misunderstanding of such cosmic disasters (Orig. *c. Cels.* 4. 11); for a similar view of Zoroastrianism, cf. p. 207.

[6] Jos. *c. Ap.* 1. 2 (9 *seqq.*); cf. p. 36.

survived the conflagration had behaved as Chrysippus had pointed out that he would be compelled to act, if he and his family were the sole survivors of such a catastrophe.[1] The scheme could of course be combined with the orthodox eschatology; all previous catastrophes could be regarded as rehearsals for the one great event, which was yet to come.[2] It was normally, however, substituted for the end of the world, where Judaism was in sufficiently close touch with Greek thought to feel the difficulty of the biblical tradition.

Such catastrophes again could be fitted into the scheme of eschatology which regarded history as consisting of a fixed number of world-periods. The Iranian tradition believed in four such periods, while the classical tradition of Hesiod believed in five.[3] But the Iranian tradition, at any rate as described by Theopompus,[4] believed in periods of 3000 years, one of which covered the reign of Ahriman and one the age of conflict. Babylonian tradition as recorded by Berossus recognised two Great Years, one of 600 and one of 3600 ordinary years.[5] Both were calculated to suggest to Judaism the belief that the duration of the world consisted of six ages, a view which corresponded admirably with the Jewish predilection for the number seven. It was popular in Hellenistic circles, since it corresponded with the value attached by Pythagoras to the number seven, the seven ages of man and the seven planets; to Judaism these were all imitations or else mystical types of the sabbath.[6] It was obvious that there ought to be six ages of the world, to precede the eternal sabbath of God;[7] the view was

[1] For Chrysippus cf. Orig. *c. Cels.* 4. 45 and the parallel versions given in v. Arn. *Stoic. Vet. Fr.* 3. 185. For the rabbinical interpretation of the story of Lot's daughters by their belief that they were the sole survivors cf. *Gen. R.* 49. 8. *Clem. Recog.* 1. 32 modifies the tradition by making the intercession of Abraham avert the world-catastrophe.

[2] 2 Pet. 2. 5 *seqq.*, and cf. the Hellenisation in Lk. 17. 26–28 of the logion of Mt. 24. 37.

[3] *Loc. cit.* p. 4, n. 4 above. For the Iranian belief cf. Lommel, *Die Religion Zarathustras* 139 *seqq.*

[4] See note on Greek writers and Persian Religion, p. 204. It may perhaps be pointed out here that for the Hellenistic age it is more important to know what Theopompus and Greek opinion thought than what Zoroaster really believed. Cf. also Bousset, *Rel. des Judenthums* 578.

[5] Syncellus 17a *ap.* Muller, *Fr. Hist. Gr.* 2. 498. 4; Jos. *Ant.* 1. 3. 9 (106).

[6] Cf. Philo *passim.* In *De Mund. Op.* 30 (89, M. 1. 21 *seqq.*) all but the first two sentences and the last section are Hellenistic; the sabbath alone is a Jewish addition. Clem. Alex. *Strom.* 6. 16. 145 (815 P) mentions a book on the subject by Hermippus of Berytus.

[7] 2 En. 33. 1; cf. the systems of Irenaeus and Augustine quoted in *Ap. and Ps.* 2. 451 *ad loc.* Irenaeus is probably following Jewish convention rather than Enoch. In 1 En. 93. 3 we have seven "generations" represented by their leading figures, from Enoch to the Messiah; in 4 Esdr. 3. 4 *seqq.* the fall of Jerusalem represents the sixth age. Cf. *Test. Abr.* 19 (*Texts and Studies* 2. 2. 101); Firmicus Maternus, *De Err. Prof. Rel.* 26. 3. In Lactantius, *Div. Inst.* 7. 14, God's religion and truth labour against evil in the present sixth day as in the first day He laboured in creation;

also easily adapted to at least one heathen view, which accepted seven world-ages, one ruled by each of the planets,[1] though naturally in the heathen view the seven ages were repeated one after the other to all eternity; the Jewish system led to an end, either after a seventh Messianic age or at the end of the sixth. In the later Christian tradition the Messianic age was essential; there must be seven ages, of which six were occupied with the history of the world to correspond to the days of creation, while Christianity could not identify eternity with anything below the ogdoad, the eighth day, which was like the first day of the week a Sunday, and corresponded to the resurrection of the Lord, the first day of the new creation, as the first day of the week was the first day of the old.[2] Judaism and Christianity agreed in a lack of serious interest in astrology, while both were concerned to fit whatever scheme of world-ages they adopted into the framework of history provided by the book of Genesis. Consequently they were compelled to abandon the astrological Great Year, whose duration was in any case a matter of dispute, while there were even sceptics who doubted its existence.[3] For this could be substituted either periods of history as recorded in the Old Testament, without regard to their real or supposed duration, or periods of 400, 600 or 1000 years,[4] while the number of periods of world-history could be adjusted accordingly: thus twelve periods corresponded to the tribes and the signs of the zodiac. The duration of history itself was of a pleasing uncertainty; calculations of the time from Adam to Moses varied from 3859 to 2450 years.[5] It was agreed that Adam fell on the same day as that on

here as elsewhere Lactantius shows affinities with Zoroastrian ideas (cf. Lommel, *Die Rel. Zarath.* 143 for the conception of the true religion labouring in the world). Although the number seven need have nothing to do with the planets it is always associated with them in Hellenistic literature; for its original independence cf. Jastrow, *Rel. Bab. et Ass.* 1. 282. For the antiquity of the hebdomad in Semitic religion cf. Jack, *The Ras Shamra Tablets* (O.T. Studies, no. 1), p. 36.

[1] Cumont, *Catal. Codd. Astr. Gr.* 4, quoted by Norden, *Die Geburt des Kindes* 15; cf. Boll-Bezold, *Sternglaube u. Sterndeutung* 158. The Mandean belief in planetary world-ages appears to be derived from Babylon (Bousset, *Rel. des Judenthums* 575). Lactantius, *loc. cit.*, ascribes a belief in seven ages of Rome to Seneca.

[2] For this kind of playing with numbers cf. the way in which Clement of Alexandria (*Strom.* 6. 16. 138 *seqq.*, 810 P) revises, without acknowledgment, the attempt of Aristobulus (Eus. *Pr. Ev.* 13. 12. 13) to equate Wisdom, as the precosmic light, with the sabbath; here Christian arithmetic fared better than Jewish. Cf. *Ep. Barn.* 15. 5, 8 and 9: the last may be taken from Aristobulus.

[3] Censorinus, *De Die Nat.* 18. 11. The Egyptians held that it was of 1461 solar years; Hellenistic views varied from 2484 (Aristarchus) to 136,000 (Cassander).

[4] For millennia, cf. *Ap. and Ps.* 2. 451, and Rev. 20. 3; the writer's predilection for hebdomads makes it fairly safe to assume that he would have accepted six periods of world-history before the millennial kingdom. In 4 Esdr. 7. 28 the Messianic kingdom lasts 400 years, while in 14. 11 we have twelve periods; cf. 2 Bar. 53. 5 *seqq.*, where each period is a mixture of good and evil.

[5] Cf. Charles' note on *Ass. Moys.* 1. 2 in *Ap. and Ps.* 2. 414.

which he was created; but it was impossible to say whether the "day" on which he was created was a mere human day of 24 hours or a "day of the Lord" of 1000 years.[1] Even history from Moses to the writer's own day was not dated with any exact precision. Thus it was possible to have six periods of 600 years, five millennia of history with a sixth millennium spent by Adam in the Garden of Eden except for the last few minutes, or twelve of 400 without going outside the limits of Holy Scripture. The substitution of periods of history for exact periods of time naturally allowed an infinity of speculation both as regards the precise numbers and their mystical meanings.[2]

Thus both Jews and Christians could fit this kind of speculation into their systems; Christianity, if it adhered to the popular system of hebdomads, was cursed with the necessity of an otiose millennial reign of Christ upon earth, while Judaism could always merge its seventh millennium into eternity; on the other hand, Christianity was not compelled to regard seven as the highest and best of numbers in virtue of its association with the sabbath. It was thus able to associate God with the ogdoad, the number of the zone of the fixed stars which was the proper home of the supreme deity who dwelt in the highest heaven. He was the Mind that ruled the whole,[3] just as mind was the ruling element in the eightfold soul of man; this remarkable correspondence between the heavens and man was a discovery admirably typical of the temper of the Hellenistic age.[4] Judaism, on the other hand, was liable to find its god identified with Saturn:[5] who could the "most High" God be, whom the Jew worshipped every Saturday, but the highest of the planets, the seventh from the earth?

A century before Paul spoke, speculations similar to those of Judaism and Christianity were finding a ready welcome in the Mediterranean world. Persian religion may have been one of the influences which led mankind to look for the speedy establishment of an age of gold, and to associate this hope with a ruler who was

[1] Cf. Str.-B. on 2 Pet. 3. 8 for this difficult question.

[2] So Orig. *In Ev. Matt.* 15. 33 *seqq.* explains the five "hours" of Mt. 20. 1 *seqq.* as five world-periods, corresponding to the five senses. Clem. Alex. *Strom.* 1. 21. 147 (409 P) explains the genealogy of Mt. 1. 17 as meaning six hebdomads of generations.

[3] *Placita* 4. 4. 4 (*Dox. Gr.* 390).

[4] The eightfold division of the soul (*Placita loc. cit.*) harmonises the microcosm with the macrocosm. The limitation of the gods to eight, the firmament and the planets, was as old as Xenocrates of Chalcedon (*c.* 300 B.C.), according to Cicero, *De Nat. Deor.* 1. 13. 34, Clem. Alex. *Protr.* 5. 66, (58 P), both from a doxographic collection (Diels, *Dox. Gr.* 130 and 540).

[5] Tac. *Hist.* 5. 4 assumes that the God of the Jews is Saturn and mentions the position of Saturn as the highest, and therefore the object of Jewish worship. A further reason lay in the equation of the God of the Jews with the El-Cronos of Phoenician religion (Philo of Byblus *ap.* Eus. *Pr. Ev.* 1. 10. 16).

an earthly king and yet at the same time a saviour sent from heaven; it is not entirely certain whether the belief of the later Avestas that the final saviour is both a son and a reincarnation of Zoroaster had appeared before Sassanid times.[1] But whatever their origin may have been, hopes of this kind had appeared in different parts of the world whenever intolerable conditions led men to hope for a miraculous deliverance, or when it seemed politic to regard the sudden emergence of a new ruler as the realisation of the best hopes of the past. Egyptian literature had described the triumphs of the rulers of the land in remote ages in language of a thoroughly Messianic type. "He shall make himself a name for all eternity...the Asiatics shall fall before his carnage and the Libyans before his flame. Right shall come again into its place and iniquity is cast forth."[2] Thus Egypt had a native tradition of apocalyptic; it will be seen shortly that it was revived in the Hellenistic age. Judaism was in close contact with the Gentile world from the time of Alexander onwards; and during this period it was transforming the hope of a prosperous reign for the latest king of the house of David, described in the language of court-poetry, into the faith that the judge of all the earth would vindicate His will and His power to uphold the right, by the establishment of a golden age on earth under a more or less divine ruler of a Messianic age. It is not clear how far the development was spontaneous, and again it is possible that language which appears to reflect the newer developments of the Messianic hope may really express a quite primitive belief in the divinity of the king. In any case contact with Judaism was quite probably a contributory factor in the development of apocalyptic hopes in the Gentile world. On the other hand, while it is clear that the main stimulus to Judaism came from its contact with Persia, early Jewish literature contained much material which could be interpreted as justifying such hopes.[3]

Yet another element in the development of apocalyptic came from

[1] Lommel, *op. cit.* 205 *seqq.*

[2] From the "prophecy of Neferrohu", apparently glorifying the recent triumph of Amenemhet (*c.* 1995–1960 B.C.) (Blackman, *Literature of the Ancient Egyptians* 110).

[3] Thus Briggs (*Int. Crit. Comm. the Psalms*) dates Ps. 2 before the exile and includes v. 7 as authentic; Ps. 45 to Jehu, but vv. 7–8a as a gloss "later than the Ps., and its Messianic interpretation was later still"; Ps. 72 is a prayer on the accession of a king, vv. 8–12 later Messianic additions; Ps. 110 is a Messianic Psalm, earlier than Ps. 2 and embodying a belief in the priestly character of the Davidic monarch. See notes *ad loc.* These views are all liable to dispute, but there seems no reason to doubt the possibility that what was originally court-poetry became, either by interpretation or by interpolation, Messianic Psalmody. The fact that this type of literature was current would assist an independent development of the Messianic ideal, even if the first stimulus came from outside.

the Hellenic world itself. The tragedy of the Peloponnesian War had led to the first deification of a man, when the people of Samos bestowed divine honours on Lysander in his lifetime:[1] it is possible that the Greek practice rested on a misunderstanding of the ceremonial of the court of the Great King.[2] The career of Alexander could scarcely fail to impress his contemporaries with the belief that he was more than man. The period of the wars of his successors and the growth of the power of Rome, culminating in the conquest of the Hellenistic world and the final agonies of the Republic, produced a state of chaos which not only convinced the world that its destinies were largely ruled by an inevitable fate,[3] but also made it ready to offer divine honours to any saviour who seemed able to offer some deliverance from the evils of the present situation. The old city life, in which the individual had at least some control over his own affairs, was at the mercy of strange rulers of whom he had hardly heard, and the old local city-gods seemed powerless to help in a hostile universe.[4] The only hope of mankind lay in a God who should prove his power to deliver.[5] The Eastern cults, which later invaded the Western world, only gradually made their way into the West, offering a faith which satisfied man's desire for religion in this world and immortality hereafter; the Ptolemaic cult of Isis and Sarapis was the first to make itself felt. This was an Egyptian cult artificially Hellenised to serve as a bond of union between the Greek and Egyptian subjects of Ptolemy I.[6] The cults of Asia were later to follow those of Egypt, adapting themselves to their surroundings as they moved Westwards; Attis offered salvation to his initiates in perfect iambic trimeters, while the ancient cults of Greece retained their primitive language and their primitive methods of versification.[7] They, and some of the ancient Greek mysteries which

[1] Plutarch (*Lysander* 18. 443 b), quoting Duris (*c.* 300 B.C.). Cf. Nilsson, *Griechische Feste*, 49.

[2] Bevan (*E.R.E.* 4. 526, Art. "Deification") holds that the Greeks invented the practice and handed it on to the East. But Theopompus' story of Nicostratus of Argos, who set a special table for the δαίμων of the Great King in imitation of the Persian court (*ap.* Athenaeus, *Deipnosophistae* 6. 60. 252 a), and the story of Themistocles in Plutarch (*Themistocles* 27. 125 c) suggest that Persian court practice may have led to Greek deifications.

[3] See below, pp. 63 *seqq.*

[4] The change has been often described; cf. Bevan, *Stoics and Sceptics* 98; Nock, *Conversion* 99; Murray, *Four Centuries of Greek Religion* 111. For the effect of the amalgamation of clans and townships in ancient Babylonia in changing social into personal religion cf. *Kyrios* 2. 48.

[5] For the development of the god of a social unit into a personal deliverer cf. *Kyrios* 3. 343 *seqq.*, with special reference to Marduk.

[6] Nock, *Conversion* 38; cf. Cumont, *Rel. Or.* 69; *UPZ* 83.

[7] Cf. Firmicus Maternus, *De Err. Prof. Rel.* 22. 1, where the verses θαρρεῖτε, μύσται τοῦ θεοῦ σεσωσμένοι, ἔσται γὰρ ὑμῖν ἐκ πόνων σωτηρία from the rites of Attis

regained their prosperity during this age, met the needs of the time by offering security from all the perils of life by land and sea, and everlasting life in the future;[1] the Cabeiri of Samothrace, with an extraordinary disregard for the highest teachings of philosophy, even went so far as to offer grace to achieve that moral dignity which man ought to attain by his unaided efforts.[2]

The last offer, however, was one which appealed only to the superstitious. The ordinary man asked primarily for deliverance from perils in this life and was perfectly ready to render divine honours to those who were able to offer it, and willing to do so if sufficiently flattered; the later Diadochi were deified as a matter of course, the Ptolemies inheriting the traditional godhead of the kings of Egypt. The honour of such deification, with the title of "saviour" and "Epiphanes", was bestowed with a freedom calculated to render it meaningless, as an expression of any religious sentiment.[3]

(Reitzenstein, *Hell. Myst. Rel.* (3), 400) show the adaptation of the commonplaces of Hellenistic religion to the versification of the classical drama. Real Greek religion was still at the stage of εὐοῖ δίκερως δίμορφε (Firmicus Maternus, 21. 2). Cf. the liturgy of the Curetes in Harrison, *Themis* 7; it seems that this extremely primitive liturgy was still being used in the third century A.D.; for a less daring interpretation cf. Nilsson, *The Minoan-Mycenean Religion* 475 *seqq.*

[1] For such "deliverances" cf. Artemidorus, *Oneirocritica* 2. 39. 139, Isis and Sarapis are helpers of those in the utmost danger; Diod. Sic. 1. 25. 3 for "epiphanies" of Isis as "helper" and "benefactor"; cf. Juv. *Sat.* 6. 531 for the prominence of dreams in Egyptian religion, and such a vision of the god Mandulis is discussed by Nock in *Harvard Theological Review* 27. 1. 53 *seqq.* Meyer, *Urspr. u. Anf.* 3. 391, regards "salvation" as a concept primarily derived from a more or less monotheistic conception of "God" attaching itself to particular gods as "saviours". It must however be noticed that particular gods were worshipped as "saviours" in classical Greece, though with reference to "salvation" from specific disasters; the thought of "salvation" in general could easily be attached to the power of particular gods to save from shipwreck or similar disasters. The temple of Zeus Soter at Troezen was said to have been built by Aetius; and he was a grandson of Poseidon (Pausanias, *Descr. Gr.* 2. 31. 10).

[2] Diod. Sic. 5. 49. 6; this can hardly be due to the Phoenician origin of the cult (Bloch *ap.* Roscher, *Lexikon*, s.v. μεγάλοι θεοί, doubted by Baudissin, *Kyrios* 3. 76), since the cult had been Hellenised long before. Greek religion demanded holiness; it did not provide means of attaining it. Cf. Plut. *De Stoic. Rep.* 31. 1048d. Polybius, 10. 5. 5, resents the view that P. Scipio Africanus owed his victories to the gods, whom he relegates in 37. 9. 2 to the control of natural phenomena. Livy, 26. 19, records his habit of meditating on the day's business in the temple of Jupiter Capitolinus, but ascribes it to his love of surrounding himself with mystery. Celsus *ap.* Orig. *c. Cels.* 3. 59 condemns Christianity for offering salvation to the wicked; Plato recognises prayer for knowledge as right (*Timaeus* 27c), but on the ground that it is perilous to embark on a cosmogony owing to the danger of offending the gods. The nearest parallel seems to be Epict. *Diss.* 3. 21. 15.

[3] Cf. the freedom with which Polybius describes men as "saviours", e.g. 18. 46. 12. He ridicules Prusias of Bithynia for addressing the Senate χαίρετε θεοὶ καὶ σωτῆρες, but it is only a slight extension of popular practice (30. 19. 5). In Dion. Halic. *Antt. Rom.* 10. 46, a cohort after winning an unexpected victory in a forlorn hope greets its commander as πατέρα καὶ σωτῆρα καὶ θεόν. This is of course ludicrous as history of ancient Rome, but presumably reasonable as Hellenistic practice; cf. Lucan, *Phars.* 6. 253.

It was in these conditions that the apocalyptic hope of a deliverer who should appear and establish an age of gold made its way into the Western world. In Egypt the fourth century B.C. was marked by the successful rebellion against Persia, to be followed by a fresh subjugation and the conquest of the land by Alexander the Great. This left a legacy of apocalyptic hopes, possibly even the tradition that Nectanebos II would one day return as a saviour, *rex quondam, rexque futurus*. A later specimen of such hopes, known as the "Potter's Oracle", foretells the coming of a hateful king from Syria, who is to be a madman; the document thus dates itself to the time of Antiochus Epiphanes.[1] In spite of its wretched workmanship the oracle, which is the "burden" of Alexandria, is quite in keeping with the style of the Old Testament when denouncing the doom of the great cities which oppressed Israel. It is distinctly stronger in its denunciation of the present and its threats of doom than in its forecast of future blessings; but this is a failing shared by greater prophets. The city by the sea (Alexandria) will become a place for fishermen to dry their nets (cf. Ezek. 26. 5), because the Ἀγαθὸς Δαίμων and Cneph have gone thence to Memphis, so that they who go by will say: "Was this the city that nourished all men (cf. Lam. 2. 15), wherein every race of men was made to dwell? Then shall Egypt be increased when the benevolent king, of fifty-five years of age, shall come from the sun, being appointed as the giver of good things by the great goddess Isis; so that men shall pray that the dead might rise again to partake in such good things."[2] The reminiscences of the Old Testament are interesting, but it is very doubtful if Ezekiel and Lamentations were translated into Greek

[1] For Nectanebos cf. *P.R.E.* 16. 11. 2237 *seqq.*; E. Meyer, *Kleine Schriften* 2. 69 *seqq.* (I owe this reference to Dr M. Braun of Manchester College, Oxford). Later Nectanebos appears as the real father of Alexander the Great in the romance of Pseudo-Callisthenes. The figure of the great man who is not really dead but will return to save the nation is a striking instance of the danger of assuming common sources for apocalyptic hopes. *P.R.E. loc. cit.* gives several instances from modern times. In 1916 there were many people in London who refused to believe that the late Lord Kitchener perished with the *Hampshire*, and expected him to win the war from Russia.

[2] The text is printed and discussed by Reitzenstein and Schäder, *Stud. z. Ant. Syncr.* 40 *seqq.* It is also discussed by Tarn in *J.R.S.* 22. 2. 146. The former suggest Iranian influence. But their main argument, the wish that the dead might rise again, is inevitable in an apocalypse of a golden age on earth. Either the dead are dead, and it is sad that they cannot share in such blessings, or they are immortal, in which case the golden age on earth is unnecessary, but expresses the yearning of an evil age for happiness on earth. Cf. Verg. *Ecl.* 4. 53; Pss. Sol. 17. 50 for a similar *motif*. If there is any Iranian influence, it must lie in the general impetus to apocalyptic, which has to be placed before Hesiod; the probability of this I must leave to others to decide. Tarn seems to demand an undue degree of consistency in apocalyptic in distinguishing between the warrior-king who precedes the age of gold and the king of that age itself. The two are merely doublets. The king in question may be Ptolemy III.

by the time of Antiochus Epiphanes, and still more doubtful whether they were well enough known to influence a prophecy which expresses the hatred of Memphis for Alexandria, i.e. the native Egyptian for the cosmopolitan immigrants who followed the Macedonian conquerors. It seems more likely that we have a common use of a conventional theme, the destruction of a great maritime city; if everything else is imagined away, the fishermen drying their nets on the shore are the only thing left; it corresponds to the "making into a sheepwalk" of an inland city.[1] The amazement of those who pass by the ruins and taunt the fallen queen of mankind is also probably derived from a general apocalyptic convention of the taunting of the imperial city in the hour of its disaster.[2]

This feature reappears in the pagan "apocalypse" which has found its way into the Jewish collection of Sibylline Oracles.[3] Here Rome is to be cast down and her locks shaved off by her mistress; but after being cast down from heaven to earth, she is to be raised up again. Asia will enjoy peace and Europe an age of gold, marked by perfect weather, and fertility both of the soil and of beasts; its blessings extend even to the creeping things of the earth. Blessed is the man who shall live to see that day, when law, justice, concord, faith and friendship descend to earth from heaven and necessity, lawlessness and all evils flee away. The prophecy appears to date from about 33 B.C., and to look forward to the triumph of Antony and Cleopatra over Rome, whose revival after her downfall is a marked contrast to the normal convention, but intelligible in view of the fact that Antony in 33 B.C. can have had no desire for the downfall of Rome. The personified virtues coming down from heaven to earth show a thoroughly Hellenistic point of view; they are also a remarkable advance on the material blessings which form the stock-in-trade of apocalyptic, which is here replaced by the ideal world-state of Hellenistic philosophy. In other features however the prophecy is true to type; Rome is drunk with her many-suitored weddings, as she is in the apocalyptic figure of the great harlot drunk with the blood of the saints.[4] The personifica-

[1] For ψυγμός as a drying-place for nets or anything else cf. Preisigke, *Wört. Gr. Pap. Urk.* s.v. At Arsinoe in the second century B.C. a Jewish house of prayer shares a site with a ψυγμός.

[2] Is. 47. 1, and see below, n. 4. For Is. 47. 1 as referring to Rome cf. Str.-B. on Rev. 14. 8.

[3] *Or. Sib.* 3. 350 *seqq.* For the origin and interpretation of this apocalypse see Tarn, *loc. cit.* 135 *seqq.* I have ventured to disagree with one or two minor details.

[4] Rev. 17. 4 *seqq.* and 18. 3, which curiously enough Tarn does not notice; this seems more likely than his explanation that the passage is a retort to Roman scandals as to Cleopatra's drunkenness. The same *motif* appears in Is. 51. 21, Jer. 51. 7 (Babylon), Nahum 3. 4–11 (Nineveh).

tion of the city is a natural result of its identification with its goddess;[1] the downfall of Nineveh would be regarded as the downfall of Nina-Ishtar, and the same sentiment would see the downfall of Ishtar in the downfall of Babylon. Jewish prophecy, which has alone survived, personifies the city, but cannot introduce the figure of the goddess, but there were many others who would rejoice in the overthrow of Babylon without feeling hampered by the scruples of Jewish monotheism; the taunting of Ishtar for her many lovers could claim a precedent in the literature of Babylon itself.[2] The prosperity of the beasts, even of the creeping things of the earth, indicates that they have undergone a change of heart similar to that of Is. 11. 8,[3] while the universal reign of righteousness, in a Hellenistic form, corresponds with that which is implied, even where it is not explicitly stated, in Jewish pictures of the Messianic kingdom.[4]

It is not, however, to be supposed that the picture is coloured by the Jewish Scriptures or even by popular Jewish beliefs. Judaism represents one particular line of development of the hope of a golden age which was felt everywhere; in one instance we can see the hopes of Israel coloured by those of the Hellenistic world. Philo has for the most part eliminated the apocalyptic element of Judaism from his writings; but he cannot eliminate the warnings and promises of the Pentateuch.[5] But when they appear, they are entirely hellenised. Neglect of the hebdomad (i.e. the sabbath) results in neglecting the law, the salt, the libations, the altar of pity (ἔλεος), and the common hearth by which friendship and concord are established. Philo here is working on a pagan source; the altar of pity is Athenian,[6] concord (ὁμόνοια) is Stoic and the whole is reminiscent of the Orphic-Stoic remodelling of the Olympian religion which appears in the *temenos* of Demeter of Pergamos.[7] But after the neglect of the hebdomads has exhausted the soil, the deserted land will recover and produce a new

[1] Cook, *Rel. Anc. Pal.* 190 *seqq.*

[2] In the taunting of Ishtar in the Gilgamesh epic, 6. 42 *seqq.* (Gressmann, *Das Gilgamesh-Epos* 31).

[3] Cf. 2 Bar. 73. 6. Kennett, *Composition of the Book of Isaiah* 75, brings this passage down to the Hellenistic age. But this appears to represent a preconceived view of the date of Messianic developments in Israel. The theme is obviously part of a widely spread convention; it might easily originate independently out of the belief in a state of original innocence when men and beasts were friends; cf. *E.R.E.* 2. 704b.

[4] E.g. *Test. Lev.* 18. 2; 4 Esdr. 6. 25 *seqq.* In any Jewish golden age the Torah would be supreme, unless the need for it was replaced by a complete change of heart.

[5] *De Execr.* 7 (154, M. 2. 434), expounding Lev. 26 and Deut. 28 *seqq.*

[6] Pausanias, *Descr. Gr.* 1. 17. 1; cf. Frazer's note *ad loc.*; Sext. Emp. *adv. Math.* 9. 187.

[7] Cf. *Orpheus* 260.

and blameless race; for the desert, as the prophet says, will abound in children. Is. 54. 1 is here used to justify a belief which can only be drawn from Greek mythology. Philo passes on to a moral allegory; his immediate source appears to have been a midrashic exposition of the Pentateuch which was so coloured by Hellenistic views that it had not even eliminated the altar of mercy. It is rare to find Jewish apocalyptic drawing so largely on Greek ideas, and the ultimate source seems to have been literature which looked for the beginning of a new world-age in which the Stoic ideals of virtue would be realised, as in the Sibylline apocalypse of Antony and Cleopatra.

The growth of hope in a supernatural deliverance and a new world-order was indeed responsible for a remarkable growth in the output of Sibylline literature. Ancient Greek tradition knew of one Sibyl; Varro is acquainted with ten.[1] The output of Jewish Sibylline Oracles is a proof of their popularity; Jewish propaganda would not have chosen this unpromising form, if it had not been suggested by the tastes of the Gentiles.[2] "Wars and rumours of wars" were common enough to lead men to look for the imminent end of a world-age, to be accompanied by the cosmic catastrophes of Plato[3] or the final conflagration of Stoicism;[4] possibly Eastern beliefs with regard to the proper portents for the end of the world reinforced those which were already familiar to Hellenic thought.[5] Prophecies were common; but prophets were not confined to prophecy as a means of self-expression. Once at least the extremes of misery expressed their faith in prophecy in a form which shook the Roman world to its foundation. Eunus the Syrian, who led the slave-rebellion in Sicily in 134 B.C.,[6] in his dreams and waking visions, in which the gods showed him the future, is true to the traditions of Semitic prophecy, as manifested by the servants of the Syrian goddess;[7] it was she who had foretold that he

[1] *Ap.* Lact. *Div. Inst.* 1. 6. For the Sibylline literature in general cf. Lanchester in *Ap. and Ps.* 2. 368. Cf. also Lucan, *Phars.* 1. 564.

[2] For another apocalypse cf. *Or. Sib.* 3. 741–95; it contains the usual promises of peace and prosperity for the righteous of Israel and their proselytes; there is a strong colouring of Isaiah. In general the oracles are more concerned to proclaim the true religion and to foretell the punishment of the heathen.

[3] Cf. Lucan, *Phars.* 1. 72 *seqq.* Naturally here the golden age is to begin with the apotheosis of Nero (*ib.* 60).

[4] *Or. Sib.* 5. 512 *seqq.*, which shows no trace of being Jewish.

[5] For the Zoroastrian world-ending cf. Lommel, *op. cit.* 209. In the *Bundahesh* Lommel, *op. cit.* 222, holds that the Zoroastrian view goes back to a primitive myth of a world-ending by fire.

[6] Diod. Sic. 34/35. 2. 5 *ap.* Photius 525. Diodorus describes him as a Syrian from Apamea; since he would not be likely to know of his race except from his birthplace, it is to be presumed that he means Apamea on the Orontes.

[7] Apuleius, *Metam.* 8. 27 (581 *seqq.*) and 1 Kings 18. 19, where the "prophets of the Asherah" appear to be, like those of Baal, Syrian importations to be attributed

would one day be a king. Even his mastery of the old conjurer's trick of fire-breathing is suggestive of a favourite feature of apocalyptic literature.[1]

But apocalyptic expectation had even found its way into official Roman religion. The prolonged trumpet-blast from a clear sky which preceded the civil war of 86 B.C. was explained by the Etruscan *haruspices* to portend a change in the state of the world.[2] For there were eight races of mankind, to each of which was assigned a Great Year. The end of one period and the beginning of the next were announced by a sign to show that a new race had appeared, caring for the gods less than its predecessor.[3] One remarkable feature of this account is its acceptance of a scheme of eight world-ages. A succession of ages should work in hebdomads, one for each of the planets,[4] whereas a system of eight should succeed in passing out of the series of planetary successions into the firmament of heaven, above the decrees of the planets and of fate.[5] This however may be merely an echo of the scheme of the *Timaeus* [39(a)] for the duration of each world-age. It is more striking that the Etruscans should explain the trumpet-blast in this way. Such blasts are part of the stock-in-trade of ancient portents.[6] But they have no obvious association with the change of world-ages, whereas in Judaism they have such an association; trumpets mark the accession of a king,[7] the beginning of the new year with the new moon of Tishri,[8] which was also the beginning of the sabbatical years and of the theoretical fiftieth year of the Jubilee, which may have been a late invention and never observed in practice, but was likely enough to suggest the beginning of a new series of world-ages after seven weeks of years were past.[9] The trumpets of the

to Jezebel. (Cf. Allen in Hastings' *DB* I. 165, s.v. *Astarte*, where the word is regarded as a mistake for Ashtoreth.) The technique in Apuleius and I Kings is remarkably similar.

[1] 4 Esdr. 13. 10; cf. Is. 11. 4 and 2 Thess. 2. 8, based on Isaiah, for the destruction of the enemy by the "breath" of the Messiah, which presumably goes back to the same source in primitive magic. Cf. Talmud, *Shabb.* 88 b. For a variation of the trick of fire-breathing cf. Hipp. *El.* 4. 33 (70).

[2] Diod. Sic. 38/39. 5 from Suidas and Plut. *Sulla* 7. 445 f.

[3] Reading θεοῖς ἧττον τῶν προτέρων μέλοντες, which appears to reflect correctly the essential clerical attitude.

[4] Cf. Verg. *Ecl.* 4. 6, *Saturnia regna*, for which see below, p. 18.

[5] Whether the Etruscans are correctly reported or not is a secondary question; it is equally surprising that Diodorus should take such a view.

[6] Pliny, *N.H.* 2. 57. 148; Lydus, *De Ostentis* 6 (22 c), where this and similar trumpet-blasts are referred to as foreboding wars.

[7] I Kings I. 39; 2 Kings 11. 14.

[8] Lev. 23. 23 *seqq.*; Num. 29. 1 *seqq.*

[9] For the origin and meaning of the *shofar* cf. Finnesinger in *Heb. Union College Annual* 8. 193 *seqq.*

New Year were also associated with the giving of the Torah, which was a proclamation to all mankind that the great event had occurred, which was intended to put an end to the wars of mankind and their counterpart, the upheavals of nature with which God visits the iniquity of man.[1] Moreover, the periods of fifty-year Jubilees, however fictitious they may have been, were prominent features in the calculation of the times by which the history of the world was determined and its future duration established.[2] Thus trumpets are naturally associated with a new world-age as in the Jewish festival of *Rosh-ha-Shanah*.[3] Hence from the time of Zechariah they form a regular feature of Jewish-Christian apocalyptic.[4] But the association of trumpets with an apparently closed system of world-ages at Rome in 85 B.C., or even in the imagination of Diodorus Siculus, is surprising, since it is hard to imagine a connection between the Etruscan *haruspices* and the Jewish colony at Rome.[5] On the other hand, a fortuitous coincidence of this kind is somewhat unlikely.

The years that followed the trumpet-blast were calculated to enhance the belief that the end of a world-age was at hand. The opportunities of the prophets were increased by the burning of the Sibylline Books in the fire that destroyed the Capitol in 82 B.C. The end of the triumvirate produced the great masterpiece of pagan apocalyptic, the Fourth Eclogue of Vergil. Its preservation is to be attributed not only to its literary quality, but to the fact that the author was on the right side at the end of the Civil Wars, and that the Eclogue could at least be interpreted as supporting the cause of Augustus. Many of the problems of this much discussed poem do not concern us.[6] The old

[1] Philo, *De Spec. Legg.* 2 (*De Sept.*), 22 (189 *seqq.*, M. 2. 295). Philo equates the giving of the Torah with *Rosh-ha-Shanah* (instead of the more usual Pentecost), and uses the trumpets in order to associate the giving of the Torah with a new world-age, which is a Hellenistic age of gold.

[2] So in the Book of Jubilees. Is this the explanation of the figures of *Ass. Moys.* 1. 2 and 10. 12, where Moses dies in 2500 A.M. and there are 250 "times" till the coming of the Messiah? Charles in *Ap. and Ps. ad loc.* takes these as periods of seven years, quoting the Talmud (*Sanh.* 97b) for a similar figure. But 1750 years from the death of Moses to the coming of the Messiah and a total of 4250 years or 85 jubilees seem pointless. I am inclined to suggest that "times" here are decads, and that we are intended to fix the death of Moses as half-way through the world, i.e. after 50 out of 100 jubilees.

[3] Cf. the Mishnah, *Rosh-ha-Shanah* 3. 2 *seqq.* (Danby 191); the same thought appears in Pss. Sol. 11. 1, *Mekilta Tr. Pish.* 14. 116 (ed. Lauterbach, 1. 116).

[4] Zech. 9. 14, where however they may be rather a sign of God going out to war; see further 4 Esdr. 6. 23; *Or. Sib.* 4. 174; Mt. 24. 31 and similar N.T. passages.

[5] It is of course possible that similar speculations were attached to a similar use of trumpets in some other Semitic religion and that these, and not the Jewish, are the source of this incident.

[6] Tarn, *loc. cit.*, deals with the poem and the literature, and is one of the few writers on it who bears in mind steadily the important point that Vergil did not know

age is at an end, the new age of Saturn is beginning; that this is also an age of Apollo or the sun is due to the association of the two planets.[1] Pollio is called on to banish the civil wars of the age, in order that the child who is to be born may enter on a peaceful age in which he can consort with the gods and heroes who will naturally be more accessible in the new time. This age is then described in perfectly conventional language (ll. 18–25); as he grows older it will actually improve (ll. 26–30). But there will remain some traces of the ancient sin of mankind, which will make it necessary for the child to repeat the exploits of the ancient heroes (ll. 31–36). This will be followed by a yet more abundant provision of the natural bounties of the golden age. The ending of the present age is already being heralded by the appropriate portents: the poet hopes for a long life in the new. It appears that Vergil is working with a type of world-age, which allowed for such a hope; the catastrophes of a collapsing world do not involve the destruction of all mankind.

That the child is a real child, or an expected child of two real parents, seems certain.[2] That, though divine, he is of human parentage need occasion no surprise. The heroes of old were of partly divine parentage, yet they were human. It was always doubtful whether they achieved their godhead by their exploits or their exploits by their godhead; the achievements of Alexander the Great had led to a belief in his divine descent.[3] To the first generation of Christians it seemed natural to ascribe the Messianic origin of Jesus to His divine origin, to His human exploits or to His resurrection, without any sense of inconsistency.[4]

the future when he wrote; hence he may have foretold a glorious future for a child who was a disappointment, or was never born. Norden, *Die Geburt des Kindes*, seems to me to exaggerate Iranian influences as against general apocalyptic convention.

[1] For the passage cf. Peterson, Εἷς Θεός 100, who shows that the age of the sun, described by Servius *ad loc.* as the last, is also the first. The *Saturnia regna* of primitive Italian mythology, or what Dionysius of Halicarnassus regards as such (*Antt. Rom.* I. 36), are conflated with the age of the sun. For the connection of the sun and Saturn see also Boll-Bezold, *Sternglaube u. Sterndeutung* 5.

[2] Tarn, *loc. cit.*, seems to me entirely convincing in his argument for a hoped-for child of Antony and Octavia.

[3] Dion. Halic. *Antt. Rom.* I. 40, where Evander has heard (1) that it is fated that Heracles, (2) being the child of Zeus and Alcmena (3) is to rise above mortal nature, and (4) to become immortal on account of his virtue. Cf. 2. 56 for Romulus, whose birth and dissolution provide a good argument for those who deify the souls of great men. Tarn, *loc. cit.*, doubts whether a Roman of 40 B.C. would combine both views as, he admits, a Greek would; Dion. Halic. suggests that such speculations were not alien to a Roman audience. For Alexander's miraculous birth cf. Plut. *Alexander* 2 and 3 (665 b), following Eratosthenes (*c.* 250 B.C.).

[4] Rom. I. 4 dates the Messiahship to the Resurrection, while Gal. 4. 4 asserts a divine origin. Heb. 5. 7 asserts a Messiahship won by achievements, but the author is beginning to be influenced by tradition and inserts the saving clause, "though he was a Son".

Hellenistic Judaism in the same way went as far as it could in investing the birth and death of Moses with a supernatural halo.[1]

The poem contains one departure from the normal convention in the three stages of the development of the golden age, one accompanying the birth of the child, one corresponding to his growth and one marking the end of his exploits. These are, however, conditioned by the fact that the poem appears to be an epithalamium. The work of salvation has to be divided between the bridegroom and the offspring of the marriage, though here the exploits of the bridegroom are transferred to Pollio, Vergil's patron, perhaps in virtue of a revision in the light of later events. The poet cannot underrate his patron's achievements, yet he must, if the child is to be human, leave him some exploits; it is also necessary to tide over the awkward period of his childhood; the apocryphal Gospels show the difficulty of describing the boyhood of a docetic Christ, which Jewish apocalyptic avoided by the convenient fiction of the Messiah's miraculous concealment at his birth,[2] or his ignorance of his office, until it is revealed to him at his anointing by Elijah.[3] Christianity was saved from the difficulty; a Messiah who could suffer death could have a normal childhood. The variations from the conventional method of establishing the golden age by the sudden appearance of the triumphant saviour are thus imposed on Vergil by his theme; the ordinary apocalyptist was too poor an artist to realise the difficulties. It is of course possible that Vergil has been influenced by some version of the Zoroaster legend, in which Zoroaster is followed by two "helpers" who produce a sudden improvement, followed by a further deterioration; it is only the third who brings the scheme of history to an end;[4] it is also possible that the curious appeal to the child to smile at his mother alludes to the legend that Zoroaster alone of all men laughed on the day of his birth.[5] But it seems unnecessary to find these allusions;

[1] Jos. *Antt.* 2. 9. 2 (205) and 3 (212); 4. 8. 48 (326). Cf. Philo, *De Vit. Moys.* I. 5 (20 *seqq.*, M. 2. 83) and 2 (3), 39 (290, M. 2. 179). For rabbinical legends cf. Str.-B. on Acts 7. 22, which presupposes these legends, and Ginsburg, *Legends of the Jews* 2. 262 *seqq.* Presumably the original Moses-legend contained a miraculous birth and death which have been modified in the Scriptures and unconsciously revived in the legends. Clem. Alex. *Strom.* I. 23. 153 (412 P) says that his heavenly name after his assumption was Melchi. (These appear to be "mystics" who know Hebrew.) Cf. Noah in I En. 106. 2; note that Noah here is the medium of a παλιγγενεσία.

[2] As in the Jewish apocalypse underlying Rev. 12. 1, cf. Gunkel, *Schöpfung u. Chaos* 198.

[3] Justin Martyr, *Dial. c. Tryph.* 8. 226b; cf. Jno. 7. 27, which implies one or other of the stories.

[4] Lommel, *op. cit.* 205 *seqq.*

[5] Pliny, *N.H.* 7. 15. 72; cf. Moulton, *Early Zoroastrianism* 91.

Heracles was always smiling, and Heracles was one of the intermediate beings of the saviour-type who had survived.[1] It is apparently as a contrast to the levity of pagan saviours that Hellenistic Judaism insists on the perpetual seriousness of the infant Moses.[2]

Thus it is possible but by no means certain that we have here the preservation of a genuine tradition of Zoroastrianism. But the figure of the child, or at any rate of the inaugurator of the new age, is necessary to the scheme. All things had begun (in so far as they could be said to have had a beginning) with an age of gold, and each world-age, or series of world-ages, was a precise reproduction of its predecessors. This was a logical necessity, for all things were determined by the divine reason immanent in the world, by a fate determined by the stars in their courses or by nature, the three phrases being different methods of stating the same truth.[3] Hence the end of one age must usher in the new, and the new must witness the primitive bliss of the kingdom of Saturn. It was therefore necessary that it should begin, as the first had begun, with a hero from whom the new race should take its origin, or with a leader of the new race with which mankind was to be peopled from heaven. Vergil indeed is quite illogical; the new race of l. 7 is incompatible with the hope of survival into the new age in l. 53, but we are dealing with court-poetry, not with a scientific prediction of the future. The reappearance of the heroes is equally necessary, for the heroes must repeat their former exploits, except in so far as they had been released by their virtue from the round of existence.[4] Indeed it was hardly politic to suppose in a poem addressed to the hero of a new world-age that he was reincarnated from a former age, since it suggested that he had not been worthy to make good his escape. But the difficulty could be avoided by supposing that he was a new hero sent from heaven to inaugurate the new age.[5] Here the conflation of the strictly Stoic scheme of a complete restart from a state of incandescence with the *Timaeus* and its widespread catastrophes left an opening both for the appearance of a new race from heaven with a new hero and for the survival of at least a chosen few into the new age; the result was lacking in logical justification, but was comforting to the

[1] Tarn, *op. cit.* 156.

[2] Philo, *De Vit. Moys.* I. 5 (20, M. 2. 83). Moses is also so quick to learn that his progress seems due to μάθησις rather than ἀνάμνησις. Since Philo does not believe in reincarnation, this comes perilously near to suggesting that he is of semi-divine origin. Ordinary souls may pre-exist as δαιμόνια but have to learn: they do not remember.

[3] Cf. below, p. 64.

[4] Cf. p. 3.

[5] Cf. Norden, *op. cit.* 46 *seqq.*, for the welcome of great men as saviours sent down from heaven. The practice seems to appear from the East in the first century B.C.

feelings of all concerned; in any case Vergil has canonised in literature the theme of the saviour of society who inaugurates a new world-age or series of world-ages. Properly the end of the series ought to be to deteriorate into the same state of chaos as that from which the new age is to be a deliverance; it is possible that the Zoroastrian tradition has suggested the hope that the new saviour is to inaugurate a series of ages which will not carry within themselves the seeds of their decay, but will lead to a state of eternal prosperity. It is however more probable that Vergil in writing court-poetry is not concerned with such a distant future, which it would indeed be hardly tactful to mention. The hope of a new age is an expression of a longing for deliverance, and in Vergil as in the inscriptions which hail such ages the strict demands of logic for a fresh degeneration are ignored.[1]

Another possible link with the religion of Persia is the figure of Hystaspes the "ancient king of Media" who was credited with prophecies of the downfall of Rome which were older than the Trojan war. His name suggests that the association of Zoroaster with someone named Vistaspa was known; he was credited with dreams in which he had foretold the destruction of Rome; in the miseries of the last days the righteous would raise their hands in prayer to Jupiter, who would hear their prayer and save them, while destroying the wicked.[2] He also foretold the destruction of the world by fire. The reference to Jupiter suggests, though it does not definitely prove, that the prophecies of "Hystaspes" were pagan and not Jewish; but Justin Martyr suggests that he was singled out for destruction with the Sibyl when Augustus suppressed inconvenient prophecies.[3] His prediction of the destruction of the world by fire might indicate an Iranian origin, but it is equally likely that he derived it from the common stock of apocalyptic literature; Justin Martyr, who records the fact, treats it as a variation of the Stoic view,[4] while the statement

[1] For an interesting variant cf. Philo, *De Migr. Abr.* 22 (125, M. 1. 455). From Noah, the survivor of the Deluge, springs the race of wisdom, which produces the "seeing Israel", as represented by Abraham, Isaac and Jacob, the "measures of the aeon", who prove that virtue is, has been and will be. It may at times be hidden by the ἀκαιρίαι of men, but καιρός the servant of God will reveal it afresh. The three patriarchs are the heroes of the new aeon ushered in by Noah, and suggest the aeon made up of equal periods which recur eternally (but are naturally commuted by Philo into the eternity of virtue). Cf. Reitzenstein, *Erlösungs-Mysterium* 176. But the conception is simply taken over from the general Hellenistic background.

[2] Schürer, *G.J.V.* 3. 592.

[3] *Apol.* 1. 44, 82b. The account is confused, since there seems no evidence of any infliction of the death-penalty on those who possessed the prophecies of the Sibyl or Hystaspes. It seems that Justin is referring to the destruction of prophecies by Augustus, for which see below, p. 24.

[4] *Apol.* 1. 20, 66c.

of Lactantius that his prophecies were in the form of dreams suggests that "Hystaspes'" origin is to be sought not in Persia but the pages of Herodotus.[1] His genuine affinities with Persia may well amount to no more than a vague knowledge that a quite different "Hystaspes" was a friend of Zoroaster. It appears that his prophecies had the quality of other prophecies of gathering round them the floating material of the age; Lactantius complains that the evil spirits have cut out of them all reference to the sending of the Son of God;[2] but Clement of Alexandria knows of a text in which the defect had been remedied long before the days of Lactantius.[3] Hystaspes no doubt resembled Enoch, Ezra and Baruch when acclimatised in Judaism and Christianity.

The same period produced at least two variations of the literature of escape in the form of Utopias, in which the Golden Age is replaced by the Islands of the Blessed. In Diodorus Siculus we read how a certain Iambulus was taken prisoner by the Ethiopians.[4] It was the custom of his captors, every 600 years (one of the varieties of the Great Year), to effect a purification by putting two men into a boat with six months' food and orders to sail southwards to the Islands of the Blessed; they were threatened with the direst punishment if they returned. Iambulus and his companion arrived at an island where the inhabitants, apart from various physical peculiarities, practised the communism of Plato's *Republic*; the island to which Iambulus came was one of seven; he was allowed to stay there seven years. The inhabitants practised the highest form of religion, worshipping the firmament, the sun and the rest of the heavenly bodies. The trees bear fruit all the year round; this is a feature borrowed from apocalyptic, though Diodorus appeals for support for his statement to the gardens of Alcinous. The numerical features of the story show its affinity with the apocalyptic convention, which is reinforced by a lively imagination and travellers' tales; the days and nights are of equal length and the inhabitants have a tongue divided down the middle, so that they can conduct two conversations at once. Here we have a complete Utopia; a curious compromise between utopian and apocalyptic survives in the sixteenth Epode of Horace, where the Islands of the Blessed, to which Horace proposes flight, are the refuge preserved by Jupiter for the righteous when he contaminated the age of gold

[1] *Div. Inst.* 7. 15; cf. Hdt. 1. 209. Lactantius credits him with a prophecy of the fall of Rome and the end of the world: it is possible that he is the source of Tertullian, *ad Scap.* 2 and *Apol.* 32, where the duration of Rome and the saeculum are bound up as in the Apocalypse. Possibly this expectation underlies 2 Thess. 2. 3 *seqq.* It may reflect a fairly widespread belief dating from the last years of the Republic; cf. *Or. Sib.* 3. 56 *seqq.*

[2] *Div. Inst.* 7. 18.

[3] *Strom.* 6. 5. 43 (762 P).

[4] 2. 55 *seqq.*

with brass, as now he has hardened it with iron, an interesting conflation of the Hesiodic world-ages with utopianism.

The battle of Actium brought the vogue of apocalyptic writing to an end. "Peace and the principate" appeared for the moment a satisfactory realisation of the age of gold, and the triumph of Augustus was duly celebrated as the fulfilment of the hopes of mankind by those who had hastened to rally to the victor's cause.[1] The deification of the saviour of the world was the natural climax of the Messianic hopes of the Gentile world. Hopes of the same kind might linger on and revive when times were bad;[2] and the language appropriate to the appearance of a Saviour might be used to greet the accession of a new Emperor, particularly if he were the young and promising successor of an unpopular ruler. The accession of Caligula seemed to many to be a new kingdom of Saturn, and his recovery from sickness shortly afterwards to be comparable to the first establishment of civilisation; even Jews of the Dispersion, who had recently been suffering from Tiberius' attempt to suppress Jewish propaganda in Rome by the expulsion of the Jews, were prepared to make use of the language of the Gentiles.[3] Otherwise pagan apocalyptic came to an abrupt ending. Augustus celebrated the establishment of peace and the restoration of religion with the *Ludi Saeculares* of 17 B.C.; Horace was commissioned to produce a hymn which should pray for the blessings of fertility for mankind, for beasts and for the soil which had figured largely in the apocalypses of earlier decads.[4] Augustus, as the saviour of the world, replaced Vergil's Messianic child; if he were a somewhat prosaic figure, it could at least be hinted that he was a kind of representative of Aeneas.[5] The Sibyl herself was employed to order the celebration, and the third stanza to some extent suggested that the new age of the

[1] For soteriological language in the cult of the Emperor cf. Friedrich in *T.W.z.N.T.* s.v. *εὐαγγέλιον*. There is an interesting blend of philosophy and apocalyptic in the inscription of Halicarnassus (Brit. Mus. 984, Wendland, *H.z.N.T. Die Hell.-Röm. Kultur* 410: ἡ ἀθάνατος τοῦ πάντος φύσις...ἀνθρώποις ἐχαρίσατο Καίσαρα τὸν Σέβαστον, σωτῆρα τῶν ἀνθρώπων γένους). For this blending cf. above, p. 13.

[2] So in *Corp. Herm.* Ascl. 3. 24b *seqq.* (Scott 341), where we have a thoroughly nationalist Egyptian apocalypse, dated by Scott on internal grounds at A.D. 270. It might contain older material, but it is interesting to find heathen apocalyptic as late as this.

[3] Philo, *Leg. ad Gaium* 2 (13, M. 2. 547) for Caligula's accession as *Saturnia regna* and *ib.* 3 (20, M. 2. 549) for his recovery. I have to thank Dr M. Braun of Manchester College, Oxford, for calling my attention to these two passages. Further parallels are given by Kittel in *T.W.z.N.T.* s.v. *αἰών*. For the expulsion of the Jews from Rome by Tiberius cf. Jos. *Antt.* 18. 3. 5 (84) and Tac. *Ann.* 2. 85.

[4] Note the fourth, fifth and eighth stanzas. For an account of the *Ludi Saeculares* cf. Warde Fowler, *Religious Experience of the Roman People* 438 *seqq.*

[5] He is neither exactly a "new" Aeneas nor a reincarnation of him, but stanzas 11 and 13 hint that he is something of one kind or the other.

sun was beginning. It was all a rather prosaic realisation of the yearnings of mankind, but it would scarcely have been decent to hope for anything further. Moreover, steps were taken to avoid the risk that might attach to such prophecies in the new era. Augustus collected all the prophecies he could find and burnt them to the number of two thousand.[1] Only suitable selections from the Sibyl's Oracles were allowed to survive. A despotism can have no liking for prophecy; but the measures of destruction would hardly have been successful, if the prophets had not been reasonably satisfied with the age of gold, which set in with the establishment of the empire of Augustus. Only in one corner of the Empire did a living tradition of apocalyptic survive. In Judaea Herod the Great could not be accepted as the fulfilment of the prophecy of a righteous king of the house of David. On the other hand he seems not to have troubled himself with the suppression of the prophets. By an interesting irony of fate the apocalyptic literature of Judaism owes to him its preservation from destruction and its further development.

Jewish apocalyptic had assumed a full-fledged form at the time of the Maccabean persecution, when Judaism first came into serious conflict with the great Macedonian Empires. In Daniel[2] it takes a more definitely Oriental colour than in the Hellenistic world in general. The ending of the world-process and the angelic rulers of the nations are apparently derived from Persian religion; yet the description of the resurrection of the dead seems to represent a mixture of the Semitic revival of the dead from the dust of the earth[3] and the Babylonian translation of some specially righteous souls (properly the souls of kings) to the firmament of heaven.[4] The authenticity of Daniel's message is vindicated by the marvellous manner in which he and his companions are rescued from utmost perils in the fiery furnace and the lions' den. The thought was essentially similar to the Hellenistic desire for gods who could vindicate their power by bringing salvation in the hour of peril;[5] the essential difference between the hope of

[1] Suet. *Augustus* 31.

[2] For the book of Daniel cf. A. A. Bevan, *The Book of Daniel* 11 *seqq.*

[3] Dan. 12. 2 *seqq.* For this as a Semitic view cf. Baudissin, *Adonis und Esmun* 418, where this, and the similar language of Is. 26. 19, are traced to the Semitic belief in a vegetation god, who dies away and rises again. The date of Is. 26. 19 is open to dispute; it suggests however the possibility that the Jewish belief in a future life was not simply borrowed from Persia but developed out of purely Jewish beliefs; the soul of the dead goes to Sheol and remains there, but in Isaiah it is miraculously reunited to its body, and therefore becomes once more capable of life. For Persian influences cf. above, p. 6.

[4] Cumont, *Rel. Or.* 265, n. 91 as against Reitzenstein, *Poimandres* 79.

[5] Cf. above for "salvation" in this practical form.

Israel and the similar hopes of their neighbours lay not in the desire for deliverance nor the language employed, but in the different conceptions of the nature of God and His relation to the conduct of man. The Exodus of Israel from Egypt had become a specimen of a divine act of salvation on the stage of history; the new deliverance must be something comparable.[1] The hope flourished in Palestine rather than in the Dispersion, where it died away as a serious factor with the establishment of the Empire. Possibly its disappearance was due in part to its doubtful legality. In Palestine it even seemed for a moment that salvation had arrived with the establishment of the Hasmonean monarchy. The identification of John Hyrcanus with the Messiah might involve the transference of the Messianic promises from the house of David to the house of Aaron, but that was a small matter; apocalyptic is not bound by the fetters of dogma.[2] It was, however, soon made clear that the time was not yet. In spite of this disappointment the hope of the Messiah remained alive in Judaism, when it was extinct in the world in general. The contact of Jew and Gentile had been strong enough to enable Christianity to describe the coming of the Lord into the world in language which reflects the common hopes of both.[3] Outside the Church, however, the apocalyptic hope continued to flourish only in Judaism; elsewhere it was so little regarded that it was only here that prophecies of a king from the East could be found to vindicate the triumph of Vespasian.[4]

Consequently it is not surprising that Paul's attempt to convert the philosophers of Athens was a failure. The commonplaces by which Judaism sought to represent itself as the divine revelation of the truths at which philosophy had guessed, his appeal to the guidebook curiosity of altars to "Unknown Gods"[5] and the commonplace-book quotation

[1] So in the late prophecy in Is. 63. 8 and cf. below, p. 28.

[2] *Test. Lev.* 18. 2 and cf. Charles' introduction in *Ap. and Ps.* 2. 282 and 294. But it is a mistake to talk of a "revolution in the Messianic hope". Apocalyptic could recognise as the Messiah anyone who appeared to be establishing the Messianic kingdom, just as the Church found prophecies to justify its own interpretation.

[3] Pss. Sol. 11. 2 *seqq.*; the "good tidings" of Is. 40. 9 is transformed quite simply into the "Gospel" of the Messianic kingdom. The opening chapters of Luke resemble the language of the Gentile world because they reflect a common hope, which has affected the language of the LXX. But the general atmosphere of the chapters is essentially Jewish, though it reflects a Judaism which had been affected both by the Eastern religions which influenced both Judaism and Hellenism and also by the Hellenistic influences which were at work on Judaism during the last two centuries B.C.

[4] Tac. *Hist.* 5. 13; Jos. *B.J.* 6. 5. 4 (312).

[5] The reference in Philostratus, *Vit. Apoll. Tyan.* 6. 3. 5, sounds like a commonplace from popular descriptions of Athens; for a full discussion cf. *The Beginnings of Christianity* 5. 240 *seqq.*; Frazer, *Pausanias' Description of Greece* 2. 33.

from Aratus[1] were scarcely likely to impress an audience of such a character, still less to convert it to a belief that the world-process could be brought to an end by a divine assize, or to a system centred not on a semi-divine being who had been translated to the heavens in the dim remoteness of antiquity but to a man who had risen from the dead within the last few years.[2] The Areopagus only laughed; Paul was faced with the necessity of reconstructing the Gospel, if he was to appeal to the intellect of the Gentile world.

That the scene in its essence is historical and that the speech contains in a Thucydidean form the kind of argument which Paul used on the occasion need not be doubted; it is an attempt to express the Gospel in the commonplace terms of Hellenistic Jewish philosophy, as Paul would naturally have learnt them. It is significant that from this point onwards his Epistles show a progressive adaptation of the Christian message to the general mental outlook of the Hellenistic world. There is no reason for doubting that he was first compelled to face the need of this restatement by his chance meeting with serious philosophy on the Areopagus.

[1] It is perhaps significant that the collection of heathen testimonies to Judaism ascribed to Aristobulus (Eus. *Pr. Ev.* 13. 12) contains the passage from Aratus, as does the similar collection in Clem. Alex. *Strom.* 5. 14. 99 *seqq.* (707 P), which is a purely Jewish defence of the "voice of God" and the narrative of Genesis; there is no reason for supposing that the series which Clement has incorporated is Christian rather than Jewish.

[2] Cf. above, p. 20. Such redeemers would be raised to the stars in the language of Chaldean astrology (Cumont, *Rel. Or.* 161), which could easily be harmonised with classical legends, and also easily adapted to old beliefs of the disappearance of heroes in thunderstorms (Frazer, *The Golden Bough*, *The Magic Art* 2. 181). Resurrection was unknown. At Athens the claim that the resurrection could be proved as a fact of recent history would not be a recommendation. For Hercules in the tragedies of Seneca as a saviour whose death ought to carry with it the destruction of the world cf. Kroll, *Gott u. Hölle* 412 *seqq.* It is entirely inconsistent with the outlook of the age (*op. cit.* 443) and with Seneca's real belief (cf. above p. 4, nn. 5 and 6). Kroll sees in its appearance as a literary *motif* the influence of a dualist religion.

CHAPTER II

THE SYNAGOGUE AND THE GENTILES

In the Dispersion Judaism had long since faced and accommodated itself to the difficulties which Paul experienced at Athens. In the past Sibyls had uttered oracles of doom on behalf of the one true God; it is possible that they continued to do so, for Judaism was recognised as a peculiar religion and allowed a good deal of latitude. But educated or semi-educated circles had by this time lost interest in such matters. The type of Judaism which might reasonably hope to influence and even to convert intelligent Gentiles was not concerned with speculations about the coming of the end of all things. In spite of their sympathies with their brethren in Palestine, the Jews of the West were not to be led away into vague aspirations for the restoration of Israel, which could only endanger the peace and prosperity which the nation enjoyed under the Empire.[1] The solidarity of the Jewish nation might be an impressive testimony to the truth of their religion;[2] but their religion was represented as concerned not with hopes of the future but with the divine revelation of those truths of cosmogony at which the cults and philosophies of the heathen world had only guessed, and with the true way of "salvation" which that knowledge enabled the Jew to give to the world.[3] "Salvation" rested on a true knowledge of the nature and origin of the world,[4] and of the ethics and worship which that knowledge implied; and what else was the content of the Torah? It was obvious that it contained the true account

[1] Judaism outside Palestine remained entirely unaffected by the rebellion of Judaea in A.D. 66. The risings in Egypt and Cyrene under Trajan (A.D. 115) may represent a revival of Messianic hopes; the study of the O.T. might always lead to such a revival. But the quiescence of Judaism in A.D. 66 seems to indicate a complete indifference on the part of the leaders of the Jews outside Palestine.

[2] Jos. *c. Ap.* 2. 19 (179), where the ὁμόνοια of the Jews is evidence that the Torah enables the Jew to realise the ideal of Hellenistic philosophy.

[3] Note the complete suppression of the Messianic hope by Josephus. In Philo it appears only in the two closely connected tracts *De Praem. et Poen.* 15 [(88 *seqq*, M. 2. 422), where we have the taming of the beasts and a warrior-Messiah of a purely human type (*ib.* 16 (95)), who is forced on Philo by the LXX text of Num. 24. 7, which reads "a man shall go forth from his seed" for "he shall pour forth water from his buckets"; the LXX appears to be an attempt to amend an unintelligible text], and *De Execr.* 9 (165, M. 2. 436), where we have a miraculous return to Palestine.

[4] Cicero, *De Fin.* 3. 22. 73, explains the impossibility of right conduct without a knowledge of nature and the gods. "Salvation" can be this view transferred from philosophy to a supposedly revealed religion. Philo, *De Ebr.* 28 (107 *seqq.* M. 1. 374).

of the creation of the world and the nature of man; the truth of its system of religion as a means for attaining to righteousness was vindicated by that supreme act of "salvation" through which God had delivered His people from Egypt and brought them to the promised land. The canonical account of the Exodus, with a superficial colouring drawn from the religious language of the Hellenistic world, became a regular form of "preaching" addressed to the Gentiles.[1] The type was established before the close of the canon of the Old Testament and embedded in the worship of Judaism, notably in the domestic Liturgy of the Passover.[2] It becomes more definitely in the Dispersion a proclamation of the "salvation" which God has wrought for His people on the stage of history, and of the "epiphanies" in which He has shown Himself to be their "benefactor".[3] In all this there was no real breach with the tradition of the Old Testament, though occasionally Alexandrine Judaism allowed itself somewhat serious lapses from the strict proprieties of monotheism;[4] as a rule, however, these are successfully observed. The theme is frequently associated with the giving of the Law on Mount Sinai, which is associated with a solemn proclamation of the past benefits and future promises of God; the whole leads up to the proclamation of the decalogue. The lacuna of Exod. 19. 25–20. 1 gave an opportunity for the insertion of such a proclamation into the narrative of the Old Testament; it was easy to

[1] The illuminating conception of the Apostolic *kerygma* in Dodd's *The Apostolic Preaching and its Developments* provides the key to the phenomena of Jewish literature here discussed. It seems that the Church adopted a method of exposition which had already been established in the synagogue. For the influence of such recitals on the Christian Liturgy cf. Lietzmann, *Messe u. Herrenmahl* 125.

[2] Apart from the canonical Exodus we have in Ps. 78 a conflation of two such *kerygmata*, and another in Ps. 136; this Psalm as forming part of the Hallel enters into the Passover Haggada, which in its modern form is a conflation of three *kerygmata* quite apart from the Psalm. The theme appears in Is. 63. 8 *seqq.*, with a distinctly Hellenistic colouring, for which see below p. 122; Judith 5. 5 *seqq.*

[3] So in Wisd. 10. 1. *seqq.*, ῥύομαι being preferred to σώζω except in v. 4. In Jos. *Antt.* 2. 15. 4 (326)–3. 1. 1. (1) σωτηρία appears eight times; cf. 2. 16. 2 (339) for the parting of the Red Sea as an epiphany. Cf. the Greek Esther 15. 2. In Philo the connection of God as "saviour" with the Exodus remains in *De Post. Cain.* 45 (156, M. 1. 255), *De Agric.* 17 (80, M. 1. 312), *De Migr. Abr.* 5 (25, M. 1. 440) and *passim*; but the phrase has become a commonplace and God appears as "saviour and benefactor" without any such reference, as in *De Mund. Op.* 60 (169, M. 1. 41), etc. The convention appears among the Gnostic Peratae, where the Exodus is, after the manner of Philo, a type of the soul coming out of the world into the desert (Hipp. *El.* 5. 16 (133)).

[4] As in Alypos' dedication of a synagogue to Cleopatra and Ptolemy XV as the great gods who give ear (ἐπήκοοι), Oesterley and Robinson, *History of Israel* 2. 411. In Philo lapses are fairly common, as in *De Mund. Op.* 7 (27, M. 1. 6), where the "visible gods" appear from *Timaeus* 41a, or a commentary on that work; cf. the virgin Victory who springs armed from the head of Zeus, *ib.* 33 (100, M. 1. 24). But in Philo we have no more than careless revision of the sources.

find appropriate words for Moses in the place which the original compilers had left open.[1] The necessity of instructing a proselyte in his duties as summarised in the decalogue would seem to have been prefaced with the account of God's works of salvation, while the decalogue itself was treated as a "mystery" too sacred to be revealed to vulgar ears, for its words were the words of God Himself.[2] Although orthodox Judaism, like Christianity, professed to regard the whole of the Scriptures as equal in sanctity, it was inevitable that in practice some parts should be more important and therefore more sacred than others; the withdrawal of the decalogue from those who were not proselytes would have the double advantage of stimulating the curiosity of enquirers and preserving the great summary of Jewish ethics from the ribaldry of Alexandrine anti-Semitism.[3] It could not be foreseen that the whole of this method of treatment would give to the Church an admirable opportunity of arguing that the real Torah consisted of the decalogue alone, and that the ceremonial law and Mishnah were only a secondary and inferior law imposed on the Jews for their sin in the matter of the Golden Calf.[4]

With a rather bold extension of this method of exegesis it was possible to assimilate Judaism to a mystery-cult to a remarkable extent. The normal cultus of the synagogue was as public as could be; Gentiles were welcomed and almost invited to attend. But the Paschal meal which celebrated the great deliverance could only be eaten by the circumcised proselyte. A fragment of Philo exploits this point in order to describe the meal in all the correct terminology of Eleusis; if cities refuse to reveal their mysteries to the uninitiated, still less should the true rites (τελεταί), which lead to piety, be cast

[1] So in Jos. *Antt.* 3. 5. 3 (84). For rabbinical enlargements on the passage cf. *Yalkut, Yithro* 279 *ad init.*

[2] *Antt.* 3. 5. 4 (90) (οὐ θεμιτόν); cf. R. Judah the Patriarch in *Judaism* 1. 335 for the correspondence between the Exodus and the circumcision, baptism and offering of the sacrifice of the proselyte. Naturally the theme appears more frequently in Hellenistic literature in view of its greater missionary interest.

[3] Cf. the Christian treatment of the Creed. Of course there was no real secrecy about the duties of a proselyte any more than about the Christian faith. Cf. *Conversion* 214.

[4] The theme underlies Acts 7. 38; the "living oracles" were rejected. Cf. *Ep. Barn.* 14. 1 *seqq.*; Ir. *Haer.* 4. 15. 1; Tertullian, *adv. Jud.* 3 *ad fin.*; it is implied in Orig. *c. Cels.* 2. 74 and worked out in *Didascalia* 6. 16. 6 (where *secundatione* is a reference to the Mishnah; cf. *Const. Apost.* 6. 20. 4 *seqq.*; Lactantius, *Div. Inst.* 4. 10). The theme reflects the rabbinical view of the Golden Calf as the great sin of Israel (*Judaism* 1. 537). It appears to be the reason for the withdrawal of the decalogue from the Jewish Liturgy "owing to the cavils of the heretics" (*ib.* 1. 291 and n. 64, where Moore fails to notice the wide extension of this argument in Christian writers who are entirely orthodox, though the Church never formally accepted this view). In *Clem. Recog.* 1. 36 Moses allows sacrifice as a means for averting a relapse into idolatry.

before ears full of ribaldry; those who desire admission to such things must possess piety towards the one true God, and have rejected idolatry and rites that are no true rites and mysteries that are no true mysteries (τελεταῖς ἀτελέστοις καὶ μυστηρίοις ἀνοργιάστοις). They must next be cleansed with purifying cleansings (καθαρθῆναι τὰς ἁγνευούσας καθάρσεις) in body and soul through the laws and customs of the fathers, and in the third place they must give a sure pledge of their worthiness to join in the revels, lest, after receiving the sacred food, they should be changed by satiety and make a drunken mockery where it is not lawful (οὐ θέμις) to do so.[1] The similarity of the Paschal meal to a Hellenistic mystery could even be extended to the point of regarding it as not merely a memorial of a past redemption but a means of present deliverance and redemption of the soul.[2]

In Hellenistic Judaism the symbolism was naturally adapted to the ideas of popular theology; it was a commonplace that mysteries were symbols of true philosophy.[3] Thus it could be explained as symbolising anything that was thought desirable. It could represent the beginning of the year when corn, the necessity of life, was ripe, but fruits, which were luxuries, were not.[4] Or it could represent the beginning of creation of which the spring equinox was an annual commemoration; the use of unleavened bread then either commemorated the hasty Exodus or was suited to the state of the crops which were still unripe; or it might be, "as the exegetes say", a reminder of the natural state of primitive man.[5] The state of primitive man was a favourite theme of

[1] Fr. *ap.* Joh. Damasc. *Sacra Parallela* 782 b (M. 2. 658). For the terms cf. Aristophanes, *Frogs* 354 *seqq.*; the last sentence is a precaution for securing εὐφημία. Philo is entirely in the classical tradition, either as mediated through the Sarapis-cult or (perhaps more probably) because his knowledge of such things is largely academic. Goodenough (*By Light, Light* 261) objects that the Paschal meal could only, at this date, be eaten in Jerusalem, quoting *Judaism* 2. 40 *seqq.* But Philo normally follows the text of the O.T., in which it is assumed that the full Paschal rite is binding on all Jews. I am inclined to doubt whether the prominence of Passover and Exodus in Hellenistic-Jewish literature does not indicate that there was some observance, apart from that of the synagogues. Cf. the observance of the Passover by the Jewish colony at Elephantine apparently under directions from Jerusalem (Vincent, *Rel. des Judéo-Araméens d'Eleph.* 281.

[2] So R. Gamaliel in Mishnah, *Pesachim* 10. 5 (Danby 151); this sentence however is omitted in the older texts; but *ib.* 6 the Passover is associated with the ransoming of the soul by R. Akiba. For the importance of the Passover symbolism cf. the Christian interpolation in Ezra (6. 21?) which Justin Martyr accuses the Jews of suppressing (*Dial. c. Tryph.* 72. 297 d): "this passover is our saviour and refuge", etc. Justin's good faith can hardly be disputed: it seems that the interpolation was made at such a date that he could suppose it a genuine reading. Cf. Clem. Alex. *Strom.* 1. 21. 124 (392 P), where the same interpolation is implied.

[3] Plato, *Gorgias* 493 a. Cf. Chrysippus *ap.* Plutarch, *Tranq. Anim.* 20. 477 d; *De Stoic. Rep.* 9, 1035 b and *Etym. Magn.* s.v. τελετή, 750. 16 *ap.* v. Arn. 2. 299 (1008).

[4] Philo, *De Vit. Moys.* 2 (3) 29 (222, M. 2. 169).

[5] Philo, *De Spec. Legg.* 2 (*De Sept.*), 19 (159, M. 2. 293).

the Stoics, but it does not appear that the rabbis associated the Passover with it. On the other hand, they sometimes regarded it as the date of creation;[1] it is likely enough that Philo has here taken over some Stoic explanation of one or other of the numerous festivals associated with the vernal equinox as relating to creation and attached it to the Passover. Or again the festival could be elaborately explained as a symbol of the soul's escape from the spheres of earth, the planets and the fixed stars to its home in heaven; for the lamb must be chosen on the tenth day, and the Passover of the soul is a passage from the sensible to the decad which is intelligible and divine; and again on the tenth of the month the moon is only two-thirds full; during the ensuing week it must grow, until like the full moon it is nothing but heavenly light and can offer the true sacrifice of propitiation, a blameless progress in virtue. The passage is interesting, as being drawn from a system of symbolism which appears to belong to the solar religion of Syria; the ennead of earth, the planets and the firmament appear to have been drawn from one of Posidonius' speculations as to the nature of the cosmos;[2] it may be doubted whether he was not almost as willing as Philo to incorporate material from any source that interested him. It is disappointing to pass from this symbolism to the mere cleansing of the soul from the body and its passions.[3]

In this way the Passover could be Hellenised into a mystery-rite, open only to the initiate who had accepted circumcision. It commemorated a past deliverance; here the "myth" differed only from the ordinary myth of a mystery-religion as being more seriously concerned with history. It was an effectual symbol of future salvation,

[1] For the Passover as the date of creation as against *Rosh-ha-Shanah* cf. *Gen. R.* 22. 3 on Gen. 4. 3. For the New Year as a counterpart of creation in Babylonian religion cf. Jeremias *ap.* Bertholet-Lehmann, *Lehrb. der Religionsgeschichte* 1. 505.

[2] *D.C.E.R.* 19 (106 *seqq.*, M. 1. 534) repeated Clem. Alex. *Strom.* 2. 11. 51 (455 P); God has been detached from the firmament to make a decad for the Paschal season; the same ennead with God identified with the firmament in Cicero, *De Rep.* 6 (*Somn. Scip.*), 17. 17; it is read by Servius into the *novies Styx interfusa coercet* of Vergil, *Aen.* 6. 439. A variation, perhaps under Iranian influence, appears in the nine world-ages, of which the last is also the first and the age of the sun (Peterson, *loc. cit.* p. 19, n. 1); for ten in Persian religious symbolism cf. the dream of Cyrus from Dinon's *Persica* (Cicero, *De Div.* 1. 23. 46). Peterson, *loc. cit.*, quotes Sethe against the probability of the ennead in literature of this type being derived from the Egyptian ennead. Cf. also Plut. *De Def. Orac.* the "demon" who slew Typho at Delphi cannot return till the end of nine great years. Philo may have used a source which followed the Syro-Chaldean view of the moon as the place of purification of the soul, cf. Plut. *De Fac. in Orb. Lun.* 30. 945 a and *Rel. Or.* 116 and notes, the full moon is the time when souls are released to rise to the sun in Manichean belief (Polotsky in *P.R.E. Supp.* 6. 255. 40), which may go back to older mythology. [It must however be noted that the association of Apollo with the ennead goes back to the religion of pre-classical Greece, cf. Nilsson, *Griechische Feste* 119, n. 3.]

[3] *De Spec. Legg.* 2 (*De Sept.*), 18 (147, M. 2. 292).

which could be interpreted in any manner that was compatible with the Torah and belief in immortality. Judaism could without difficulty substitute schemes of this kind for belief in a catastrophic winding-up of history, which was an alien accretion of comparatively recent date. Judaism, like Babylonian religion, did not really look forward to an end but backward to a beginning. Religion began with the creation and ended with the revelation on Mount Sinai.

Thus the Torah, which recorded the story of creation and culminated in a system of religion and ethics, could easily be made to wear a Hellenistic dress. It is never absolutely equated with the creative Wisdom of God by the Alexandrines as it is by the rabbis; for the Alexandrines were concerned, as the rabbis were not, to commend Judaism as a system of cosmogony to the Gentile world. But it is given an exalted place in the scheme of things; the Law is in harmony with the cosmos and the cosmos with the Law;[1] when Moses received it, he was prepared by forty days of fasting for initiation into the mysteries of the true religion.[2] When he received it, he actually listened to the music of the spheres.[3] Nor was the ritual side of Judaism, apart from the one stumbling-block of circumcision which was repulsive to Greeks and Romans, very difficult to justify. Ceremonial purity, as enjoined in Exod. 19. 15, was a feature of Greek and Egyptian religion; it is duly emphasised by Josephus and Philo in the technical language of Greek cultus.[4] The ceremonial lustrations of Judaism could be transferred in the same way,[5] together with other features which had been drawn from the common stock of primitive religion or borrowed in prehistoric times.

One element in Jewish cultus offered a curious opening for proving that Judaism contained the full truth at which the Gentiles had guessed, but only guessed. The one Temple at Jerusalem was sufficiently remote to allow Jewish propaganda to borrow the arguments by which Gentile philosophers proved the futility of all sacrifice, and to use them as their own.[6] Yet it was the centre of the national life so long as it stood, and though there is considerable evidence of slackness in paying the tithes and offerings due from the

[1] *De Mund. Op.* 1 (3, M. 1. 1) 153.

[2] *De Vit. Moys.* 2 (3), 2 (70 *seqq.*, M. 2. 146); cf. p. 153.

[3] *De Somn.* 1. 6 (36, M. 1. 626). Here also is an allusion to Moses' fast.

[4] Herodotus 2. 64 for the tabu as shared by Greeks and Egyptians; it is of course common, but apparently unknown to the other religions observed by Herodotus. For Judaism cf. Jos. *Antt.* 3. 5. 1 (78) and Philo, *De Decal.* 11 (45, M. 2. 188).

[5] Cf. the use of such terms as ἁγνεύω, περιρραντήριον, etc.; for parallel practices in later Hellenistic religion cf. Tertullian, *De Bapt.* 5.

[6] Philo, *De Plant.* 30 (126, M. 1. 348).

Jews of Palestine, there is also ample evidence for enthusiasm among the Jews of the Dispersion in regard to the annual tax for its upkeep.[1] The fact that it was the only Temple in the world where sacrifice might be offered constituted an impressive testimony to the unity of God.[2] In the ritual of the Temple the High Priest was an impressive central figure; the ordinary Jew from abroad on a pilgrimage to Jerusalem or the proselyte would not realise how far the holders of the office had fallen from the ideals, which they should have represented in the opinion of the representatives of the Pharisaic tradition.[3] Their robe of office had indeed acquired that special sanctity which can only be acquired by a sacred object when it becomes a matter of political controversy: the procurators had on several occasions taken the robe into the Tower of Antonia as a security against disturbances, only allowing it out of custody when it was actually needed for ceremonial purposes.[4] It thus became a sacramental expression of the hope of the deliverance of Israel.

But it could also receive a mystical significance. Our three principal sources for Hellenistic Judaism all mention the cosmic significance of the robe. In Wisd. 18. 24 it is assumed as sufficiently familiar to be understood in an allusive reference, while Josephus gives a symbolical interpretation of the robe and of the Tabernacle and its furniture as a sufficient reply to those who criticise Judaism as lacking in due respect for the divine;[5] cosmic symbolism was *de rigueur* in the religion of

[1] For the difficulty of securing the due payment of tithes in Palestine cf. Mishnah, *Demai*, *passim*, and Danby 20, n. 9; the Mishnah is confirmed by Philo, *De Spec. Legg.* 1 (*De Sacerd. Hon.*), 5 (153, M. 2. 236) and Judith 11. 12 *seqq.* For the payments by Jews of the Dispersion cf. *De Spec. Legg.* 1 (*De Templo*), 3 (78, M. 2. 224).

[2] *De Spec. Legg.* 1 (*De Templo*), 1 (67, M. 2. 223); Jos. *c. Ap.* 2. 23 (193). For this conventional panegyric of "unity" cf. p. 194. There is a curious puzzle as to the temple of Onias at Leontopolis, which appears to have stood until the time of Vespasian. Philo ignores it completely, though it was partially recognised by official Judaism (Mishnah, *Men.* 13. 10; Danby 512). However unimportant it may have been, it is hard to suppose that Philo was unaware of its existence, since it is known to Josephus (*B.J.* 7. 10. 2 (420 *seqq.*)). Presumably orthodox Jews of Alexandria disapproved of it very strongly, though the rabbis could not entirely deny the validity of its cultus.

[3] Mishnah, *Yoma* 1. 3 and 5 (Danby 162 and 163).

[4] Jos. *Antt.* 18. 4. 3 (90).

[5] *Antt.* 3. 7. 7 (179). Cf. *B.J.* 5. 5. 4 (213 *seqq.*). Goodenough, *By Light, Light* 23, says that it is impossible "to imagine how intense must have been the emotional associations of the Jews of antiquity with the secret ark of the covenant". The impossibility is enhanced by the reticence of the authorities. Philo and Josephus only refer to it when they come upon it in the natural course of their exposition of the narrative of Exodus. The rabbis seem to have regarded the problem of the accommodation of the wings of the cherubim in the confined space of the sanctuary as providing light relief from more serious discussions, cf. Str.-B. on Rom. 3. 25 (3. 168 *seqq.*), while the whole of this note shows how little relation the ancient object

educated circles. Naturally Philo gives it in greater detail and in several places. The long robe of blue or black represents the air, the flowers (from the LXX version of Exod. 28. 34 (30)); pomegranates and bells stand for earth and water at the bottom of the cosmos; the ephod is heaven, the two emeralds the two hemispheres, the six names of tribes on each are the six signs on each side of the sun's path through the zodiac, while the twelve names of the breastplate are the signs themselves. The double breastplate (*λογεῖον* in LXX) stands for the double function of the Logos in the universe, as Logos of the ideal and the material world, and in man as *ἐνδιάθετος* and *προφορικός*; the same symbolism applies to "truth" and "showing", the LXX attempt to render Urim and Thummim. On his head is the golden mitre, engraved with the tetragrammaton, the symbol of the goodness of God which holds the cosmos in being. The whole dress shows that the High Priest who is consecrated to the Father of the universe must have as his advocate God's son the Logos, and that the servant of God must be worthy, if not of God, which is impossible, at least of the cosmos; if it is permissible to say so, and it is right to speak truly concerning the truth, he must be a small cosmos. Since Philo elsewhere uses the analogy of macrocosm and microcosm with complete freedom, the apology of the last clause shows that he is incorporating matter from an earlier source.[1]

Here the figure of the High Priest has replaced Zeus, who is conventionally represented with a *nimbus* of blue to represent the heaven or a mantle of blue with the same meaning; the mantle of blue is sometimes spangled with stars.[2] The ornaments of Zeus could be attributed to other deities; they appear in Attis, Men and the Zeus Oromazdes of the monument of Antiochus of Commagene; it does not appear how far in particular cases they represent the transference of the attributes of Zeus to other deities or a conflation of the proper character of these deities with that of Zeus.[3] They reappear in a late Orphic hymn to the sun which has a curious connection with Judaism[4] and in the

of veneration retained when it was no longer present in the sanctuary. The High Priest's robe plays a far larger part in the Hellenistic writers. It must be remembered that the whole Temple-cultus was more calculated to impress visitors from the Dispersion than Jews of Palestine, in view of the opposition to the Sadducees. The surviving literature reveals very little veneration for the ark.

[1] *De Vit. Moys.* 2 (3). 11 (109 *seqq.*, M. 1. 151). For further references to this symbolism by Philo cf. p. 49.

[2] Cook, *Zeus* 1. 33 *seqq.*, 1. 56 *seqq.* This primitive feature of Zeus as the sky-god was preserved in the art of the Hellenistic era.

[3] Cook, *op. cit.* 2. 386 *seqq.*

[4] Macrob. *Sat.* 1. 18. 22, following immediately on the oracle of Apollo of Claros describing Iao as the supreme deity. The hymn and the oracle with the other verses quoted by Macrobius come from an older collection; the position of Iao seems to be due to the influence of Jewish Gnosticism.

Egyptian deities Cneph and Phthah described by Porphyry, both deities being dressed in robes similar to those of Zeus and the High Priest, while Phthah also wears a crown of gold which represents among other things the stars.[1] The borrowing of the figure of Zeus for the High Priest was rendered possible by the Stoic practice of finding allegories of the one divine principle in the cosmos in the mythology and cultus of Hellas.[2] In a form which may have had a widely different origin but was not dissimilar in its total effect the cosmos could be regarded as the body of the deity, a conception which appears to have been derived from the solar religions of the East but was naturally read into the religion of Egypt by the imaginative powers of the Alexandrines.[3] The Stoic convention appears to have associated its cosmic symbolism with the name of Orpheus, the traditional founder of Greek mythology,[4] possibly under the influence of religious sects which claimed to be the heirs of the Orphic religious tradition.[5]

This was a godsend to Judaism. If Orpheus had visited Egypt, it was obvious that he had learnt there the Orphic system of religion, which was not monotheistic; yet "at heart it worshipped one God, Dionysos".[6] Other wise men of Greece had in one form or another believed in the unity of God; it was significant that they too had visited Egypt. It was obvious that their knowledge of the one true God was an unacknowledged borrowing from Moses, whose teaching they had learnt there.[7] It was even possible by a rather bold conjecture to identify with Moses the shadowy figure of Musaeus, the

[1] *Ap.* Eus. *Pr. Ev.* 3. 11. 29. Cneph was identified with the Ἀγαθὸς Δαίμων, the patron deity of Alexandria (*Conversion* 40); Phthah, the creative word of Memphite theology, goes back to the pyramids (Breasted, *Religion and Thought in Ancient Egypt* 43). Phthah in Porphyry's account has his legs joined together, a feature which appears in Eudoxus' story of the myth of Zeus and Isis (Plut. *De Is. et Os.* 62, 376 c). It seems that the cult-images of Zeus and Phthah were identified as early as Eudoxus (*c.* 350 B.C.). Cf. also the robe worn by Demetrius Poliorcetes at Athens (Douris *ap.* Athenaeus, *Deipnos.* 12. 50. 535 f.).

[2] Cf. p. 30 and below, p. 53.

[3] Diod. Sic. 1. 11. 6, where Osiris is the sun and Isis the moon, and the rest of the universe is the body of which they are the head. The explanation is associated with "Orpheus" (11. 3); it appears to go back to Manetho (Eus. *Pr. Ev.* 3. 2. 9). Cf. also the oracle given by Sarapis to Nicocreon of Argos (Macrob. *Sat.* 1. 20. 16) and Pantaenus' description of the cosmic body of Christ (Clem. Alex. *Ecl. Proph.* 56 (1003 P)).

[4] Cicero, *De Nat. Deor.* 1. 15. 41; cf. *Orpheus* 255. See also Galen, *De Hipp. et Plat. Plac.* 3. 4 (120), p. 281 M. (v. Arn. 2. 255).

[5] *Orpheus* 253 as against Cumont, *Rel. Or.* 303 and Nock in *Essays on the Trinity and the Incarnation* 65, a view which he has perhaps modified slightly in *Conversion* 30. I have not the courage to express an opinion in such a conflict.

[6] *Orpheus* 251.

[7] Pseudo-Justin, *Cohortatio* 14. 15b, who quotes Diodorus Siculus (1. 96. 1) for the visits of the wise men of Greece to Egypt; but the tradition goes back to Judaism, see note following.

legendary son or disciple of Orpheus, who could easily be transformed into his teacher.[1] The question of chronology was easily settled; the necessity of proving the priority of Moses to Orpheus was one of the chief themes of the wearisome calculations of dates by which Judaism and later Christianity proved the superiority of the Bible to the philosophy of Greece, which possessed nothing of value but its unacknowledged borrowings from Moses.[2]

The essence of Orphism was its offer of a true understanding of the origin of the cosmos and of man and of the means by which he might hope to escape from the material world.[3] This was what the Judaism of the Dispersion offered, and once it had been established that Orpheus had borrowed from Moses it was perfectly safe to produce "Orphic" literature which presented the teachings of Judaism in an Orphic-Stoic dress and represented him at the same time as acknowledging the debt which he owed to the instructors whose assistance he had failed to mention in the versions of his writings current among the Gentiles. Thus it is not surprising to find at least one considerable "Orphic" fragment of Jewish origin and composition going back to a date earlier than Aristobulus[4] in the second century B.C. In this, the universe is described as the body in which God may be seen by those who have the wisdom to see Him.[5] The fragment is addressed to Musaeus. The ancient account of Him tells that He is one and the maker of all things, and Himself moves in them; no mortal soul can know Him, but mind alone. So far the texts agree; here (line 13 in Aristobulus) we are told that He does not bring evil out of good to men, but grace and hatred follow Him, and war and pestilence. The language here is uncertain, since Christian-Jewish thought wavered between preserving the original protest of Is. 45. 7 against Zoroastrian dualism

[1] Artabanus *ap*. Eus. *Pr. Ev*. 9. 27. 1.

[2] Cf. p. 5. Cf. also Jos. *c. Ap*. 1. 22 (161). In Eus. *Pr. Ev*. 10. 7. 12 this passage is immediately followed by Diod. Sic. 1. 96. 1, which also appears in Pseudo-Justin (see above, p. 35, n. 7). Diodorus appears to be a fixed part of propaganda as to the antiquity of the Jews. The construction of chronologies for this end goes back to Demetrius (*c*. 222 B.C.; cf. Schürer, *G.J.V*. 3. 473; Meyer, *Urspr. u. Anf*. 2. 33), quoted by Clem. Alex. *Strom*. 1. 21. 141 (403 P). The whole chronology begins *ib*. 101 (378 P); for the borrowings of Orpheus and Plato from Moses, cf. also 5. 12. 78 (692 P). For the theme, cf. Tatian, *Or. adv. Gr*. 31. 118 *seqq*.; Eus. *Pr. Ev*. Book 10.

[3] Cf. Aristophanes, *Birds* 692, where a parody of the Orphic cosmogony is offered as a means of escape from Prodicus.

[4] For Aristobulus cf. p. 68.

[5] For the whole of this literature cf. Schürer, *G.J.V*. 3. 599. The Orphic fragment appears in Aristobulus *ap*. Eus. *Pr. Ev*. 13. 12. 4 *seqq*. Part of it appears in Clem. Alex. *Protr*. 7. 74 (63 P); further parts at *Strom*. 5. 12. 78 (692 P) and 14. 123 (723 P). The greater part of it has by this time passed into the stock of Christian collections and reappears in Pseudo-Justin, *Cohortatio* 15. 15c and *De Mon*. 2. 104e. There is an allusion to it in Tatian, *Or. adv. Gr*. 8. 39.

and softening down the charge that God creates evil.[1] Orpheus himself cannot see Him for a cloud cuts Him off from sight, and ten *πτυχαί* (folds or layers) conceal Him from men;[2] none can see Him but those who like Abraham rise above the sphere of the stars.[3] It is God who rules the spirits (or winds) in the air and the water and brings the flash of fire to light; the author has here tried without much success to put Gen. 1. 2–3 into Orphic verse. God Himself sits in heaven on a throne of gold and His feet stand on the earth (Is. 66. 1).[4] His right hand is stretched out over the Ocean, and the mountains tremble at His anger and cannot stand before His might. He is Himself in heaven and fulfils all things on earth, being Himself the beginning and middle and end of all things; the last thought is an adaptation to Jewish tradition of the recognised conception of Zeus in popular philosophy which saw in Zeus the divine power immanent in the fate which ruled the cosmos through each world-age; but it was an "ancient word" in the time of Plato and had its roots in the ancient Zeus cult of Dodona.[5] This is the ancient word expounded by him who was born from the water, who received it from God in accordance with the ordinance of the two Tables.[6]

The poem is of Jewish origin, though following Gentile models.[7]

[1] In Aristobulus the lines run

αὐτὸς δ᾽ ἐξ ἀγαθῶν θνητοῖς κακὸν οὐκ ἐπιτέλλει
ἀνθρώποις· αὐτῷ δὲ χάρις καὶ μῖσος ὀπηδεῖ
καὶ πόλεμος καὶ λοιμὸς ἰδ᾽ ἄλγεα δακρυόεντα,

while the version of Pseudo-Justin is

οὗτος δ᾽ ἐξ ἀγαθοῖο κακὸν θνητοῖσι δίδωσι
καὶ πόλεμον κρυόεντα καὶ ἄλγεα δακρυόεντα,

which Schürer regards as original, as does Peterson, Εἷς Θεός; the latter overlooks the fact that the dualism in any case is modelled on Isaiah; the Iranian influence lies behind the O.T.

[2] Apparently the ten *πτυχαί* are the ennead of Philo (cf. p. 31), God Himself being the last; astral mathematics are always liable to insert additional units, and the author had to make his line scan.

[3] Peterson, Εἷς Θεός 298, denies the reference to Abraham and sees a reference to the speculations of the Iranian-Chaldean cult of the Aeon; but he overlooks the reputation of Abraham as the father of astrology, who rose above the planets to find the one true God in heaven (p. 101). Pseudo-Justin omits the astrological lines and the reference to Abraham, and merely emphasises the impossibility of seeing God with mortal eyes: Clement quotes a variant of his version, but also that of Aristobulus.

[4] Schürer, *loc. cit.*

[5] Cf. p. 160.

[6] Moses, who is eliminated from the Christian versions.

[7] It does not appear in the collection of hymns to the sun associated with the name of Cleanthes in Macrob. *Sat.* 1. 18. 14, although Cleanthes followed Chrysippus in reconciling Orpheus to the Stoa (Philodemus, *De Piet.* 13. 80 g (*Dox. Gr.* 547)). It is interesting to note that in Macrobius' collection the line Εἷς Ζεύς, εἷς Ἀΐδης, εἷς Ἥλιος, εἷς Διόνυσος appears; it is found in Pseudo-Justin, *Cohortatio*, *loc. cit.* immediately after our fragment, but not in the other versions; it would seem that the line which may reflect the Oriental conception of the sun as the one divine Aeon expressing himself in the four seasons and so representing the division of eternity

The figure of God is modelled on the Old Testament and yet approximated to Gentile pantheism. Judaism could never be really pantheistic, yet it could accommodate itself to any monotheistic system, since it was not concerned with the niceties of philosophy; Aristobulus could proceed from his Orphic lines to quote Aratus' description of all things as filled with Zeus, "for we are also his offspring", which Paul used on the Areopagus. The imagery of the Orphic lines could be safely adopted and it was not necessary to enquire as to its immediate source, since it came in the last resort from Moses himself. The thought was in reality a commonplace; it declined in the last days of paganism into a formula of magic to describe the Ἀγαθὸς Δαίμων whose head is the heaven, the aether his body, the earth his feet and the water about him the Ocean.[1] But in its day the Orphic-Stoic convention was reputable theology and could safely be employed to describe the one true God.[2] Its teaching was to be found in the philosophy of Greece; Orphism may have been one of the contributory factors in the early development of Greek philosophy;[3] but the Hellenistic age had long since forgotten that the resemblances between Orpheus and the philosophers might not be merely fortuitous or providential. Judaism was simply adapting itself to general practice in availing itself of the name of Orpheus to advocate a system of monotheism. Orpheus proclaimed the mysteries of the one God who pervaded the Stoic universe; he could also proclaim the one God of the cosmogony of Genesis. Judaism could also borrow from him the convention of calling on mankind to wake from the slumber and drunkenness of ignorance and turn to the daylight and the sobriety of the truth.[4] It was a simple matter to avoid the extremer forms of

into recurring cycles of time has not penetrated to the earlier sources. The Jewish Gnosticism which introduced Iao into this scheme appears to be later than Aristobulus and Clement. For similar Orphic poetry cf. Valerius Soranus *ap*. Aug. *De Civ. Dei* 7. 9.

[1] *Papp. Mag. Gr.* 12. 243, 13. 771 and 21. 6, in a more or less fixed formula, in which *παντοκράτωρ* and *ὁ ἐμφύσησας πνεῦμα ἀνθρώποις εἰς ζωὴν* and the *ὄνομα ἄρρητον* all suggest Jewish influence. Does the imagery of the papyri come from that of Cneph as described by Porphyry (see p. 35)?

[2] Philo does not use it, but in *De Vit. Moys.* 2 (3). 4. 82 (M. 2. 147) is an elaborate explanation of the geometry of the Tabernacle, where the Holy of Holies is the head and mind, the outer court the feet and sense; here we have the same symbolism applied to man as the microcosm.

[3] *Orpheus* ch. VII.

[4] Aristophanes, *Birds* 685, where the description of mankind as *πλάσματα πηλοῦ* shows how easily fortuitous parallels occur in widely separated religions; the phrase might easily be supposed to come from Gen. 2. 7. For the convention cf. *Corp. Herm.* 1 (*Poimandres*), 27 (Scott 132); it is the theme of *Corp. Herm.* 7 (Scott 170), Philo, *De Somn.* 2. 44 (292, M. 1. 697); cf. the "initiate's" prayer for enlightenment, *ib.* 1. 26 (164, M. 1. 645); see also the Oxyrhynchus Logion, *Pap.* 1. 8 (*Apocr. N.T.* 27), Rom. 13. 11 *seqq.*, 1 Thess. 5. 6 *seqq.*, Eph. 5. 14. The absence of rabbinical parallels in Str.-B. is significant.

pantheism in accommodating the history and cultus of Judaism to this cosmic philosophy; even the shadowy figure of Phanes, a double, it would seem, of Dionysos,[1] but not like him associated with the cult and mythology of the Olympian pantheon, could be introduced as a guess by Orpheus at the cosmic word or wisdom or spirit of God.[2]

Thus Judaism followed the example of contemporary religion in general in reading the mysteries of the cosmos into the institutions of religion. Incense was a peculiarly favourite theme for such treatment; Egyptian incense was made out of sixteen ingredients, and so furnished an impressive testimony to the Pythagorean admiration for the number four; Jewish incense was at least made of four ingredients, and could therefore claim to prove that Judaism was acquainted with this part of the wisdom of Pythagoras; it was fortunate that Moses should have noticed in compounding the incense the need of alluding to a number which the book of Genesis otherwise treats with little respect.[3] Incense was naturally a favourite theme with the exponents of the Pythagorean tradition of Alexandria. For the master had forbidden the sacrifice of animals;[4] naturally it was necessary to prove the

[1] *Orpheus* 95 *seqq.*

[2] In one instance at least Phanes appears as an anticipation of Christianity, Lactantius, *Div. Inst.* 1. 5. So in *Clem. Hom.* 6. 4 *seqq.* Appion makes Phanes the immanent spirit in the cosmic egg; Clement's reply hardly touches him and confines itself to the conventional attack on pagan mythology, as borrowed by Judaism from the Academics (cf. Cicero, *De Nat. Deor.* 3. 21. 53 *seqq.*). Cf. Ps.-Just. *Cohort.* 15. 16b for Orpheus' borrowing of the creative Word of Genesis from Moses during his stay in Egypt. Since Phanes was derived from φαίνω, "because he first shone forth", he was obviously capable of identification with the "light" of Jewish cosmogony. Phanes was also Protogonos (*Orpheus, loc. cit.*): and Protogonos is one of the manifestations of the Logos in Jewish Gnosticism (p. 49); as a regular title of the Logos in Philo it probably reflects the general language of the age. But in Athenagoras, *Leg. pro Christ.* 20. 96, Phanes is merely condemned as a typical heathen deity.

[3] Philo, *Q.R.D.H.* 41 (196 *seqq.*, M. 1. 500), and Plutarch, *De Is. et Os.* 79, 383a, both make incense a symbol of the Pythagorean virtue of equality and the value of four; Plutarch adds the superiority of the morning to the evening air, which is also Pythagorean (Diog. Laert. 8. 26). The tetragrammaton is treated in the Pythagorean vein in *De Vit. Moys.* 2 (3). 11 (115, M. 2. 152), but only with a brief allusion; cf. p. 48.

[4] So in Epiph. *adv. Haer.* 3. 8 (*Dox. Gr.* 590). This doxographic collection is no doubt wrong in the statement in view of the varying accounts of Diog. Laert. 8. 20, which fairly clearly imply that Pythagoras did not reject all sacrifices, but that the later Pythagoreans did, and tried to claim his authority. According to Egyptian tradition, as recorded by Macrob. *Sat.* 1. 7. 15, animals were not sacrificed in Egypt till the cults of Sarapis and Saturn were introduced by the Ptolemies. That burnt-offerings were not a regular feature of Egyptian religion until a fairly late period appears to be correct: but animal food-offerings were made and apparently burnt-offerings were offered when it was impossible to make a food-offering at the temple (Erman, *Die Religion der Ægypter* 176). The Pythagoreans seem to have read their views into this system. For the Orphic rejection of animal sacrifice cf. Plato, *Laws* 782c. For their retention to some extent in Pythagoreanism cf. also Athenaeus, *Deipnos.* 7. 80 (308c). [Wilcken *UPZ* 87 ascribes the tradition of Macrobius to a misunderstanding of the practice of locating temples of Sarapis, as a god of the underworld, outside cities.]

mystical value of the incense which was the only offering welcome to the gods. Philo is aware of this tradition; indeed he shows some skill in conflating it with the view of the prophets that God demands mercy and not sacrifice, when he writes that the smallest offering of incense by the righteous is better than the holocaust of the wicked.[1]

In one point indeed Judaism could claim that its cultus contained that element of mystery which always has a potent appeal to the human instinct of curiosity. The name of God had been withdrawn from the public worship of the synagogue about the beginning of the Christian era, and was only uttered in the Temple on occasions of special solemnity.[2] The withdrawal was indeed comparatively recent, since Philo has incorporated sources which still admitted its use in oaths of a solemn kind.[3] On the other hand, he is acquainted with the rabbinical substitutes and the interpretations placed on them.[4] Philo is entirely ready to make the use of the name in the Temple worship into a mystery of the approved type, in which the priests, who hear the name when the High Priest utters it, have to play the part of allegorical initiates.[5] He is even prepared to hold that the true meaning of the tetragrammaton, "I that am" (ὁ ὤν), is that nothing which exists can "consist" (συστῆναι) without calling upon the name of God. Here Philo has abandoned the LXX use of Κύριος as the rendering of the name of God, presumably because he is a good enough Greek scholar to know that this is impossible.[6] In Josephus Moses desires to be told the name of God in order that he may call on Him by name to be present at the time of sacrifice;[7] the tetragrammaton carved on the mitre of the High Priest had even won the worship of Alexander the Great.[8] After this it is no great thing that Artabanus should relate that the mere whisper of it in Pharaoh's ear had caused him to fall lifeless; written on a tablet, it had slain an Egyptian priest who mocked.[9] All

[1] *De Spec. Legg.* I (*De Sacr.*), 4. 275 (M. 2. 254). That this is so is proved by the fact that the altar of burnt-offerings is of stone and outside the Tabernacle, the altar of incense inside and made of gold.

[2] Mishnah, *Yoma* 3. 8 and 6. 2, *Tamid* 3. 8 (Danby 165, 169 and 585); cf. Philo, *De Vit. Moys.* 2 (3). 11 (114, M. 2. 152).

[3] *De Decal.* 19 (93, M. 2. 196).

[4] *Q.R.D.H.* 35 (170, M. 1. 497), where the reference is to Adonai and Elohim as symbolising the two divine attributes of mercy and justice; see below, p. 45, for his reversal of the rabbinical order.

[5] *De Vit. Moys. loc. cit.* n. 2 above.

[6] *Loc. cit.* 14 (132). The thought is suspiciously reminiscent of the statement of Theopompus *ap.* Diog. Laert. 1. 9 that according to the Magians all things that are continue in existence through their incantations (if this is the correct translation; cf. Hicks' translation and note *ad loc.* in the Loeb version).

[7] *Antt.* 2. 12. 4 (275), where it is οὐ θεμιτόν for Josephus to reveal the name.

[8] *Antt.* 11. 8. 5 (331); the passage is an interesting glorification of the High Priest's robe, but the emphasis is on the name inscribed on the mitre.

[9] Eus. *Pr. Ev.* 9. 27. 13. It seems a recognised trick of magic; cf. Simon Magus' killing of a boy by whispering in his ear, *Acts of Peter* 25 (*Apocr. N.T.* 325). For a

this was quite in accordance with pagan ideas; Valerius Soranus had approved of the making public of the secret name of Rome, and come in consequence to an evil end.[1] But Judaism itself was perfectly well aware of the importance and value of names, and of a knowledge of the correct name of God; one of the reasons urged by the rabbis for the withdrawal of the name, and its disclosure in the days of the Temple only to suitable people, was that it might be used by "violent" men for purposes of vengeance.[2] In Christianity the belief is still to be found, either, as in Paul's case, surviving in phrases which imply it, but have lost all real meaning,[3] or, as in the Apocalypse, expressing the popular belief in the potency of a name which is known to none but God and its bearer, who is thus immune from the assault of hostile powers.[4] Later Christianity, even in its most enlightened exponents, recognised the value of the right name in addressing the powers of the unseen world;[5] it was even held that the name of Jesus Christ was not the real name, but only that used by Him on earth, but here we are in circles of an unorthodox character.[6]

In one respect at least Jewish insistence on the supremacy of the God of Israel with the ineffable Name produced unfortunate results. The underworld of Hellenistic magic could not afford to ignore so potent a deity. The name itself, in its Greek form, Iao, was suggestive, for it contained the first, middle and last of the vowels (unfortunately in the wrong order), and the vowels possessed a magic efficacy of their own as the means by which the voiceless consonants could express what would otherwise be unutterable.[7] The wrong order

magical use of the name (to locate the coffin of Joseph in the Nile) cf. *Mekilta, Tr. Besh.* 1. 93 (ed. Lauterbach 1. p. 176).

[1] Pliny, *N.H.* 3. 9. 65. For Roman views on the secrecy of divine names cf. Warde Fowler, *Religious Experience of the Roman People* 120, Lucan, *Phars.* 6. 732.

[2] Talmud, *Kiddushin* 71 b; cf. Rashi, *ad loc.* for the view that its withdrawal "when violent men multiplied" refers to those "who made practical use" of the name; it was revealed while the Temple stood to those who did not stand on their rights, because they would not use it for vengeance. No doubt the tablet of Rheneia (Deissmann, *Licht v. Ost.* 305) praying for vengeance to the most High God, the Lord of the spirits of all flesh, would have acquired an added potency from the insertion of the name. The name or rather names of Aoth, Abaoth the God of Abraham, Iao of Isaac and Aoth, Abaoth the God of Israel appear in a "defixion" adjuring the demon in a grave to bring Urbanus to his lover Domitiana; the tablet appears to date from the third century A.D. (Leclercq, *Dict. d'Arch. Chrét.* 1. 527, regards it as possibly Christian, but a comparison with the papyri suggests that it need not even be Jewish).

[3] Phil. 2. 9.

[4] Rev. 2. 17; the references to "new names" in this book *passim* reveal a real belief in their efficacy.

[5] Cf. p. 208.

[6] *Acts of Thomas* 163 (*Apocr. N.T.* 435).

[7] Philo, *De Mund. Op.* 42 (126, M. 1. 30). Such a statement shows how close "sympathy" can come to magic.

was not a decisive objection, since in magic the repetition of the vowels in every possible permutation and combination of order was a regular practice; the spirits, even the stars themselves, would not obey any but the correct address.[1] It seems that the mysterious name of the God of Israel was taken as a sort of summary of all the potency of the mystical sounds of the vowels which themselves represented, among other things, the planets; for the planets and the vowels were correlated by the ancient learning of the Chaldeans.[2] Since then the name could be a symbol of the hebdomad, it summarised that mystical correspondence between the nature of the heavens and the whole cosmos, and the nature of the microcosm man, which was the ultimate secret of all wisdom.[3] Hellenistic magic could not fail to recognise that such a name possessed a peculiar potency of its own; Judaism appears to have adopted the theme by adding the last letter of the alphabet and so making the name Iaoth, which could symbolise, not very accurately, the position of God as the beginning, the middle and the end of all things.[4] Moreover, the God of Israel had other names, whose number could be brought up to seven by the addition to the ordinary four names of God, as found in the Scriptures, of others drawn from the sphere of magic.[5] Thus He could be made to play a prominent part in this realm, the more so in view of His court of angels, whose outlandish names were calculated to attract the attention of the vulgar, and to increase the effectiveness of the magician's incantations.[6]

[1] For the importance of the right name cf. Boll-Bezold, *Sternglaube u. Sterndeutung* 125. Cf. *Papp. Mag. Gr.* 13. 208 for the position of Iao in regard to the seven vowels in the Gnostic cosmogony of the Monad or Eighth book of Moses; I suspect that this was one of the main reasons for the popularity of Iao.

[2] Plut. *De Ei ap. Delph.* 4. 386a and the oracle Porphyry *ap.* Eus. *Pr. Ev.* 5. 14. 2, and the "great name with seven vowels", *Papp. Mag. Gr.* 13. 39.

[3] Cf. the whole passage on the hebdomad in Philo, *De Mund. Op.* 30 (90, M. I. 21)–42 (127, M. I. 30), especially the "physical sympathy" of 117. Here we have a harmless Stoic-Pythagorean play with numbers which is hardly intended seriously; contrast the system of Marcus in Ir. *Haer.* I. 14. 7, where the same scheme as that which appears in Philo, possibly drawn from the same source, is fitted into the magic which is the basis of Marcus' system. (Cf. *Papp. Mag. Gr. passim* for the letter-magic described in Ir. *Haer.* I. 14. I, and "Uphor" in 12. 316 with the "Ouphareg" of Ir. *Haer.* I. 21. 3.)

[4] Photius, *ad Ampl. Q.* 89. 7, where it symbolises that God is without beginning and without end; but properly Tau as the last letter should show that He is the end of all things, as Omega does in Greek. Iao has travelled into Greek and there been used to show that He is the end, in virtue of the Omega, and returned to Hebrew where He has had to assume the Tau in order to retain His character.

[5] Orig. *c. Cels.* 6. 32. Origen appears to be well informed.

[6] For the value of Hebrew or Babylonian names cf. Lucian, *Alexander* 13, and *Papp. Mag. Gr.* 3. 119 *κατὰ τῆς Ἑβραϊκῆς φωνῆς* as a means of adjuration; for the superior efficacy of prayer in a barbarous tongue Clem. Alex. *Strom.* I. 21. 143 (405 P).

The prestige of the Jewish God was enhanced by the success of Jewish exorcisms, which were undoubtedly effective, both in the more definitely "magical" form in which they were associated with the use of the herbs and fumigations handed down by Solomon, which orthodox Judaism recognised as effective, while doubtful of their orthodoxy,[1] and in the liturgical or "kerygmatic" form which sought to overpower the demons by the recitation of the mighty works of the God of Abraham, Isaac and Jacob in the creation of the world and in the deliverance of His chosen people; the predilection for His mighty works in bringing His people through the Red Sea and Jordan may have been intended to overawe the demons yet further, for they knew that they could not cross running water; *a fortiori* they could not resist the God who was able to bring His people through it dryshod.[2]

How far this magical efficacy of Judaism led to the abandonment of religion in favour of magic by members of the Jewish nation is perhaps a doubtful question; Jews who lapsed in this way would leave no trace on the religious literature. The influence of Judaism on the magical literature of the Hellenistic world is very strong,[3] but it would be perfectly easy for Gentiles, who were impressed with the potency of the Most High God of the Jews, to attach themselves to the synagogue and so acquire a good working knowledge of the Jewish Scriptures.[4] The Greek bible could probably be purchased at Alexandria, as it could certainly be stolen at Ephesus.[5] In any case it is clear that

[1] Jos. *Antt.* 8. 2. 5 (46) records such an exorcism by the herbs of Solomon enclosed in a signet-ring which he witnessed in the presence of Vespasian and his staff; cf. *B.J.* 7. 6. 3 (180) for a specially valuable herb, which can only be gathered at grave personal danger. For fumigations cf. the burning of the fish's liver, Tobit 6. 17, and 8. 2 *seqq.* The doubts of the rabbis as to these methods appear in the Baraitha to Mishnah, *Pes.* 4. 8 (Danby 141), where the sages approved of king Hezekiah for hiding away the "roll of healings" no less than for destroying the brazen serpent. For adjurations written by Solomon cf. Orig. *In Matt. Comm. Ser.* 110; Justin Martyr, *Dial. c. Tryph.* 85 (311c), accuses the Jews of the use of fumigations and binding spells; he holds that exorcisms in the names of kings, righteous men, prophets or patriarchs (presumably Solomon) are not effective, but has to admit the efficacy of those by the "God of Abraham, Isaac and Jacob" (see below, p. 208). It may be suspected that Justin's orthodoxy here is more reliable than his account of the facts. The Q-Logion Mt. 12. 27 = Lk. 11. 19 is a testimony to the effectiveness of Jewish practice. (For the Hezekiah story cf. McGown *The Testament of Solomon* 92 *seqq.*)

[2] See Note II on Jewish influences in magical literature.

[3] Nock, *Gnomon* 12. 11. 607.

[4] A class of persons of this type appears to be implied in Acts 19. 18; they would seem to have gone over from Judaism to Christianity as a more efficacious system, and subsequently to have undergone a genuine conversion. Apart from a possible exaggeration of the value of the literature burnt, the story seems perfectly probable. Cf. below, p. 148.

[5] Jos. *Antt.* 16. 6. 2 and 4 (164 and 168). It is hard to see why a gentile should steal a copy of the Bible or the roll of the Torah and fly to asylum out of a mere excess of anti-Semitic zeal; it would be more effective either to destroy it or deface it, cf. *Antt.* 20. 5. 4 (115).

Judaism was a leading factor in the magical world, in so far as its God, in virtue of His wonderful names and His position as the creator of the universe, and His proved power to deliver His people in the past, and those possessed with demons in the present, showed that He controlled vast spiritual forces.[1] Here there was a link which connected Judaism with the lower side of the religion of the Hellenistic world, which was always ready to absorb the practices of religion and convert them to magic purposes; naturally the line between religion and magic was even less fixed than in modern times, and prayers and forms of worship with a perfectly reputable origin, or exorcisms based on belief in the power of God to heal those possessed by evil spirits, would easily degenerate into magic of the crudest type, which bound the spirits of evil to work the will of those who knew the correct formula.[2]

Nor was Judaism of a more purely religious type always strict in its adherence to the limits of Jewish monotheism. In the main stream of Palestinian and Alexandrine tradition there is no evidence of any real deviation from orthodox Judaism. The Hellenistic writers in general know of Iao, the God of the Jews, as being another name for Saturn,[3] or as being the God who is above the seven spheres.[4] According to others he is "the unknowable"[5] or more often "the invisible". The last title is significantly associated with the name of God by Paul in his opposition to the more or less Gnostic teachers at Colossae; in itself it was entirely unexceptionable, while the frequent anthropomorphisms of the Old Testament made it necessary for

[1] The importance of cosmogony seems to lie in the fact that a recitation of creation proves to the demons that the magician has an intimate knowledge of the methods of the supreme being. The efficacy attached to the Jewish knowledge of cosmogony appears from the fact that the Gnostic cosmogony contained in *Papp. Mag. Gr.* 13 (cf. Jacoby quoted in the introductory note) is described as the Eighth book of Moses, though it has on the whole rather less than the average amount of Jewish influence. In 12. 92 *seqq.* the adept transforms himself into Moses, who is conceived in the style of Philo as chief of a body of initiates.

[2] Cf. Dieterich, *Abraxas* 2 for the view that the religious elements in the magical papyri are borrowed from the liturgical books of various religious communities.

[3] See above, p. 8.

[4] So in an unnamed writer *ap.* Lydus, *De Mens.* 4. 53 (ed. Wunsch), where the name Sabaoth implies that he is the God who is above the seven spheres (from a source which recognises the similarity of sabaoth and sabbath). The view that the Jews worshipped the firmament was a natural way of expressing the fact that they had only one god, whom they did not identify with any particular figure or factor in the cosmos, and who dwelt in the firmament, which was, according to the general Stoic view, the ἡγεμονικόν in the cosmos. So in Hecataeus *ap.* Diod. Sic. 40. 3. 4 (*ap.* Photius *Bibl.* 244. 58) and (presumably) Posidonius *ap.* Strabo 16. 2. 35 (761), where God is either the firmament or the cosmos or the nature of the world. The same opinion appears in Celsus *ap.* Orig. *c. Cels.* 5. 6.

[5] Cf. Norden, *Agnostos Theos* 58 *seqq.*

Judaism to insist on the invisibility of God against the criticism of the Gentiles.[1] Moreover, the invisibility of the soul and the invisibility of God were two elements in that correspondence of macrocosm and microcosm which played a leading part in the apologetics of Stoicism. But it was easy to pass from the invisibility of God to the visible forms in which the divine manifested itself to the world. In general Judaism was content to do so by means of such abstractions as the "Wisdom" of God, or His "powers" or attributes.[2] But it would seem that speculation sometimes went further than this. Later Gnosticism used the Jewish names of God to describe the spheres through which the soul must pass in its ascent to the firmament.[3] It is stated by Lydus that according to Herennius (Philo of Byblus), Varro identifies Iao, the God of the Jews, with "intellectual light".[4] The line of descent is not perhaps above suspicion. If it be true, it would seem that the "mystical writings of the Chaldeans", which are Varro's alleged source, equated the tetragrammaton with that light which God created in the beginning (Gen. 1. 3). Aristobulus equated Wisdom with that light,[5] and had at the same time identified it with the sabbath by a rather unsuccessful attempt to equate the first and seventh days of the week with one another; in his glorification of the hebdomad he had pointed to the recognition of the seven planets as a tacit recognition of the importance of the sabbath. This was all quite harmless propaganda; but it is hard to feel so certain of Varro's "Chaldeans", who are clearly not Chaldeans or even Babylonian Jews. They can only be Greek-speaking Jews, for whom the tetragrammaton is represented by the LXX *Κύριος*; this again represents God's second attribute of justice, not the attribute of goodness which is His pre-eminent character as *Θεός*.[6] For Hebrew-speaking Jews the tetragrammaton

[1] Cf. p. 159. For Iao as "invisible" cf. the *Onomastica* (ed. Wutz), *passim*. For God as invisible as against charges of anthropomorphism cf. Philo, *De Conf. Ling.* 27 (138, M. 1. 425), *De Cher.* 30 (101, M. 1. 157), with an allusion to Plato (*Phaedo* 79a). But the conception was easily found in the O.T., cf. Exod. 33. 20.

[2] Cf. pp. 50 *seqq.*

[3] See below, p. 154.

[4] *Loc. cit.*

[5] *Ap.* Eus. *Pr. Ev.* 13. 12. 13 *seqq.*

[6] For Κύριος as justice and therefore secondary to *θεός* cf. Philo, *Leg. Alleg.* 3. 23 (73, M. 1. 101). The change could hardly be avoided in view of the connotation of the Greek words. Hence in Philo, *De Conf. Ling.* 28 (146, M. 1. 427), the Logos can be the name of God, i.e. Κύριος, the LXX rendering of the tetragrammaton. The whole of this passage is very curious. The Logos appears as the chief of the angels; for this there are two parallels, *Q.R.D.H.* 42 (205, M. 1. 501), a passage where the Logos is unusually personal and concrete (cf. p. 123), and *De Somn.* 1. 25 (157, M. 1. 645), where Jacob's dream implies the archangel as lord (*τὸν ἀρχάγγελον Κύριον*), standing at the head of the ladder; the phrase is obscure; it suggests that it comes from a source where Iao as = Κύριος was a secondary manifestation of God. For the passage in *De Conf. Ling.* see below, p. 49.

was inevitably the supreme name, and the secondary attribute of justice was represented by Elohim.[1]

Thus Varro's reference must be to Greek-speaking Jews whose description as "Chaldeans" implies that they dabbled in astrology, even if they did no more. If they identified the tetragrammaton with the first-created light and combined this view with astrology, it is hard to avoid the suspicion that they carried out the scheme to its logical conclusion; the seven days of creation would naturally represent seven aspects of God, each represented by one of the seven planets,[2] and each represented by one of the names of God. Again, the planets could be regarded as the manifestation in action of the divine unity concentrated in the firmament of heaven; Jewish speculations of this kind obtained the approval of no less an authority than Apollo himself.[3] The oracle is undated but bears a suspicious resemblance to an ostensibly harmless passage in Philo, dealing with the affinity which exists between the monad, the number of the firmament, and the hebdomad, which possesses a peculiar affinity to the monad, and provides the divisible element in it, while the firmament provides the indivisible.[4] Beneath the Pythagorean mathematics and the Platonic distinction of the two varieties of substance there seems to lie a system which really was concerned with astral speculation of the type indicated in the oracle of Apollo, though Philo has reduced it to harmless proportions; a similar suspicion is excited when we read elsewhere[5] that the two cherubim represent the fixed sphere and the planets respectively, and the flaming sword none less than God Himself. Now here the flaming sword should obviously be the Logos, as in other systems it can be Mithras;[6] but the appearance of God and the contro-

[1] *Kyrios* 3. 707.

[2] Naturally astrological allegory would find no difficulty in the lack of any planets till the fourth day of creation.

[3] Quoted by Porphyry *ap.* Eus. *Pr. Ev.* 9. 10. 4.

[4] *De Decal.* 21 (102 *seqq.*, M. 2. 198). I am not sure if the correspondence of unit and hebdomad to firmament and planets can be paralleled in Philo; the fact that by preserving their proper relations they "prolong the aeon", i.e. make up the Great Year, is hardly to be found elsewhere in his writings. Cf. below, p. 49.

[5] *De Cher.* 7 (24, M. 1. 143), where God committed the reins to none but Himself for fear of a rebellion; this seems to reflect an Iranian dualism, where the Logos took the place which Philo assigns to God at this point as a controversial reply to an unorthodox view. The flaming sword between the trees of Paradise appears in the Ophite system, *ap.* Orig. *c. Cels.* 6. 33. Cf. also *Papp. Mag. Gr.* 13. 254 and 335, where the adept proclaims himself to be "He that sitteth upon the two cherubim", i.e. identifies himself with Iao, and summons the archangel (= the Logos?) to appear.

[6] Orig. *c. Cels.* 6. 22. Celsus explains Mithraism as the spheres of the fixed stars and the planets, and the descent of the soul between them; presumably here the planets belong to the material. For Mithras as mediator between Ahura Mazda and Ahriman cf. Plut. *De Is. et Os.* 46. 369e.

versial note seem to show that Philo is combating unorthodox speculation which saw the action of the Logos embodied in the planetary spheres. It is also likely enough that Philo's controversy with "Chaldeans" (ostensibly the natives of Ur, as opposed to Abraham)[1] represents the need of refuting Jews who dabble in astrology; it need hardly be said that Philo elsewhere incorporates such speculations as his own, though reduced to a harmless form in which the three cities of refuge beyond Jordan represent the three "powers" of God which man cannot imitate, the Logos, creation and government; the three on the near side, mercy, commandment and prohibition, represent those which he can.[2] Similarly we find an apparently controversial statement that God had no helper when He imposed the element of order on the chaos of matter, which may be an allusion to unorthodox speculations as to the rôle of Wisdom in creation (Philo has forgotten that in associating the chaos of matter with the creation of the ideal world, with which he is ostensibly concerned at this point, he is confusing two completely incompatible cosmogonies, the ideal world of the *Timaeus* which is not as yet related to the chaos of matter and the book of Genesis).[3] An equally unorthodox line of thought appears to have made itself felt in his admission of the distinction of the *Timaeus* between the immortal side of man's nature, created by God Himself, and the mortal and material side created by the "powers".[4] It may be that he is merely airing his knowledge of Plato; but the "powers" have a tendency to identification with the planets, and it is quite possible that there lies behind this passage a

[1] *De Migr. Abr.* 32 (178, M. I. 464).

[2] *De Fug. et Inv.* 19 (103 *seqq.*, M. I. 561). Bousset, *Rel. des Judenthums* 404, sees here Ahura Mazda and the six Amhaspands. It is of course possible that Philo's source was inspired by a memory of the Persian tradition; but the real point of the passage is to find a peculiarly elaborate symbolism to justify the obvious problem presented by the six cities of refuge. An omnipotent god of perfect holiness ought to have been able to save an involuntary homicide from the perils of the blood-feud without this curious machinery. The rabbinical "positive" and "negative" commandments show how hard pressed the writer was to find a symbolism which he could read into his text. The same applies to the cherubim in *Quaest. in Exod.* 2. 62 *seqq.* Philo has produced a hebdomad out of God and His two chief attributes united by the Logos, two parallels of the first two attributes and the "intellectual world" symbolised by the mercy seat. He has thus secured a celestial hebdomad to correspond to the planets and at the same time transferred the awkward figures of the winged beasts from the sanctuary to heaven; the motive is obvious in view of the apparent conflict between the figures of the cherubim and the Jewish view of idolatry.

[3] *Timaeus* 48 A; the position of matter in the *Timaeus* is sufficiently ambiguous, but Philo's view of it here reflects the chaos of Genesis and perhaps the Stoic view in the form described by Diog. Laert. 7. 134. For Philo see *De Mund. Op.* 6 (23, M. I. 5).

[4] *De Fug. et Inv.* 13 (69, M. I. 556). Cf. Justin Martyr, *Dial. c. Tryph.* 62 (285 D), for Jewish heretics who hold that the body of man was made by angels (*Timaeus* 41 C).

rather dangerous speculation. If the "powers" were the planets, or even if they were angelic beings corresponding to them but able to overrule them in virtue of their higher order in the heavens, it might easily follow that the true Gnostic was no longer bound to the burden of the literal observance of the Torah, which need only apply within the limits of the material world; the observance of the seventh day was after all the quintessence of the Torah, and the importance of the hebdomad in the natural sympathy of the cosmos need not apply to those who were above it.[1] Similar conclusions could be drawn from the identification of the seven archangels, powers or manifestations of God in the days of creation, with the Logos, a speculation which may be implied in the equation of Iao with the "intellectual light" created on the first day; the ultimate God of the universe had no name.[2] Similarly, the equation of Iao with Saturn may reflect such speculations,[3] which could easily lead to the assimilation of Judaism to Gentile religion by introducing a lower order of the divine nature accessible to the ordinary man, but not to the Gnostic.

It is far from clear how widely such speculations were diffused. It would seem that they lie behind the teaching which Paul opposes at Colossae and some of the curious contacts between paganism and Judaism which meet us in later literature, usually in connection with the fourfold aeon.[4] It would of course be natural that Jews of such unorthodox views would join hands with the Gnostics who cared little for Christianity; it is probable that some of the contacts

[1] Cf. p. 46; Jews who reject the Torah on the ground that it does not apply to them because they are "above" the material world seem to be implied in *De Migr. Abr.* 16 (90, M. I. 450).

[2] This was the inevitable result of the substitution of Κύριος for the tetragrammaton. Philo's inconsistencies on this point (the supreme God cannot have a name (see references on p. 40); the name on the mitre "is said" to be of four letters; it is not the real name, but that applied to the powers, *Q.R.D.H.* 35 (170, M. I. 497)) represent different sources and the gradual withdrawal of the name from use during the last century B.C. and the first century A.D.

[3] But see p. 8.

[4] Cf. p. 37 and the further hymn in Macrob. *Sat.* I. 18. 20, where Iao takes the place of Adonis as the fourth manifestation of Helios-Aion; cf. Peterson, Εἷς Θεός 243. Such speculations would enter Judaism more easily, since the sun was created on the fourth day; hence Philo, *De Plant.* 28 (117 *seqq.*, M. I. 347), allegorises the number four in relation to the light of the sun and the seasons in a manner which suggests such speculations, but is simply based on Genesis and the Pythagorean tetrad. So in *Q.R.D.H.* 34 (165, M. I. 496) the four first days belong to the aeon, the last three to time (Genesis and the *Timaeus*). Origen, *In Ev. Jo.* 13. 40, conflates the two lines of speculation by making the present age a tetrad, corresponding to the four elements; eternity and heaven begin with the sphere of the moon. But these speculations would easily associate themselves with the less orthodox views later associated with the chariot of Ezekiel.

between allegorical interpretation of the Philonic type and the Gnostic systems represent the work of Jewish heretics, though they have been overlaid by the anti-Semitism of later generations.[1] In any case all this allegorising in its Philonic form is entirely harmless; but it seems difficult to suppose that a description of the Logos in *De Conf. Ling.* 28 (146, M. 1. 427) in which he appears as "protogonos", the archangel, the beginning, the Name of God, the archetypal man and "the seeing Israel", does not represent a sevenfold division of the Logos accommodated to Gnostic speculation and to astrology.[2] It is interesting to note that it is associated with the view that if we are not yet worthy to be called the sons of God, we must seek to be sons of His image, the Logos, language which is neither Jewish nor Greek, but suggests a Gnostic ascent of the soul to God through the Logos, while elsewhere[3] the title of Protogonos is associated with the Logos as the High Priest who inhabits the cosmos [he is symbolised by the High Priest's robe, which represents the stars], just as the rational soul dwells in man. The latter passages are innocent enough; the sevenfold Logos is suspicious, especially in view of the magical formula which we meet elsewhere in which the seven names of archangels (ending with Israel) form a "sword" of peculiar potency and of a purely Jewish character.[4] The apocryphal "Prayer of Joseph" preserved by Origen[5] represents a similar speculation: "Jacob" is the patriarch's human name: to God he is known as Israel, the first of all creatures to whom God has given life. When he leaves Mesopotamia (LXX) the angel Uriel opposes him: Jacob points out that Uriel is only eighth in order, while he is first; here we have a rebellious hierarchy below the seven angelic beings of whom Jacob is first. He is distinctly superior to Abraham and Isaac;[6] who the other angels are does not appear.

[1] Thus the system of the Peratae (Hipp. *El.* 5. 16 *seqq.* 133) combines an entirely Philonic allegory of the Exodus with the view that Cain is righteous as against Abel, who serves "the master of this world", and Esau as against Jacob. There is no hint of the method by which Moses was retained as on the side of the two higher elements, Father and Son, as against the lowest element of "becoming" which is subject to the stars: I suspect that a Jewish system has been incorporated.

[2] Cf. God as = the monad = the firmament mirrored in action in the planets = the hebdomad in *De Decal.* 21 (102 *seqq.* M. 2. 198). Properly God in action also = the Logos, but Philo does not say so here.

[3] *De Somn.* 1. 37 (215, M. 1. 653).

[4] For the "sword of Dardanus" see p. 203.

[5] *In Ev. Jo.* 2. 25. There is no hint of Christianity in the fragments preserved by Origen, who regards it as an orthodox Jewish work of an almost canonical character. But Origen's standard of orthodoxy is not high.

[6] This appears to be the meaning of the statement that as Israel "the man who sees God" he is *πρωτόγονος παντὸς ζώου ζωουμένου ὑπὸ θεοῦ* while Abraham and Isaac *προεκτίσθησαν πρὸ παντὸς ἔργου*. But Abraham and Isaac may be referred back to a pre-angelic order of creation.

Another way of expressing God's action on the world was to speak of His "powers". This conception was drawn from the Stoic attempt to combine a theoretical monotheism with a practical conformity to established religion.[1] From the Stoics the word passed into the Jewish exegesis of Alexandria, where it provided a convenient method of explaining away the remnants of polytheism embedded in the cosmogony of Genesis and the stories of the patriarchs. In the case of the story of Creation the use of the plural indicated the fact that God consulted His powers in regard to the formation of man, the only creature capable of moral evil.[2] It was ingeniously argued that the use of the two titles of "God" and "Lord" implied the two main attributes of God, His goodness and His justice; for the orthodox exposition of Alexandria tended to reduce the attributes of God to these harmless ethical qualities, though angels and the celestial bodies could also, in more incautious moments, be included among them, or their number could be increased if the exigencies of allegory demanded it.[3] By a fortunate coincidence the visitations of divine anger in Gen. 11. 3 and 18. 20 (cf. v. 1) were associated with the remnants of polytheistic language; consequently it was possible here too to draw the lesson that God by Himself is only the author of good; where He is compelled by the sin of man to inflict punishment He only does so after consultation with His powers. The source of this ingenious explanation appears to be the treatise of Posidonius on divination [or a tract of a similar type], which was concerned with the view of the Etruscan *haruspices* that lightnings sent by Jupiter alone are harmless; those which do harm are sent only after consultation with the rest of the gods.[4] The Etruscan view was dismissed as absurd from the Stoic standpoint; yet it contained a salutary lesson for kings that they should only punish their subjects after due deliberation; Philo draws precisely the same lesson from the plural manifestation of God at the destruction of the cities of the plain, in a manner which clearly reveals that he is drawing on the same source as that which explained away the lore of Etruscan divination.[5] The whole of this ingenious explanation was

[1] Diog. Laert. 7. 147, where they are described as οἰκειότητες; "powers" appear in Plut. *De Is. et Os.* 67 (378 a) as also in Sext. Emp. *adv. Math.* 9. 40, Aristides (Keil), 45. 8, Aug. *De Civ. Dei* 4. 11, cf. Cumont, *Études Syriennes* 197.

[2] Cf. p. 84.

[3] Philo (*De Conf. Ling.* 34 *seqq.* (171, M. 1. 431)) equates the powers employed in creation with the world of ideas, which is also the world of the heavenly bodies, and with the traditional angels; normally, however, he limits them to goodness and mercy, as in the passages referred to on p. 45. For a curious variation cf. p. 47.

[4] Seneca, *N.Q.* 2. 43. 1; I can hardly doubt that this is drawn from Posidonius in view of the extent to which he and Philo follow him.

[5] *De Abrahamo* 28 (143 *seqq.*, M. 2. 22); here the powers are goodness and punishment.

taken over by the rabbis of Palestine, who replaced the "powers" by the term *middoth* (measures or attributes);[1] the rabbinical exegesis was able to use language which suggested that goodness and mercy were "qualities" of God, a view which was impossible for the Alexandrines, since it was a dogma of Greek thought that God was "without qualities".[2] Naturally the terms which described the attributes were reversed; in Hebrew the tetragrammaton had to stand for goodness, the supreme attribute of God.[3]

The "powers" explained the somewhat polytheistic cherubim of the ark: the mercy seat between them represents the Logos,[4] whose position as uniting and ruling the powers here, as compared with the position of God between the powers on the road to Sodom, proves that the figure of the Logos has no real meaning; God Himself might just as well have taken its place.[5]

There was, however, a further use for the powers. The natural sympathy which holds together the universe could be regarded as a system of "powers" emanating from God into the cosmos.[6] This terminology was drawn from Gentile sources, not from the Jewish attributes of God.[7] Gentile convention could regard the mysterious "powers" which upheld the cosmos as being in sympathy with, if not governed by, the planets which foretold or ruled the fate of man; the cosmos itself was divine, or ruled by a divine world-soul immanent in it.[8] Here we have a consistent Stoicism which omits the transcendent elements of deity in the firmament; it would appear to represent a reaction to the original Stoic scheme, though it is quite possible that it was adopted in one or another of the writings of Posidonius or his followers. Naturally Judaism could not allow this: but it was easy to explain that the planets were endowed with a celestial nature, like the rest of the angelic beings who peopled the upper air.[9] In that capacity

[1] The powers appear as "measures" in *De Sacr. Ab. et Cain.* 15 (59, M. I. 173).

[2] Cf. *Leg. Alleg.* I. 15 (51, M. I. 53). For the rabbinical conception of the attributes cf. R. Meir, quoted in *Judaism* I. 387.

[3] See p. 45.

[4] For the Logos as a "power" employed in creation cf. p. 83: for Wisdom as a "power" see *Leg. Alleg.* 2. 21 (86, M. I. 82).

[5] *De Fug. et Inv.* 19 (101, M. I. 561). Cf. *De Cher.* 9 (27, M. I. 144) for the two cherubim of paradise and the flaming sword; Philo seems to regard this as peculiarly his own.

[6] *De Migr. Abr.* 32 (181, M. I. 464), with a definite allusion to *Timaeus* 41 a.

[7] Cf. Plut. *De Anim. Procr. in Tim.* 26, 1025 c, where the principles of identity and diversity appear as "powers" of the world-soul.

[8] *De Migr. Abr. loc. cit.* (179).

[9] *De Conf. Ling.* 34 (173, M. I. 431); in the parallel passage, *De Somn.* I. 22 (141, M. I. 642), they are called "demons" by "other philosophers" but angels by Scripture. Actually Philo tends to avoid angels, except where he is explaining the

they could be employed by God to do His will, but it was useless for man to try to read the secrets of these higher beings.[1]

But when once the position of Judaism had been safeguarded against the perils of astrology, it was safe to read the heavens and their movements as the work of the "powers" of God. Thus without denying the astral wisdom of the age to the extent of rejecting entirely the belief that there was a direct connection between the heavenly bodies and the life of man, it was possible to reduce such speculations to comparatively harmless dimensions by seeing in both spheres the action of the divine powers of mercy and justice embodied in the Torah and in the history of Israel. All Jewish speculations were by no means so harmless; in general however Alexandrine Judaism, as represented by Philo, confines the planets to the position of conventional angels of the Jewish type; they are free agents, but they have no desire to do anything but the will of God. The danger of heretical speculation was too pressing to allow for any trifling in this matter; the rabbis of Palestine were more secure, and were quite ready to agree that the Gentiles were subject to a fate that was determined by the hostile powers which ruled the heavens.[2] This Alexandrine orthodoxy dared not allow; at the most they could foretell cosmic disasters, a view which the rabbis also admitted.[3]

Thus the powers of God could be employed for almost any purpose. It is indeed possible that in methods of exegesis less elaborate than that of Philo the conception of a single "power" representing God's dealings with the universe was already current. This power could be equated with the Memra or the Shekinah or any other of the periphrases by which Judaism endeavoured to avoid an excessive measure of anthropomorphism in describing God's dealings with the universe, without for a moment supposing that the introduction of such a figure in any way interfered with the absolute unity of God.[4] The use of such terminology was a mere periphrasis, except in so far as it served to demonstrate Moses' familiarity with the esoteric truths of

nature of the stars and other disembodied souls of the Platonic type. In *De Vit. Moys.* 2 (3). 39 (291, M. I. 179) the angels who bury Moses are "immortal powers".

[1] P. 63. [2] Cf. p. 100.

[3] Cf. Tosefta, quoted below, p. 100.

[4] Cf. Justin Martyr, *Dial. c. Tryph.* 128 (358a). Justin points out that the Jews allow one power, which is an angel when it brings messages, the glory when it appears in a vision, a man when sent in human form, the Logos (Memra) when it reveals God to man. Justin opposes the view that it is put out from God yet inseparable from Him, as the light from the sun, and urges that it is ἀριθμῷ ἕτερον. But it is possible that this conception of one "power" represents Jewish controversy with the Church as to the Logos, not independent speculation.

religion, as known to the philosophers and read by them into the mythology of paganism.

All this range of speculation might originate in a perfectly harmless desire to show that the true doctrine of the one God manifested in creation and in history was not to be found, as the heathen vainly supposed, in a belief in a divine principle, permeating the whole as fate and nature, and capable of being identified either with the greatest of all the gods, or with a particular deity in so far as the divine principle was being considered in one particular manifestation;[1] God was in the one God of Israel, manifesting Himself either in person or through His angels or powers under different aspects expressed by different names. This belief could be regarded as orthodox, though it had a suspicious resemblance to polytheism; clearly it could not be safeguarded from such a danger when the manifestations of God were related to the planets and so to the general astrological scheme of paganism. It would be equally dangerous if related not to the seven days of creation and the seven planets, but to the four seasons in which the sun manifested himself, and so to the one unending aeon manifested in the succession of four world-ages; yet the Jewish Scriptures could be urged in support of such teachings, since Ezekiel's vision of the chariot of God could easily be made to symbolise such a teaching, and had in fact probably been derived from it.[2]

It must, however, be noticed that this tendency to Gnosticism, while it makes itself felt on the borders of Judaism and Christianity in the heresy of Paul's opponents at Colossae, was in most cases, except indeed in the lower class of magical practice, confined to mystery-mongering of the most innocent variety. Judaism, especially in Palestine, felt sure of itself. The worship of the synagogue, consisting mainly of the

[1] The conception of one God manifested in the whole cosmos as fate, nature and Jupiter, and as the various gods of the pantheon in particular aspects of nature, was a commonplace of Stoicism, and was vital to it as a means of upholding the general practice of religion while avoiding the crudities of mythology (Cicero, *De Nat. Deor.* 2. 13. 36, 24. 63 *seqq.*; Varro *ap.* Aug. *De Civ. Dei* 7. 6; Seneca, *De Benef.* 4. 7. 1 *seqq.*). It is of course possible that the Stoic view represents Oriental influences quite apart from the astrological; but the general Hellenistic scheme provides a quite adequate explanation of the Jewish views suggested here, which meet us later in Colossians (cf. c. 7 below). There is no need to look for an Oriental source for the theory.

[2] Cf. p. 207. Ezek. c. 1. may be derived from Iranian speculations of the aeon manifesting itself in four ages (cf. Peterson, Εἷς Θεός 250). But it appears to leave Jewish speculation quite unaffected, apart from providing four beasts for the conventional imagery of apocalyptic, until after the Christian era. I cannot believe that Philo could ignore the whole chapter, if it had been a popular theme for mysticism in his day; his omission would imply that it was being used for entirely unorthodox purposes, but if this had been the case, we should expect a polemic against it rather than a complete silence. I am inclined to think that it came into fashion when Christianity had made speculation on Genesis 1 too dangerous.

recitation or exposition of the Old Testament Scriptures or the exposition of them and of prayers closely modelled on the tradition of those Scriptures, could be trusted to preserve the transcendent omnipotence of the one God of Israel. It is a striking proof of the security which the Pharisees felt, that they were willing to adopt cosmic speculations, which might seem to be dangerous, and to read them, as the Alexandrines did, into the cultus of the Temple, without fear that they might lead to a syncretism of Judaism with the religion of the Gentiles.[1] In Alexandria there was little danger, for the cultus of the Temple was known only to Jews of the Dispersion and proselytes at second hand, except in the case of those who were both wealthy and devout enough to go on pilgrimage to Jerusalem for the great festivals. It appears, however, that even in Jerusalem itself the whole theology of Hellenistic convention could be read into the cultus of altar, candlestick and incense or anything else: "Hermes" could be called as a witness to the truth of the Torah. The Pharisees were willing to go to lengths which excited the affected horror of their Sadducean opponents, precisely because they felt entirely secure of the system of Judaism. There is no evidence that their confidence would have been misplaced, apart from the historical incidents which gave rise to Christianity.

[1] Cf. Tosefta, *Hag.* 3. 35, where the Sadducees, seeing the Pharisees cleaning the candlestick in the Temple, exclaim, "Come and watch these Pharisees cleaning the radiance of the moon". But the Jerusalem Talmud reads (79d) "the orb of the sun". In Philo, *Q.R.D.H.* 45 (221, M. 1. 504), the main candlestick in the middle, with three smaller lights on each side, represents the sun in the middle with three planets on each side, and the divine Logos (i.e. mind as a divine element in man) dividing the six parts of the soul. Here again there may be a reminiscence of the six Amhaspands, but it is purely formal and artificial; the object is to find something which the candlestick can symbolise. For the possible relation of this symbolism to Hermetic speculations among the Pharisees cf. below, p. 113.

CHAPTER III

THE DIVINE WISDOM

As long as the unity of God and the supremacy of the Torah were preserved, Judaism was prepared to adopt any argument and any form of thought that seemed suited to the purpose. Naturally Paul was willing to do the same. In this, as in his whole theological outlook, he was thoroughly true to the tradition of the Judaism which he had learnt at the feet of Gamaliel, apart from the one decisive change. It had been said by one of the great figures of early Judaism that the world stood on three things, the Torah, the worship of the Temple and acts of love.[1] For Paul the world stood on Jesus, faith in Him and love as the fulfilling of the Law.

Paul, in common with the leaders of rabbinical Judaism in his day, assumed the apocalyptic outlook of the Scriptures and the conventions of apocalyptic writing.[2] But if the Greek world, while rejecting the Gospel[3] as a system of eschatology, was prepared to accept it as a system of cosmogony, Paul was perfectly prepared to meet their wishes. Either system of exposition was from the Jewish point of view midrashic rather than dogmatic; in other words it was to be regarded not as a statement of ultimate truth in the sphere of metaphysics, phrases which would have meant nothing to the mind of a Jew of the period, but as means of bringing home to the mind and conscience of the hearer the paramount claims of Jesus on the obedience of all mankind, claims which rested on His resurrection as the guarantee of the divine authority of the whole of His earthly life and teaching.

Judaism had already provided a terminology in which Paul could expound the position of Jesus in the scheme of the universe. To understand his language it is necessary to go back to the time of the return from the exile. At that time Judaism was arriving with infinite

[1] Simeon the Just, Mishnah, *Aboth* I. 2 (Danby 446).

[2] Cf. below, p. 90. The attempt of Christian writers (e.g. Charles, *Ap. and Ps.* 2. xi) to distinguish between the ethical outlook of apocalyptic and rabbinical Judaism seems as unfounded as the counter-statement of Travers Herford (*Talmud and Apocrypha* 235) that "the Apocalyptic and the ethical spirit do not get on well together". Paul's case shows how easily they can be combined in the same mind. Cf. below, p. 112, n. I.

[3] For the contents and structure of the primitive Gospel see Dodd, *The Apostolic Preaching and its Developments*. I am inclined to think that he underestimates the importance of the eschatology in the form of an imminent second coming.

labour at an absolute monotheism; but outlying colonies still worshipped a pantheon of at least five figures, apparently without fearing that the authorities of the Temple at Jerusalem would disapprove of their action.[1] The Jews of Elephantine burnt incense to Anath, as their grandparents had burnt incense to the Queen of Heaven in the cities of Judah and in the streets of Jerusalem, at the end of the fifth century B.C. It is possible that Ezra had not yet arrived from Babylon, and that the Judaism of Jerusalem was still of an unreformed type.[2] It is perhaps more likely that the exiles of Elephantine were ignorant of the change of affairs at Jerusalem and that their appeal fell on deaf ears. In any case Jewish monotheism was a recent growth at the beginning of the fourth century B.C.

In that century the face of the Eastern world was changed by the conquests of Alexander the Great, and by the year 300 B.C. Judaea had become an outlying province of the Ptolemaic Empire. Judaism was in consequence brought into contact with the cult of Sarapis and Isis. The central figure of the cult as it affected the public at large was Isis, not mainly as the sorrowing wife and sister, but rather as the divine agent, who created and sustained the universe, and the teacher who had revealed to mankind the principles of morality and the laws and arts of civilisation. Isis proclaimed her greatness to the world in a style which was new to Greek religion; her panegyric of herself attained a canonical form and was widely diffused throughout the dominions of the Ptolemies.[3] The panegyric was old enough for a copy inscribed in stone to have become largely illegible by the end of the first century B.C.[4] The cult was attractive, and although the Ptolemies were too wise to attempt any systematic persecution of Judaism as a religion, their policy provided the temptation of full citizenship and the consequent opportunities of advancement in public life to those who were initiated into the mysteries.[5]

[1] Cowley, *Aramaic Papyri of the Fifth Century B.C.* xviii, 72 and 148. Cf. Cook, *The Old Testament* 150, Vincent, *op. cit.* p. 30, n. 1.

[2] Oesterley and Robinson, *History of Israel* 2. 114 *seqq.*, date the return of Ezra about 400 B.C., which is about the date of the papyri. On the other hand, Ezra makes no reference to polytheism in the strict sense at Jerusalem; it seems unlikely that he would have ignored it.

[3] For the aretalogy of Isis at Cyme and Ios see Peek, *Die Isishymne von Andros.* The text appears in my article on the Divine Wisdom in *J.T.S.* 38. 151. 230 *seqq.*

[4] Diod. Sic. 1. 27. 4. Although the "tomb" of Isis at "Nyssa" in Arabia is open to suspicion (Nyssa is the legendary birthplace of Dionysus: Arnobius, *adv. Gentes* 5. 28), the accurate quotation of the opening clauses of the aretalogy makes it clear that he or his source was acquainted with an inscription in which the inscription was illegible through age. For the prominence of Isis as against Sarapis or Osiris in the Hellenistic cult cf. *UPZ.* 29.

[5] For settlements of Jews in Egypt under the Ptolemies, cf. *Letter of Aristeas* 12, and Andrews' note *ad loc.* in *Ap. and Ps.* 2. 95. The persecution of Ptolemy Physcon

In any case the temptation to relapse into polytheism, either as more attractive in cultus,[1] or as politically more advantageous, was constantly present before the Maccabean rebellion.[2] Consequently it is not surprising that the new cult, which combined official support with missionary propaganda, should have appeared a serious danger to the men who were concerned to maintain the purity of the reformed religion as established by the successors of Ezra.[3]

It was to meet this danger that the personified figure of Wisdom was introduced into the literature of the third century B.C. Wisdom as an expression of the nature of God and the ideal character of man is naturally a conception which might easily occur independently in different civilisations; it expresses the ideals of an established order in Church and State as against dangerous revolutionary tendencies on the part of the younger generation. In Judaism "wisdom-literature" as a whole may have been inspired by Egyptian models, which show a close similarity to the Jewish.[4] This is merely the adoption of a form of writing and a conception of the nature of God and man that is natural to a certain stage of development. But the personified Wisdom is a female figure definitely on the divine side of the gulf which separates God from man; the gulf is made more conspicuous by the absence from the earlier Wisdom-documents of the angelic hierarchy; this

(so Jos. *c. Ap.* 2. 5 (53 *seqq.*) as against Philopator in 3 Macc. 1. 1) was accompanied according to the latter book with an offer of citizenship to those who were initiated into the mysteries (2. 30); 3. 21 suggests rather that a formal compliance on state occasions was enough. The book dates apparently from *c.* 100 B.C. (Emmet, *Ap. and Ps.* 1. 158), and represents the temptation to obtain full citizenship by sharing in the religion of the city, even if there was no particular offer at the time; the writer of 3 Macc. admits that some accepted it (2. 31).

[1] Cf. Is. 65. 1–15 and 66. 17. For the official encouragement of the cult cf. *Rel. Or.* 74 and 235, n. 21. Wilcken, *UPZ* 83, admits the political purpose of the cult in its hellenised form.

[2] 1 Macc. 1. 13; the distinction in the text would not necessarily present itself so clearly to the worshipper, who would ascribe the superior attractiveness and the political advantage to the superior powers of the deity.

[3] A specimen of their methods appears in the Passover, a nomad pastoral festival blended with an agricultural festival of unleavened bread (W. J. Moulton in Hastings' *D.B.* 3. 684 *seqq.*, Art. "Passover"). But it has been transformed into a commemoration of the Exodus with such success that hardly a trace of the original remains in the scriptural account. Pentecost remains in the O.T. a harvest festival, and Philo has no knowledge that it has any other meaning. But Acts 2. 2 *seqq.* represents Pentecost as the giving of the new Law, which implies a knowledge of the rabbinical view that Pentecost is the festival of the giving of the Torah (*Judaism* 2. 48, but Moore here has overlooked the implications of the scene in Acts; for this cf. *The Beginnings of Christianity* 5. 115 and below, p. 195). For the survival of the external ritual of primitive rain-magic in the feast of Tabernacles, and for possible Dionysiac elements in it, cf. Cook, *Rel. Anc. Pal.* 194; it was known in magical circles, cf. *Papp. Mag. Gr.* 13. 997.

[4] Cf. Peet, *Literature of Egypt, Palestine and Mesopotamia* 99 *seqq.*

absence is natural, since it represents a borrowing from Persian as against Egyptian sources.[1] She appears abruptly in interpolated passages as a figure who utters a panegyric of herself.[2] The style of the panegyric is entirely out of keeping with the tradition of Jewish writing, where Psalmists praise God, but God does not praise Himself, except in a few cases where this is necessitated by dramatic convention.[3] The subject-matter of the panegyric is even more alien to Jewish orthodoxy. Wisdom appears as the source of good counsel, strength and justice, through whom kings reign and do justice, and from whom all prosperity is derived. But she is more than this, for she is the first of God's creatures, made by Him before He created the universe, yet delighting to dwell among the sons of men.[4] As such Wisdom has no function to play in creation and no reason for appearing at all. But these functions are precisely those which Isis claims for herself in her aretalogy, except that there she is the agent of creation and the divine power manifested in the maintenance of the cosmos; the latter function was impossible for Wisdom in view of the essentially deistic view of creation which is characteristic of Judaism as against the pantheism of Hellenistic Egypt,[5] while the former could hardly be ascribed to her in a Jewish document. Hence she remains the delight and darling of God, just as the Isis of the aretalogy is the eldest daughter of Cronos,[6] and in some sense a link between God and man, as Isis in the aretalogy is the real intermediary between the gods and the world of men, for it is through her that man has learnt the

[1] The tantalising Wisdom-fragment of 1 En. 42. 1 *seqq.* combines the angels of Persian origin with the personified Wisdom; but it is an isolated fragment to whose date there seems no clue.

[2] Prov. 8. 1–31 has been inserted so clumsily that the contrast between Wisdom's invitation to her banquet and that of the "strange woman" is entirely interrupted. Wisdom's house with the seven pillars does not belong to the main panegyric and the personification here is entirely different. It is quite unnecessary to see in the house with seven pillars an allusion to the seven-storied temple of Babylon (so Rankin, *Israel's Wisdom-Literature* 252, following Reitzenstein, *Ir. Erl. Myst.* 208). If the seven pillars are not part of the normal equipment of an Eastern house (Oesterley and Robinson, *History of Israel* 2. 311) they are probably the seven planets, for the cosmos is the natural home of Wisdom. But Judaism at this date shows little interest in astrology. In Ecclus. 24 we have no actual interruption; but it would be hard to find a train of thought to interrupt. In Prov. 3. 19 we have a casual interpolation of the figure apparently suggested by the allusion to "rubies"; cf. below.

[3] Thus in Pss. 50. 7 *seqq.* and 81. 10 *seqq.*, but the purpose is not that God should praise Himself, but that He should convict His people.

[4] LXX "when he delighted" (Prov. 8. 31) is meaningless and can only be due to failure to understand the Hebrew.

[5] So in the aretalogy *ἐγὼ ἐν ταῖς τοῦ ἡλίου αὐγαῖς εἰμί* and *ἐγὼ παρεδρεύω τῇ τοῦ ἡλίου πορείᾳ* (clauses 44 and 45); the conception is entirely alien to Judaism.

[6] So in Apuleius, *Metam.* 11. 5. 761, Isis is *saeculorum progenies initialis*.

knowledge of the gods and the method of serving them.[1] The similarity of the style and subject-matter and the interpolated character of the whole passage show that we are dealing not with a natural expression of Jewish piety but with a personification of the attribute of Wisdom as the highest characteristic of God and man, designed as a counterblast to the figure of Isis, as she meets us in her panegyrics of herself.[2] The figure was sufficiently familiar to the compiler of the opening chapters of Proverbs to be present before him in two versions, since we have an anticipation of her in 3. 19 *seqq.*, though in a less definitely personal form. But although Wisdom is not definitely personified here, her identity with the personal Wisdom appears from the mention of the "tree of life"[3] and the superiority of Wisdom to "rubies".[4] The former identification is a regular attribute of Wisdom; the superiority seems to have been an attribute of the virtuous women of Israel before ever the personal Wisdom made her appearance.

This portrait of Wisdom would appear to date from about 250 B.C.[5] In Ecclus. 24 we get another version, again interpolated into the text, and again in the form of a panegyric by Wisdom on herself. But the portrait is very different. Instead of the colourless and correct Isis of the aretalogy who has no particular character of her own but does everything which a good goddess ought to do, we have a figure who proceeded from the mouth of the Most High and wandered through all the earth seeking for a suitable abode; this she was unable to find until her creator gave her an inheritance in Israel. She is eternal; she was established in the Tabernacle and the Holy City. Wisdom proceeds

[1] In the aretalogy ἐγὼ μυήσεις ἀνθρώποις ἐπέδειξα; cf. Wisd. 8. 4 and *Corp. Herm.* Exc. 23 (Κόρη Κόσμου), 65 *seqq.* (Scott 492), on which see *Conversion* 279.

[2] The "egoistic" style appears to be characteristic of the missionary propaganda of Isis; cf. Apuleius, *loc. cit.*, which is another specimen of this type of literature. The writer of Proverbs may not be following the aretalogy, but a different version to which he may be adhering more closely.

[3] The "tree of life" appears in Prov. 3. 18 and Wisd. 10. 4, where, curiously enough, it is the ark, as also in 14. 7, which is a different document. But in Philo, *Leg. Alleg.* 3. 17 (52, M. 1. 97), Wisdom is the tree of life. The association of Wisdom and the first man reappears in Job 15. 7 *seqq.* For the text cf. Rankin, *Israel's Wisdom-Literature* 237; but there is no need to introduce the myth of a "cosmic man" to explain the passage, which can be quite adequately explained from Gen. 3. 6, though it may reflect an older version of the myth.

[4] The phrase occurs six times. In Lam. 4. 7 it is used of the Nazirites. It is applied to the personal Wisdom of Prov. 3. 15 and 8. 11 and to "lips of knowledge" (20. 15); it is used of the quasi-personal wisdom in Job 28. 18. The reason seems to be that it is already proverbially applied to a virtuous woman. The virtuous wife of Prov. 31. 10 appears in 1 Sam. 1. 2 *seqq.*, where Hannah is better than Peninnah ("Ruby"). Properly the word means corals.

[5] Cf. Oesterley and Robinson, *History of Israel* 2. 201 and Nowack in Hastings' *D.B.* 4. 142, Art. "Proverbs".

to compare herself to the forest trees of Lebanon and the trees and shrubs of the low countries, with a special reference to those used for making the incense of the Tabernacle.[1] From comparing herself to the vine she passes to an invitation to come and feast on her, which is perhaps modelled on the theme of Proverbs. Here the panegyric ends, and we pass to explicit identification of Wisdom "as described above"[2] with the Book of the Law of Moses, which is then compared to the four great rivers of Eden, with Jordan added in deference to Palestinian tradition. This is the first specific equation of Wisdom and Torah, which plays a great part in rabbinical theology. Here it is obviously quite unharmonised with the earlier description of Wisdom in the character of the great nature-goddess. Moreover it reflects a conception of Wisdom later than that of Ecclesiasticus, in which Wisdom has been equated with the Stoic reason pervading the cosmos. Law, which ruled in the affairs of gods and men alike, was simply the divine mind or reason at work in the sphere of conduct.[3] It would seem that it was the conflation of Wisdom with the deity pervading the cosmos that led to the further identification of the Torah with Wisdom; for if the Gentiles held that the true law was that immanent in the cosmos, it was obvious that they must be referring to the Torah.

Thus the passage appears from its content to be a late interpolation, perhaps intended to soften down the startling figure. Yet a further mark of its unauthentic character is the abandonment of the "I-Style" and still more the impossible comparison of the feminine Hokmah or Torah of the Hebrew to a river, which is always masculine and always a god in classical or Semitic mythology.[4] The comparison can only have been added to the panegyric by a writer who thought in Greek and equated the rivers with the masculine νόμος.[5]

Apart from this there can be little doubt as to the original of this highly coloured portrait. The lady who dwells in the city of Jerusalem and in its Temple, who is also to be compared to all the forest trees

[1] Possibly an allusion to the cosmic symbolism of the four ingredients of the incense; cf. above, p. 39. But there is no necessity for such a reference.

[2] Note the very clumsy transition ταῦτα πάντα in 24. 23, which is merely the interpolator's transition to a totally different theme.

[3] Cf. Chrysippus *ap.* Marcianus 1 (1. 11. 25, v. Arn. 3. 77) and cf. the extracts from Cicero, *De Legibus* quoted by v. Arn. *ib.* (3. 78 *seqq.*). The equation of Wisdom with the Torah though due to Stoic influences may have been assisted by Deut. 4. 6, which however does not seem to be quoted in this sense. I owe this suggestion to the Rev. H. St J. Hart.

[4] For Semitic river-gods cf. Cook, *Rel. Anc. Pal.* 174. In Philo Wisdom is always associated with springs, but never with a river, except in *Q.R.D.H.* 62 (315, M. 1. 518); here Euphrates symbolises the wisdom of God as against the Nile, which represents the body and its passions, but wisdom is not in any way personified.

[5] Actually the passage is not found in the Hebrew, but this proves nothing. Philo, *De Ebr.* 9 (32, M. 1. 362) seems to be an echo of it.

of Hermon and the luxuriant verdure of the Jordan valley, is the great Syrian goddess Astarte or Atargatis, at once the goddess of great cities,[1] and the mother manifested in the fertility of nature.[2] The search for "rest" throughout the universe seems at first sight inappropriate for Astarte as against Isis. But the two goddesses had been practically merged into one another for centuries before this,[3] and the particular feature of the quest of Isis had been adopted on behalf of Astarte.[4] The change in the portrait appears to represent Isis in the character of Astarte or Astarte in the character of Isis, the ambiguous figure who appears on coins of Antiochus Epiphanes.[5] This transformation in the character of Wisdom dates from the beginning of the second century B.C., the time of the transfer of Palestine from the Ptolemaic to the Seleucid Empire.[6] It would seem that this panegyric was written at a time when the danger to Judaism came from a propaganda which centred on Antioch rather than Alexandria; the more highly coloured figure of Syria might have less attraction for the Greeks; but it had a greater affinity to the Jewish point of view. The character of Wisdom as searching throughout the cosmos remains a feature of later writings,[7] though the difficulty of the personification of a female figure led the author of Job to rationalise the theme of the quest of Wisdom throughout the cosmos into a quest of the whole cosmos for Wisdom.[8] The final appearance of the search of Wisdom

[1] Especially of Byblus. For the Baalath Gebal cf. Cook, *op. cit.* 93. [Properly Astarte is the goddess of Sidon, Atargatis of Syria.]

[2] For cedars as associated with Astarte cf. Baudissin, *Adonis und Esmun* 193; cedars are sacred to Irnîni-Ishtar in the Gilgamesh Epic (Gressmann 5.6, p.27); the monster Humbaba reappears as Combabos in the Stratonice romance of Lucian's *De Dea Syria* 19; cf. Harmon's note *ad loc.* in the Loeb edition and Garstang, *The Syrian Goddess* 58, n. 35. Gressmann, however (*op. cit.* 112), denies the connection. For cypresses cf. Furtwängler in Roscher, *Lexikon* 1. 395, Art. "Astarte", and Elmslie's note on Mishnah *Abodah Zarah* (*Texts and Studies* 8. 2.60). For Astarte as a goddess of fertility Roscher *ib.* 397.

[3] Cook, *op. cit.* 108; for the Hellenistic age cf. *Kyrios* 2. 268. On the offering of Dionysius of Sidon 130 B.C. cf. Roussel, *Cultes Égyptiens à Delos* 132.

[4] "Sanchuniathon" *ap.* Philo of Byblus *ap.* Eus. *Pr. Ev.* 1. 10. 21.

[5] Baudissin, *Adonis und Esmun* 196. For the reverse process cf. the inscription of Carvoran, Bücheler, *Anth. Lat.* (*Epigr.*) 1. 24, where the Syrian goddess who is "inventress of justice, foundress of cities, weighing life and good rights in the balance" has become the colourless Isis of the aretalogies.

[6] Ecclesiasticus appears to date from 200 to 175 B.C. (Box and Oesterley in *Ap. and Ps.* 1. 293). The conquest of Palestine by Antiochus appears to have been completed in 199 B.C.

[7] Cf. 1 En. 42. 2. Rankin, *op. cit.* 258, compares the quest of Dike in Aratus, *Phaen.* 96 *seqq.* But it is a far cry from Aratus to Enoch, and we have not a quest of Dike but her gradual withdrawal from earth to heaven. Isis-Sophia is a good deal nearer.

[8] This seems more likely than a cosmic myth. We have a vague parallel for such a myth in *Ad. et Ev.* 36 (*Ap. and Ps.* 2. 143), where Seth is sent to find the oil of mercy from the Tree of Life (cf. above, p. 59). But it seems more likely that the search of Wisdom throughout the cosmos for something entirely unspecified has been transformed into a search for wisdom throughout the cosmos, a rational and therefore probably secondary feature.

in theology is in the romance of Valentinus, where she figures as the divine element sunk in the material world, and seeking to return to her home in the *pleroma*.[1]

There were two ways in which orthodox Judaism could assimilate this embarrassing female figure. She could be identified with the Torah, which could be described in the language of midrashic piety almost as a personal figure; but the Torah could never lose its character as a written book and become a real person.[2] There was, however, another line of development open for the figure of Wisdom. In Alexandria from the middle of the second century B.C. Judaism was in contact with Hellenistic philosophy, with which it was bound to come to terms, if it was to retain its hold on the intelligent and educated members of the nation. The sacrifices which loyalty to the religion of Israel demanded[3] could not be asked of any but the most ignorant, unless Judaism could find means of reconciling itself with the attitude of the intelligent and cultured outlook of mankind.[4] Wisdom provided the means of reconciliation.

The general philosophy of the Hellenistic world was a compromise between Platonism, Pythagoreanism and Stoicism, a philosophy which may reflect the rather shadowy personality of Posidonius.[5] The differences of the schools of philosophy, which were a sign of intellectual vigour in classical Greece, were no recommendation to the Hellenistic age, which asked rather for a practical guide of life, which would enable man to feel at home in a strange and hostile universe.[6]

[1] Ir. *Haer.* 1. 2. 2 and 1. 4. 1 *seqq.*; cf. Plut. *De Is. et Os.* 78, 383 a, for Isis as the divine element in the cosmos seeking for the pure principle of divinity.

[2] The identification goes back to Ecclus. 24. 23 and may be implied in Aristobulus. The personification of the Torah appears to be implied in Θουρώ in "Sanchuniathon" *ap.* Philo of Byblus *ap.* Eus. *Pr. Ev.* 1. 10. 28; cf. *Kyrios* 3. 446. (My thanks are due to Professor S. A. Cook for calling my attention to this reference.) It appears that Cronos (= El (*ib.* 16), = Israel (*ib.* 29) and therefore presumably = Iao = Saturn) left Thot to teach religion to mankind. Thot = Moses in Artabanus (*ib.* 9. 27. 2). Thouro explains his teaching to mankind (= Isis of the aretalogy clauses 19–22).

[3] Philo dismisses circumcision in the short tract *De Circumcisione* (*De Spec. Legg.* 1, M. 2. 210). Elsewhere he hardly mentions it (Cohen-Wendland, index, notes three references. He admits that it is ridiculed everywhere). It is very much softened down in the LXX version of Deut. 10. 16, "Cut off the hardness of your heart" and 30. 6, "The Lord will cleanse your hearts". For Stoic objections cf. Orig. *in Ep. ad Rom.* 2. 13 (ed. Lommatzsch 6. 137).

[4] Cf. *De Conf. Ling.* 2 *seqq.* (2, M. 1. 405). The use of the myth of the Aloades to discredit the story of the Tower of Babel appears to be a stock argument already: it recurs in Celsus (Orig. *c. Cels.* 4. 21; cf. Cyril, *c. Jul.* 134 *seqq.*).

[5] I have here followed Bevan's view (*Stoics and Sceptics* 85). Reinhardt's *Poseidonios* seems to give him a quite exaggerated importance as a real philosopher.

[6] Cf. Bevan, *op. cit.* 25; naturally the state of affairs in the third century was only intensified by developments between that date and 100–50 B.C. Bouché-Leclercq, *L'Astrol. Gr.* 354, n. 2, points out the influence of the wars of the Diadochi on the acceptance of astrology by the Hellenistic world; after all astrology is not much more complicated or meaningless than the politics of the period.

Posidonius urged that the differences of philosophers were no reason for abandoning philosophy, since at that rate we should have to abandon life altogether;[1] it would seem that he solved the problem of their divergences by amalgamating as many philosophies as possible into a single system without enquiring too closely into their consistency. He hoped in this way to provide mankind with a system which would withstand the confusion of the first century B.C. At the same time he was a scientific observer of real ability; he had travelled to Gades, and there established by strict observation the dependence of the tides of the Atlantic on the moon.[2] Few discoveries have been so disastrous. If the moon could dominate so vast a thing as the Atlantic, it was difficult to doubt that there was "a tide in the affairs of men". If, as he held in accordance with the whole Stoic tradition, the cosmos was governed by a divine power of reason pervading the whole, which was also the natural "sympathy" which united all things to one another,[3] nothing could be more natural than to suppose that the wisdom of the Chaldeans had indeed discovered in the movements of the planets through the fixed stars the signs which foretold, to those who could read them aright, the future destinies of the world, and indeed of every individual in the world; for all were bound together by that natural "sympathy", which was also providence and fate and the will of God. Hence Posidonius, though he does not appear to have accepted the belief that the planets governed the fate of man, or that the fate of mankind was determined by hostile powers, accepted the belief that the future could be read in the stars by those who were skilled to do so, in virtue of fate,[4] which was simply the causal con-

[1] *Protreptica ap.* Diog. Laert. 7. 129. For philosophy as a means of escape from the disasters of the time cf. Cicero, *De Nat. Deor.* 1. 4. 7; *De Div.* 2. 2. 6.

[2] Strabo 3. 5. 8 (173).

[3] The view goes back to Chrysippus (Stob. *Ecl.* 1. 153. 24, v. Arn. 2. 152, and Alex. Aphr. *De Mixt.* 216. 14, *ib.* 154). Cf. Verg. *Aen.* 6. 724 *seqq.*; Servius, *ad loc.*; Seneca, *De Benef.* 4. 7. 1 *seqq.*, *Ad Helv. Matr. de Cons.* 8. 3. In Sext. Emp. *adv. Math.* 9. 79 the influence of the moon on natural phenomena proves that the cosmos is a single body, whose nature must be rational, since it includes rational natures and the whole is greater than the part; cf. Cicero, *De Nat. Deor.* 2. 7. 18 *seqq.* and *De Div.* 2. 14. 34, where sympathy is admitted but divination denied in a parody of the conventional argument; it would seem that Posidonius was not willing to let his great discovery die. For Philo cf. *De Prov.* 2.76 (A. 95); in *Leg. Alleg.* 1. 4 (8, M. 1. 45) in a brief panegyric on the hebdomad the moon is the "most sympathetic" to the earth of all the stars; the theme is developed in *De Spec. Legg.* 2 (*De Sept.*), 17 (140 *seqq.*, M. 2. 292). For the general theme cf. *Corp. Herm.* Exc. 12 (Scott 434).

[4] For this limited influence cf. Philo, *De Mund. Op.* 38 (113, M. 1. 27) and 19 (58, M. 1. 13); for disasters cf. *Timaeus* 40 a, omitting *οὐ*. In Clem. Alex. *Strom.* 5. 6. 37 (668 P), in a revised version of Philo's account of the High Priest's robe the rulers of the planets assist in the "becoming" of things on earth (or "in the birth of men on earth"?). According to Origen, *in Gen. Comm.* 3. 5, the stars are used by

nection which governed the course of all things, and might equally well be described as nature or Zeus.[1] Divination, of which astrology was a branch, was the system of judging the future on the basis of past experience, similar to the power of the astronomer—an ominous analogy—to foretell the movements of the heavenly bodies. The argument opened the way for the dominion of astrology for centuries to come.[2] Although it has been urged that in accepting astrology within this rather limited sphere, he betrayed his Oriental affinities—for he was a native of Apamea in Syria—it may be doubted whether in his attempt to find a single principle of order to explain all natural phenomena and in his willingness to argue from one branch of knowledge to another on the basis of superficial analogy, he did not show himself a true child of the spirit of classical Hellas.[3] But his admission of astrology, even though he seems only to have admitted it as a branch of the science of divination, on the strength of a cosmic sympathy, seems to have opened the floodgates.[4] His more temperate disciples might limit the range of astrology severely; Philo accepts it only as a branch of meteorology of value in foretelling natural catastrophes and as a guide to the farmer and the navigator,[5] but the Hellenistic world in general was delighted at the discovery of a science which offered a single consistent explanation for all the phenomena of the universe; the temptation was one which the Greek mind could hardly resist.[6]

God to direct the powers who execute His will; they can only be read in so far as the rebel angels have betrayed the secrets entrusted to them. Cf. 1 En. 8. 3, Clem. Alex. *Ecl. Proph.* 53 and 55 (1002 P). They still have no power over men; but in *Clem. Recog.* 1. 28 they foretell the future and can be read by the learned; they can also (10. 12) determine man's evil desires, but he has power to resist. This is a long way from Philo's incautious admission (cf. *De Migr. Abr.* 33 (184, M. 1. 465), where the meaning of the stars is simply beyond man's understanding). (For the possibility of Chaldean influences on the *Timaeus* cf. Boll-Bezold, *Sternglaube u. Sterndeutung* 93.)

[1] Cf. p. 51. For fate as the causal connection of all things cf. Cicero, *De Div.* 1. 55. 125, following Posidonius; a rhetorical version of the same theme in Seneca, *ad Marc. de Cons.* 18. 2.

[2] It appears from Boll-Bezold, *op. cit.* 26 that the way had been prepared by others. Bouché-Leclercq, *L'Astrol. Gr.*, seems unduly severe in regarding him as the villain of the piece (545).

[3] Reinhardt is right to this extent in calling him a great "vitalist", in so far as he tried to find a single rational principle pervading all phenomena.

[4] Thus in Cicero, *De Div.* 1. 19. 36, astrology is defended only as one specimen of divination and not the most important. Cf. *ib.* 42. 93 (for the reasons for its vogue in Egypt and Babylon) and 52. 118 for natural "sympathy" as explaining the possibility of divination.

[5] Cf. p. 63, n. 4. A queer bit of genuine astrology has crept into *De Somn.* 2. 16 (114, M. 2. 673), but Philo does not vouch for it (the greater stars vie with one another for escorts of the smaller).

[6] The influence of Oriental contacts, in causing the general acceptance of astrology, seems very uncertain; Diogenes of Babylon reduced the influence of the stars to a

The main interest of this school of philosophy was, however, the reconciliation of Stoicism with the teaching of the Bible of the Hellenistic schools of Alexandria, the *Timaeus* of Plato.[1] There were several reasons for the position which this dialogue enjoyed. It is Plato's only formal cosmogony; but it is put into the mouth of the Pythagorean Timaeus of Locri, and so could be regarded as the synthesis of Plato and Pythagoras.[2] It was monotheistic in so far as it recognised one transcendent deity. But besides the "father of the universe" there is the living and divine pattern of the universe, which is projected from the mind of the God to be either the ideal world of which the actual is a copy, or the ideal world from the union of which with the material the universe derives its existence. The ambiguity of the relation was characteristic of Plato: the Hellenistic age was not of course likely to regard a lack of consistency and clarity at a vital point as a disadvantage. In terms of Pythagorean mathematics God was the pure monad who expanded himself into the duad; and from this act of expansion the universe came into being.[3] Yet again this divine pattern could also be equated with that element of reason, which was the refined and ethereal fire which pervaded the universe and was itself divine. By means of this amalgamation of the *Timaeus* with the older Stoic tradition, it became possible to combine a system of transcendental monotheism with the pantheism of the early Stoa.[4] Thus the *Timaeus* attained an almost canonical position: it had, no less than Stoicism, always found a place for the gods of the Greek pantheon and for the cult of the pagan world. But while the supreme deity of Plato was, at least in many passages, not merely the "idea of the good" but a genuinely transcendent personal being, in the older

minimum (Cicero, *De Div.* 2. 43. 90), and Seleucus of Seleuceia on the Tigris even supported the impious view of Aristarchus that the earth moved round the sun (Plut. *Plat. Quaest.* 8. 1. 1006c). The ultimate belief in the immanence of God in the cosmos, which underlay the whole scheme, goes back to Zeno, who is credited with such affinities in virtue of his Phoenician origin; but an interest in God as source of the law of nature is quite alien to the Semitic mind (cf. *Kyrios* 3. 461 *seqq.*).

[1] Bouché-Leclercq, *op. cit.* 20.

[2] The actual question of the relation of the *Timaeus* to Pythagoreanism is irrelevant from the point of view of the Hellenistic age, which accepted it as representing the two great masters.

[3] *Placita* 1. 3. 8 (*Dox. Gr.* 280); cf. Zeller, *Phil. der Gr.*[4] 3. 2. 129 *seqq.*

[4] According to Diog. Laert. 7. 142 and 156, Zeno, like Heraclitus (*ib.* 9. 7 *seqq.*), regarded fire as the principle of which all things are composed; the cosmos comes into being as it contracts into air, moisture and earth and then returns to fire. Cf. Ar. Did. *Epit.* 36. 2 (*Dox. Gr.* 468): the fire is ethereal, intelligent and divine (*Placita* 1. 6. 1, *Dox. Gr.* 292 and Diog. Laert. 7. 137). But in Diog. Laert. 7. 134 God, as reason, is the artificer, acting on an independent matter. It seems uncertain whether the inconsistency is due to Zeno or his followers. Bevan, *op. cit.* 43, holds that Zeno left room for a transcendent element of deity.

Stoicism he was often difficult to distinguish from the reason immanent in the cosmos; and a pure pantheism offers no possibility for worship. The later Stoics however, if not the earlier ones, distinguished between the element of divine fire immanent in the cosmos and the concentrated element of fire in the firmament of heaven. Their favourite analogy between the universe as the macrocosm and man as the microcosm helped them here; for as man has a dominant element of reason in his head (or usually his heart), yet pervading his whole body and enabling the dominant element to be aware of sensations,[1] so there was in the cosmos a dominant element of aether or fire concentrated in the firmament (the highest part of the cosmos being naturally superior to the lower), and also a diffused element of divinity, diffused throughout the cosmos, but present in different parts of nature in different degrees; that which was present in inanimate objects as a mere "force" was present in man as reason.[2] The argument was invaluable to the astrologers;[3] but in itself it was a serious attempt to vindicate the existence of God as a being whom man could know and worship in virtue of that affinity between God and man which was proclaimed by the very structure of his body, which enabled him alone of all the beasts to contemplate the stars without difficulty.[4]

It would be hard to imagine a system which has less in common with the religion of the Old Testament, with its utter insistence on the transcendence of God as the ruler, first of the nation He had chosen, and later of the world which He created in the beginning. From His Temple at Jerusalem He had been transferred to the firmament of heaven some centuries before, when the destruction of the Temple and the exile had compelled Judaism to raise Him to be ruler of the

[1] For an incredibly literal account of the way in which the "breath" of life, as inspired into Adam, penetrated his whole body cf. Tert. *De Anim.* 9, but Tertullian had the advantage of a revelation from a prophetess. For a similar account from a less ambitious source cf. Philo, *De Fug. et Inv.* 32 (182, M. 1. 573). Tertullian (*De Anim.* 32) justly claims that the extension of the soul through the body proves the impossibility of its transmigration into another body which would not fit it.

[2] Diog. Laert. 7. 139. It should be observed that from the point of view of Hellenistic Judaism it is less important to ask what the great figures of the Stoa really taught than what the doxographers and journalists of the type of Diogenes said that they taught. Cf. Cicero, *De Nat. Deor.* 2. 6. 17 for the view that the "higher" part of the cosmos must be "better" than the "lower" and 11. 29 for the rational nature of the ἡγεμονικόν; it is not clear whether the ἡγεμονικόν is the aether or firmament or a reason residing in one or other of them.

[3] For the commonplace macrocosm-microcosm analogy cf. Philo, *De Mund. Op.* 23 (69, M. 1. 16) and 27 (82, M. 1. 19). For its use by the astrologers see p. 174.

[4] The thought appears in the *Timaeus* 90a; it was a favourite among the later Stoics, cf. Philo, *Quod Det. Pot. Ins.* 23 (85, M. 1. 207); Cicero, *De Nat. Deor.* 2. 56. 140; Seneca, *ad Ser. de Ot.* 5. 4, and the literature of the period *passim*.

cosmos, if He was not simply to be one among the many gods of the nations who had signally failed to deliver their worshippers from the kings of Assyria and Babylon. Judah, under the influence of the prophets, had taken the heroic course; the sky became "heaven" and the God of Israel the "God of heaven".[1] Here Judaism could easily accommodate itself to philosophy; for Judaism God was a perfectly holy spiritual being who dwelt in the firmament; for philosophy the firmament was an intelligent being, who was perfectly good in an ethical sense; the "numinous" quality of holiness could hardly be applied to the supreme deity of philosophy. Thus there was little difference, especially as the Stoics were quite liable to substitute the "mind" in the aether or firmament for the aether or firmament itself;[2] the apparent materialism of Stoicism, which could not deny that even God Himself was in some sense "material", did not detract from the entirely spiritual character of their conception of God.[3] But as against this possibility of agreement it might have seemed that the further conception of a divine power or a "second God" immanent in the cosmos presented an insuperable difficulty to the strictly unitarian monotheism of Judaism. Judaism was the cult of a God of the tribe, who had never been a nature-God,[4] and it had attained to its monotheism by a rigid elimination of the deities in whom the Semites saw the bestowers of the bounties of nature. In consequence it had singularly little interest in nature as such; even where it comes nearest to such an interest, it is limited to the animal world.[5]

[1] Cf. Cook, *The Old Testament* 132, for the relation of earth and sky as the abode of Yahweh. But the "God of heaven" in Neh. 1. 4 has replaced the Lord of Is. 6. 1, who, though "high and lifted up", is still in His Temple. The religions of Babylon and Persia were no doubt partly responsible for the change. A general tendency to transfer gods from earth to heaven appears in the growing use of the title "most High" (Hypsistos); for this cf. Roberts, Skeat and Nock in *Harvard Theological Review* 29. 1. 56 *seqq.* (Jan. 1936). Both Jewish and pagan usage imply a definitely monotheistic conception (*ib.* 66), as against the Syrian and Phoenician titles of El Elyon and Baal-Shamayim, which may be merely complimentary and not suggest that the deity in question is in any sense a supreme God (*Kyrios* 3. 83 and 115). The "lord of Heaven" may be merely a local deity resident in the sky above his city, not ruler of the whole firmament (*ib.* 37 and 43). Naturally astrology told in favour of the prestige of any deity who could prove an established connection with the sky (*Rel. Or.* 118).

[2] Cf. above, p. 44, for the God of the Jews as equated by intelligent Gentiles with the firmament itself, and *Placita* 1. 7. 33 (*Dox. Gr.* 306) for νοῦς ἐν αἰθέρι as God.

[3] Cf. Tarn, *Hellenistic Civilisation* 272 *seqq.*

[4] Cf. *Kyrios* 3. 463 *seqq.* for the distinction between tribal Gods and nature-Gods in Semitic religion.

[5] Ps. 104 is a startling exception to the general outlook of Judaism (*Kyrios* 3. 487). But the peculiarity of its outlook may be due to Greek influence (for its late date cf. Briggs, *Int. Crit. Comm.* 2. 331). Even so the "breath" of God, as the source of life, does not extend beyond the animal world (vv. 26 *seqq.*); the vegetable world exists for the benefit of the animal (vv. 14–18).

But Judaism was provided with a figure which could easily be employed in the rôle of the divine element immanent in the cosmos. The divine Wisdom, like her prototype Isis, could easily assume this character; it was indeed easier for Wisdom. She had never been more than an otiose personification, invented to divert attention from the attractions of Isis and equated with the Torah, whereas Isis was a sharply personal and transcendent deity, who needed all the capacity for accommodation, characteristic of Egyptian theology,[1] to exchange her rôle of the sorrowing wife and sister, who was also queen and saviour of mankind, for that of an immanent principle of deity.[2]

The earliest writer to attempt the identification of Wisdom with the divine power immanent in the cosmos is, or professes to be, Aristobulus, tutor of Ptolemy VI Philometor (2 Macc. 1. 10). His writing takes the form of a letter to the king, explaining away the anthropomorphisms of the Old Testament.[3] The interest of his letter lies in his statement that God, in creating the cosmos, gave the sabbath to man as a day of rest. This day might also be called in nature the first coming into being of the light in which all things are contemplated. The same title might be transferred to Wisdom, for all light comes from her.[4] Hence some of the Peripatetic school have described her as a beacon,[5] while Solomon describes her as being older than heaven and earth. This leads on to an explanation of God's rest on the sabbath, which is not to be taken literally but as symbolising the Jewish use of the sabbath for obtaining the knowledge of things human and divine; this again leads up to a selection of verses in praise of the hebdomad, including some from "Linus" which mention the sevenfold construction of the spheres of heaven. It is clear that we have here a Jewish writer, not a Christian, since the sabbath has to play the part both of the first day on which light was created and also of the seventh; but a correspondence between the first and seventh days is only a desperate attempt to read the correspondence of the beginning and the end into Judaism, which is committed to a seven-day week. It is rendered possible by the fact that the first day of Gen. 1. 3 is a creation of

[1] *Rel. Or.* 81; cf. Erman, *Die Rel. der Ægypter* c. 6.

[2] Cf. Plut. *De Is. et Os.* 54. 373a *seqq.*; Osiris is the monad or pure idea, Isis is matter, which is however not lifeless but intelligent; Horus is the cosmos, who as child of the two is not eternal but continuous through a cycle of rebirths. Cf. 77. 382c for a variant of the theme; cf. also the rôle of "nature" in *Corp. Herm.* Exc. 23 (Κόρη Κόσμου), 10 (Scott, 463). For the real character of Isis in Hellenistic religion cf. Apuleius, *Metam.* 11. 3. 756 *seqq.*

[3] Eus. *Pr. Ev.* 13. 12. 13; cf. 7. 14. 1 and 8. 10. 1.

[4] Or "the whole is light as a result of her (action)".

[5] Aristotle, *Eth. Nic.* 6. 7. 1141a, 17. It is perhaps doubtful whether Aristobulus has any other claim to his usual title of "the Peripatetic".

precosmic light.[1] None the less it remains unconvincing; Clement of Alexandria takes over the passage without acknowledgment and reconstructs it into the Christian ogdoad, in which the first day of creation and the first day of the resurrection have a far more natural "correspondence".[2] Thus Aristobulus is certainly Jewish, while it is unlikely that he is later than the more elaborate treatment of the theme in the Wisdom of Solomon.[3]

In Aristobulus Wisdom has derived her character of precosmic light from the book of Genesis, yet it was also a character of Isis.[4] The attempt to place her at the beginning of all things and yet to identify her with the sabbath suggests that he has in mind the equation of Wisdom with the Torah, as described in the interpolation in Ecclesiasticus and in rabbinical tradition.[5] His panegyric on Wisdom enables him to introduce the argument that the philosophers of Greece had really borrowed from Moses;[6] unfortunately it also reveals the paucity of his acquaintance, and that of his successors, with the philosophy of the classical age, since he like the rest of them fails to notice the one passage in that philosophy in which a cosmic figure of Wisdom really appears, in the *Philebus* of Plato;[7] the omission is a striking proof of the extent to which the philosophy of Judaism depended on doxographers' handbooks.

The Wisdom of Solomon is a composite document of Alexandrine

[1] Cf. above, p. 36. In Philo, *De Mund. Op.* 8 (30, M. I. 6), the light of the first day is a νοητὸν φῶς, which is the image of the Logos: but since it corresponds to mind as the ἡγεμονικόν of the soul, it really is the Logos. Cf. *De Somn.* I. 13 (75, M. I. 632). Philo's obscurity is due to his attempt to combine the cosmogony of Genesis with the *Timaeus*, and shows the obscurity of the latter as to the relation of the archetypal divine pattern to the actual heaven.

[2] Cf. above, p. 7, n. 2.

[3] His authenticity is defended by Schürer, *G.J.V.* 3. 512; cf. Meyer, *Urspr. u. Anf.* 2. 366. The only question seems to be whether the mixture of Orphic and Stoic elements which he represents, both of them coloured by the Pythagorean value of the hebdomad, and the introduction of a scrap of Peripatetic teaching, can really go back to 150 B.C. If not, it remains perfectly probable that a Jew of Alexandria should have written under his name fifty or a hundred years later; after all it would suggest that the prominent figure of Alexandrine Judaism had anticipated the philosophers of that city. Apparently *Ep. Barn.* 15. 9 is borrowed from him with suitable revision.

[4] *C.I.G.* 3724.

[5] Cf. *Genesis Rabba* on Gen. I. I, which would seem to represent an older tradition of cosmogony adapted to the necessity of Christian controversies. For the sabbath as "last in time but first in thought" cf. the hymn לכה דודי from the Jewish liturgy (Singer's *Authorised Jewish Prayer-book*), which shows the tradition persisting till the 16th century.

[6] Cf. p. 35.

[7] *Philebus* 30c is, so far as I know, the only reference to "wisdom" as a cosmic power in classical philosophy; in Aristotle, quoted by Aristobulus, wisdom is really the habit of mind acquired by philosophy. There is no allusion to it even in Philo, or the Jewish writers used by the apologists and Clement of Alexandria.

origin,[1] the relevant part of which (6. 12–11. 4) may safely be regarded as older than Philo. Philo substituted the term Logos for Wisdom as the title of the divine power immanent in the cosmos, and so eliminated the awkward female figure from the theology of Alexandrine Judaism; she had by now fulfilled her purpose as a counter-attraction to Isis, who could safely be disregarded.[2] This section is simply one representative of a whole school of Jewish exegesis of the pre-Philonic era. On the other hand, it is later than the amalgamation of Plato and the divine reason of the Stoics, which seems to be the work of Posidonius.[3]

The glories of Wisdom as described in 6. 12 *seqq.* open with a well-known and entirely inappropriate borrowing from Stoicism; Wisdom is easily seen by those who love her;[4] the saying was applicable to the Stoic God diffused through the material world, and it was justified by the language of Prov. 3. 15b. It was however quite inappropriate to the Jewish conception of God as entirely transcending the universe, a conception which Wisdom really shares in this book in spite of the writer's attempts to place himself in the Stoic tradition.[5] The section which follows (6. 13–16) is modelled on the tradition of Proverbs[6] and leads up to the *sorites*, which proves that by following wisdom man can attain to that immortality which comes from being near to God and is the true kingdom.[7] Solomon proclaims her to mankind; for he is himself a mortal and all his wisdom only comes from the gift of wisdom which was granted to him as an answer to his prayer for her.[8] Here he is of course true to the tradition of the Old Testament; yet it was also the view of the later Stoics that the great man is great by the

[1] Meyer regards 1. 1–6. 11 as a separate book (*Urspr. u. Anf.* 2. 362). It is far more certain that 11. 4 begins a separate book, by a writer of a far lower spiritual level and intellectual outlook. For the arguments against its unity cf. Holmes in *Ap. and Ps.* 1. 521 *seqq.*, where they are stated with great moderation.

[2] For Wisdom in Philo see below, p. 81.

[3] It is, however, quite possible that it was begun by earlier writers.

[4] *Comm. Bern.* Lucan 63[a]. 5. 28, p. 305. 23 (ed. Usener): *Ait enim Posidonius Stoicus θεός ἐστι πνεῦμα νοερὸν διῆκον δι' ἁπάσης οὐσίας, hoc est terram, aquam, aera, caelum. Hunc spiritum summum deum Plato vocat, artificem permixtum mundo, omnibusque quae in eo sunt. Quod si ita est, omnes eum videmus.* Cf. *Corp. Herm.* 11 (2), 22a (Scott, 222).

[5] But cf. the equation of nature with Zeus in the passages referred to p. 64.

[6] 6. 14=Prov. 8. 34b and 3a, 6. 16=Prov. 8. 2b; 7. 8–9=Prov. 8. 10–11. "Precious stones" was as near as the LXX could get to the "rubies" of the Hebrew.

[7] For the wise man as king cf. Diog. Laert. 7. 122; as divine *ib.* 119; the theme is of course a commonplace. Cf. Epict. *Diss.* 2. 17. 33. In *Quod Omn. Prob. Lib.* 7 (42 *seqq.*, M. 2. 452) Philo manages to work it into Judaism on the strength of Exod. 7. 1.

[8] Note the repudiation of envy in 6. 23 and 7. 13, going back to the Platonic tradition as in *Phaedrus* 247a.

gift of God.[1] The effect is that we have the Spirit of God, as it appears in the Old Testament, transformed into the quality of intellectual mysticism[2] and represented as the character by which the world is to be governed and the individual advanced in virtue, learning and piety. "Solomon" becomes an idealised philosopher-king,[3] with a complete understanding of cosmogony and the problem of time in relation to philosophy and history,[4] meteorology and astronomy (or astrology; it must be remembered that meteorology and astronomy were one science for the Greeks), zoology, demonology,[5] psychology and botany (with special reference to the magic of which Solomon was a master). Here Solomon has somewhat ousted the Greek philosopher; but to the Jewish mind the wisdom of Solomon was in no way incompatible with his reputation as a magician.

This brings us to the description of Wisdom (7. 22 *seqq.*); there is in her an intelligent spirit. Properly she is herself that infinitely subtle spirit which pervades all things, but the Wisdom of the earlier tradition is too strongly personified to allow her to be treated in this way. But the spirit which is "in" Wisdom is really Wisdom herself, an infinitely subtle spirit, which is capable of pervading all other spirits however subtle they may be.[6] Her subtlety and holiness are described at length in twenty-one epithets, possibly a mystical number, while the long list follows the tradition set by Cleanthes.[7] She is an exhalation of the power of God, the emanation of His glory, a beam of the everlasting light and a perfect reflection of the action of God. She is thus described in terms of all those varieties of "emanation" which were a standing puzzle to the philosophical physics of

[1] Cicero, *De Nat. Deor.* 2. 66. 165; cf. p. 75, n. 4. [2] 7. 10. [3] 7. 17 *seqq.*

[4] For the problem of time cf. Ar. Did. *Epit.* 26 (*Dox. Gr.* 461), where Posidonius figures largely; it is clear that the problem of time was a theme of interest at Alexandria. Note the connection of ἐνιαυτῶν κύκλους (world-periods) with ἀστέρων θέσεις.

[5] So Holmes rightly in *Ap. and Ps. ad loc.* "Violence of winds" is a possible translation, but an impossible displacement of the order of learning; Solomon's reputation as an exorcist was quite reputable and his botany was mainly magical. διαλογισμοί are the secret thoughts of men which Solomon's supernatural powers enabled him to read. Cf. Lk. 2. 35, Mk. 2. 8 and parallels, and similar passages; also *Papp. Mag. Gr.* 1. 176 and *Clem. Recog.* 2. 50, 65, 3. 45 and elsewhere for ability to read the thoughts as a proof of magical ability. But on the other side the thought goes back to the conception of God as καρδιογνώστης (Acts 1. 24, etc.).

[6] An allusion to the conception that the soul is πνεῦμα ἢ λεπτομερέστερόν τι πνεύματος. (Cleanthes *ap.* Sext. Emp. *Pyrrh. Hypot.* 2. 70.)

[7] Cf. Holmes in *Ap. and Ps. ad loc.*, who quotes Cleanthes' catalogue of epithets of goodness. The catalogue appears in the selection of extracts from heathen writers in Clem. Alex. *Strom.* 5. 14. 110 (715 P), which has all the appearance of being a Jewish collection, expanded from Aristobulus (or an earlier compiler); cf. above, p. 26, n. 1. The author of Wisdom seems to be imitating Cleanthes, as known through the medium of the commonplace book.

the ancient world,[1] and provided the Stoics with standing examples of the possibility of the permeation of one "material" body by another;[2] for light though "material" permeates air, which is no less "material". The original and rival of Wisdom, Isis, was in the same way transformed by the theology of Alexandria into the image and emanation of Osiris in the material world, or the power which brought into the material world that order which is the imitation and image of Osiris.[3] Wisdom is again (v. 27) the Stoic principle of divinity, which at stated periods of time absorbs all substance into itself and creates it anew;[4] the writer would have found it hard to justify this conflation of the God of Israel with the God of Zeno; but he has ascribed to Wisdom the Stoic commonplace of God as immanent in the cosmos without regard to the implications of the concept or the range of speculations to which it might lead.[5] This conception of the divine action on the cosmos is introduced to lead up to her function of entering from generation to generation into the souls of holy men and making them friends of God and prophets.

In this sudden transition from the immanent deity of Zeno to the Spirit of God in the Old Testament there is implied the whole development of the teaching of the later Stoics as to the relation between God and the human soul. Zeno was a logical thinker, and admitted the logical implication of his view by agreeing that God permeates all the material world, even in its most repulsive elements.[6] If so, he is not particularly present in the soul of man, which has no particular divinity; but the divinity of man's nature and his duty of living up to his true nature were articles of faith on which the Stoic creed insisted. Chrysippus tried to meet the difficulty by holding that while the divine element is present in all things as "habit", it is present in the highest part of the soul of man as "mind"; Posidonius

[1] Cf. Theophr. *Physic. Opin. Fr.* 23 (*Dox. Gr.* 494); *Placita* 4. 13. 1 *seqq.* (*ib.* 403 *seqq.*); and index *ib.*, s.v. ἀπόῤῥοια. Cf. also the ἀπόῤῥοιαι of the sun's rays, which are all that the human eye can behold, owing to its inability to look direct on the sun, Philo, *De Spec. Legg.* 1 (*De Mon.*), 5 (40, M. 2. 218). It is interesting to note that Orig. *De Orat. Lib.* 9 explains 2 Cor. 3. 8 as meaning that the soul, when reflecting God, partakes of a "more divine" νοητὸς ἀπόῤῥοια.

[2] Chrysippus *ap.* Alex. Aphr. *De Mixt.* 216. 14 (v. Arn. 2. 154). Normally they are content with the fire and the red-hot iron (e.g. Ar. Did. *Epit.* 28 (*Dox. Gr.* 463, l. 25)), a legacy which the Church found invaluable.

[3] Cf. p. 68, n. 2.

[4] Diog. Laert. 7. 137.

[5] In combination with Pythagorean arithmetic it could prove that God was the beginning and end of all things, for He is the monad from whom all numbers start as He is the myriad with which they end, for the monad runs through all numbers (Philo, *De Plant.* 18 (76, M. 1. 341)). For the monad and hebdomad in astral gnosticism cf. p. 42.

[6] Clem. Alex. *Protr.* 5. 66 (58 P). Clement's pious horror is characteristic; Plut. *De Stoic. Rep.* 34 (1050 d) (Chrysippus).

was prepared to make this one of his many solutions of the problem.[1] This, however, was open to the same objection as the original view of Zeno; if reason is a divine gift, specially vouchsafed to man, it is present in the wicked, who use the divine gift of reason for bad ends, just as the good use it for good ends.[2] The position was further complicated by the desire of Posidonius to amalgamate Stoicism with Platonism. In Plato the soul of man was an independent spiritual being, which had descended from the heavenly spheres to be imprisoned in the material body, and was doomed to a perpetual round of reincarnations from which it could escape only by serious devotion to philosophy.[3] The strict Stoic view of Zeno and Chrysippus held that the soul, as part of the divine fire, returned to it at death, though the righteous were allowed a relative survival until the next conflagration; but by an inexorable necessity each soul reappeared in each world-age.[4] Posidonius modified this belief by holding that the element of "soul" present in all things as "life" was present in the beasts as sense as well as life, while in man it was present as "mind" and became an independent "genius".[5] These souls dwelt in the air, which was full of souls; it was absurd to suppose that the rest of the cosmos was full of living beings, but that the air, the most lively of all elements, was empty.[6] Apparently it was possible for this to take place because the substance of mind was drawn from the aether, the material of the "mind" of gods and men,[7] which by a further piece of eclecticism could be equated with the Aristotelian quintessence of which the stars and firmament were made.[8] This view had obvious advantages. It could be adapted to the Orphic tradition,[9] which believed in a round

[1] Diog. Laert. 7. 139. In *Corp. Herm.* 13. 18 the λόγος of God praises Him through the worshipper "through" the various elements, i.e. the divine element present in Him by a special grace is continuous with the deity present in the cosmos (Scott, p. 252, but without his rearrangements).

[2] Alex. Aphr. *De Anima Libri Mantissa* 113. 12 (v. Arn. 2. 307); Cicero, *De Nat. Deor.* 3. 26. 66; 27. 69, 70; 28. 71.

[3] *Phaedo* 69c and 114e; *Phaedrus* 249a.

[4] Ar. Did. *Epit.* 39. 6 (*Dox. Gr.* 471); Diog. Laert. 7. 156; in Seneca, *ad Marc. de Cons.* 26. 6, the belief is retained but the next conflagration is deferred to a date so remote as to secure the practical advantages of immortality. Verg. *Aen.* 6. 744; cf. Bevan, *Stoics and Sceptics* 108.

[5] I.e. δαιμόνιον: Varro *ap.* Aug. *De Civ. Dei* 7. 13 and 23.

[6] Cicero, *De Nat. Deor.* 2. 15. 42 and 44, following Aristotle; the argument appears in Philo, *De Gigant.* 3 (12, M. 1. 264) and *De Somn.* 1. 22 (137, M. 1. 641), with obvious reference to the Platonic passages quoted in n. 3; it seems that we have independent redactions of Posidonius. Cf. Ar. Did. *Epit.* 39. 4 (*Dox. Gr.* 471); Sext. Emp. *adv. Math.* 9. 86. Rohde, *Psyche* 499 *seqq.*

[7] Macrob. *Sat.* 1. 23. 7, quoting Posidonius "On heroes and demons".

[8] Philo, *Q.R.D.H.* 57 (283, M. 1. 514).

[9] *Orpheus* 186.

of reincarnation but allowed the initiate a possibility of escape. It could be accepted by Judaism, which could simply omit the doctrine of reincarnation, as it omitted any serious belief in a cycle of world-ages; Judaism might divide history into such ages, but it had no belief in them as recurring cycles.[1] It could retain the Platonic tradition of reincarnation as the punishment of the lowest class of "earth-bound" souls.[2] On the other hand, it had the advantage of offering a hope of immortality by its introduction of the belief that some particular souls are of divine origin and return at death to the gods.[3] Such divine souls were not reincarnated; it was a great advantage for an age which was seriously concerned with the task of flattering its rulers that it could hold before them the prospect of being translated at death from earth to heaven, while it was easy to explain that others of a similar quality would be sent from heaven for the benefit of mankind and for the fulfilment of that exact correspondence between each successive world-age which was a necessity both of Stoic physics and Chaldean astrology.[4] If a soul was withdrawn from the round of reincarnation, it was logically necessary that it should be replaced; the loss of a single soul would be as fatal to the order of fate as a grain of sand in a delicate machine; in Christian thought it was urged that the Incarnation, and the new star which announced it, had overthrown the power of fate and the stars and abolished all magic for ever.[5]

This divinity of the souls of the great and good may have been

[1] Varro *ap.* Aug. *De Civ. Dei* 22. 28. ascribes to some *genethliaci* the belief that the same soul is joined to the same body in recurring periods of 440 years. This is impossible astrology; it might represent a curiosity from the collections of Posidonius, taken from a Jewish system which allowed 400 or 440 years to the world-age (cf. p. 7); it is possible that there were unorthodox Jewish speculations which recognised reincarnation for the wicked in each Jewish world-age of this very brief duration.

[2] Cf. Servius on Verg. *Aen.* 6. 127, Cicero, *De Rep.* 6 (*Somn. Scip.*). 26. 29.

[3] Cicero, *De Rep.* 6 (*Somn. Scip.*), 24. 26; *De Legg.* 2. 11. 27; Philodemus, *De Piet.* 7b (*Dox. Gr.* 539). In Philo the belief is adapted to Judaism; *De Somn.* 2. 34 (229, M. 1. 689) represents the good man as midway between God and man, while *De Spec. Legg.* 1 (*De Sacerd.*), 12 (116, M. 2. 230) applies this conception to the High Priest. Origen, *In Ev. Jo.* 13. 43, applies Ps. 126. 5 *seqq.* to the descent of the nobler souls to earth in sorrow and their return to heaven in joy.

[4] In Cicero, *De Rep.* 6 (*Somn. Scip.*), 13. 13, the great men of all time come from heaven and return there. Cf. Horace, *Odes* 1. 2. 45 *seqq.*; Lucan, *Pharsalia* 1. 46 *seqq.*, where however flattery has become too extravagant for any possible meaning; *quis deus esse velis* is meaningless. But Antony as a "new Dionysus" (cf. Tarn, *J.R.S.* 22. 2. 149) is entirely logical; if there was a Dionysus in a past world-age, there must be one in the rest; cf. the "men from heaven" of the first century B.C. (p. 20). Boll-Bezold, *Sternglaube u. Sterndeutung* 203, is inclined to accept the view that Zeno was influenced by astrology in accepting the belief in the reappearance of the individual in each world-age. This may be right; but it was a necessity of Stoic physics, and Zeno was logical.

[5] Ignatius, *ad Eph.* 19. 2 *seqq.*, and cf. below, p. 93.

derived from the Oriental belief in the divinity of kings and the practices by which they were immortalised after death; but it found plenty of support in the traditions of classical Greece.[1] It was not far removed from the Orphic view, which may have believed in a divine element present in all men and capable of being nourished until it dominated the nature of the individual, but could easily be represented as a doctrine of the divinity of particular souls, which enabled them to recognise the truth.[2] This conception seems to have been dictated by the practical necessities of the ethical teaching of Stoicism, which was on the one hand concerned to urge the necessity of living in accordance with the dictates of the highest element in man's nature, because it was the divine element; yet experience showed that many men had so little care for that element that it was useless to appeal to it. One solution of the difficulty was to hold that not all men possessed a δαιμόνιον of divine origin, but that only the δαιμόνια of the best came from the gods and that others came from some lower stage in the celestial spheres.[3] Yet another explanation was that there is some special divine *afflatus*, which enables the great and good to be great and good, a view which was apparently conflated with the view that they are also great and good in virtue of a special divine character already present in them.[4]

It was from this range of conceptions that it was possible to combine the Spirit of God with the "mind" of Hellenistic philosophy, the divine element which was given to those of mankind, who either by

[1] Cf. *Rel. Or.* 117 and 265 n. 91.

[2] Cf. *Orpheus* 156; for deliverance at death the tablets from Southern Italy translated *ib.* 172 (texts in Kern, *Orphicorum Fragmenta* 32 (pp. 104 *seqq.*)). Philo, *De Gigant.* 13 (58, M. 1. 270), explains that Moses did not intend the myth of the giants to be taken literally; it is an allegory of three types of men, the man of earth, the man of heaven and the man of God. Abraham is the man of heaven who rises to be the man of God, Nimrod the man of heaven who "deserts" and becomes a man of earth. Here Philo seems to be working on a Stoic-Orphic allegorisation of the giant myth. But *De Vit. Moys.* 1. 50 (279, M. 2. 124), the LXX version of Num. 23. 10 ("may my seed be like his") is interpreted as meaning that the bodies of the Israelites are fashioned from mortal seed, but their souls are divine; therefore they are ἀγχίσποροι θεοῦ, i.e. analogous to the heroes of Aeschylus Fr. 162 *ap.* Plato, *Rep.* 391e, which has an Orphic ring (cf. *Timaeus* 40d).

[3] Plutarch, *De Def. Orac.* 10. 415a, suggests a hierarchy of gods, demons, heroes and men, the last three being able to rise or sink in the scale. Cf. Max. Tyr. 9. 1. 49b, *Corp. Herm.* 10. 19a (Scott 200), Exc. 23 (Κόρη Κόσμου), 16 (*ib.* 466), 24. 2 (*ib.* 496); in the last, souls of kings are divine, others from lower spheres. On the other hand the Gnostic Julius Cassianus *ap.* Clem. Alex. *Strom.* 3. 13. 93 (553 P) regards the incarnation of the soul as a punishment for yielding to desire in the heavenly state.

[4] For a combination of the views cf. Cicero, *De Nat. Deor.* 2. 13. 34 and 66. 165 and 167; *Corp. Herm.* 1 (*Poimandres*), 22 (Scott 126); mind is given to the pure in heart to make them capable of deification (26a, Scott's omission has no justification). For the possibility of O.T. influence here cf. Dodd, *The Bible and the Greeks* 170.

nature or their own efforts were worthy of it. The power which made men great was a divine *afflatus*;[1] it was easy to identify this divine inspiration with that peculiar gift of inspiration which enabled certain men to foretell the future under the influence of divine frenzy. That power, like the power of foreseeing the future in dreams, was derived from the kinship between the soul of man and God, and consequently the capacity for foreseeing the future was only found in that rare class of men who abandoned the cares of the world and devoted themselves to the knowledge of divine things.[2] The argument, which was intended to justify the possibility of foretelling the future, furnished an excellent proof of the inspiration of the great prophets of the Old Testament; for prophecy of the frenzied form associated with the oracles of Apollo and the worship of Dionysus was not easy to distinguish from the early forms of Hebrew prophecy.[3] The introduction of the ascetic and contemplative state as a necessary condition of prophecy increased the resemblance between the Greek and the later Hebrew tradition; the need of purity and detachment for veridical dreams was recognised by pagan tradition, and even extended as far as the true interpretation of the signs of the stars, the flight of birds and the entrails of the sacrifices.[4] It was an easy thing for Judaism to reject all other kinds of divination as untrue, or, if true, as the work of evil spirits, and to claim that the only true form of divination was that power to foresee the future and to guide the destinies of the nation which God had vouchsafed to His servants the prophets.[5]

[1] The word is used by Cicero, *De Nat. Deor.* 2. 66. 167; cf. Philo, *Q.R.D.H.* 11 *seqq.* (56 *seqq.*, M. 1. 481).

[2] Cicero, *De Div.* 1. 49. 111. The mind is divine and all things are filled with a divine mind; hence mind, when free, can be influenced by divine minds; but men who turn away from the body to devote themselves to divine things are rare; hence as a rule divination only occurs in sleep or frenzy. Judaism could ask no better account of the prophets. Cf. Plut. *De Def. Orac.* 40. 432b; *De Gen. Socr.* 20. 588d. Josephus puts a long exposition of this view into the last speech of Eleazar (*B.J.* 7. 8. 7 (345 *seqq.*)).

[3] For the connection between Apollo and Dionysus cf. *Orpheus* 41 *seqq.*; Rohde, *Psyche* 287 *seqq.* Plutarch, *De Def. Orac.* 51. 438a, deals with the necessity of the "spirit of enthusiasm" for the giving of oracles. Oesterley and Robinson, *History of Israel* 1. 179, suggest that the resemblance between such "prophesying" as that of 1 Sam. 10. 10 and 19. 24 is due to a common Phrygian element in Hebrew and Greek religions. (For Dionysiac enthusiasm cf. Rohde, *op. cit.* 255. But this kind of prophetic enthusiasm is a widespread feature of primitive religion, cf. James, *Origins of Sacrifice* 231 *seqq.*)

[4] Cicero, *De Div.* 1. 53. 121.

[5] Cf. Philo, *De Spec. Legg.* 1 (*De Mon.*), 9 (60, M. 2. 221), for Moses' prohibition of the *artificiosa divinatio* of Cicero as against the true prophecy promised in Deut. 18. 15, and *ib.* 4. 8 (49, M. 2. 343) for "enthusiastic" prophecy as the only means for predicting the future. Cf. also *Q.R.D.H.* 53 (264, M. 1. 511) and *De Migr. Abr.* 34 (190 *seqq.*, M. 1. 466); here prophecy by dreams is equated with the contemplation induced by "philosophy" in the waking state; "prophecy" has been transformed

Thus Wisdom is the divine element of inspiration which enters into men who are already holy,[1] and makes them friends of God and prophets. The language is covered by the tradition of the Old Testament (Exod. 33. 11 and 2 Chron. 20. 7); but the reference is to the Stoic wise man, if not to the man who is made divine by a supernatural gift of Wisdom. For none but those who possess Wisdom are beloved of God, since Wisdom is fairer than the sun and higher than the stars; she is found to be prior to the light, which is succeeded by the darkness, whereas vice cannot prevail against Wisdom.[2] The language suggests that Wisdom, as the pre-cosmic light, is also that divine power which is the ἡγεμονικόν of the cosmos, concentrated either in the sun, according to Cleanthes and the tradition of Syrian religion,[3] or in the sphere of the fixed stars in the firmament, according to the more usual Stoic view.[4] It is natural that God should only love those who dwell with Wisdom, if Wisdom is the power that raises them up to Himself.[5] The description closes (8. 1) with an identification of Wisdom with the orthodox Stoic reason, the divine element of fire, aether or intelligence which pervades and orders the cosmos. Thus the identity of the divine power which inspired and sanctified the prophets and great men of Israel with the divine reason of philosophy is placed beyond a doubt.[6]

The purpose of the verse appears to be to lead up to the brief outline of the history of the world, as adapted to the traditional Jewish

into mysticism. So of the Therapeutae in *De Vit. Cont.* 2 (12, M. 2. 473), where the language of Dionysiac religion is applied to the "heavenly love" of the mystic.

[1] The ambiguity is characteristic of the Hellenistic tradition. For the wise man as the friend of God cf. Philo, *Quod Omn. Prob. Lib.* 7 (42, M. 2. 452), where Philo has forgotten to delete the "Olympian gods" from his source, and Epictetus' epitaph on himself as *φίλος ἀθανάτοις* (Macr. *Sat.* 1. 11. 45). Cf. also Polybius 10. 2. 7 for wise men as *θειοτάτους καὶ προσφιλεστάτους τοῖς θεοῖς*, and 21. 23. 9.

[2] 7. 28–30.

[3] For Cleanthes cf. Diog. Laert. 7. 139; for Syrian religion cf. *Rel. Or.* 123 and p. 270, n. 116.

[4] For the normal Stoic view cf. Diog. Laert. *loc. cit.* In Cicero, *De Rep.* 6 (*Somn. Scip.*) 17. 17, the sphere of the fixed stars is *summus ipse deus*, and the sun is *dux et princeps et moderator luminum reliquorum, mens mundi et temperatio*. Apparently here the firmament takes the place of the supreme deity of the *Timaeus* and the sun of the divine pattern; is this another of Posidonius' methods of reconciling the divisions of philosophy? Or is his attempt to find a place for the sun a mark of his Syrian origin?

[5] Cf. Philo, *Leg. Alleg.* 1. 13 (38, M. 1. 51). If man is to rise to God, three factors are needed, God, the mind which receives inspiration, and the spirit which is inspired.

[6] Cf. Chrysippus *ap.* Stob. *Ecl.* 1. 79 (v. Arn. 2. 264); Diog. Laert. 7. 138: *τὸν κόσμον διοικεῖσθαι κατὰ νοῦν...εἰς ἅπαν αὐτοῦ μέρος διήκοντος τοῦ νοῦ καθάπερ ἐφ' ἡμῶν τῆς ψυχῆς* (Chrysippus and Posidonius); Philodemus, *De Piet.* 11. (*Dox. Gr.* 545).

kerygma form; but at this point the main thread of the argument is broken by the panegyric on Wisdom. It is a remarkable testimony to the strength of the Isis-convention that the writer should feel it necessary to insert this chapter, which is simply a fresh version of the conventional Jewish revision of the aretalogy. The origin of the convention has been so far forgotten that the first person singular has been dropped. But Wisdom's habit of praising herself remains;[1] while her character, as the spouse of God, who was with Him when He created the world,[2] and as initiating men into the mysteries of the knowledge of God,[3] can only be derived from the same source as the Wisdom of Proverbs and Ecclesiasticus. Here, too, Wisdom is the source of virtue, though as against the aretalogy and Proverbs she is the source of virtue in general, rather than of those virtues which are indispensable for social life.[4] Wisdom is now the source of the conventional quaternion of Stoic virtues (v. 7) and the teacher of divination (v. 8); Solomon's reputation for magic harmonised well with the recent rehabilitation of this aspect of religion.[5] She is naturally the source of honour and reputation in society and government, and also of immortality;[6] for it is by the union of the element of mind with the divine *afflatus* that man attains to the sphere of heaven.[7] Realising her attractions Solomon sought her; he was a child of noble birth and endowed with a good soul, or rather he was a spiritual being of the highest order and entered into a body which had no defects to impair his natural goodness (vv. 19 *seqq.*). Thus Solomon belongs to the order of divine beings from which Oriental kings and the noblest of mankind were supposed to come.[8] His bodily perfection would seem to be

[1] 8. 3. [2] 8.3 b implies this.

[3] For 8. 4 cf. the aretalogy of Isis, clauses 19–22; and cf. 9. 8.

[4] In the aretalogy clauses 16, 28, 35, 37 and 38 deal with "justice", as does Prov. 8. 20. But the Jewish version suggests "righteousness" in general rather than social justice. The remaining virtues of the aretalogy except for clause 32, ἐγὼ τὸ καλὸν καὶ αἰσχρὸν διαγεινώσκεσθαι ὑπὸ τῆς φύσεως ἐποίησα, are all the virtues essential for social life; and clause 32 bears a suspiciously Stoic colouring and may be a comparatively late insertion into the story of the triumphs of Isis.

[5] Philo's rejection of artificial divination is true to the tradition of the O.T., and Solomon's power of discerning the future is somewhat unorthodox.

[6] V. 13a might mean no more than an eternal reputation, but v. 17b must refer to immortality in the proper sense.

[7] *Corp. Herm.* 1 (*Poimandres*), 25 *seqq.* (Scott 128), where there may be Jewish influence, is clear on this point; Mind is given to raise the soul to heaven; it leaves the bad psychic qualities behind as it ascends. Jewish writers are as obscure as Gentiles on the question of whether (*a*) the highest element in the soul is naturally immortal because divine (Philo, *De Mund. Op.* 46 (135, M. 1. 32); cf. Cicero, *Tusc. Disp.* 1. 17. 40), or (*b*) it attains to immortality by piety (Philo, *op. cit.* 55 (154, M. 1. 37), where the "tree of life" may imply a Jewish source, which equated the tree of life with Wisdom, cf. above, p. 59).

[8] Cf. above, p. 74.

a Jewish feature, since Philo insists strongly on the physical perfection of Moses in accordance with the general midrashic exposition of the narrative of Exodus.[1] The change from being endowed with a good soul to being naturally good suggests that the writer feels he is in danger of unorthodoxy; the former implies the distinction of "mind" as a more or less divine element from the soul, the latter the more usual division of soul and body, which replaces the former here and in v. 15. Yet it was only by a divine inspiration that he knew that it was wisdom which he needed; since he needed it, he prayed that it might be granted to him; Hellenistic thought has reached a stage in which the prayer of 1 Kings 3. 6 *seqq.* is perfectly respectable from the intellectual point of view; prayer is no longer confined to such natural blessings as man may need.

Solomon's prayer (9. 1 *seqq.*) is influenced by the Isis-tradition, since Wisdom helped to teach him to build the Temple after the pattern of the eternal tabernacle. For Isis revealed to mankind the right method of building temples to the gods; but here again Moses had preserved the truth of the matter; God had showed the pattern of the tabernacle to Moses on Mount Sinai.[2] But the real purpose of the prayer appears at the close. Man is made up of soul and body, and the corruptible body weighs down the soul and mind (which is here identical with soul). Thus the old tradition of the σῶμα-σῆμα of Plato and the Pythagoreans[3] replaces the newer conceptions; the writer shows his fidelity to Hellenistic tradition and midrashic Judaism by the complete indifference with which he employs entirely different systems as though they were identical. The change enables him to revert to the standpoint of orthodox Judaism. None can know the mind of God, unless He sends His Holy Spirit from on high; for it was only through it that men learnt the will of God, and so were saved by Wisdom.

This leads up to the *kerygma* of the Old Testament; but Solomon has made it clear by his reversion to the old distinction of soul and body that it is not only the king who needs wisdom in order to rule justly, but the ordinary man who needs it in order to be delivered

[1] *De Vit. Moys.* 1. 3 (9), 4 (15) and 5 (18) (M. 2. 82–83), but cf. Plato, *Rep.* 402 a.

[2] Exod. 25. 9 and 40. In Philo, *De Vit. Moys.* 2 (3), 3 (74, M. 2. 146), the pattern of the Tabernacle as shown to Moses has a distinct flavour of the *Timaeus*, but after all the Tabernacle is a type of the cosmos; in *Q.R.D.H.* 23 (112, M. 1. 488) it is a copy of Wisdom (from a source which equated Wisdom with the divine pattern of the *Timaeus* and the world of ideas). For the rabbinical views cf. Str.-B. on Heb. 8. 5. Cf. pp. 65 and 112. For Isis and Osiris as teachers of the correct method of building temples cf. *Corp. Herm.* Exc. 23 (Κόρη Κόσμου), 65 (Scott 492); here the rites they reveal are copies of the mysteries of heaven, though the temples are not.

[3] *Gorgias* 493a. In *Cratylus* 400c it is ascribed to Orpheus: in Clem. Alex. *Strom.* 3. 3. 17 (518 P) to Philolaus.

from the burden of the body which crushes down the soul. Wisdom is not a manual for kings but a book of devotion for the intellectual Jew of Alexandria, who needs the divine gift of the spirit of God not as a special gift of government but as the means of attaining to immortality. The fiction of the manual for kings is carried out in c. 10; but any reader would know that the *kerygma* is intended to describe the history of Israel as the story of man's salvation through the Torah.

Thus Wisdom is revealed as the power of God which has saved mankind in history, and continues to do so now. It was she who delivered mankind from the three great world-catastrophes of the Fall,[1] the Deluge[2] and the destruction of the cities of the Plain,[3] and carried them safely through the perils of murder and perverted "homonoia", the forms of barbarism which naturally beset mankind during the recovery from the catastrophes which from time to time obliterate civilisation. It was she who delivered the father of the chosen people from his perils and finally established his righteous son in the kingship.[4] Thus allowing for the somewhat refractory character of the Old Testament narrative we have a description of the growth of civilisation from a world-catastrophe up to the establishment of the ideal form of government, a righteous monarchy. The only difference between this narrative and the philosophical convention for such narratives is that we have a summary based on what the author regards as real history; consequently Wisdom plays an active part, whereas in the Hellenistic convention, although in theory God, providence or fate is the power at work in history no less than in the physical universe, yet history is not regarded seriously as a field of divine activity; men act for themselves, or as the puppets of fate, governed at best by an entirely impersonal power of reason.[5] Moreover, the early chapters of Greek history are confused with a mythology in which the author hardly believes; consequently the professional historians rarely give

[1] Rom. 8. 20, and cf. Str.-B. *ad loc.* Philo, *De Conf. Ling.* 3 (6, M. 1. 405), is aware of a fable that men and beasts understood one another's language before the fall: cf. Jos. *Antt.* 1. 1. 4 (41). The end of the state of innocence is an end of the golden age.

[2] For διέσωσεν of deliverance at sea cf. *Pap. Par.* 29 (*UPZ.* 41. 4), Acts 27. 44, 1 Pet. 3. 20.

[3] Cf. above, p. 5. The author's purpose appears from the space of three verses devoted to Lot out of fifteen for the whole of Genesis.

[4] Polybius 6. 5. 4 *seqq.* after Plato, *Laws* 677a. History culminates in constitutional monarchy (*ib.* 6. 6, 12), which explains the position of Joseph as a king in v. 14.

[5] In Polybius, *loc. cit.*, we have no divine government, only a growth in λογισμός. But Isis furnished a precedent for a more personal supervision of history, as in the euhemerised version of her story in Diod. Sic. 1. 22. 1. The large space devoted to Jacob is partly due to the fact that he received a revelation of the true religion at Bethel, partly to the fact that he is the victim of πλεονεξία; cf. below, p. 173.

us such a philosophy of history; the Jewish writer was able to represent the story of Genesis not merely as history, but as edifying history, without an undue strain on his sources.[1] With the establishment of the "kingdom" of Joseph over the "tyrants"[2] a point is reached at which serious history begins, and we proceed with the story of the Exodus, only to meet with a disappointment; the book breaks off suddenly and a new document of far less interest and importance begins. We are left to speculate as to the relation of Wisdom to the Torah, a matter which should have been settled in a few verses; it is possible that the suppression of the rest of the book was deliberate; the synagogues of the Dispersion seem at this time to have disapproved of the publication of the words of the decalogue.[3] It is, however, clear that the Torah must in some sense have been the work of Wisdom, though it is hardly possible that the writer could have equated the two absolutely after the manner of Ecclesiasticus and the rabbis.

In Philo Wisdom has no real place at all. The divine power at work in the cosmos,[4] which is also the living pattern after which the cosmos was created according to the *Timaeus*,[5] the image of God after which man was created,[6] the spiritual man who was created after that image[7] (except indeed when the spiritual being is identical with Adam and the fall is a fall into matter),[8] the immanent reason which governs and holds together the cosmos,[9] are all included among the various titles of the Logos. In himself the Logos is merely a substitute for Wisdom. Wisdom herself had been transformed from her original character of Isis into the divine reason immanent in the cosmos. The

[1] Apart from Joseph's "kingdom" the only serious departure is Abraham's association with the tower of Babel, drawn from the cycle of Abraham legends (cf. Alexander Polyhistor *ap.* Eus. *Pr. Ev.* 9. 18. 3; for his authenticity cf. Schürer, *G.J.V.* 3. 469 *seqq.*); he is known to Jos. *Antt.* 1. 15. 1 (240). The association of Abraham with Nimrod in Philo, *De Gigant.* 15 (65, M. 1. 272), implies the same legends.

[2] Cf. Polybius, 6. 6. 12, for the distinction here.

[3] Cf. above, p. 29.

[4] *De Mund. Op.* 6 (24, M. 1. 5), where it is also the intelligible world, and *passim*. The remaining explanations are also found frequently.

[5] *Ib.* 5 (20, M. 1. 4).

[6] *Leg. Alleg.* 3. 31 (96, M. 1. 106).

[7] *Ib.* 1. 12 (32, M. 1. 49).

[8] *Quaest. in Gen.* 1. 53 and by implication in *Leg. Alleg.* 3. 22 (69, M. 1. 100); cf. Orig. *Hom. in Gen.* 1. 13 (following Philo), *De Princ.* 2. 3. 3; *c. Cels.* 4. 40; *In Ev. Jo.* 1. 17 (of the serpent in the first instance; cf. his exegesis of the mill-stone of Mt. 18. 6 as a material body into which a spiritual "power" may be put as a punishment (*In Ev. Matt.* 13. 17)). In Philo, *De Op. Mund.* 46 (134, M. 1. 32), we are told that the man who is formed of the dust in Gen. 2. 7 is far inferior to the ideal man whom God made in His own image (*ib.* 23 (69, M. 1. 16)). Unfortunately at this point the fall is omitted and we do not hear how the spiritual man is related to the material. The fault is really that of Plato in the *Timaeus*.

[9] *De Plant.* 2 (8, M. 1. 330), which might be a paraphrase of Wisd. 8. 1.

change of terminology simply substituted one of the common words for describing the divine reason for an unusual one.[1] At the same time it harmonised with the narrative of the book of Genesis and the general Jewish conception of creation as due to the word of God, a concept which had no doubt once been understood in the most literal sense of primitive mythology but had long since been transmuted into the conception of creation as dependent simply on an act of the divine will. The figure of the Logos in Philo is in general distinctly less personal than Wisdom even in her latest manifestation; the decline of "personality" renders it unlikely that Philo, or his source, was influenced by Hellenistic religion.[2] He has followed Posidonius in conflating the Stoic reason with the divine pattern and the Platonic idea, adding the image of God from Hebrew cosmogony.[3] Yet the conception has so little real importance that his summary of the various values of the cosmogony of Genesis[4] forgets to mention the existence of the Logos at all. The variety of functions represents the variety of sources, the book of Genesis, the *Timaeus*, the earlier Stoicism and its later harmonisation with Plato, which have all contributed to this inclusive figure. But Philo's only real interest in the Logos is to show that the true cosmogony of the *Timaeus*, as interpreted by Posidonius in terms of Stoicism, is really to be found in Genesis;[5] in consequence the divine pattern of the *Timaeus* takes the form of the precosmic light as the image of God in accordance with the Jewish Wisdom-tradition. But since man was made in the image of God, that image was also an ideal man; the pattern of the *Timaeus* was a living being and divine. This conflation was made easier by the two accounts of the creation of man in Genesis, where only the second mentions the earth; but the lack of consistency or importance of these speculations appears from the fact that the first creation in Gen. I. 26, in which God says

[1] For Logos in this sense cf. Diog. Laert. 7. 88, 134; *Placita* I. 28. I (ascribed to Heraclitus) and 3 (Chrysippus) (*Dox. Gr.* 323; the use is commonplace).

[2] The "holy word" of *Corp. Herm.* I (*Poimandres*), 5a (Scott 116) is the Jewish word of creation, not the Philonic Logos (Dodd, *The Bible and the Greeks* 115 *seqq.*).

[3] The extent, if any, to which the Logos in Philo is connected with the Memra of the Targums is discussed in *Judaism* I. 416 *seqq.* Moore is entirely negative, but does not consider the possibility that the Memra of the Targums is a survival from an earlier stage of speculation which was abandoned with the growth of Christianity. In any case the Memra as it survives in the Targums has no relation to the Logos of Philo except in so far as both are used as circumlocutions to avoid awkward anthropomorphisms. But Alexandrine speculation may have left a trace of its influence in this survival: cf. pp. 50 and 52.

[4] *De Mund. Op.* 61 (170 *seqq.*, M. I. 41).

[5] Reinhardt's view that Posidonius did not produce a commentary on the *Timaeus*, or expound his views in language which professed to be an exposition of that work, seems entirely untenable in view of the explicit statement of Sextus Empiricus (*adv. Math.* 7. 93).

"Let us make man in our image", is normally not the creation of the ideal man, but of actual man; the plural is an address to the powers or the Logos, as sharing in the creation of man, the only being capable of sin.[1] The image of God is again the divine element of mind, the specific quality of the divine element present in all things in that special form in which, according to the later Stoics, it manifested itself in man.[2] In *Quaest. in Gen.* 1. 53 this element of Mind is symbolised by Adam, whose union with Eve ("life" or "soul") results in the fall into the material body, symbolised by the coats of skin; again in *Leg. Alleg.* 3. 22 (69, M. 1. 100) the statement of Gen. 38. 7 that "Er was wicked in the sight of the Lord and the Lord slew him" is explained to mean that "Er", whose name means "skin", symbolises the fall into the body not of the mind but of the soul.[3] The passage shows how little Philo is really concerned to distinguish between the highest element of "mind" and the "soul"; he is only concerned to show that the Old Testament contains the truths of philosophy, and the source which he is following here was following the normal distinction of soul and body and ignored the distinction of the higher element of mind from the lower element of psyche. It is also interesting to note here as elsewhere the habit of reading the deepest truths of philosophy into the more difficult passages of the Old Testament; the Lord's apparently arbitrary dislike of Er clamoured for explanation.

Here we have a line of exegesis which is of interest as recalling the widespread myth of an "original man" of heavenly origin and purely spiritual character, whose fall into the material world is the explanation of man's double character. The general conception has many parallels in ancient mythologies; it can be found in varying forms in Indian and Norse folk-lore. It is an essential element in the system of the Mandeans and Manichees. But it was also an essential element of Orphism;[4] the devouring of Dionysus by the Titans explained the

[1] So in *De Mund. Op.* 46 (134, M. 1. 32) and *Leg. Alleg.* 1. 12 (31, M. 1. 49) the man who is made of earth is contrasted with an ideal man. Yet in *De Mund. Op.* 24 (72, M. 1. 16) God says "Let us make" in order that others may bear the blame of man's sin. These are the powers in most cases, but in *De Migr. Abr.* 1 (6, M. 1. 437) the Logos is employed πρὸς τὴν ἀνυπαίτιον τῶν ἀποτελουμένων σύστασιν.

[2] *De Mund. Op.* 23 (69, M. 1. 16).

[3] For the raiment of skin cf. *Od. Sol.* 25. 8 and the parallels quoted by Bernard, *ad loc.* (*Texts and Studies* 8. 3. 107); Ir. *Haer.* 1. 5. 5. "Er" is a mysterious figure; Philo interprets his name as "skin" (עור); properly it seems to mean "watcher". The giants of Gen. 6. 4 are "watchers" (1 En. 1. 5 and *passim*). Does the name go back to a primitive demon of Semitic mythology?

[4] *Orpheus* 82, 156. This element of Orphism belongs to its oldest stratum, or at least to a period earlier than Plato.

presence of the divine spark in man; it could be read into the Narcissus myth by the author of the Hermetic tract *Poimandres* or into the Attis myth by the Emperor Julian; it was found before him by the Naassene Gnostics in all the myths on which the various mysteries were based.[1] It was possible to read it into the received mythologies just as Philo reads it into the mythology of Genesis; Mani introduced it by means of inventing a new mythology; Valentinus combined the methods, introducing a fall into the heavenly places as a parallel to the fall of Eve and so explaining the descent of a heavenly being into the material world. In all these cases the purpose was the same, to explain the presence of the divine element in man in the material cosmos, which was evil in virtue of its material character. It is possible that the dualism was of Oriental origin; it was certainly intensified by the influence of Chaldean astrology. But in itself it is no more than the Platonic view of the material as the source of evil, intensified by the despair of the natural world which was characteristic of the first century B.C. This was the common property of all religions; it was natural to read the imprisonment of a heavenly being in the material body into the narrative of the fall of Adam, but it was equally possible to attach it to the giants of Gen. 6;[2] this impartiality shows how little importance attached to the myth. The same experience expressed itself in terms of any mythology that was available and could be forced into symbolising the fact.[3]

An ancillary duty of the Logos, which it shares with the divine "powers" or attributes of goodness and justice, is to avoid the awkward anthropomorphisms of the Old Testament.[4] The fact that the Logos and the powers are practically duplicated shows how little Philo really means by either. Both can be incorporated and equated with the Platonic and Stoic conceptions, for the simple reason that none have any real value as compared with the faith and practice of the synagogue.

The real effect of the introduction of the Logos was to make the divine Wisdom unnecessary; the fact that Logos is masculine made it

[1] A full discussion of the "Original Man" is to be found in Professor J. M. Creed's article "The Heavenly Man" in *J.T.S.* 26. 102. 113 *seqq.*, on which the above is largely based. For the Mandeans see Note III.

[2] Cf. p. 75, n. 2 and Orig. *In Ev. Jo.* 6. 25.

[3] In Athenagoras, *Leg. pro Christ.* 24. 130, Satan is the ruler of matter and the "forms" in it. The fall of the angels entrusted with the firmament and the spheres below it is as described in Gen. 6 and Enoch: Satan's fall is the result of his culpable negligence in governing his charge. Here the fall of a spiritual being into matter and the sin of the watchers are combined.

[4] *De Cher.* 11 (35, M. 1. 145), the angel of Num. 22. 31; *De Fug. et Inv.* 1 (5, M. 1. 547), as God speaking to Hagar. Cf. above, p. 50.

a convenient substitute for the awkward feminine figure. None the less Wisdom has survived in Philo's writings; it is a testimony to the tenacity and wide diffusion of this type of exegesis that it cannot be eliminated. Philo has indeed preserved one reminiscence of the origin of Wisdom which has vanished from the earlier literature. Wisdom appears as "many-named".[1] To this title she has no right whatsoever, but it was a standing title of Isis, won by her capacity to absorb any and all of her rival goddesses; she was not merely many-named but "myriad-named".[2] She could be at the same time the Virgin-goddess of the Parthenon and the many-breasted mother-goddess of Ephesus.[3] She could so far forget her original history that she could cease to be equated with the questing mother Demeter, who was her natural counterpart,[4] and become the lost daughter, Persephone.[5] Lists of her titles show that she could be equated as a matter of form with any goddess;[6] after all, it was easy to explain that just as different races of mankind had different names for the sun and moon, yet referred to the same luminaries, so they might have different names for Osiris and Isis, yet refer to the same deities.[7]

But apart from this incidental survival Wisdom has no real function to differentiate her from the Logos. Her sex enables her to appear as the cosmic reality symbolised by the virtuous women of the Pentateuch, sometimes with rather surprising results. In *De Cher.* 12 *seqq.* (42, M. I. 146) we have an elaborate imitation of the philosophical tract, expounding the mysteries of pagan religion as a cosmic allegory, applied to the wives of the patriarchs.[8] The profane are solemnly warned to withdraw;[9] the "mystery" to be revealed is that the virtues, of which Sarah, Rebekah and Leah are types, are fertilised by God but bear children to men; this is the great "mystery" into which Philo has been initiated by Moses; but he has learnt another from the lesser hierophant Jeremiah, who writes: "hast thou not called me as it were the house and the father and the husband of thy

[1] *Leg. Alleg.* I. 14 (43, M. I. 51).

[2] Plut. *De Is. et Os.* 53. 372e.

[3] Apuleius, *Metam.* 11. 5. 762 *seqq.*

[4] Demeter appears as "many-named" in a papyrus of about 300 B.C. (Roberts in *Aegyptus* (1934), 447 *seqq.*). This looks like an attempt on the part of Demeter to hold her own.

[5] Apuleius, *loc. cit.*

[6] Cf. *Conversion* 151 for such a list.

[7] Plut. *op. cit.* 67. 377f.

[8] For allegories of this type cf. Cicero, *De Nat. Deor.* 2. 24. 63 *seqq.*; Dio Chrys. 36. 55 (v. Arn. 2. 189). Cf. Dion. Halic. *Antt. Rom.* 2. 20 for a grudging admission of allegory attached to a condemnation of Greek mythology borrowed from Plato, *Rep.* 377e. Plut. *De Is. et Os.* is simply a tract of this kind. Cf. Macr. *Sat.* I. 23. 9 for Adad and Atargatis in this allegory.

[9] For the general imitation of this Eleusinian demand cf. Lucian, *Alexander* 38, 244; Apuleius, *Metam.* 11. 23. 803.

virginity?"[1] The words show that God is the "house" of the ideas, the father of all things and the husband of Wisdom; union with God produces virginity, for all the virtues are virgins.[2] This is a rather extreme specimen, but similar uses of Wisdom for the mothers of Israel or for women mentioned in the Torah are not uncommon. One of them indeed is of considerable value as a means for estimating the importance to be attached to Philo's use of the cosmic Wisdom. In *De Fug. et Inv.* 20 (109, M. 1. 562) the High Priest may not defile himself for his father or mother; for the High Priest represents the Logos, whose robe is the cosmos, while his mother is the cosmic Wisdom.[3] Here we have an exact reproduction of the symbolism of the Egyptian triad, Osiris, Isis and Horus-Harpocrates.[4] Unfortunately a few sections before, *ib.* 18 (97, M. 1. 560), the Logos has appeared as "the source of wisdom". This shows that the whole conception of the sacred marriage of God and Wisdom with the Logos as their child is not to be taken seriously; its function is to provide a meaning for the families of the Old Testament and particularly where they are at first sight hard to explain or explain away.[5] At best they are to be regarded as attempts to provide a picture of the true Holy Family to preserve restive young Jews from succumbing to the attractions of Osiris, Isis and Harpocrates (or any other triad of Hellenistic religion). Hellenistic religion was defending and rehabilitating its triads by finding a cosmic meaning in the myth which would justify the retention of the cult;[6] Plutarch used this means for defending Isis and Osiris, and Varro for defending the Cabeiri of Samothrace.[7] On the other hand Judaism could also use them to appeal to the Gentile

[1] Jer. 3. 4 in LXX, but with ἄνδρα for ἀρχηγόν of received text.

[2] Norden, *Die Geburt des Kindes* 78, sees here an allusion to the belief that Re visits the queen of Egypt, so that each new Pharaoh is a son of the God. This seems to imply a reality in the allegory which it has no claim to possess. It is simply an imitation of any Stoic tract about any "sacred marriage". Cf. *Quod Deus Imm.* 1 *seqq.* (4, M. 1. 273) for a similar treatment of 1 Sam. 1. 28. The allusions to Jeremiah and 1 Samuel suggest that Philo is working on material taken from an earlier Jewish source. For "sacred marriages" cf. p. 201.

[3] Cf. *De Ebr.* 8 *seqq.* (30, M. 1. 361), where the non-Pentateuchal references to Prov. 8. 22 and Ecclus. 24. 30 suggest a non-Philonic source. In a similar vein is *De Fug. et Inv.* 9 (51, M. 1. 553).

[4] Plut. *De Is. et Os.* 54. 373 a and *De Anim. Procr.* in *Tim.* 27, 1026 c.

[5] *De Ebr.* 8 (30) deals with the well-known crux of the stubborn and rebellious son. For rabbinical attempts to avoid the necessity of punishing him in accordance with Deut. 21. 18 *seqq.*, cf. Mishnah, *Sanh.* 8. 1 (Danby 394). Possibly it seemed hard that the High Priest might not mourn for his family.

[6] Plut. *De Is. et Os.* 8. 353 e and 11. 355 c. Cf. p. 68.

[7] Varro *ap.* Aug. *De Civ. Dei* 7. 28; the Cabeiri as "Jupiter, Juno and Minerva" stand for the firmament, earth and the realm of ideas or the divine pattern of the cosmos.

world on the principle of "Whom then ye ignorantly worship, him we declare unto you".

In the case of the "sacred marriage" the retention of Wisdom is necessary. If the stories of the patriarchs are to be a cosmic allegory, there is no other figure to represent the mothers of Israel. But the strength of Wisdom appears from the retention of her figure as a piece of conventional symbolism in a number of cases where she is not necessary. Any allusion to the Temple, Tabernacle, house or city of God is liable to introduce an allusion to Wisdom, usually in a cosmic sense (the distinction between the cosmic Wisdom and wisdom as a quality of God or an ideal for man is more obvious to the modern reader than to the ancient writer, who was not concerned with such niceties). This symbolism appears to rest on the philosophic commonplace of the cosmos as the house of the gods,[1] or the temple of God.[2] In virtue of the analogy between macrocosm and microcosm this can be extended to the soul of the righteous; but it seems that the tradition of Judaism was too strong to allow the soul of man to be the house of Wisdom; it is always the house of God.[3] This symbolism is almost invariably associated with Wisdom, rarely with the Logos.[4] Wisdom as a city is normally associated with the soul of the righteous, which dwells in Wisdom.[5]

A further convention is that which equates Wisdom with the famous waters of the Old Testament. Only once is a river used for this equation.[6] Normally the convention that a spring is feminine but a river masculine is strictly observed; thus we find a surprising accuracy in describing Wisdom as the spring from which the river of the Logos flows.[7] Any other famous water, whether a well, a spring, or the

[1] Chrysippus *ap.* Cicero, *De Nat. Deor.* 3. 10. 26.

[2] Cicero, *De Rep.* 6 (*Somn. Scip.*), 15. 15: *Deus cuius hoc templum est omne quod conspicis*; Plut. *De Tranq. Anim.* 20. 477 C.

[3] Philo, *De Spec. Legg.* 1 (*De Templo*), 1 (66, M. 2. 222), attempts to combine the Stoic view that the cosmos is the true temple of God with the Temple at Jerusalem.

[4] For the association of the Temple or Tabernacle with Wisdom cf. *D.C.E.R.* 21 (116, M. 1. 536); the Logos appears as the house of God in *De Migr. Abr.* 1 (3, M. 1. 437), but with no allusion to the Tabernacle; the "house" here is "thy father's house" in Gen. 12. 1. Cf. *Q.R.D.H.* 14 (69, M. 1. 482).

[5] E.g. *Leg. Alleg.* 3. 1 (3, M. 1. 88). For the curious use of the Logos of the cities of refuge cf. above, p. 54.

[6] Cf. above, p. 60.

[7] Cf. especially *De Somn.* 2. 36 (241 *seqq.*, M. 1. 690), another instance of the association of Wisdom with a non-pentateuchal reference (Ps. 37. 4). In *Leg. Alleg.* 1. 19 (63, M. 1. 56) the introduction of generic virtue leaves a confusion of this concept with Wisdom and the Logos which makes it difficult to see which is the garden of Eden, which the river and which the spring from which the river flows. Philo is less careful than his Jewish sources. The two passages seem to have a common source: γάνυμαι (*Leg. Alleg.* 1. 19 (64) and *De Somn.* 2. 37 (248)) is rare

miraculous rock in the desert, is liable to introduce an allusion to the Wisdom of God.[1] For this convention there are several possible sources; the equation of the Torah with the rivers of Eden in Ecclus. 24. 25 and its rather clumsy attachment to Astarte-Sophia may have led to the equation of Wisdom with the fountain of Eden and so to springs in general. On the other hand it is a regular Stoic view that "the good" is the "source" of goodness, the term for source being πηγή;[2] this may have suggested the equation of springs with Wisdom as the quality of divine goodness. Another Stoic use of the term, to describe the ἡγεμονικόν[3] in man, appears in Philo, drawn apparently from a source which had greater scruples than Philo naturally displays in the matter of verbosity.[4] The same passage treats God as a source, or fountain, reinforcing the argument with a reference to Jer. 2. 13; again the reference outside the Pentateuch suggests that Philo is incorporating earlier Jewish exegesis, while a reference to "Olympian and heavenly actions"[5] suggests careless incorporation from the same source as *De Somn.* 2. 36 (242). This equation between God, as the source of being or goodness, and the ἡγεμονικόν in man, as the source of sensation, falls within the normal Stoic convention of macrocosm and microcosm. Since, however, there does not appear to be any direct evidence for the use of the word πηγή in precisely this application of the analogy, it is possible that it was first used by the Jewish exegetes of Alexandria, who were compelled to find a mystical meaning for the numerous water-supplies, which the needs of their Bedouin ancestors had caused to be written large on the religious literature of their race. More probably they found the word πηγή used in this sense on a larger scale than we can trace, though it is possible that they read into the word a more definite reference to "sources" of water than it naturally bore in the Hellenistic age. In any case the Jewish writers normally transfer the character of the "source" from God, as the ἡγεμονικόν of the firmament, to Wisdom, which really corresponds to the divine principle immanent in the cosmos: this is merely another

and common to both. In *De Somn.* the "Olympian and heavenly shoots" of virtuous souls show a contact with heathen sources, while the midrash on Pss. 65. 9 and 46. 4 (where again the Logos is filled with the flow of Wisdom) shows a Jewish source behind Philo.

[1] E.g. Rebecca's well, *De Post. Cain.* 41 (136, M. 1. 251); *De Fug. et Inv.* 35 (195, M. 1. 575); for the rock in the desert cf. *Quod Det. Pot. Ins.* 31 (115 *seqq.*, M. 1. 213). On this cf. next page, n. 3.

[2] Stob. *Ecl.* 2. 69. 17 (v. Arn. 3. 18), and Sext. Emp. *adv. Math.* 11. 25.

[3] Chalcidius, *ad Timaeum* 220 (v. Arn. 2. 235).

[4] Philo, *De Fug. et Inv.* 32 (181 *seqq.*, M. 1. 573). Philo can hardly be responsible for στοχαστέον γὰρ τοῦ μὴ μακρηγορεῖν.

[5] *Ib.* 36 (199).

proof of the fact that Judaism had no real need of the concept and attached no serious importance to it. Wisdom had a general association with wells and springs, and springs had an association with the mind of man and with God in contemporary Stoicism, and no Jew could ask for better proof that the Pentateuch contained all the mysteries of Greek philosophy.[1]

Among the famous sources of the Old Testament the greatest of all was the rock that miraculously followed the children of Israel through the desert. It appeared in the early days of their wanderings (Exod. 17. 6) and continued with them until they were on the edge of Sihon's country (Num. 21. 17). Since there was no water in the desert, it was obvious that the rock accompanied them.[2] Consequently it was inevitable that it should receive considerable attention from the exegesis of Alexandrine Judaism. In two passages we find the rock equated with the divine Wisdom; in the later of the two we have an equation of the water from the rock with the manna, which again is equated with the Logos;[3] we could need no clearer evidence that here the Logos and Wisdom are merely different names for the same thing, the divine element diffused throughout the cosmos. Since this conception is merely introduced to reconcile Judaism with Hellenistic thought, it can be described by either term and symbolised by anything that needs a symbolic explanation; it does not bear any serious reference to Jewish thought or religion.

[1] Springs appear to be associated with temples of Astarte in Syrian religion (Lagrange, *Études sur les Religions sémitiques* 158), as with nymphs in classical Hellas. But it is doubtful whether post-exilic Judaism or Alexandrine philosophy took any serious interest in such aspects of religion.

[2] Cf. Str.-B. on 1 Cor. 10. 4. In Mishnah, *Aboth* 5. 6 (Danby 456), it appears among the things created on the eve of the first sabbath; it has no cosmic significance in rabbinical literature and does not symbolise the Torah. Since the Torah is often a well in this literature it is probable that the equation of it with the rock in the desert was common in the pre-Christian era but abandoned under the stress of controversy with the Church.

[3] *Leg. Alleg.* 2. 21 (86, M. 1. 82) and *Quod Det. Pot. Ins.* 31 (115, M. 1. 213). Cf. further *De Fug. et Inv.* 25 (137, M. 1. 566), where the manna "rained down" from heaven is not the Logos but Wisdom, as again in 30 (166, M. 1. 571) wisdom is "rained down" from heaven. The convention of wisdom as drink is the older and stronger; the Manna-Logos convention represents Philo's attempt to fit his own concept into an existing symbolism.

CHAPTER IV

FROM OMEGA TO ALPHA

PAUL was entirely at home in the apocalyptic convention of the primitive community. He accepted it as a matter of course, and was prepared to insert into his letters prophecies of the return of Jesus in glory which, in virtue of their position in the tradition of the primitive community, he regarded as part of the Gospel, "the word of the Lord".[1] Or such prophecies could be "mysteries", part of the divine plan hitherto concealed but now made known to those who had eyes to see.[2] He incorporated in his teaching a prophecy of the return of Caligula in the character of anti-Christ.[3] Yet he was perfectly well aware that the second coming was only to be the consummation of a state which was already in existence; so much had been done that he could use language which seemed to leave no room for that further completion, the necessity of which he realised in actual practice.[4]

Consequently he was perfectly willing to express the Gospel in any other terms which might seem likely to be more effective in the work of saving mankind. The wisdom of the world might indeed be foolishness, but he was quite ready to use it to glorify Jesus, just as Judaism was ready to use it to glorify the Torah. Of philosophy in its proper sense he was entirely ignorant; the wisdom of the Greeks meant for him a collection of fragments, in part forgeries, from Greek writers, whose unconscious admission of the unity of God and the supremacy of the Torah provided missionary propaganda for the synagogues of the Dispersion.[5] He had also a slight and superficial acquaintance with the conceptions of popular philosophy of the type

[1] I Thess. 4. 15. The phrase "word of the Lord" may imply that it was ascribed by tradition to Jesus, but it need be no more than part of the general "word of the Lord" in the sense of the Gospel as Paul had received it. For an actual quotation ῥῆμα would be more natural than λόγος, as in Acts 11. 16.

[2] I Cor. 15. 51.

[3] Cf. *Jerusalem* 187, n. 9.

[4] Rom. 8. 1 *seqq.*, Gal. 2. 20; contrast Rom. 8. 23, Phil. 3. 13.

[5] Paul's two quotations from the classics are from Aratus in Acts 17. 28 and Menander in I Cor. 15. 33. Of these the former figures in the collection of Aristobulus (cf. p. 26). The latter does not appear, but Menander was a popular figure in Jewish propaganda literature; he figures in the similar collection of Clement of Alexandria (*Strom.* 5. 14. 99 *seqq.*, 707 P), at 119 (720 P), 120 (*ib.*) and 130 (727 P). I suspect that Paul's quotation also figured in such a collection; it was important to prove that the provisions of the Torah with regard to intercourse with Gentiles were recognised by the best pagan writers. In Ps.-Just. *De Mon.* 5 (107b) he figures with twelve fragments, again in a collection which shows no trace of Christian interest as against Jewish.

which was commonly employed in expounding the religions of the age to more or less educated circles; it is at least probable that Judaism had at its disposal a doxographic selection of the views of the chief schools of philosophy, which purported to show how all that was true in Greek thought was borrowed from Moses and the rest an aimless and incoherent statement of conflicting errors.[1] Paul himself may have been acquainted with such a collection, though again it is possible that he was acquainted with the Book of Wisdom; this work, together with the smattering of philosophical language which was the common property of the Hellenistic synagogue, would have provided all the background of his theology.[2] It is possible, as will be seen later, that speculations of a "Hermetic" type combining popular philosophy with a smattering of astrology were current in the circle of Gamaliel, and that it was in part to these that Paul owed his knowledge of the learning and wisdom of the Greeks.[3] In any case that knowledge was of the most superficial kind.[4]

Moreover, any value which it might have possessed vanished with his conversion. Thenceforward all that mattered was the fact of his deliverance. That deliverance could be stated in terms of the Messianic kingdom of God already established on earth. Later Paul was to state it in the language of Hellenistic cosmogony as understood by the synagogues of the Dispersion. Between these two extremes there were, however, various forms in which the truth could be expressed, which involved a less absolute breach with the whole tradition of Jewish monotheism than that which Paul adopted in his later writings.

The adoption of a different terminology from that of Palestinian Christianity was in any case rendered necessary by the danger of speaking of the kingdom of God to the Greek-speaking world; that world "had no king but Caesar".[5] The conception was not even

[1] Cf. p. 35 for the Jewish use of "Orpheus". Jos. *c. Ap.* 2. 16 (167 *seqq.*) shows the influence of such summaries; the summary incorporated by Cicero, *De Nat. Deor.* 1. 10. 25 *seqq.*, reappears in various forms in Clem. Alex. *Protr.* 5. 64 *seqq.* (55 P); Minucius Felix, *Octavius* 19. 4 *seqq.*; Ps.-Just. *Cohort. ad Gent.* 3 *seqq.* (4c). A collection of this kind underlies Philo, *De Somn.* 1. 4 *seqq.* (21, M. 1. 623); cf. Wendland in *Sitzungsberichte der K. Pr. Akad.* 1897, pp. 1074 *seqq.*, where the collection is identified with the *Placita* of Aetius. The wide distribution of the collection of Cicero in Christian literature suggests that these writers are all using a common Jewish compilation.

[2] It is to this tradition that the resemblances between Paul and Philo are to be traced; there is no means of deciding how far it was committed to writing or how far it was simply a general convention of the pulpit.

[3] Cf. pp. 54 and 113.

[4] Cf. Burkitt, *Christian Beginnings* 107 (perhaps slightly underrating his Greek culture).

[5] See *Jerusalem*, 271, n. 7, for the reasons for the abandonment of the "kingdom of God" after Paul's disastrous use of it at Thessalonica.

particularly intelligible to the Greeks, for the kingship of a god—as against the deification of a king—belonged to Semitic rather than to Greek religion.[1] But there were many other conceptions ready for use in the Greek world.

A natural equivalent for the kingdom of God, familiar both to Jew and to Gentile, was that of the new world-age. Palestinian Judaism only knew of the present age and the age to come at the end of the world-process;[2] there was no precedent in Jewish thought for the inauguration of a Messianic world-age in which the Messiah was not visibly triumphant, an age in which sinners existed on equal terms by the side of the redeemed. Apart from a possible reign of the Messiah in glory on earth, Judaism adhered to a single ending to the present age. But the apocalyptic hope as such was entirely fluid. In the Hellenistic world the thought of a new age continuous with the present was familiar. Some fifteen years before Paul's visit to Athens the accession of Caligula had been acclaimed by the world in general as the establishment of a golden age; Judaism outside Palestine had been prepared to adopt the language with which the world acclaimed "the best of aeons" though meaning by its language even less than the world in general; it expressed no more than a profound relief at the removal of Tiberius and the end of an anti-Jewish policy.[3] Judaism had indeed suffered a greater disillusionment under Caligula than the rest of mankind; he might be mad, but his madness did not injure the ordinary provincial. It was another matter for the Jew when he threatened to desecrate the Temple; the peril had been so narrowly averted that in Palestine he could be regarded as the great enemy of God, the anti-Christ who must yet return.[4] Neither Judaism nor Christianity in Palestine had ever used language which implied that

[1] *Kyrios* 2. 286 *seqq.* and 3. 634 *seqq.*

[2] The normal Jewish conception is that of the parable of the Tares (Mt. 13. 24 *seqq.*); cf. Mishnah, *Sanh.* 10. 1. (Danby 347). The Gospel shows that the Mishnah here preserves the dominant view. Jewish speculation imagined world-ages on the stage of history (cf. p. 6); but the Messianic kingdom on earth seems always to be preceded by the triumph of the Messiah and the defeat or annihilation of the Gentiles.

[3] For the accession of Caligula as a new world-age in Jewish circles cf. above, p. 23. For such language elsewhere cf. the inscription of Assos (Dittenberger *Sylloge* 797. 9) and Seneca, *De Morte Claudii* 1. 1: *anno novo initio saeculi felicissimi*, a passage which is of interest as showing that such language was still a commonplace at the time when Paul used it. For aeon in the sense above cf. Ps-Arist. *De Mund.* 5. 397a. 9.

[4] Anti-Christ appears to be developed from a conflation of the Jewish enemies of the Messiah, kings, empires or their supernatural rulers (cf. Str.-B. on 2 Thess. 2. 3) with Satan, whose part in the final conflict is taken over from the Zoroastrian tradition (Lommel, *Die Rel. Zarath.* 209, 218). For the development of the Christian myth cf. Charles, *Int. Crit. Comm. Revelation* 2. 76 *seqq.*

his accession was a new world-age; Judaism was too near to an attempt to establish the kingdom of God on earth by the appeal to arms to trifle with such conceptions. The Church was concerned with a new age of a different sort. But Paul was perfectly prepared to adopt the language of the Hellenistic world. The only difference was that the new age was not that of Caligula or any other Caesar but that of Jesus. The age of Caligula, whether new or not, was not an age of gold; it was an age of evil, and the god who dominated it was Satan.[1]

From this age of evil the Christian was delivered into the new age inaugurated by the death of Jesus. This was simply a means of expressing the fact of which the Christian was conscious, that he lived in a new order in which the whole system of values of the old life had been reversed. The next generation of Christian thought was to associate the new age with astral portents of a suitable character, though with some doubt as to whether the decisive moment was the birth or death of the Lord. A new age could hardly be ushered in without a portent; on the other hand the appearance of a new sign in heaven must inevitably upset the whole of the order which would otherwise have been determined by the stars in their courses. Yet the appearance of such astral portents was more an invention of pious fancy, and an expression of the Christian's freedom from the powers that ruled the fate of mankind outside the Church, than an expression of a serious belief either in the power of the stars or in the portents which were supposed to have overthrown their domination.[2] The new life in Christ was the certain fact; it was perfectly legitimate to use any language that could come near to expressing it. Paul himself was not concerned to embroider his acceptance of the plain and obvious facts

[1] Gal. 1. 4 and 2 Cor. 4. 4, where "the god of this age" as a description of Satan is quite inexplicable as a part of the ordinary Jewish-Christian vocabulary. The phrase appears to be an echo of *Test. XII Patr.* (Symeon) 2. 7. But the substitution of "god" for "ruler" apparently is intended as a satire on the fact that the kind of being whom this age worships is Satan, as embodied in such emissaries as some of the emperors.

[2] Cf. above, p. 7. In Ignatius, *ad Eph.* 19. 1 *seqq.*, the star of Mt. 2. 2 (possibly of a different version of the story) is associated both with the birth and death of Jesus. This is absurd astrology; obviously Ignatius does not really understand it. The new star overthrows astrology; for *μαγεία* in this sense cf. Orig. *c. Cels.* 1. 58, where Celsus regards the Magi as astrologers. Origen, *loc. cit.*, quotes Chaeremon for comets as portending new world-ages; cf. the eclipse of Lk. 23. 45, if the eclipse of the sun represents the genuine text. (Cf. Creed's note *ad loc.* in *The Gospel according to St Luke* for the text here.) For the star of the Magi as the end of astrology cf. also Tert. *De Idol.* 9; Clem. Alex. *Exc. ex Theod.* 74. 2 (Casey 650 *seqq.*). For the birth of Augustus as a new creation cf. the inscription of Priene, Dittenberger, *Or. Gr. Inscr. Sel.* 458 (ll. 5 *seqq.*). Normally the Augustan age was initiated by the *Julium sidus* (Horace, *Odes* 1. 12. 46; Pliny, *N.H.* 2. 24. 93).

with midrashic legends, which could not enhance the certainty of the Gospel.

Thus in describing the Christian dispensation as a new age, Paul was on ground familiar to Judaism. He was on equally familiar ground in describing it as a new creation (Gal. 6. 15; 2 Cor. 5. 17).[1] Rabbinical Judaism was quite prepared to explain the Messianic language of Ps. 2. 7 ("this day have I begotten thee") as implying that the appearance of the Messiah was accompanied by a return to the beginning of all things. Even the Scriptures of the Old Testament had accepted the widespread belief that the end of all things must correspond to the beginning. The belief belonged naturally to a system which believed in a series of world-ages, each corresponding to its predecessor.[2] Judaism was under no obligation to expect that the beginning of the new age would resemble the beginning of the old. Yet the beginning of man had been a divine creation and it was reasonable to hold that the ideal was a return to the original perfection that man had lost. It was sometimes held by pious fancy that the original garden of Eden had been removed to the heavens as the abode of the righteous.[3] It was tenable that it would be restored to earth, possibly in an improved form.[4] Again, the first Adam was created in a state of perfection; here Judaism could join hands with one school of Stoicism and hold that subsequent ages represented a degeneration from the ideal man made by God Himself,[5] a belief which seems to have been widely held until Christian emphasis on the fall led to a

[1] For the Messianic age as a new creation cf. *Midr. Teh.* 2. 9 (ed. Buber, p. 28) where the view is ascribed to R. Huna (d. 297). For the association of the new creation in 2 Cor. 5. 17 with the Day of Atonement see below, p. 144. It is probable enough that the conception came to Judaism from Iranian or Hellenistic religion; but Paul would seem to have adopted it from the general background of Judaism, as a thought which suited the ideas of Hellenistic hearers.

[2] Gunkel, *Schöpfung und Chaos* 367; Is. 11. 6 *seqq.* repeated 65. 25, which suggests that the theme was popular. Box, *The Book of Isaiah, ad loc.*, ascribes the prophecy to Isaiah, while Kennett, *Composition of the Book of Isaiah* 75, places it in the Hellenistic age.

[3] Jubilees 4. 23; 4 Esdr. 8. 52. Cf. Bousset, *Rel. des Judenthums* 324 *seqq.*

[4] *Test. XII Patr.* (*Levi*) 18. 10: it is simply opened to the righteous; it has been glorified in Rev. 21, but retains the Tree of Life (22. 2).

[5] For rabbinical views cf. *Judaism* 1. 451 *seqq.* The Stoics varied between Panaetius, who held that the life of primitive man was "nasty, brutish and short" (Schmekel, *Phil. der mittleren Stoa* 65; cf. Polybius 6. 5. 5 *seqq.*) and Posidonius, who held to the *Saturnia regna* of mythology and the Platonic tradition (*Philebus* 16c; *Rep.* 391e). Plato's view appears in Philo, *De Mund. Op.* 47 (136, M. 1. 32), with a curious allusion to the suitable (ἐπιβάλλοντας) numbers employed in his composition, a Pythagorean conception which suggests that Philo is drawing on Posidonius. For Posidonius' view of the virtue of the first men see Seneca, *Ep.* 14. 2 (90). 5; cf. *N.Q.* 3. 30. 8. For the belief in apocryphal writers cf. *Vit. Ad. et Ev.* 13. 14 (where the fall of Satan is due to his refusal to obey God's command to worship Adam at his first creation), 2 En. 30. 11. Cf. Heb. 2. 7.

tendency to minimise it in rabbinical Judaism. It was possible that if Adam, like the angels, had stood fast in the first moment of temptation, he would never have known death; it was his failure, which was shared by the rest of the animals, that had brought death on all, except the phoenix, which had refused to yield and remained immortal.[1] On the other hand if it was desired to glorify the Torah, it could be held that all evil inclinations were from the first present in man, but that the Jews were delivered from them on Mount Sinai;[2] God could not be accused of injustice, since the rest of the nations had heard the Law; it was Israel's merit to have accepted it, while the rest did not. In any case death was due to Adam and deliverance from sin came by the Torah.

These conceptions were all familiar to Judaism. Romans is Paul's *apologia* to his own nation and seeks to conciliate Jewish-Christian readers so far as it is possible to do so. The human origin of Jesus from the house of David appears in the preface;[3] His Messianic office is established by the power of God in raising Him from the dead.[4] The normal Pauline phraseology of "Christ in us" is kept in the background; it appears, perhaps by a calculated indiscretion, in 8. 10 and is immediately equated with the harmless "spirit of Christ dwelling in you".[5] Thus the general conceptions with which Paul works in this Epistle may be presumed to be such as Christians drawn from a normal Jewish synagogue would regard as tolerable; he would not damage his case by using arguments which his readers would reject from the outset, or arguments which they would entirely fail to understand. This remains true even if it was not originally addressed to the Church of Rome, but was a general letter to the world; it remains an *apologia* as against the Jewish nation with a postscript

[1] *Gen. R.* 19. 6 on Gen. 3. 6, where the insertion of "also" implies that she gave it to the rest of the beasts; the immortality of the phoenix proves that it did not eat. So the *Clementine Homilies* 2. 52 hold that Adam, who was made by the hands of God, did not sin. For Adam's sin as the cause of death cf. 4 Esdr. 3. 7; 2 Bar. 17. 3 and Str.-B. on Rom. 5. 15. For the reference to *Gen. R.* I am indebted to Dr D. Daube of Caius College, Cambridge.

[2] Talmud, *Abodah Zara* 22b. All evil inclinations, including the desire for sodomy, were naturally present in the Jews, but the Torah delivered them (R. Johanan, *c.* 250 A.D.). For the general promulgation of the Torah and its rejection by the Gentiles cf. *Judaism* 1. 277 *seqq.* A similar view seems to be implied in Rom. 5. 13, since sin is presumably imputed to the Gentiles. In Rom. 2. 15, however, we have the Stoic explanation of the unwritten law of conscience or nature. Cf. Philo, *De Abr.* 1 (5, M. 2. 2).

[3] Rom. 1. 3.

[4] 1. 4; cf. above, p. 81.

[5] The spirit of Christ, properly the spirit of God as manifested in Christ, could be transferred to others as easily as the spirit of Elijah could rest on Elisha. Christ could not be "in others" except as being more than a Messianic king.

(11. 13 *seqq.*) to the Gentiles.[1] It possesses therefore, with Galatians, a claim to consideration here as being logically prior to the development of Paul's thought in the Corinthian Epistles, which are earlier in date. None the less there is one element in the Epistle which appears to be entirely alien to Judaism, and to the rest of the New Testament, in Rom. 7 with its insistence on the utter corruption of human nature and its incapacity to achieve its own salvation. Yet even this was merely an extension to all mankind of the doom which the Torah brought on all who rejected it.[2] Paul's own experience had convinced him that the truth was not that the Torah brought life to Israel and to the proselyte, but that it could not bring life even to them; consequently man's last hope was gone, unless some new intervention on the part of God came to his rescue. This was a rationalisation of his own experience of conversion and a logical inference from his rejection of the Torah. Naturally this belief was a complete contradiction of Judaism; but the terminology and the method of exegesis were both familiar. There was indeed a revolutionary element in the teaching which substituted Jesus for the Torah as the centre of the Christian life, but this was not specifically Pauline; even those Christians who observed the Torah with the utmost strictness recognised that Jesus had superseded the Torah as the centre of the whole of the Christian life:[3] the question as between Paul and his Jewish-Christian opponents was whether the Torah still remained necessary as a safeguard against the sins of the Gentile world.

Thus for Jewish or Jewish-Christian readers there was nothing strange in the argument that the sin of Adam had brought death on all mankind. The Torah revealed the nature of the righteousness which God demanded. This was common ground to Paul and the strictest rabbi. Paul went beyond them by denying that it was possible to attain to that righteousness, except in virtue of the one act of righteousness, the life and death of Jesus, which was the exact reversal of the

[1] That it is a genuine letter to the Church of Rome seems to me quite certain. Cf. Meyer, *Urspr. u. Anf.* 3. 465 *seqq.*; Dodd, *Epistle to the Romans*, intr. pp. xvii *seqq.* A letter to Rome, as the centre of the world, would suggest itself naturally; the position of Rome was a commonplace; cf. Diod. Sic. 1. 4. 3 and the variation on the theme in Ir. *Haer.* 3. 3. 2, Dion. Halic. *De Orat. Ant. Prol.* 5.

[2] Cf. Str.-B. on Rom. 7. 10 and 2 Cor. 2. 16.

[3] For the Sermon on the Mount as the proclamation of a new Torah cf. Windisch, *Der Sinn der Bergpredigt* (2), 97 *seqq.* The same writer (*ib.* 94) notes that Rom. 7 is unique in the Bible in its expression of man's inability to obey the will of God; he fails to notice that the whole theology of this part of Romans is far more an expression of Paul's experience and an argument against Judaism than a system of dogmatic theology. Paul would have seen no incompatibility between his own teaching and the thought of the Sermon on the Mount as a new Law, cf. Rom. 13. 9.

sin of Adam (Rom. 5. 15–21). However much Jews might reject such an argument, and however hard Jewish-Christians might find it to accept, it was cast in a form of thought with which the Jews were entirely familiar.

The argument might be stated in various forms, based on the midrashic exegesis of the Old Testament as expounded by the tradition of the synagogue. In Rom. 6 it is stated in terms of the Christian revision of the *kerygma* of Judaism, in which the death and resurrection of Jesus replace the Exodus from Egypt. The proselyte through circumcision and the proselyte's bath was enabled to come out of Egypt and pass through the Red Sea into the promised land of Israel.[1] This original salvation of the people was re-enacted in every Gentile who was prepared to come out of Egypt, the natural type of evil in a religion whose literature was dominated by the utterances of the prophets who had counselled submission to Babylon. Paul transfers the argument to the death and resurrection of Jesus. Those who share in it through faith and pass through the waters of baptism are delivered from the old Egyptian bondage to sin and pass instead into a new slavery to righteousness which results in sanctification.[2] Here the union of the Christian with Jesus is stated in terms of an exchange from one slavery to another, on the strength of the Christian conception of the passion and resurrection as the new Passover. The fact that the Christian *kerygma* dealt with recent facts of history, and that the risen Lord was the centre of the faith and devotion of the Church, gave a life and reality to the conception of deliverance, which was wanting in Judaism. Judaism was centred on the Torah, and the preaching of the deliverance of the proselyte by a mystical sharing in the Exodus was a devout play of fancy, which enhanced the Israelite's sense of gratitude to God; it also provided a note of "deliverance" which

[1] Cf. p. 28. For Egypt as a permanent type of evil cf. *Q.R.D.H.* 62 (315, M. I. 518), where the Nile stands for the body and its passions, Euphrates for the wisdom of God, an interesting survival of the pro-Babylonian policy of the prophets. The association of Egypt with the evil and the material is a standing convention in Philo; cf. the appearance of Egypt as a convention for evil among the Peratae, and Euphrates and Babylon as relatively good among the Naassenes (Hipp. *El.* 5. 16 (131) and 9 (121)). In the Hymn of the Soul in the *Acts of Thomas* (108, *Apocr. N.T.* 411) Egypt and Babylon are both evil; apparently this reflects the Persian view, cf. Reitzenstein, *Erlösungsmysterium* 71 *seqq.*

[2] Meyer, *Urspr. u. Anf.* 3. 472, regards this as referring to the practice of voluntarily entering into slavery to secure a living. It is, however, possible that it is simply a reference to the practice of the devotee who brands himself as a mark of slavery to his god. Philo quotes this (*De Spec. Legg.* I (*De Mon.*), 8 (58, M. I. 221)) but regards it as folly, on the assumption that it is done in the service of an idol; Paul refers to the scars of his persecutions as such stigmata (Gal. 6. 17). Such voluntary "slavery" would be reprehensible or laudable according to whether it was offered to idols or to the one true God.

might attract the Gentile who sought for a religion of salvation. But it was not the central and most vital element of his faith, as it was for Paul. None the less the method of argument was the same; a past event of history (or mythology), embodied in a ritual action, became an "effective symbol" for producing a change in the character of the believer.[1] This conception had passed from Hellenistic religion into the devotional language of the synagogue; Paul transferred it to the faith of the Church. The essential difference was that Paul really believed in salvation by an act of God wrought in the person of Jesus, while Judaism believed in salvation through the observance of the Torah; deliverance by an act of God was not the foundation of Judaism, but only a devotional accessory. The result was a complete revolution; the Lord had said that the new wine could not be put into old bottles and the Christian was conscious that he walked in an entirely new life.[2]

Rom. 6 represents an exposition of salvation in terms of the liturgical practice of the Church as contrasted with that of the synagogue. It could also be expressed in reference to the experience of deliverance by faith as a result of conversion in the form of a revised version of the story of Abraham, in which sonship by adoption was contrasted with physical descent. This argument[3] was necessary in order to vindicate God's fulfilment of His promises, and as a means of answering the natural Jewish claim that if salvation was promised to the Jews it must find its fulfilment within the traditional system of Judaism. From this point of view the Torah was the means by which God preserved the chosen people from the sins of the Gentiles, and consequently it must still hold good if the Christian was not to relapse into them. This Paul denied on the basis of his own experience. The Torah had failed in practice to produce that righteousness which God demanded. Rom. 7 is an impressive statement of Paul's experience of failure before his conversion. It introduces his whole conception of the relation of the old dispensation of the Torah to the new dispensation of the Spirit, which is set forth in a midrashic exposition of the fall of Adam, as it had already been interpreted by the Judaism of the Dispersion in its attempt to read the philosophy of the Gentile world into the writings of Moses.

Judaism had already interpreted the fall of Adam as the fall of a

[1] Cf. p. 29. The Hellenistic influence lies in the conception of "salvation" as a divine gift; both Judaism and Christianity offer primarily "salvation" from sin, not from fate, though fate is liable to be thrown in as an accessory.

[2] Mk. 2. 22; cf. Rom. 6. 4. The thought of the Gospel as a revolutionary novelty appears to belong to the earliest stratum of the N.T.

[3] Rom. 9. 1 *seqq.*; Gal. 3. 7 *seqq.*

spiritual being into the sphere of matter.[1] Paul accepted this conception;[2] if the fall of Adam represented a fall into matter, the triumph of Jesus over death restored man to the sphere of the Spirit. The Spirit might be a divine gift which liberated the "soul" or it might be the highest element in the nature of man and of a divine origin, yet needing a special divine *afflatus* to enable it to obtain deliverance from its association with soul and body.[3] In either case the "new creation" could be expressed as a divine reversal of the old disaster; the effect of the gift of the Spirit was to restore man to his original condition of eternal life. The misery of man under the Law lay in the fact that he desired to serve God, but was unable to resist the lusts which resulted from his association with the flesh. His mind might serve the law of God, but his flesh served the law of sin. Unless a gift of the spirit reinforced the spiritual element of "mind", man was unable to overcome the natural "disposition" which was allied to the flesh.[4] It was only in virtue of the union of the mind of man with the Spirit of God that it was possible for man to hope so to die to the sins of the body that his spirit alone remained alive through the righteousness resulting from union with the Spirit of Christ[5]. Once man had achieved that union with the Spirit of God, he could hope that as the Spirit had raised Jesus from the dead, so it would even raise his mortal and material body to eternal life. Man must die to the flesh, if he hoped to attain to life: the last thought adjusted Paul's argument to the tradition of Heraclitus as current in the Hellenistic synagogues.[6]

At this point Paul anticipates his argument; the Christian has received a spirit of adoption in virtue of which he is once again the son of God and a fellow-heir with Christ; he must share His sufferings,

[1] Cf. p. 83.

[2] For this implication in Rom. 8. 18 *seqq.* cf. p. 107. See also 1 Cor. 15. 45.

[3] Rom. 7. 23 and 25 distinguish fairly clearly between "mind" as the spiritual or divine element in man, imprisoned by the sin of Adam, and the divine *afflatus* of the Spirit of God, which appears in 8. 2.

[4] φρόνημα is used in 8. 6 instead of ψυχή because the "soul", although it ought logically to be neutral and capable of following the Spirit no less than the flesh, is in practice always quasi-material and allied to flesh. Cf. *Corp. Herm.* 13. 1 (Scott 238) for a similar use of the word, and Plut. *De Ser. Num. Vind.* 23 (563e), τὸ φρονοῦν.

[5] The antithesis of the body as being dead δι' ἁμαρτίαν and the spirit as alive διὰ δικαιοσύνην (8. 10) is hopelessly obscure, as a result of the confusion of the spirit of man with the Spirit of God; I am inclined to interpret it as in the text, the body of man being dead on account of sin, while his spirit is alive because of the righteousness imparted by the Spirit of Christ. Cf. Sanday and Headlam, *ad loc.*

[6] For 8. 13 cf. Philo, *Leg. Alleg.* 1. 33 (108, M. 1. 65) and Str.-B. on Mt. 10. 39, where the saying of Talmud, *Tamid* 66a, "What must a man do to live? He must put himself to death. What must a man do to die? He must bring himself to life" appears as a rabbinical answer to Alexander the Great; does this betray a reminiscence of its Hellenistic origin? Cf. also *De Vit. Cont.* 2 (13, M. 2. 473).

but through doing so he will share His glory. The argument as to sonship through the Spirit as against sonship through physical descent from Abraham is however diverted by the allusion to suffering, in a passage which shows the willingness both of Judaism and Christianity to borrow the ideas of the world around them. The sufferings of the Christian are expounded in language which reflects the attitude of the age to the stars which ruled the fate of man in the theologies which offered him deliverance from their dominion. Alexandrine Judaism was indeed afraid to admit this dominion, for the peril of idolatry was close at hand.[1] But the Pharisees of Palestine had no such hesitation. They were sufficiently sure of their hold on the Torah to be perfectly willing to admit that the heathen might be right, so far as they themselves were concerned. But Israel was free from the stars; by a rather courageous interpretation of Gen. 15. 5 it could be shown that God had raised Abraham "forth abroad" to the firmament of heaven, so that he might look "down" upon the stars and learn to despise them both for himself and for his descendants.[2] But there was no objection to identifying the gods of the nations with the angels to whom they were originally entrusted by God. These angels had rebelled against God; it was quite reasonable to suppose that they were the lords of the planets and determined the fate of those who were subject to them.[3] This was indeed the natural meaning of Deut. 4. 19, and of the "angels of God" in the LXX version of Deut. 32. 8.[4] It was only natural that eclipses of the sun and moon should portend evil to the nations of the world, for it was right that if a nation was punished, its gods should be punished as well; was it not written that "on the gods of the Egyptians will I do judgment"?[5]

Naturally, again, Israel was free from the power of the stars; at any rate if it studied the Torah devoutly it was free from them; in this way

[1] Cf. above, p. 52, and *Q.R.D.H.* 60 (300, M. 1. 516) for an allusion to "weaker people", who read fate into Gen. 15. 16.

[2] *Gen. Rabba* 45. 12, *ad loc.* Cf. Jos. *Antt.* 1. 7. 1 (156) for Abraham as the discoverer of that "sympathy" of which the stars are a symptom; Philo, *De Abr.* 15 (69, M. 2. 11), gives the same story in a partly allegorised form. In Eupolemus and Artabanus (Eus. *Pr. Ev.* 9. 17. 2 and 18. 2 and in the ἀδεσπότα quoted *ib.*), Abraham is the inventor of astrology, but learns to rise above it.

[3] *Judaism* 1. 227; there were properly seventy such rulers, cf. 1 En. 89. 59; the Jewish tradition preserved by Origen, *In Ev. Jo.* 2. 3, holds that the heavenly bodies were given as gods to the Gentiles to preserve them from serving idols and demons.

[4] *Judaism* 1. 226 and 403 *seqq.* It seems probable that the LXX preserves the original reading of Deut. 32. 8 (*ib.*).

[5] R. Meir in Tosefta, *Sukkah* 2. 6. It is possible that Josephus has this in mind in *Antt.* 18. 1. 3 (13), where he describes the Pharisees as believing that the universe is partly ruled by fate. More probably, however, it is only Nicolas of Damascus' way of explaining the Pharisaic belief in providence.

belief in the power of the heavenly bodies could be given a definitely homiletic value;[1] the Christian Gnostics later were uncertain whether it was baptism that delivered man from fate and the power of the stars, or whether Gnosis was needed as well.[2] Judaism was not alone in believing that it possessed the secret of delivering man from their dominion. At the lowest stage magic offered to the adept the power to raise himself from earth to heaven, so that from that superior eminence he might control the stars themselves, precisely as Abraham had been able to tread them under foot.[3] More commonly the initiate into a mystery was offered in this life deliverance from the hostile powers, together with the knowledge of the methods which would enable him after death to pass through their spheres to the firmament of heaven;[4] the systems which offered these forms of deliverance varied almost indefinitely between genuine religion and the cruder forms of magic, largely in accordance with the individual believer's interpretation. They could rise to a mysticism which attained the heights of contemplation or they might remain at a level of ecstatic emotion; in either case the experience was to the believer coloured with details drawn from the pictorial cosmography of the age, so that he appeared to be conscious of himself as passing through the heavenly spheres.[5] The language is used by those who are aware that it is not necessary

[1] Tosefta, *loc. cit.*

[2] Clem. Alex. *Exc. ex Theod.* 76. 1 *seqq.* (Casey 661 *seqq.*).

[3] *Papp. Mag. Gr.* 4. 537 *seqq.*, a document which has sunk from religion into magic (cf. 514 *seqq.*). See also the repudiation of magic as a means of obtaining deliverance from fate in *Corp. Herm.* Fr. 21 (Scott 540). Deliverance from fate is included among the forms of deliverance to be obtained by the spell in *Papp. Mag. Gr.* 1. 197 *seqq.*, where there is a strong Jewish colouring. In Talmud, *Sanh.* 67*b*, R. Johanan (c. 250 A.D.) holds that magic interferes with the "upper family", i.e. the fate decided by God in the court of the angels (so Rashi, *ad loc.*).

[4] Cf. Ir. *Haer.* 1. 21. 5 (Marcus); Orig. *c. Cels.* 6. 27 and 31 (Ophite); Epiphanius, *Panar. Haer.* 36. 3 (Heracleon). Cf. pp. 154 *seqq.* The followers of Marcus are on high and above every power even in this life (Ir. *Haer.* 1. 13. 6); if brought to trial they can make themselves invisible to the judge (cf. *Papp. Mag. Gr.* 1. 102 *seqq.*). The same result can be achieved by a descent of the god with a name of seven letters to correspond to the seven vowels, etc. (*ib.* 13. 762 *seqq.*). For a specimen of the "ascent" to heaven in this life see also the "Mithras-Liturgy" (*ib.* 4. 510 *seqq.*). Here the adept prays for a ἱερὸν πνεῦμα to replace his own ψυχικὴ δύναμις, which he arranges to receive again after his ascent. He then proceeds to a quite literal ascent; the planets which seek to oppose him are silenced by the "symbol of the living and incorruptible god". The formulae in Marcus and Heracleon may have been influenced by the Orphic tradition.

[5] *De Mund. Op.* 23 (71, M. 1. 16); *De Spec. Legg.* 1 (*De Mon.*), 1 (17, M. 2. 214). The same conception appears in *Corp. Herm.* 11 (2). 19 (Scott 220), where it is really irrelevant, since the author is concerned with God as present everywhere for those who have the courage to seek for him, but the commonplace is really concerned with a God who is in heaven for those who have the courage to ascend to Him. For the literal ascent cf. *Corp. Herm.* 4. 5 and 8 (b) (Scott 152 and 154).

to ascend to heaven in order to know God,[1] but it was natural for those interested in mystical religion to picture their union with God in the form of an ascent to heaven, though it was equally possible to think of it as due to a descent on the part of God.[2] The tradition of contemplative mysticism seems to have made itself felt originally in Egyptian religion.[3] In Hellenistic literature it was naturally coloured by the belief that the abode of God is in the firmament in a literal sense. But it could be identified with the flight from this world and the assimilation to God, which Plato had canonised as the highest ideal.[4] It could be held that it was the desire to attain to contemplation which was the object of the silences of the Pythagoreans.[5] Posidonius, whose views dominated the world of philosophical religion, had taught that it was the true end of man.[6] It could easily be introduced into Hellenistic Judaism, which claimed to be the true philosophy; it could be offered as the true meaning of the visions of the prophets. Judaism indeed tended to visions of a definitely pictorial type, rather than to mystical contemplation which transcended all visual imagery; but this difference could be overlooked in adapting Judaism to philosophy. Paul himself was conscious of having been caught up to the third heaven;[7] it was natural to suppose that Moses was raised to heaven when he received the revelation of the Torah, which was nothing less than the music of the spheres.[8] Rabbinical Judaism was aware of such ascents to heaven, but later regarded them with suspicion. Mysticism was associated with an interest in cosmogony which might easily lead to theosophy or even to Christianity.[9]

[1] *Corp. Herm.* 11. (2). 19 (Scott 220); but we need courage, as if to rise to heaven or cross the sea, to know God; this is based on Deut. 30. 11 *seqq.*, which is a favourite text with Philo, who however always uses it to prove that virtue of thought, word and deed is easy, not with reference to the mystical vision of God (e.g. *De Post. Cain.* 24 (84, M. 1. 241). Its frequency in him and its appearance in Rom. 10. 6 *seqq.* prove that it is a recognised synagogue argument in favour of the simplicity of Judaism. Cf. also 4 Esdr. 4. 8; Baruch 3. 29.

[2] Philo, *De Sobr.* 13 (64, M. 1. 402); man must pray that God will dwell in him and raise the little dwelling of his mind to heaven.

[3] *Rel. Or.* 89 and 242, n. 89. But Livy's story of Scipio Africanus (p. 11 above) suggests that the search of an "origin" for contemplative prayer is dangerous. The practice may simply be a natural result of taking religion seriously. For solitude in Egyptian religion cf. Nock, "A Vision of Mandulis-Aion", *Harvard Theological Review* 27. 1. 59.

[4] *Theaet.* 176b, quoted by Philo, *De Fug. et Inv.* 12 (63, M. 1. 555).

[5] Clem. Alex. *Strom.* 5. 11. 67 (686 P).

[6] Clem. Alex. *Strom.* 2. 21. 129 (497 P). Cf. Epictetus, *Diss.* 1. 3. 3. It is the common view of the Hermetica, cf. *Corp. Herm.* 7. 2a (Scott 172) and Ascl. Epil. 41b (*ib.* 376).

[7] 2 Cor. 12. 2.

[8] *De Somn.* 1. 6 (36, M. 1. 626), where Moses is taken out of the body for the purpose. Paul seems aware of controversies on the point, and to dismiss them as unimportant.

[9] *Judaism* 1. 413. Bousset, *Rel. des Judenthums* 590, regards such "ascents of the

From yet another point of view this power to rise to heaven and so to attain to superiority over fate was the prerogative of the philosopher or the philosophic theologian. For he was not concerned with the material world;[1] mind, in virtue of its divine affinity, raised man above all things, even if it could also lower him to the depths.[2] The stricter Stoic tradition might indeed hold that all things were determined by fate, and that the value of philosophy lay in its power to enable man to face the decrees of fate nobly;[3] but it might equally be held that it was only the material side of man that was subject to the power of the stars; the sympathy that pervaded the whole world need not apply to the divine element which was above the material; it was a variation of this that the lower psychic qualities were derived by the soul from the stars as it descended through them. In so far as it was dominated by these qualities, the soul was at the mercy of the stars; in so far as it made itself superior to them, it was able to attain to a freedom which they could not affect; it could pass at death to its eternal home above the spheres which were subject to their control.[4]

There were indeed various views as to the precise relation of man to the planets as the powers which affected man with evil. It might be held that they were themselves evil powers; this was the Zoroastrian tradition: the five planets, with two imaginary ones added to make the conventional seven, could be regarded as creatures of Ahriman; in this case the sun and moon were good.[5] This view could be accommodated to the widely held belief that the moon was the place of purification for the soul, before its final passage to the sun or to the aether.[6]

soul" as due to Iranian influence. But they are a necessary corollary of the belief that God is "in heaven".

[1] *Corp. Herm.* Fr. 20 (Scott 540). Cf. Clem. Alex. *Strom.* 4. 25. 159 (636 P).

[2] *Corp. Herm.* 12 (1), 9 (Scott 228): the view that mind is responsible for evil is quite inconsistent with the general outlook of the Hermetica, including this tract.

[3] Seneca, *Quare aliqua* 5. 7; *Ep. Mor.* 2. 4 (16), 5.

[4] Cf. Philo, *De Mund. Op.* 40 (117, M. 1. 28), where the sympathy of macrocosm and microcosm is proved by the correspondence between the seven planets and the seven lower parts of the soul; Servius *ap. Aen.* 6. 714; *Corp. Herm.* Exc. 29 (Scott 530); Macrob. *Somn. Scrip.* 1. 12. 13. In Mandean literature the planets each contribute part of their respective "mysteries" to Adam, *G.R.* 241, Lidzb. 242. 28. Cf. above, p. 46, for the whole conception of the two celestial spheres and the descent of the world-soul between them in Mithraism and in the unorthodox Jewish-Iranian speculations condemned by Philo; also *Corp. Herm.* 1 (*Poimandres*), 1. 13 b (Scott 120).

[5] Meyer, *Urspr. u. Anf.* 2. 86. The distinction of the sun and moon from the other five planets, the latter alone determining the fate of man, appears in Seneca, *ad Marc. de Cons.* 18. 2, and in the consistent association of "the five" no less than "the seven" with Ruha in the Mandean religion (*G.R.* 11, Lidzb. 13. 27).

[6] Cf. p. 18 and the *σύστασις πρὸς ἥλιον* of *Papp. Mag. Gr.* 3. 495 *seqq.* ending in the prayer which also appears in *Corp. Herm.* (Ascl.). Epil. 41 b (Scott 376 *seqq.*). The rite belongs to religion, not to magic (cf. 585 *seqq.*). Cf. also Sext. Emp. *adv. Math.* 9. 73 for souls as *ἔκσκηνοι ἡλίου* and Cumont, *Fouilles de Doura-Europos* 103 *seqq.*, for this belief in Syrian religion.

Frequently, again, the seven planets of orthodox astronomy were included together as the source of evil by those who refused to recognise the power of the stars to control the fate of man, or who offered to mankind a deliverance from the material world.[1] Alexandrine Judaism of the orthodox type, as represented by Philo, refused to recognise fate and astrology at all; yet it was perfectly ready to adapt itself to the language and thought of the age that the essential thing was to escape from the domination of the material world, and even to use this view as a means of avoiding standing problems of the exegesis of the Old Testament.[2] Rabbinical Judaism, as has been noticed, was less careful; it was perfectly willing to recognise the supremacy of the stars over man, but not their supremacy over the Torah. Paul was perfectly ready to use not merely the cosmography which was the common form of his age, but also those implications of it which the Alexandrines rejected. He had been brought up to boast that the Torah delivered mankind from the power of the stars which rule the material world; he was perfectly ready to hold that, while the Pharisees were wrong in attributing this salvation to the Torah, their error lay not in their conception of salvation, but in their ascribing to the Torah what could only be found in Jesus. In Rom. 8. 15 *seqq.* he expounds the relation of the Christian to the fate determined by the celestial bodies.[3] As a result of the condemnation of sin by Jesus in the flesh, he is now able to live after the spirit and not after the flesh. He has received a spirit of adoption in virtue of which he is a son; he has not received, as he did from the Torah, a spirit of bondage, which works only by fear. The Spirit of God testifies to his own spirit that he is the son of God and therefore an heir to a future glory, as compared with which his present sufferings are merely trivial.[4] The

[1] *Corp. Herm.* 1 (*Poimandres*), 25 (Scott 128). Normally fate only rules the sublunar sphere (*Placita* 2. 4. 12, *Dox. Gr.* 332, of Aristotle; Hipp. *El.* 1. 4 (10), of Empedocles; Epiph. *Haer.* 3. 8, *Dox. Gr.* 590, of Pythagoras). Cf. Cicero, *De Rep.* 6 (*Somn. Scip.*), 17. 17. In the Ophite system of Orig. *c. Cels.* 6. 31 the soul on reaching the lowest sphere is already "part of the light of the Father and of the Son" but needs a proper outfit of spells to pass through the spheres of the planets.

[2] The story of Nadab and Abihu in Lev. 10. 2 appears in this light in *Leg. Alleg.* 2. 15 (57, M. 1. 76); *Q.R.D.H.* 61 (309, M. 1. 517); *De Fug. et Inv.* 11 (59, M. 1. 555); *De Somn.* 2. 9 (67, M. 1. 667). The reason for the frequency appears to be that it was an obvious difficulty; but rightly understood it showed that Moses recognised the true nature of the soul as pure and ethereal fire. Cf. p. 83.

[3] This passage is of crucial importance for the interpretation of Gal. 4. 3 and 9 (see below p. 108), where it is the Torah that is "weak and beggarly". The stars can be described as "vanity" in virtue of the O.T. language as to the gods of the heathen: but I doubt if Paul regarded the planets as either "weak" or "beggarly".

[4] The "spirit" in v. 16 shows clearly the double character of the divine element of "spirit" of "mind".

Christian (vv. 19 *seqq.*), in common with the whole of creation, has indeed, as a result of Adam's sin, been made subject to "vanity"; yet he has a hope of being delivered from the bondage of corruption into that glorious liberty which awaits the children of God. At present the creation groans and travails, just as the Christian does, who possesses indeed the first-fruits of the Spirit, but is compelled still to wait in hope for the full redemption that awaits him. In this period of waiting (vv. 23 *seqq.*) the Spirit is present to assist him; the Spirit even shares in the groaning of the creation, for the Christian's wrestlings in prayer are not merely the groanings of his own "spirit", but the groanings of the divine Spirit within him; this experience of prayer as an agony of unutterable yearning, which is unintelligible to the human mind, does not mean that the prayer so offered is mere vanity; it is offered by the Spirit, and God knows that the "mind" of the Spirit (here we have a noticeable ambiguity, as between the mind which is governed by the Spirit of God and the mind which is dominated by the spiritual as against the fleshly element as in v. 6) always prays in accordance with His own will.[1]

The allusion to the work of the Spirit was in the nature of a digression; Paul returns at v. 28 to his main theme. Although creation as a whole may groan in its subjection to vanity, those who love God are subject not to a fate dominated by the stars but to a loving providence, in which all things co-operate in order to enable those who love God to attain to that likeness of the Son for which they were predestined (or with the reading ὁ θεός in which God co-operates in all things with those who love Him).[2] This was the whole purpose of God in calling the Christian; He had foreknown and foreordained him, thus

[1] Cf. Kirk in *The Epistle to the Romans* (Clarendon Bible), *ad loc.*

[2] With the reading τοῖς ἀγαπῶσι τὸν θεὸν πάντα συνεργεῖ εἰς ἀγαθόν the meaning must be that all things work together for them that love God; I cannot believe that it is possible to extract ὁ θεός understood as the subject of the sentence. πάντα as the subject makes perfectly good sense, though with a formal inconsistency in so far as here all things help, whereas in v. 38 we find that they are unable to hinder. Dodd in Moffatt's commentary, *ad loc.*, objects that the traditional reading finds in Paul an evolutionary optimism, which he rightly sees is no part of the Pauline outlook. But it is not a question of evolutionary optimism but of the powers of evil being conquered. The variant ὁ θεός seems extremely difficult in view of τὸν θεόν preceding. Sanday and Headlam, *ad loc.*, prefer ὁ θεός as the harder reading; it should be noted that while Origen appears to imply the reading ὁ θεός (*In Ev. Jo.* 20. 20, Lommatzsch 2. 250), he follows the traditional reading in his commentary on Romans (*In Ep. ad Rom. Comm.* 7. 7, where even the Spirit of God is reckoned among "all things", and 9); but this may represent a revision by Rufinus. Is it possible that the reading of the Chester-Beatty papyrus τὸν θεὸν πᾶν συνεργεῖ ὁ θεός represents an original τὸν θεὸν τὸ πᾶν συνεργεῖ "the universe co-operates with those who love God"? τὸ πᾶν in this sense is not found in the N.T. but is common in Philo.

transferring him from the sphere of fate to the sphere of providence, which carried with it predestination to the attainment of the likeness of Jesus; God's purpose in sending Him was that He should be the first-born among many brethren;[1] the calling of the Christian was a predestination to righteousness and glory. The traditional privileges of Israel were thus transferred to the Church; the emphasis of the whole passage is not on predestination as such, which was taken over from the commonplace language of rabbinical theology, but on the fact that the Christian is subject to a divine providence, not to a blind fate, ruled by the stars.[2] Thus the Christian is sure of final victory, for God is on his side, and has proved His willingness to save by giving His own Son; naturally He will give with Him everything else that can be needed. Christ Jesus, who has died and been raised from the dead, is present in heaven to be his advocate.[3] Consequently no affliction that he may suffer can separate the Christian from the love of Christ; he merely sees in his sufferings the fulfilment of prophecy. In all these things he conquers through the love of Christ, knowing that neither death nor life nor angels nor the rulers of the heavenly spheres, neither the present position of the stars in their courses[4] by which the future is determined, nor those future positions by which all the future thereafter is determined,[5] nor the powers which hold them in their courses,[6] nor the exaltation of the planets in the heavens, the moment at which the hostile planets are most potent for harm, nor their declension when the friendly are least powerful to save, nor yet any other created thing can separate the Christian from the love of God revealed to him in Jesus. It is doubtful perhaps whether Paul was very clearly conscious of the precise meaning of the terms ὕψωμα and βάθος, but there can be no doubt that he is borrowing his rhetoric

[1] Normally neither the Messiah nor the Logos can be regarded as merely an elder brother; Heb. 2. 11 suggests that there is something unusual in describing the sanctifier and sanctified as "brethren". Possibly the language originated with the Logion of Mk. 3. 34; it would be assisted by the words of Ps. 22. 22, a Psalm inevitably associated with the Passion and Resurrection. In the N.T. it survives only in the passages noted with the parallels to Mk (in Mt. 25. 40 and 28. 10 = Jno. 20. 17). Its use here suits the general caution of the Epistle in regard to Christology.

[2] Cf. above, p. 100.

[3] Cf. Philo, *De Spec. Legg.* 1 (*De Templo*), 12 (116, M. 2. 230), where the High Priest is halfway between God and man. It his is function to intercede for the whole cosmos (*ib. De Sacerd.* 6 (97)). He is also a symbol of the Logos, cf. p. 49. In *De Vit. Moys.* 2 (3) 14. (134 M. 2. 155) he symbolises the cosmos which is the advocate of man in approaching God.

[4] For the importance of the "present" moment cf. *Papp. Mag. Gr.* 7. 506; the point is obvious in astrology.

[5] The phrase is rhetorical; obviously the position of the stars at any given moment determines everything else. For a parallel cf. Bardaisan *ap.* Eus. *Pr. Ev.* 6. 11. 41.

[6] Cf. Philo, *De Migr. Abr.* 32 (181, M. 1. 464); Clem. Alex. *Exc. ex Theod.* 69 *seqq.* (Casey 618).

from the language of astrology in which "height" and "depth" are the apogee and perigee of the planets, the decisive moments of their courses.[1]

In view of this use of astrological terms, there can be no doubt as to the meaning of vanity. It is not the general sense of futility of Ecclesiastes, nor yet the imperfection which replaced the original perfection in which God created the world.[2] Vanity is a "bondage of corruption" because with the fall of Adam there came either a fall of the ideal first man created in the image of God into the material, or a fall which involved the whole ideal world of God's creation, with the result that man, who was by his proper nature entirely above the stars and fate, put himself beneath them and into their power.[3] "Vanity" is another name for the gods of the heathen, the rulers of the angels, into whose power man fell when he sinned. These rebel angels are at once the rulers of the stars and the gods of the heathen, for whom the adjective *μάταιος* is a standing term in the Greek version of the O.T.[4] It has become so firmly fixed that it can be used, as here, to describe the rebel angels who rule the planets and are worshipped by the heathen, though their power to inflict persecution and nakedness and famine and peril and sword suggests that they are scarcely "vanity", but rather very real and potent lords of evil. Yet they are unable in the last resort to separate the Christian from the love of God, just as for the rabbis they were unable to inflict more than external harm on the Israelite who was faithful in the study of the Torah.

The question as to the reason why Jesus was able to deliver man in this way Paul does not discuss at this point. Rom. 8. 18 *seqq.* is a profession of faith based on immediate experience; it is the

[1] I cannot believe that it is merely by accident that Paul has hit on four technicalities and a fifth possible technicality (*δύναμις*) in five terms. For *ὕψωμα* and *βάθος* or *ταπείνωμα* cf. Sext. Emp. *adv. Math.* 5. 35, Theo. Smyrn. 179 *ap.* Bouché-Leclercq, *L'Astrol. Gr.* 194; *ὕψος τε καὶ βάθος ὅτε μὲν ἀπογειότερα ὅτε δὲ προσγειότερα θεωρούμενα.* Cf. Reitzenstein and Schaeder, *Stud. z. Ant. Syncr.* 224, where Gayomard cannot die until Jupiter is in *ταπείνωμα* and Saturn in *ὕψωμα.*

[2] For this view cf. *Gen. R.* 12 on Gen. 2. 4.

[3] Cf. above, p. 83. It is hardly likely that Paul was sufficiently acquainted with philosophy to think of the first man as falling into the material and carrying the world of ideas with him. Probably he is merely thinking of Adam's fall as having enslaved him to the planets, without exactly asking how this was done. For the whole passage cf. Origen, *In Ep. ad Rom.* 7. 4. Cf. above, p. 100. There is a curious variant in Tatian, *Or. adv. Gr.* 8. 35 *seqq.* The rebel angels brought man into the dominion of fate by revealing to him the courses of the stars; but the Christian is above fate, for he worships one unwandering master instead of the wandering planets.

[4] Cf. 1 Kings 16. 2 and 13; in Jeremiah *passim* as a translation of הבל, e.g. 8. 19. For the same thought in the Jewish Liturgy, cf. Singer's *Authorised Jewish Prayer-book,* intr. p. lxxxvii, Abraham's note on Alenu prayer.

quintessence of Paulinism, cast in terms of a particular conception of the cosmos. For an exposition of the reason for this power of Jesus to triumph over the stars in their courses we must turn to the equally Jewish Epistle to the Galatians, a letter which is somewhat earlier than Romans. Here (3. 7 *seqq.*) we read that the promises made to Abraham were given in virtue of his faith. The Torah brought a curse on all who disobeyed it; since no man could obey it, it brought a curse on all men. Jesus had redeemed man from it, "being made a curse for us; for it is written 'cursed is every man that hangeth on a tree'". The reason is obscure until it is recognised that the tabu of Deut. 21. 23, an obvious crux of Old Testament exegesis, since it appeared to sanction the punishment of crucifixion and yet to regard it with horror, was explained by the conventional exegesis of the synagogues of the Dispersion as meaning "cursed is the man who clings to corruptible matter instead of to God".[1] Thus Jesus, being a denizen of the spiritual world, had accepted of His own free will the curse of a material nature, and so liberated from that curse, and the consequent subjection to the Torah, those who had been plunged into matter by the sin of their first parent. The Torah was indeed divine in its origin; but it was merely a check on the sins of mankind, not a means of delivering them from the power of the "elements", the material world, which in virtue of its material character was subject to the power of the stars under which it lay.[2] Man was compelled to serve them while he was still in the state of childhood, before he passed by adoption into the proper enjoyment of his rights as a son.[3] The Torah itself was not the work of the elements; the angels who delivered it on Mount Sinai were the righteous angels who serve God, not the rebels who rule the world; but it did not deliver man from the power of the stars, and any attempt to insist on the observance of the Torah represented a foolish desire to return to the power of the elements, which represented an "elementary" stage of religion.[4] The fact that

[1] *De Post. Cain.* 8 (26, M. 1. 231) and 17 (61, M. 1. 236); cf. *De Spec. Legg.* 3. 28 (151, M. 2. 324).

[2] For "elements" as the celestial bodies cf. *Voc. Gr. N.T.* s.v. and Dibelius in *H.z.N.T.* on Col. 2. 8. See also *Clem. Hom.* 10. 9. The *Kerygma Petri ap.* Clem. Alex. *Strom.* 6. 6. 41 (760 P) entirely misses the sense in saying that the Jews "worship" the elements. The Torah is not a worship of the elements, but a partial check on the power of the elements over the fate of man.

[3] Gal. 4. 3 and 9.

[4] The reference to childhood suggests that the thought of the ABC of religion is present to Paul's mind; אות means properly a "sign", hence a letter of the alphabet. It is hard to see what word Paul could have used for the "elementary" stages of learning other than στοιχεῖον. There is a curious parallel to his ambiguity in Philo, *Q.R.D.H.* 46 (226, M. 1. 505), where the furniture of the Temple symbolises that all things in the cosmos ought to render thanks to God, not only the στοιχεῖα but also

the same Hebrew word, properly meaning a "sign", could be used both for the letters of the alphabet and for the signs written on the face of the heavens enabled Paul to dispose of the Torah on the double ground that it was "weak and beggarly" and a childish stage of religion, and also that it was merely a check on man's tendency to sin, not a means of deliverance from his bondage to the planets.

In this exegesis the Torah, in spite of its divine origin, assumes almost the position accorded in the later Pauline writings[1] to the rulers of the heavens, who fail to recognise Jesus and so attack His material nature, which alone is subject to them; but owing to His celestial origin and His freedom from sin they have no jurisdiction over Him, and by asserting a wrongful claim against Him they forfeit a legitimate claim against those of mankind who are "in Him". Here there is an obvious approximation to the typical redemption-myth of Hellenistic theology: that myth expresses the thought that the element of "spirit" in man derives its "psychic" and material qualities from the planets, and is justly bound to restore them as it ascends to its home in heaven; in Pauline literature the drama centres on the Cross and the "psychic" nature of Jesus is ignored, only His material body being considered. The material body is thus the price which Jesus pays to those who really have no claim against Him. In paying this price He not only liberates His own spirit (as the adept of a Gnostic tradition might do), but also all those who, being in Him, are no longer "material" or psychic but spiritual. But in the more Jewish letters the mythology is not worked out. The Torah had a just claim on man, but that claim had been met by Jesus, who had Himself paid the price of man's redemption; the recipient of the price is not considered.[2]

All this exegesis was cast in a form which was derived from Hellenistic religion. But in the form which it assumes in the Galatian

the ἀποτελέσματα. The latter word can mean either the "finished product" (Artemidorus, *Oneiroc.* I. 9. 15; Plutarch, *Lycurgus* 30, 58 a) or the position of the stars (Plutarch, *Romulus* 12. 24 c). In Philo the candlestick symbolises the heavenly bodies (cf. p. 54). Cf. Jer. 10. 2 for the celestial bodies as "signs of the heavens": in the Targum in Is. 44. 25 the "tokens of liars" (LXX, ventriloquists) are "signs of astrologers" (for אות cf. Jastrow, *Dict.* s.v.). For στοιχεῖα as "letters" in grammar cf. Philo, *De Mund. Op.* 42 (126, M. I. 30), where they are associated with the sympathy of the universe, as revealed by its predilection for the hebdomad manifested in the vowels and the stars (see p. 42). Thus the association of "letters" as the ABC of religion and as the planets suggested itself both from the Jewish and from the Hellenistic side.

[1] I Cor. 2. 8; Col. 2. 15; cf. Jno. 14. 30 and cf. p. 220.

[2] Cf. the slavery metaphors of Rom. 6. 15 *seqq.*, 7. 14, 8. 21. The recipient of the price could only be the Torah, an obvious absurdity. The angels of Gal. 3. 19 are of course not the rebel rulers of the planets, but the virtuous angels of rabbinical tradition.

and Roman letters it does not pass beyond the capacities of the Jewish Messiah. The Messiah could be regarded as the "Son of God" in a sense which might seem to imply that He was a being of a celestial order.[1] But Jewish exegesis was willing to use a line of argument as far as it would serve without any thought of pressing it to its logical conclusion; and Paul was perfectly prepared to follow rabbinical precedent. In the same way he could, like the Jewish preachers of the Dispersion, proclaim a deliverance from sin in terms which were borrowed from the promises of salvation held out to the initiate in Hellenistic religion.[2] But the promise was not one of deliverance from fate; the lords who ruled the world could still subject the Christian to such trifling inconveniences as persecution and nakedness and famine and peril and the sword. But the Christian was delivered from all dangers that were really serious, for nothing could separate him from the love of God which was in Christ Jesus the Lord. The form might be Hellenistic; the faith was the Jewish faith in the Torah transferred to Jesus as the Lord who had conquered death on the stage of history.

But if Jesus was thus superior in the order of creation to the Torah, and if He were able, as the Torah was not, to deliver mankind from the power of the lords of the planetary spheres, it was difficult to avoid the logical conclusion that He was superior to them in the order of space, a denizen by right of the sphere of the fixed stars, and prior to them in the order of time.[3] Judaism might care little for logical conclusions, and Paul might be equally willing to ignore them. But he was the Apostle of the Gentiles: and the Greek world demanded a consistent scheme of thought; and if Paul was pressed to provide one, he could only do so by assigning to Jesus a position in the order of reality which could scarcely be made acceptable to the unitarian monotheism of Judaism.

[1] Cf. Str.-B. on Rom. 1. 3. The Messiah appears as the son of God in the Marcan tradition, as also in 4 Esdras and in rabbinical literature, where it is necessitated by such passages of the O.T. as Ps. 2. 7. It seems probable that it was avoided elsewhere as being likely to furnish a handle to Christian controversialists.

[2] Cf. Apuleius, *Metam.* 11. 15. 783: *In tutelam iam receptus es fortunae sed videntis.*

[3] In cosmic matters "superiority" in space implies general superiority: cf. Cicero, *De Nat. Deor.* 2. 6. 17; Philo, *De Mund. Op.* 7 (27, M. 1. 6); *Clem. Recog.* 2. 53 and 68.

CHAPTER V

"AND THE ROCK WAS CHRIST"

In his first visit to Corinth Paul would seem to have been content to confine himself to the ordinary eschatological tradition of Palestinian Christianity; he was mainly concerned with Jews, proselytes and adherents of the synagogue. But his visit to Athens had shown that the emphasis must be transferred from the end of all things to the beginning if the educated Greek world was to be won for the Gospel, and he was perfectly aware of the necessity when he arrived in Corinth; when at a later stage the Corinthians began to display an excessive pride in their intellectual gifts, he was able to point out that he had merely preached to them an elementary version of the Gospel, not the deeper mysteries reserved for the more advanced Christian; he had given them milk and not meat.[1] He had already realised the need of a presentation more suited to the learned world, and had already worked it out.

The change of system involved no serious difficulty. The figure of the Messiah was drawn from circles of Jewish thought which were concerned not with the beginning of all things but with the end. But the apocalyptic hope of Israel had been fitted into the general scheme of Judaism by the rabbis. If the Messiah was destined to appear as a full-grown man in a future so near at hand that it was worth while endeavouring to compute the times and seasons, it followed that he

[1] 1 Cor. 3. 2; cf. Philo, *De Agric.* 2 (9, M. 1. 301), where "the man" in each of us is mind; the lower "soul" must be fed with the ordinary studies, represented by milk; instruction in the Stoic virtues is the perfect teaching reserved for men; so also in *Quod Omn. Prob. Lib.* 22 (160, M. 2. 470). Macrobius, *In Somn. Scip.* 1. 12. 3, ascribes to Pythagoras the view that souls are fed on milk because they come from the Milky Way. Reitzenstein (*Hell. Myst. Rel.* (3), 329) derives Paul's language from the practice of the mysteries of Attis (Sallustius, περὶ Θεῶν 4); of course such practices as feeding on milk are part of the regular stock-in-trade of initiation rites (Nock, *Sallustius* p. lv; James, *Origins of Sacrifice* 114 *seqq.*). But Paul is using the philosophic commonplace, as Philo does; it is possible that the commonplace was derived from initiation rites, but it is equally possible that both the commonplace and the rites were derived from independent observation of the same phenomenon. Similarly the conception of the teacher as the "father" of his pupil is a commonplace of primitive initiations (Frazer, *The Magic Art* 1. 74 *seqq.*); it appears in *Corp. Herm.* 13. 2 (Scott 238, and cf. his note *ad loc.*); it also appears in the Mishnah (*Bab. Metz* 2. 11, Danby 350) and Gal. 4. 19, cf. Mt. 23. 9; for the mysteries cf. Apuleius, *Metam.* 11. 25. 808. Here again we have a commonplace; for the various conceptions cf. Epict. *Diss.* 2. 16. 39, 3. 22. 81, and 24. 9.

must already exist in the scheme of things.[1] It might be held that he had already been born and was waiting until the time when Elijah should reveal to him the knowledge of his vocation, or that he had been caught away to a place prepared by God until the time for his manifestation should come.[2] If he were already in existence, it could do no harm to put his origin back to the beginning of all things; if he were part of God's eternal purpose, he must always have had a kind of existence. It was generally agreed that the Torah had existed from all eternity, and if the Torah had existed from all eternity, it followed that Moses had existed in the same way, for it was hard to suppose that the Torah could be dissociated from him.[3] But such beliefs were mere expressions of midrashic piety, analogous to those in which Judaism was prepared to glorify the heroes of the Old Testament, to whom it attributed exploits suspiciously similar to those of the divine heroes of the Hellenistic world.[4] In the same way the Temple might have pre-existed from all eternity; the view may have been derived from the Oriental belief that earthly sanctuaries are a copy of heaven, which seems to underlie the language of Exod. 25. 9.[5] Naturally Hellenistic Jewish writers associated this view with Plato's doctrine of ideas; here again he had borrowed from Moses.[6] All this was a mere glorification of the religion of Judaism; it was not intended to be taken seriously, except in so far as it implied the unique character of God's revelation to Israel; or in the case of the Messiah it was a fanciful attempt to explain the problem of his sudden appearance as a full-grown man.[7]

[1] Cf p. 17, n. 2. The speculations referred to appear to imply that the end of all things is near; so in *Ass. Moys.* 9. 1 the martyrdom of Eleazar and his seven sons is a sign of its imminence and must have been regarded as a recent incident. (Cf. Charles' note *ad loc.* in *Ap. and Ps.* for this passage.) The attitude of Zadok the Pharisee to Judas of Galilee (*Antt.* 18. 1. 1. (4)) and of Akiba to Bar-Cochba (*Judaism* 1. 89) shows that Pharisaical circles were quite liable to accept Messianic pretenders, though many Pharisees discouraged them.

[2] For these views cf. above, p. 19.

[3] *Ass. Moys.* 1. 14, with an obvious allusion to Prov. 8. 22.

[4] For Abraham cf. the stories which I have collected in *Harvard Theological Review* 28. 1. 55 *seqq.* For Moses cf. Artabanus *ap.* Eus. *Pr. Ev.* 9. 27. For their relation to the Egyptian figure of Hermes-Thoth cf. Dieterich, *Abraxas* 70, but they appear to be part of a general convention of Hellenistic literature; cf. Osiris *ap.* Diod. Sic. 1. 14 *seqq.*, and Heracles *ap.* Dion. Halic. 1. 41. For Philo and Josephus cf. the passages referred to p. 19, n. 1.

[5] *Judaism* 1. 526, Wisd. 9. 8, with Holmes' note *ad loc.* in *Ap. and Ps.* For the Babylonian belief cf. Burrows in *The Labyrinth* 59, and for Egypt Cook in *Rel. Anc. Pal.* 54; it appears that the original belief was that the temple on earth was an earthly heaven rather than a copy of a heavenly sanctuary. The belief reappears in 2 Bar. 4. 2 and Rev. 21. 2 *seqq.*; cf. Odes of Solomon 4. 3, Hermas, *Vis.* 2. 4. 1.

[6] Cf. above, p. 79.

[7] For the pre-existent Messiah cf. 1 En. 46. 1 and 4 Esdr. 13. 26 *seqq.*, *Judaism* 1. 526 and 2. 344, where however Moore exaggerates the difference between the pre-existence of the Messiah and of the name of the Messiah. But he rightly insists that the importance of his pre-existence only arises with Christianity.

It could never have led to an association of the Messiah with the work of creation, for this belonged to an entirely different aspect of Jewish thought. The unimportance of his pre-existence is shown by the ease with which the celestial pre-existences were at a later stage, perhaps in answer to Christianity, increased to seven by the addition to the Torah, the Temple and the Messiah, of heaven, hell, repentance and the throne of God.[1] By himself the pre-existent Messiah could never have obtained a rôle in the cosmogony of Judaism.

But it was easy for Paul to find a terminology in which he could adapt the figure of Jesus, regarded as the centre of the life of the Church, to the fashionable cosmogony of the Hellenistic world. The speculations of Alexandrine Judaism had accommodated the book of Genesis to the syncretised system of philosophy in vogue at Alexandria; and these speculations would seem to have been fairly well known in Jerusalem itself. The later rabbinical writings recognise the existence of a cosmic "beginning" which is at once the Wisdom of Proverbs 8. 22 and the Torah; it seems likely that they are survivals of an earlier time when speculation on these matters was less hampered by the necessity of avoiding the danger of Christian arguments that the cosmic "beginning", in which God had made the world, was Jesus the divine Logos.[2] In any case this "beginning" was equated with the Torah. There is some evidence that speculations of an Alexandrine type, associated with the name of "Hermes", had been known to rabbinical Judaism at a time when it was sufficiently sure of its position to admit the speculations of the Egyptian sage, presumably in view of his unconscious testimony to the truth of the divine revelation given to Moses.[3] Such speculations, however, were never concerned with the Messiah, who belonged to a circle of ideas which had no contact with cosmogony; by the middle of the second century A.D. they were

[1] *Judaism, loc. cit.*

[2] For the Torah as the "beginning" of Gen. 1. 1 cf. *Gen. R.* 1. 1, where we may have fragments of earlier speculations as to the cosmic rôle of the divine Wisdom reduced to a harmless form as a reply to Christian identifications of the "beginning" with Jesus (cf. Orig. *In Ev. Jo.* 1. 22).

[3] In Mishnah, *Yadaim* 4. 6 (Danby 784), the Sadducees object to the Pharisees for not saying that the books of "Hamiram" render the hands unclean. The phrase implies that the books in question might conceivably have been regarded as sacred by somebody, hence such conjectures as "Homeros", "ha-Minim" and ἡμερήσια do not seem to meet the case; Kohler in *J.E.* 6. 354 conjectures "Hermes", which gives excellent sense; the Sadducees mean that the Pharisees take so much interest in this literature that they ought to include it in the Scriptures. There is a confirmation in the incident of the cleaning of the candlestick referred to on p. 54, which suggests that the rabbis were fond of speculations of the Philonic type; Philo's failure to mention Hermes may reflect the fear of Alexandrine Judaism of anything that might tend to syncretism between Judaism and heathenism: the rabbis of Palestine were less cautious, cf. p. 100.

too closely identified with Christianity to be familiar to the Judaism of Palestine;[1] they were regarded as the property of the Alexandrines, in whose speculations the Messiah had little or no place. For at Alexandria the Messiah was relegated to the background or even explained away as a prophetic type of the Logos;[2] he had no real reason for existence in that sphere of Jewish thought, which was quite without interest in the end of the world-process and only concerned with its beginning. Thus it is possible that Paul was acquainted even before his conversion with Jewish speculations which substituted for the Messiah the divine reason immanent in the cosmos and identified it with the Spirit of God which inspired Moses and the prophets, and regarded it as possessing some special affinity with the element of mind or spirit which was the highest element in the soul of man, or at any rate in the soul of the righteous. In any case he was bound to meet them in the synagogues of the Dispersion, where the popular philosophy of the age was the common property of educated Jews.

Since Jesus, as the Messiah, raised man above the power of the planets, it was natural to suppose that He came from the sphere above them, which was eternal; consequently He was not merely superior to them in space, but also before them in the order of time, or rather eternal, whereas they were temporal.[3] It was therefore an easy matter for Paul in writing his first letter to Corinth to transfer the person of the historical Jesus from the category of the heavenly Messiah of Palestinian Judaism and Christianity into that of the divine Wisdom which was the centre of Hellenistic-Jewish speculation, where the term Logos had not yet ousted it under the influence of Philo.[4] The panegyric of the wisdom of God, as manifested in the Cross, shows the ease with which the Messianic and the cosmic lines of thought could be conflated; it is possible that they show the process by which Paul

[1] Gen. 1 ranks with Ezek. 1 in the Mishnah, cf. p. 207. Aristo of Pella in his *Dialogue of Jason and Papiscus* represented Papiscus as a Jew of Alexandria (see the preface of Celsus to the dialogue, Routh, *Rel. Sacr.* 1. 97); according to Jerome, *Quaest. Hebr. in Gen.* 305, Migne 2. 937, Aristo read Gen. 1. 1 as *In filio fecit deus caelum et terram.*

[2] Philo, *De Conf. Ling.* 14 (62, M. 1. 414), where the "man from the East" of Zech. 6. 12 (LXX) becomes the Logos in order to support the explanation of Gen. 11. 2 as a journey away from virtue. See p. 118.

[3] Cosmogonies based on the *Timaeus* had to regard the celestial bodies as coming into being with the creation of time (37d). This suited Judaism very well, for the heavenly bodies were not created till the fourth day (to show the folly of astrology Philo, *De Mund. Op.* 14 (45, M. 1. 9)).

[4] It is interesting as showing the gradual diffusion of language in the synagogues of the Dispersion that Paul is not acquainted with Philo's far more convenient word, while the author of the Fourth Gospel is. The latter writer has even less real contact with Philo's outlook than Paul himself, but Philo's term has become by his time a commonplace of the synagogues.

arrived at his conflation. Formally he is concerned to contrast the wisdom of God with the wisdom on which the Corinthians pride themselves (1 Cor. 1. 18 *seqq.*). The Cross might appear foolishness to the Greeks and be a stumbling-block to the Jews; but it was Christ, the power and wisdom of God; the quarrels of the Corinthians and their love for the manifestation of the spiritual gifts on which they prided themselves were examples of the foolishness and weakness of the world, which wrongly regarded itself as wisdom and power. The contrast was dictated by the circumstances in which the letter was written. The description of Jesus as the power and wisdom of God might simply describe the Messiah,[1] who could be associated with the wisdom of God's purpose as easily as with the more normal thought of His power.[2] In particular Paul used the outpouring of the power of God in Jesus as the Messiah to point out the contrast between the fear and weakness of his own preaching at Corinth and the outpouring of the Spirit and the signs and wonders which accompanied that preaching.[3] He still retained the Messianic category, when he described Jesus as the wisdom of God, which had been hidden even from the spiritual rulers of the universe, who in their ignorance had crucified the Lord of glory, but was now made manifest by the revelation of the secret purposes of God: the word "mystery" here retained its proper Jewish sense of a divine secret, hitherto concealed, but now revealed.[4]

[1] For Wisdom as a mark of the Messianic age cf. 1 En. 48. 1 and 49. 1; 4 Esdr. 8. 52. The "Wisdom of God" in Lk. 11. 49 may refer to a lost apocalyptic work; if the language is intended to refer to a written work it was clearly of an eschatological character. Creed in *The Gospel according to St Luke*, *ad loc.*, quotes Bultmann as still holding this view, which he rejects while recognising the difficulty of the passage. I am inclined to suggest that the passage is a quotation from such a work which was incorporated by Q into the sayings of Jesus and that Luke recognised it, while Matthew did not. In 1 Cor. 1. 30 wisdom is still the result of the Messianic work of Jesus, as are righteousness (Rom. 5. 18), sanctification (Rom. 6. 22) and redemption (Rom. 3. 24).

[2] For the natural association of the "power" of God with the Messiah cf. Mk. 14. 62, where the rabbinical substitution of *ha-gebhurah* for the tetragrammaton is used to describe Him as manifested with the Messiah. (For the use cf. Jastrow's *Dict.* s.v. Lk. 22. 69 adds "of God", as he does not understand the usage.) The Gospel of Peter, 5. 19 (Akhmin Fr., *Apocr. N.T.* 91), substitutes ἡ δύναμίς μου for the *Eloi, Eloi* of Mk. 15. 34 in a docetic sense, "power" being the divinity of Jesus. "Power" would naturally be attributed to Jesus as the Messiah in virtue of His miracles (Mk. 6. 14) and those associated with the ministry of the Apostles (1 Cor. 2. 4). Cf. the title ἡ δύναμις θεοῦ ἡ καλουμένη μεγάλη adopted by Simon Magus (Acts 8. 10).

[3] 2. 3. There is no reason to suppose that Paul is referring to his disappointment at Athens. He is anxious to discredit worldly "wisdom", so he emphasises his own weakness. There is no need to look for any motive beyond homiletic necessity and the natural fear which Paul would feel in approaching an audience, which from past experience he would expect to find hostile.

[4] 2. 6 *seqq.*; for the whole passage cf. Notes IV and V.

Up to this point the exposition had not necessarily implied that Jesus was the "power" and "wisdom" of God in any sense in which these terms might not be used of the Messiah as the revelation of God's purpose and the means of its fulfilment. But at 2. 10 Paul turned abruptly from Jesus as the Messianic revelation of the Wisdom and the power of God to the apparently irrelevant spirit by which the Christian was able to understand the deep things of God. The "spirit" is the highest element in man, in virtue of which he knows his own affairs. In the same way man could not know the things of God except by the Spirit of God.

The "spiritual" man had received that gift; the man who possessed only the natural soul had not received it and therefore could not understand the things of God. Paul claimed for himself, and for all other Christians who like himself were "spiritual", that they had received a gift of the Spirit, which enabled them to understand the gifts which God had bestowed on man and to teach with a wisdom higher than human wisdom, a wisdom that was taught them by the Spirit.[1] The ordinary man, having a soul but not the Spirit, could not receive such teaching, which needed the Spirit if it was to be understood. No man knows the mind of the Lord, so as to be able to instruct Him; but the natural man who criticises the spiritual man is in effect trying to do so, for he is criticising the mind of Christ, as possessed by the spiritual Christian.

The force of the argument depended on the conception by which the prophetic spirit of God in the Old Testament was equated with the divine Mind or Spirit permeating the cosmos, and also with that divine *afflatus* which was present in the best and wisest of mankind.[2] Thus Paul and those like him possessed that immunity from criticism which was the prerogative of the Stoic wise man,[3] but they possessed a far

[1] "We" here is vague, as normally in Pauline writings; presumably it covers all Christians who like Paul are "spiritual".

[2] Cf. p. 75. The extent to which this thought of the highest element of mind in man, or the good man, as divine is a commonplace of philosophy appears from Seneca (presumably following Posidonius, one of those *qui plurimum philosophiae contulerunt, Ep.* 14. 2 (90). 20); thus *Ep.* 4. 12 (41). 2: *sacer intra nos spiritus sedet, ib.* 5: *animus magnus ac sacer et in hoc demissus, ut propius quidem divina nossemus, conversatur quidem nobiscum, sed haeret origini suae,* and 9. 2 (73). 16: *deus...in homines venit; nulla sine deo mens bona est.* Seneca is at least as confused as Paul over the question whether "mind" is a divine element present in the good man or a divine inspiration which assists the mind to become good. It is possible that the Pauline language as to "Christ in us" is drawn from this kind of philosophic commonplace. But it is used to express an immediate experience and it seems more likely that the phrase is his own independent coinage, to express a fact of his own consciousness which could hardly be put more simply or directly.

[3] Diog. Laert. 7. 125; cf. v. Arn. 3. 148 (557 *seqq.*).

higher right to it. For the divine element in the Stoic wise man was with difficulty differentiated from the divine element present in human nature as such; the distinction was made, but not very clearly maintained, except where the divine element was a special prerogative of those exalted souls whose powers or virtues seemed to raise them above normal humanity. Paul's equation of the Spirit with the mind of Christ made it abundantly clear that the Spirit was a special gift of God, not a property of the soul of man as such. The further question of the relation of the historical Jesus to the divine power immanent in the cosmos and specially manifested as a divine gift in the highest type of Christian was one which Paul did not raise, any more than he asked how it was possible to relate the element of "spirit" which was an essential part of human nature (2. 11 ascribes a "spirit" of some kind to all men who are capable of managing their own affairs) to the Spirit of God, or how it was possible to describe the Corinthians as merely psychic, if they actually possessed a human "spirit". The lack of clarity was characteristic of Hellenistic Judaism, which was bound to retain the Spirit of God, which inspired the prophets, as something separate from human nature as such, but yet was quite ready to accept the idea of a divine element in man representing the "image of God" in which man was created. Paul, if pressed for an answer, would probably have retorted that the question was one which only concerned the wisdom of the world, and that the wisdom of the world was foolishness with God. He would at least have had the justification that the wisdom of the world was entirely chaotic in its attempt to answer precisely these questions.[1]

Thus Paul's claim for immunity from criticism was based on the possession of a divine gift of the Spirit, which was nothing less than the mind of the Lord (2. 16). The words of Is. 40. 13 proved the folly of trying to teach God; His purpose in creation was entirely above

[1] For a satirical account of the confusion of philosophy on the point cf. Orig. *c. Cels.* 8. 49. The "Mithras-Liturgy" of *Papp. Mag. Gr.* 4. 510 is quite consistent; a "sacred spirit" replaces the *ψυχικὴ δύναμις* (524) of the adept for the period of his ascent to heaven. In Wisd. 7. 23 Wisdom is a spirit which penetrates all spirits, however subtle. In Philo, *Leg. Alleg.* 1. 12 (32, M. 1. 50), man has an earthy "mind" in virtue of which he has a soul; he would have no more, if God did not inspire him. In *Q.R.D.H.* 13 (64, M. 1. 482) divine mind is inspired from heaven, but in *ib.* 53 (265, M. 1. 511) mind is expelled by the entry of a divine spirit in ecstasy or prophecy; in *De Mund. Op.* 46 (135, M. 1. 32) the "soul" given to Adam is a spirit which is the divine element of reason which makes him immortal; in *De Gigant.* 6 (27, M. 1. 266) the spirit of God is that which is "completely and entirely filled", i.e. the Logos of *De Somn.* 1. 11 (62, M. 1. 630). The papyrus and *Q.R.D.H.* 13 (64) go back to the same tradition.

man's comprehension.[1] But that purpose in creation was simply the divine Wisdom; and that Wisdom was the possession of the spiritual Christian, who possessed in the Spirit the mind of Christ, the Wisdom of God. Thus the purpose of God, His Wisdom hitherto concealed but now revealed in the Messianic figure of Jesus, is also the creative Wisdom which was with God in the first beginning of creation; the whole argument depends for its force on this equation of Jesus with the cosmic Wisdom, and the further equation of that Wisdom with the divine Spirit immanent in the cosmos, yet vouchsafed to the Christian, or at least to the spiritual Christian. The transformation of the Messiah into the divine Wisdom was thus complete; it is at least possible that Paul had arrived at his reinterpretation of the person of Jesus in terms of cosmogony through an established convention, which equated the hidden Wisdom of God's purpose in the Messiah with the Wisdom which was His counsellor in the creation of the cosmos. The claim to a specially privileged position for the Apostle and other "spiritual" Christians was of course only introduced to rebuke the Corinthians for their spiritual pride; their "psychic" condition was a mark of their inferiority to the normal Christian who was "in Christ" and therefore possessed His "spirit" or "mind".[2]

At a later stage in the Epistle Paul made it clear that the possession of the gifts of the Spirit ought to be a mark of the normal Christian as such. He was concerned to correct the disorders, which had grown up at Corinth as a result of an excessive concern with the abnormal spiritual manifestations familiar to primitive Christianity. Such mani-

[1] The passage reappears in Rom. 11. 34 in combination with Job 41. 11 (=41. 2 LXX). The variation from LXX noted by Sanday and Headlam *ad loc.* appears to be an allusion to the Targum rendering: "Who hath been before me on the day of creation that I should repay him?" Thus Is. 40. 13 appears to be quoted with a reference to its original context; it would naturally be useful as a Christian proof-text, implying that God had a counsellor in creation, namely Wisdom.

[2] The confusion of the passage shows that Paul is here operating with conceptions which he has taken over without troubling to rationalise them; we are dealing with a midrashic exposition of the divine Wisdom in relation to the gifts of the Spirit, not with a consistent theology. The *Poimandres* appears to be secondary, since it tries to work out a consistent scheme analogous to those of the Christian Gnostics, and represents mind as given to the good. Cf. above, p. 75, n. 4. In Ir. *Haer.* 1.7.5 we seem to have two accounts, one recognising three classes of spiritual, psychic and material, the other distinguishing between those who are naturally good and capable of receiving the spirit, and those who are naturally bad and incapable of doing so. Heracleon seems to have been equally inconsistent, cf. Foerster, *Von Valent. zu Heracl.* 75. In Clem. Alex. *Exc. ex Theod.* 56. 2 (528 Casey) the spiritual element is present in very few, the psychic are not many and most men are material. The inconsistency is inevitable in systems which try to win converts and therefore have to act as though all were capable of possessing the special spiritual nature. But the Gnostic systems appear to be trying to introduce a consistency to which Paul is indifferent.

festations had ceased to play any considerable part in the religion of educated circles in the Hellenistic world. Ecstatic prophecy was confined to a few of the less reputable cults, especially those of Syrian origin.[1] Prophecy as one form of the power of divining the future had been accepted by Posidonius and therefore was philosophically respectable, and Judaism naturally welcomed this confirmation of the Old Testament.[2] But Judaism was careful to minimise the ecstatic element of prophecy; mystical contemplation and piety rather than frenzied eloquence are the mark of the prophet as described by Philo.[3] In the synagogue prophecy had ceased except in so far as it lingered, an impressive but peculiar phenomenon, among the Essenes and similar sects.[4] Christianity had however revived the tradition of the Old Testament in this respect, though the temper and tradition inherited from the synagogue kept it within reasonable limits in most of the Churches. At Corinth, where that tradition had grown weak with the influx of Gentile converts and the departure of the Jewish refugees from Rome who had formed a large part of the original community,[5] such enthusiasms threatened to become a serious nuisance. Paul found himself compelled to work for the suppression of the more dramatic manifestations of the "Spirit" even at the cost of a good apologetic argument. The simple-minded observer in such a city as Corinth was hardly likely to be so deeply impressed by ethical gifts as by those frenzied outpourings which had in the past won classical Greece for the worship of Dionysus, and could not fail to attract the mixed Levantine population of a great port. But if the educated world was to be converted, the "Spirit" must be a divine power, animating the world in general with a divine life, and animating the virtuous man and raising him to a higher stage of goodness.

Paul was perfectly prepared for such a sacrifice. The gifts of the

[1] Cf. above, p. 15, n. 7, and Orig. *c. Cels.* 7. 9, where Celsus mixes up the ecstatic prophecies of Syrian religion with the enthusiastic preaching of Christian missionaries. (The Syrian prophets may be genuine, but the sound ante-Nicene theology is transferred to them from Christian missionaries by Celsus. Cf. further the references in *Conversion* 82 and note *ad loc.*) The story of Medea in Diod. Sic. 4. 51. 2 is illuminating as to the attitude of mind of the cultured Greek to prophetic frauds. See also *Rel. Or.* 43 *seqq.* for the vogue of ecstatic Phrygian and Thracian cults, and Dion. Halic. 2. 19 for the contempt of the educated for such cults and their popularity with the uneducated.

[2] Cf. p. 76, n. 5.

[3] *Q.R.D.H.* 52 (259, M. 1. 510), where prophecy is given to all good men; the allusion to "enthusiasm" is a reference to Plato rather than to the O.T.

[4] Josephus, *B.J.* 2. 8. 12 (159), credits them with power to foretell the future; naturally he does not refer to frenzy of the O.T. type. See also *D.C.E.R.* 20 (112, M. 1. 535), where enthusiasm and prophecy are sandwiched into a catalogue describing the true goods of the soul of which the chief is τοῦ κατορθοῦν ἔρωτα.

[5] Cf. *Jerusalem* 268 and 280, n. 41.

Spirit which took the form of speaking with tongues and prophecy could not for a moment be allowed to compete with the essential gifts of faith in Jesus, as expounded by the Church, the hope of His return and love for God and man. The arrangement of the essential gifts into a group of three Paul borrowed from the style of the Hellenistic age,[1] their content was strictly defined by the primitive Gospel of the earliest disciples and the teaching of Jesus Himself. Speaking with tongues, even the tongues of angels,[2] power to understand and expound the mysteries of the return of the Lord,[3] knowledge of the secrets of creation and their relation to the present position of man in the cosmos,[4] even the faith of which the Lord had said that it could move mountains, were nothing as compared with the essential virtue of love.[5] This was the essential Gospel as preached by Jesus; in comparison with it spiritual gifts of the dramatic kind were nothing, and if they interfered with it they must be abandoned. On the other hand the conception of "the Spirit" was too firmly fixed in the tradition of the Church to be abandoned in the same way. Since, however, the synagogues of the Dispersion had already identified the Spirit, which inspired the prophets, with the divine Mind, which permeated the cosmos and had at all times entered into holy souls and made them friends of God as well as prophets, it was easy for Paul to follow suit. If Judaism could transform the prophets of Israel into intellectual mystics and patterns of holiness, he could equally transform the Christian gifts of the Spirit into faith, hope and love. It is probable enough that he was unaware of the extent to which the synagogue had paved the way for him; Judaism and Christianity were faced with the obvious necessity of substituting ethics for ecstasy if they were to appeal to any but the least educated classes of society.

In transforming Christian worship from an exhibition of ecstatic

[1] For 1 Cor. 13. 13 cf. Norden, *Agnostos Theos* 352 *seqq.*

[2] Presumably this was a proverbial expression: for its application to R. Jochanan b. Zakkai cf. Str.-B. *ad loc.*

[3] As in 1 Cor. 15. 51, which is a "prophecy" expounding a "mystery". The Apocalypse is the same on a larger scale.

[4] For Gnosis in this sense cf. Clem. Alex. *Exc. ex Theod.* 78. 2 (Casey 677; see his parallels *ad loc.*) and Seneca, *Ep.* 11. 3 (82). 6. The transfer of the power to remove mountains from learning, to which it was applied by rabbinical Judaism, to faith appears to be an allusion to Mt. 17. 20; it is, however, possible that both the N.T. passages incorporate a popular proverbial expression, which reappears in the rabbinical tradition (for this cf. Str.-B. on Mt. *loc. cit.*).

[5] The style may show Hellenistic influences, but the substance is entirely dictated by the O.T., though it is probable that Paul has in mind the combination of Deut. 6. 5 and Lev. 19. 18 in the logion of Mk. 12. 29. There is a striking contrast in the triad of *Corp. Herm.* 11 (2), 21b (Scott 222), where knowledge, will and hope are the means of attaining to God. It is possible that this tract has been influenced by Pauline literature, in view of the reference to Deut. 30. 12 *seqq.* Cf. above, p. 102, n. 1.

phenomena into an orderly system based on that of the synagogue, Paul was only restoring it to its normal character; for it is clear that he regarded the state of affairs at Corinth as a mere parody of what Christian worship should be. Speaking with tongues and prophecies were only tolerable if they were isolated incidents in a generally orderly procedure. He supported his reformation by an appeal to the conventional argument of Hellenistic Judaism; the synagogue was commonly represented as a meeting for the discussion of the true philosophy; it had been instituted by Moses in his character of the father of philosophy;[1] it was therefore to be desired that the meetings of the Church should impress the visitor with that shame and penitence which all but the most abandoned would feel on entering a meeting at which a philosopher was delivering an ethical homily of the kind which was popular at the period.[2]

But while Paul was prepared to borrow arguments from philosophy, and to present Christianity in terms of the cosmogony of the age in which he lived, he was entirely indifferent to philosophy as such. Love alone was eternal; for love was the fulfilling of the Torah (Rom. 13. 8) and therefore could abide, when prophecies had ceased to have any meaning,[3] when speaking with tongues had ceased and when knowledge, whether in the form of rabbinical learning or the mystical knowledge of God, had been done away. For all such partial means of knowing[4] were only intended for the present life, in which

[1] Cf. Philo, *De Vit. Moys.* 2 (3), 27 (211 *seqq.*, M. 2. 167).

[2] 1 Cor. 14. 23; cf. Musonius *ap.* Aulus Gellius, *Noct. Att.* 5. 1, apparently a commonplace which has been adopted by the synagogue.

[3] For the cessation of the prophecies of the O.T. in the Messianic kingdom as opposed to the prevalent rabbinical view of the eternity of the Torah cf. Str.-B. on Mt. 5. 18.

[4] Kittel in *T.W.z.N.T.* maintains that a mirror need not be an inferior form of seeing (s.v. αἴνιγμα). But to see God even in a single mirror, as in the rabbinical story of Moses, is inferior to direct vision which is impossible for man (Exod. 33. 20). So in *Leg. Alleg.* 3. 33 (101 *seqq.*, M. 1. 107) Moses' prayer that he may not κατοπτρίζεσθαι the form of God in any creature but in God Himself (a prayer that he may not see a reflection of God, but may see Him directly) is associated with the belief of Num. 12. 6 *seqq.* that Moses did see God directly, not "through riddles". Cf. *De Decal.* 21 (105, M. 2. 198), where the mind sees God in the hebdomad, which is a mirror of God: but He is the monad. It would appear that seeing in a mirror may imply either "to see as clearly as in a mirror" (so in Polybius 15. 20. 4) or "to see, but only as in a mirror", according to the context. Paul appears to be following the view that Moses himself, no less than the prophets, saw only as in a mirror. It seems unlikely that there is any allusion to the magic mirror in which God reveals Himself (Kittel, *loc. cit.*). Cf. Plut. *De Is. et Os.* 76, 382a, where God may be seen as in a riddle in lifeless things, and in living things as in the "clearest" mirrors, and *De Gen. Socr.* 20. 589b and 22. 591e, where the relation of mind in man to a higher mind is that of reflection to reality, *Plat. Quaest.* 3. 1. 1002a. For the thought cf. *Corp. Herm.* Ascl. 3. 32b (Scott 356) and Seneca, *Ep.* 10. 3 (79). 12: the whole imagery is drawn from Hellenistic commonplace.

man was still in the state of a child. Here, like the prophets,[1] he had only glimpses of God seen as in a mirror through riddles; naturally Moses' vision was no better. Full knowledge could only come when man could see God face to face and attain to that knowledge of Him which He possessed of man; it was only in virtue of God's cognisance of him that man had any knowledge of God.[2] The thought was drawn from popular theology, which here harmonised with the outlook of Judaism; for Judaism was essentially a religion which emphasised the divine initiative in the relations between God and man;[3] God had "known" Israel and the prophets, and it was natural that His "knowledge" of the prophets should be extended to all Christians who possessed the "Spirit", for they were greater than the prophets. It was perhaps an advantage of the thought that it made "Gnosis" depend upon an act of God towards man and therefore depreciated the value of that knowledge on which the Corinthians prided themselves.

The effect of 1 Cor. 13 was to harmonise the "Spirit" of God as manifested in the Church with the Wisdom of God as interpreted in the light of the later Stoic tradition by the author of Wisdom; there is no evidence that Paul was acquainted with this work, but the book of Wisdom was merely one specimen of a larger body of traditional exegesis. Paul's familiarity with this exegesis and the decisive proof that in writing to the Corinthians he had in mind the equation of the historical Jesus with the Wisdom of the Hellenistic synagogues appear in 1 Cor. 10. 1 *seqq.* The *kerygma* of the mighty works of God in delivering His people from Egypt was an established form of missionary preaching. It could not be doubted that this deliverance was the work of God Himself; rash speculations which ascribed it to an angel could only be condemned, as they were actually condemned by the writer of Is. 63. 9, or at any rate by his translator in the LXX.[4] It

[1] Kittel, *loc. cit.*, rightly sees that Paul is alluding to the comparative obscurity of the prophetic view.

[2] Philo, *De Plant.* 15 (64, M. 1. 339); *De Ebr.* 11 (43 *seqq.*, M. 1. 363) and 17 (72, M. 1. 367), where not to be refused recognition by God is to be accounted worthy of complete salvation; cf. *De Cher.* 32 (115, M. 1. 160), where the soul (here only in Philo a divine element which is reincarnated in successive "regenerations") knows us without being known.

[3] Cf. Norden, *Agnostos Theos*, 287; he quotes *Corp. Herm.* 1 (*Poimandres*), 31 (Scott 130), which is hardly the same (God wishes to be known and is known), and 10. 15 (Scott 196), which is a genuine parallel, but seems to stand alone in the Hermetic writings. He may be right in ascribing the conception to the Hellenistic theology of Oriental origin, associated with Posidonius; but it was a conception native to Judaism (Exod. 33. 12, 17; Jer. 1. 5; for Israel, Amos 3. 2); for rabbinical parallels cf. *Judaism* 1. 373 *seqq.*

[4] The LXX version "it was not a messenger or angel, but He Himself that saved them" may represent the true text (so Box in *The Book of Isaiah, ad loc.*). Meyer,

was of course possible to ascribe the deliverance to the Wisdom or Logos of Alexandrine thought, for such figures had no real personality apart from God; and it was at the same time possible to identify them with the actual manifestation of the cloud, and so avoid the awkward consequences of a literal interpretation of Exod. 13. 21.[1]

With the use of the Old Testament *kerygma* as a means of expounding the Gospel the Church had been familiar from the beginning. Paul adopted it as a means of warning the Corinthians against the danger that awaited those who had once been delivered; they were always in peril of relapsing. The fathers were delivered from Egypt; they were sheltered by the cloud and they passed through the Red Sea; the cloud and the sea represented the baptism by which they passed from the complete bondage to sin represented by Egypt into that relative freedom which was represented by Moses and the Torah.[2] They received the spiritual food of the manna and the spiritual drink of the water from the rock;[3] and the rock from which they drank was Christ. The equation of the rock with Christ was simply the equation of Jesus with the Wisdom of God, for which the water from the rock was a standing type in the midrashic exegesis of the synagogues of the Dispersion;[4] Paul slipped into an expression of

however (*Urspr. u. Anf.* 2. 99), would read: "The angel of His presence saved them." In any case the Greek text seems to be a controversial statement, denying the view that an angel was responsible for the deliverance. What the speculations rejected were is a doubtful matter; they might simply represent an attempt to avoid the undue anthropomorphism of God's action in the Exodus. They might, however, arise from attempts to harmonise Judaism with Gnostic ideas of the various forms of the divine manifestation; different acts of God in the O.T. could be ascribed to His various "names". Cf. above, p. 53. Or they might be due to beliefs of Iranian origin as to a succession of "saviours", Moses being one; for such beliefs and their possible contacts with Judaism cf. Reitzenstein, *Erlösungsmysterium* 99 *seqq.*

[1] This may have been the reason for supposing that it was an angel, the view contradicted by Is. 63. 9. In Wisd. 10. 17 Wisdom becomes the cloud and the pillar of fire. In Philo, *Q.R.D.H.* 42 (205, M. 1. 501), we have a remarkable description of the Logos as symbolised by the cloud; he is the chief of the angels, the suppliant of the mortal to the incorruptible and the ambassador of the ruler to the subject; in *De Vit. Moys.* 1. 29 (166, M. 2. 107) the cloud is actually an archangel, but not the Logos. Naturally it would be entirely orthodox to make the cloud an angel, provided that the deliverance was the work of God; but in the former passage Philo seems to be attempting to reduce to orthodox limits a speculation in which the Logos appeared as an archangel, cf. p. 49.

[2] Presumably this is how Paul would have adapted this midrashic exegesis of the deliverance of Israel from Egypt as a type of the Christian deliverance. It must be remembered that to escape from Egypt is always a deliverance from sin in the convention of this literature.

[3] "Spiritual" here is a play on the two thoughts that the manna and the rock have a "spiritual" meaning, and that the true meaning is Christ, who is the Spirit, to which the Torah points.

[4] See above, p. 87.

the thought which occupied his mind,[1] without remembering at the moment that the readers, who had only received milk and not meat, might be unable to follow him in his speculations as to the cosmic position of Jesus as equated with the Wisdom of God.[2]

[1] For a similar lapse under the influence of the association of ideas cf. the completely irrelevant allusion to the Law in 1 Cor. 15. 56. The thought of Jesus as the divine Wisdom makes itself felt with equal irrelevance in the allusion to Jesus followed by *δι' οὗ...δι' αὐτοῦ* of 8. 6, which has no relevance to the unity of God as precluding the eating of *εἰδωλόθυτα*.

[2] For the easiness of the equation cf. the *Kerygma Petri ap.* Clem. Alex. *Strom.* I. 29. 182 (427 P), where Jesus is both Logos and *νόμος*, i.e. the Torah as the "beginning" of Genesis and the "Wisdom" of Proverbs in rabbinical convention.

CHAPTER VI

THE LIFE OF THE WORLD TO COME

THE first Epistle to the Corinthians was written some two years after the end of Paul's first visit to Corinth. It would seem that he failed to allow for the extent to which the Jewish element in the Church had declined; at any rate a considerable section of it was sufficiently acquainted with the outlook of popular philosophy to refuse to believe in the resurrection of the dead in the form in which he had presented it. That rejection was natural. No intelligent and educated person believed in a subterranean Hades;[1] even the authority of Homer and Plato was unable to save it. Vergil had been compelled to conform to the classical tradition, but could only do so by placing a duplicate set of celestial spheres in the traditional inferno.[2] The priests of Osiris himself were hard put to it to maintain his traditional position as lord of the dead.[3] Reincarnation after the next period of incandescence, and purification in the stars with a possible escape to the firmament, was the general form in which the Stoics offered a future life to mankind; they were far from consistent in their presentation, but none believed in Hades.[4] Belief in the ancient realms of the dead continued to be a living force in the less educated classes; it was naturally a potent element in magic which was largely concerned to evoke demons and the souls of the dead from the lower regions.[5] But educated opinion, more particularly in Greece, was entirely clear on the point; it is perhaps significant of the social class from which the more important converts of the synagogue and the early Pauline missions were drawn, that Paul was compelled to abandon the traditional

[1] Cicero, *Tusc. Disp.* I. 5. 10; Seneca, *Ad Marc. de Cons.* 19. 4; Juv. *Sat.* 2. 149; the rejection is a commonplace.

[2] *Aen.* 6. 640, 730 *seqq.*; cf. Servius on *Aen.* 6. 127. Lactantius, *Div. Inst.* 7. 20, claims that Vergil, as the representative of Stoicism, believes in heaven or the Elysian fields for the righteous and eternal punishment for the wicked; but he ignores the extent to which the Stoic tradition has forced Vergil to conflate the beliefs of the classics with the astrological conception.

[3] Plut. *De Is. et Os.* 78, 382e. Plutarch himself transfers Osiris to the firmament.

[4] It is instructive to attempt to make a consistent view out of the passages quoted v. Arn. 2. 223, 812 *seqq.*

[5] Cf. Kroll, *Gott u. Hölle* 466 *seqq.* Outside magic Hades survives mainly in Latin works which revise the Greek traditions under Oriental influences (*op. cit.* 392). The return of Christianity to a subterranean hell may simply reflect popular belief in the less Hellenised parts of the Church or it may be due to the reaction against Gnosticism: naturally both influences may have been at work.

Jewish conception of Sheol, just as the synagogues at the same time were beginning to substitute the lower spheres of heaven for a subterranean Sheol, as the place of punishment reserved for the wicked.[1] Here as elsewhere Judaism was not bound to any rigid system and was free to adapt itself to the beliefs and language of Gentile literature and to the tastes of potential converts.[2]

It was only natural that the more educated Corinthians should refuse to believe in a system which logically implied that the soul at death departed to Hades or Sheol, and that at the day of judgment it would be reunited to the body. Christianity had accepted this conception from Judaism without question, so long as it remained on the soil of Palestine, mainly because it was not concerned with the rather unimportant issue of the state of the dead during the brief period of world-history that had still to run. At Corinth it was otherwise. A section, apparently of some importance, refused to accept the traditional view. They seem to have accepted the Gospel as the inauguration of a new world-age, which was shortly to be consummated by the appearance of Jesus in glory. Those who lived to see that day would enjoy a life of such blessedness and of such length that they could afford to ignore the possibility of its coming to an end; the age of gold could be regarded as being for practical purposes eternal.[3] Possibly Christians who died before it were supposed to suffer death on account of their misdeeds, on the lines suggested by Paul's own teaching in 1 Cor. 11. 30. The conception of a new age which had already begun and was shortly to be completed by the appearance of the Lord was fairly prominent in Christian preaching; apparently it commended itself as against the immortality of the soul, a belief which was natural

[1] In *Test. Lev.* 3. 1 the lowest heaven is gloomy because it has to behold the deeds of the wicked, and contains the spirits of vengeance. In 2 En. 9. 1–10. 6 both paradise and hell are in the third heaven; but the location of hell on the North side of the third heaven allows it to be described in the same terms as the subterranean hell of tradition; here we have the opposite of Vergil, a hell located in the heavens instead of heavens located below the earth. In 3 Bar. 3. 3 the builders of the Tower of Babel are punished in the third heaven, presumably as a type of the hopelessly wicked. Curiously enough there seems no instance of the use of the lower air for this purpose in Jewish literature.

[2] Cf. Jos. *B.J.* 2. 8. 11 (155) and 14 (163 *seqq.*), where the Essene view is depicted as a correct classical system; the Pharisees believe in the transfer of the righteous to "another body"; this may be intended to suggest that the Pharisees believe in transmigration (I owe this suggestion to Dr M. Braun). They believe also in hell for the wicked. The one thing that both Pharisees and Essenes believed in, the final judgment, has been dropped overboard for the benefit of Greek readers.

[3] This is the hope of Vergil, *Ecl.* 4. 53. Behind the language of those who welcomed the establishment of the principate or the accession of an emperor as a new aeon (cf. above, pp. 23 and 92), there must have been some genuine religious expectation of a real age of gold, involving a practical immortality for those who survived into it. Cf. also the Sibylline oracle discussed on p. 13 above.

to the Hellenistic age, but not easily to be harmonised with the apocalyptic version of the Gospel.[1]

Paul met this aberration by a restatement of the conventional apocalyptic scheme; the most striking feature of it is the appearance of the Adam-myth which is used in Romans; the sin of Adam had brought death on mankind, since it caused him to fall from the state of a pure spirit into that of a mere "living soul"; Jesus as the last Adam had returned from the state of a "living soul", which was His during His life on earth, into that of a pure spirit, which not only lived but had the power to give life to others (1 Cor. 15. 45). It followed that the resurrection of the dead was a resurrection not to the material body, but to a body suited to its new conditions as a pure spirit, instead of a more or less material and fleshly soul.[2] This thought was defended on the lines of a common rabbinical argument: if the seed, which is sown naked, rises clothed, how much more would God provide raiment for the soul.[3] Yet, again, the glory of the heavenly bodies differed; so would the glory of the risen body differ from the body sown in corruption; the two analogies combined the two traditions of the Old Testament, the Chaldean imagery used by Daniel and the Semitic used by Isaiah. The function of the present body was to provide a vehicle for the earthy and material soul into which the first Adam fell; the new body was to be a suitable vehicle for the heavenly spiritual nature which the second Adam from heaven would confer in due course on those who were His.[4] From the point of view of eschatology the material and the psychic preceded the spiritual; the argument, however, from the narrative of Gen. 2. 7 was only valid if the verse was interpreted to mean that Adam possessed a spiritual body from which he fell, or at any rate a body capable of becoming spiritual.[5] In any

[1] Paul shows no objection in 2 Corinthians to abandoning the resurrection of the dead in favour of the immortality of the soul (see below, pp. 136 *seqq.*). The arguments of 1 Cor. 15. 14 *seqq.* and 29 imply a view derived from the common language of the "new age" coupled with an intense experience of conversion and "spiritual" enthusiasm. A similar view seems to have been taken by Hymenaeus and Philetus in 2 Tim. 2. 18, or to have been taken by the author of that letter as the meaning of this passage.

[2] Cf. above, p. 109.

[3] For 1 Cor. 15. 37 cf. Talmud, *Sanh.* 90b; probably the two passages are independent versions of a rabbinical commonplace.

[4] Is the reading πνευματικός of the Chester-Beatty Papyrus in v. 47 of the "second man" an Alexandrine emendation or does it preserve the original reading? It gives an excellent meaning: the true "spiritual man" is not Adam but Jesus.

[5] So Philo, *Leg. Alleg.* 1. 13 (42, M. 1. 51), makes the πνοή breathed into the material Adam a mere emanation of the πνεῦμα of the ideal man (=the Logos). In Clem. Alex. *Strom.* 5. 14. 94 (703 P) the "image" of God is the Logos, the impassible man, the "likeness" is the "image of the image", the mind of man. In Tert. *adv. Marc.* 2. 9 the *afflatus* of God in Adam is capable of sin, but the spirit is not, cf. *De Bapt.* 5. Tatian, *Or. adv. Gr.* 20. 89, makes man fall not, like the demons, from heaven but from a better earth than the present.

case it was not the material flesh and blood that would inherit the kingdom of God; the resurrection of the dead would be accompanied by a change to a body of radiant glory. The final catastrophe would raise the dead to this state, while the living would be suddenly transformed into a similar condition. It does not appear how this transformation of the righteous (the fate of the wicked is ignored) was to be harmonised with the view expressed in v. 28 that the final ending will be one in which God is all in all, a phrase which was easily carried over into the theocentric religion of Judaism, in which it had no real place, from the current view of popular philosophy, in which the end of each world-age resulted in the reabsorption of all things into the divine fire;[1] in that state even the divine element permeating the cosmos was to be reabsorbed in the one element of divinity;[2] it is not to be supposed that Paul had any serious belief that Jesus and His disciples would cease at the end of all things to retain their individual being;[3] but his language was drawn from a system of belief which implied it.

It appears that Paul's admission of the immaterial nature of the risen body and his suggestion of some kind of reabsorption of all things into God were not enough to satisfy the difficulties of the Corinthians. The second Epistle is largely devoted to a complete revision of Pauline eschatology in a Hellenistic sense. The circumstances in which the Epistle was written as a vindication of his past conduct and his authority as an Apostle have tended to obscure the importance of this

[1] There is a close parallel in Ecclus. 43. 27, where the author, after describing God's works in creation in the anthropomorphic style of the ordinary Jewish tradition, suddenly remarks: "to sum up, He is all." At first sight we have here a surprising piece of pantheism; actually we have a scrap of Greek erudition thrown in to increase the praises of God by a writer to whom pantheism would have been entirely unintelligible.

[2] The "deification" at death of those who possess "mind" in such passages as *Corp. Herm.* 1 (*Poimandres*), 26a (Scott 128) seems to conflate the Stoic reabsorption and the Oriental deification of the king (cf. p. 75); it is hardly the magic identification of the adept with the deity. It is noticeable that such language only appears in Christianity with the Alexandrines, in whom it has entirely lost its meaning; cf. Clem. Alex. *Strom.* 4. 23. 149 (632 P), and note that *ib.* 152 it is simply the same as "being made as like God as possible"; Orig. *De Orat. Lib.* 27 (Lommatzsch 17, p. 220), where we also find (26, *ib.* p. 201) that man can "become heaven". The language of Hellenistic piety has been carried over into Christianity, but the meaning has disappeared.

[3] The rabbinical parallels quoted by Str.-B. on this verse are not parallels at all in the strict sense; there seems no Jewish basis for this belief in the reabsorption of everything into the nature of God, which is drawn from popular theology, cf. Seneca, *Ep.* 1. 9. 16, where Jupiter *resoluto mundo et dis* (i.e. the various manifestations of God in the processes of nature) *in unum confusis paulisper cessante natura adquiescit cogitationibus suis traditus*. There seem to be traces of a similar conception in Zoroastrianism (Lommel, *Die Rel. Zarath.* 218 and 222); but the source of the Pauline language is more naturally to be found in the Stoic tradition, which is not strictly applicable to Christian eschatology; cf. also Epict. *Diss.* 3. 13. 4 *seqq.*

aspect of the letter;[1] it is introduced as a secondary matter, but it may be doubted whether it was not more important for the propagation of the Gospel in the Hellenistic world than any other part of the Epistle.

Formally the subject is introduced as a digression on the nature of Paul's "ministry". His first letter was followed by a visit intended to reduce the rebellious elements of the Church of Corinth to order. The visit was unsuccessful; it was followed by an angry letter, part of which survives in the last four chapters of 2 Corinthians in its present form.[2] The result was a complete triumph; but it was still desirable to remove any impression of high-handedness which his conduct might have produced.[3] It was vital that the collection for the Saints at Jerusalem should succeed; but a large part of his difficulties had been caused by Jewish Christians who were not Apostles in any sense, but were content to describe themselves as "ministers of Christ".[4] Paul was ready to borrow, and almost to parody their language.

He opened the letter with an outburst of triumphant thanksgiving over his victory, and proceeded to an account of his motives and actions which led up to a justification of his authority as stated in terms of ministry, a justification which carried with it a vindication of the superiority of the Gospel to the Torah. His very journey to Corinth was a procession of triumph in Christ, which manifested the fragrance of the knowledge of Him wherever Paul went (2. 14 *seqq.*). The fragrance was at the same time the incense of the triumph[5] of the sufferings of Jesus, offered in the person of the Apostle as a sacrificial

[1] Meyer, *Urspr. u. Anf.* 3. 104, rightly emphasises the objection of the educated Greek world to the idea of the "revivification of the corpse"; but he ignores the fact that this idea is thrown overboard in 2 Cor. 4. 7 *seqq.*

[2] For the course of events cf. Strachan in Moffatt's *Commentary*, pp. xvi *seqq.*

[3] 2 Cor. 1. 12, 3. 1, 5. 12, 7. 2 *seqq.*

[4] For the Jewish element in the opposition at Corinth cf. *Jerusalem* 311. For their use of the term "ministers" see 2 Cor. 11. 23 (note that there is no reference to "Apostles" here). But in the section 10. 1—end Paul is an Apostle four times; a minister only here and in 11. 15 by implication; the language is that of his opponents. "Ministry" appears in 11. 8 but in its literal sense. In Rom. 11. 13 Paul alludes to the apostolate as a "ministry", but not elsewhere in the earlier Epistles. Similarly he is an Apostle eight times in 1 Corinthians; he is a "minister" only once, in 3. 5, where he is deprecating all human authority as against that of Christ. But in 2 Corinthians 1. 1–9. 15 he is an Apostle only in the formal opening verse; he introduces his activity as a "ministry" in the long midrash on the subject 3. 3 *seqq.*, and has further allusions to his "ministry" in 5. 18 and 6. 3 and 4 quite apart from the "ministry" of collecting for the Saints. On the other hand his helpers become "apostles" in a quite indiscriminate fashion in 8. 23.

[5] Appian, *Punica* 66; cf. the unofficial triumph of Valerius in Dion. Halic. *Antt. Rom.* 9. 35 and the reception of the Magna Mater at Rome in Livy 29. 14 for incense as the adjunct of a triumphal procession. For the use of incense in royal and religious processions in the Hellenistic age cf. Athenaeus, *Deipnos.* 5. 27, 197e and 6. 62, 253c. These were not strictly "triumphs", but it is doubtful whether a Hellenistic-Jewish writer would have differentiated them.

fragrance to God,[1] and the knowledge of God revealed in the Gospel, the fragrant spice which really brought life to the righteous and death to the wicked, as against the Torah for which the rabbis wrongly claimed that virtue.[2] The wealth of haggadic allusion was worthy of the pupil of Gamaliel; it is difficult to suppose that Paul's Corinthian readers were very clear as to his meaning.

Paul had been accused of "commending himself" by claiming a personal authority instead of relying on the authority conferred by the Church of Jerusalem and established by letters of commendation. To this charge, which his triumphant language might seem to justify, he replied that for such a ministry as his no human being could be "sufficient". The question of "sufficiency" could not be put to those who like himself preached the full truth in the sight of God, and were not content to sell a cheap and inferior imitation for their own personal advantage.[3] He was not beginning to commend himself; he had no need of letters of commendation, such as his opponents had produced to justify their claims; the Church of Corinth itself was his letter of commendation, a letter for all to read, written not on tables of stone but on the tables of men's hearts. It was thus one instance of the fulfilment of the prophecy that a time would come when all men should know God because there would be a new Torah, written on the hearts of all men.[4] Thus he was able to speak and write with complete confidence, not because he had any sufficiency of his own, but because God had bestowed on him a measure of the "sufficiency" which was an essential element of His own nature. Through this divine "sufficiency" Paul was able to be a minister of the new Torah, which was

[1] *Gen. R.* 34. 21, where God smells the fragrance of Abraham in the furnace of Nimrod, of the Three Children in the fiery furnace and of the martyrs under Hadrian. The last item appears to be an addition to an existing scheme; it is not likely that any martyrs were actually burnt under Hadrian. For *ὀσμὴ εὐωδίας* as a sacrificial fragrance, cf. *Test. Lev.* 3. 6. For the merits of the righteous in the Messianic age as a sweet savour see Str.-B. on this passage.

[2] Cf. Str.-B. *ad loc.* and Buxtorf, *Lexicon*, s.v. סַמָּא, for the word as a transliteration of *ὀσμή*. Firmicus Maternus, *De Err. Prof. Rel.* 22. 1, describes the anointing of the throats of the initiates in the mysteries of Attis with fragrant ointment; it is possible that the Torah as the סַם חַיִּים is derived from Hellenistic religion; cf. Diod. Sic. 1. 25. 6 for the *φάρμακον ἀθανασίας* in Egyptian legends.

[3] Cf. Windisch in *T.W.z.N.T.* s.v. *καπηλεύω*.

[4] Jer. 31. 33; the allusion to that prophecy follows naturally on the knowledge of God, which was the subject of 2 Cor. 2. 14 *seqq.*, since the new Torah of Jeremiah consisted in a personal knowledge of God, planted by Him in the hearts of all men. The description of the Gospel in terms of "knowledge" may be due to the popularity of gnosis of a Hellenistic type at Corinth, but Paul confines it here strictly within the limits of the O.T. The prophecy of Jeremiah was valuable as an anticipation of the Stoic idea of the unwritten law; cf. Philo, *De Spec. Legg.* 4 (*De Just.*), 3 (149, M. 2. 361).

not of the letter, which led to death, but of the spirit, which led to life.[1]

With this apology for his apparent boasting Paul passed to the ministry of the new covenant. The glory of the old was such that the face of Moses shone when he came down from the mount, so that the children of Israel could not look on it. By comparison with the exceeding glory of the new, the glory of the old was no glory at all.[2] For the glory of the new covenant was permanent and not transitory; in virtue of this hope the ministers of the new covenant could speak with absolute boldness and had no need to veil their faces, as Moses did because the children of Israel could not look even on the lesser glory of the old covenant. Even to the present time they could not do so; the veil which covered the ark of the Law in every synagogue[3] preserved the memory of the veil over the face of Moses and symbolised the veil laid over the hearts of the people until it was revealed to them that it had been done away in Christ. As Moses removed the veil when he turned to the Lord, so was the veil removed from all who turned to Him. For the Lord was the Spirit; consequently all who were converted turned from the letter to the Spirit. To turn from the letter to the Spirit was to find freedom, for where the Spirit was there was complete freedom of access to God. Thus the Christian could remove all veils from his face and be free to reflect the glory of the Lord; he was changed from glory into glory through the power of the Spirit which governed the process.[4] The comparison of the transformation of

[1] *ὁ ἱκανός* as a title of God is used to translate the "Shaddai" of the O.T. as if it were שֶׁדַּי, "He who is sufficient". For the term cf. the LXX rendering of Shaddai in Ruth 1. 20, 21; Job 21. 15, 31. 2, 40. 2 and Ezek. 1. 24 in the A text; it is frequent in Aquila and Symmachus, cf. Hatch and Redpath, *Concordance*, s.v. *ἱκανός*. The thought is common in Philo, cf. *Leg. Alleg.* 1. 14 (44, M. 1. 52); *De Cher.* 13 (46, M. 1. 147); *De Mut. Nom.* 4 (27, M. 1. 582) and 5 (46, M. 1. 585). A different explanation is given in *Gen. R.* 46. 3 on Gen. 17. 1; here it is not God that is sufficient; He says to creation "it is enough".

[2] 3. 10.

[3] This appears to be intended by 3. 14; for the veil cf. Str.-B. 4 (1), 137. The veil of the sanctuary in the Temple was a favourite theme of the synagogues of the Hellenistic world, both on account of its cosmic significance (Jos. *Antt.* 3. 7. 7 (183), cf. above, p. 33, the symbolism being that of the High Priest's robe), and because it concealed the sacred things from the gaze of those who were unconsecrated (Philo, *De Vit. Moys.* 2 (3), 5 (87, M. 2. 148), cf. *De Spec. Legg.* 1 (*De Sacr.*), 4 (274, M. 2. 253)). This was a *motif* with an obvious value; since the veil of the ark of the Law could obviously be regarded as a counterpart of the veil in the Temple, it seems likely that the symbolism was extended to the veil in the synagogue. But the symbolism would inevitably be abandoned in view of the opening it offered to Christian propaganda.

[4] The *κυρίου πνεύματος* of 3. 18 cannot mean the Spirit of the Lord; it could only mean "the Lord of the Spirit", which is nonsense. If the reading *κύριον* in v. 17 were correct, the word *κύριος* would in both cases be used to mean that the Spirit controls or governs the process. In v. 18 the adjectival sense seems the only possible

the soul, which reflects the glory of God without a veil, into the likeness of that which it reflects, depended on the solution given by philosophy to the standing problem of ancient physics of the reflection produced in a mirror; one explanation was that it was produced by a series of emanations proceeding from the object and establishing the resemblances of themselves in the polished surface of the mirror.[1] The conception was eminently suited to Paul's conception of the action of the Spirit on the soul, however doubtful the accuracy of the physics on which it rested. It was rendered still more easy and suitable by the fact that the immanence of the divine element in the multiplicity of the phenomenal world could be expressed in popular philosophy by the analogy of the one face reflected in many mirrors.[2] The relation of the spirit of man to that divine element could again be described, in view of the quite undefined nature of the relation of the spirit of man to the Spirit of God, as a reflection; the mind which withdrew from the world and contemplated itself was beholding God, reflected in itself as in a mirror.[3] Paul could easily adapt this metaphor to the Jewish-Christian thought of the Spirit of God, which had some kind of affinity with the spirit of man, in virtue of which it was able

one; cf. Plut. *De Ser. Num. Vind.* 30, 567 b: ἐν τῷ λογιστικῷ καὶ κυρίῳ; Ps.-Plut. *De Fat.* 6. 570e: τὸ δ' ἐφ' ἡμῖν, ὡς κύριον, χρῆσθαι τῷ ἐνδεχομένῳ; Polybius 31. 7. 12 and *passim*; Hermias, *Irr. Gent. Phil.* 6 (*Dox. Gr.* 652, l. 26), where mind is αἴτιος καὶ κύριος τῶν ὁλων; Clem. Alex. *Exc. ex Theod.* 70. 2 (Casey 625), the stars have no power of their own, but reveal the action of κύριοι δυνάμεις; *Papp. Mag. Gr.* 2. 78 τὸ δὲ κύριον, of the decisive words of a spell. In theological literature we might expect an avoidance of the adjectival use of the word to avoid confusion; but in Philo, *De Mut. Nom.* 2 (13, M. 1. 580), the ὄνομά μου Κύριος of Exod. 6. 3 is interpreted as meaning that God did not reveal to the patriarchs His κύριον ὄνομα. He allows them to address Him as ὁ ὤν, but the κύριον ὄνομα is not revealed, for God cannot have a name. Philo here ignores the tetragrammaton. So in *Papp. Mag. Gr. loc. cit.*, after three magic names, the spell proceeds κύριε θεέ.

[1] Cf. above, p. 71; for the mirror *Placita* 4. 14. 1 *seqq.* (*Dox. Gr.* 405). For a variation of the theme cf. Epict. *Diss.* 2. 23. 3 where sight is a πνεῦμα proceeding from the eye to the object.

[2] Macrob. *Somn. Scip.* 1. 14, 15.

[3] Cf. p. 76, n. 2; Philo, *De Migr. Abr.* 34 (190, M. 1. 466), from the same source as Cicero, *De Div.* 1. 32. 70, 49. 110 and 51. 115, presumably Posidonius' defence of divination, though Philo uses the analogy between the immaterial nature of mind in man and the mind of God for an attack on astrology; but his argument that the mind by consorting with itself sees truth as in a mirror depends for its force on the view that the mind is a mirror of God, though Philo cannot admit this and in 193 denies that the mind of God, the Father, can be contained in man, the son; but he has forgotten to cut out the allusion of his source to the mirror. Cf. Plutarch, quoted p. 121, n. 4, for the relation of the mind of man to a higher mind as that of light to reflection or to the reflection of an object in a mirror. For this meaning of κατοπτρίζεσθαι cf. Orig. *c. Cels.* 5. 60. In the Syrian writers who identify the element of "spirit" in man with the Holy Ghost the Lord becomes a mirror, *Od. Sol.* 13. 1; cf. Ephraim, quoted by Bernard *ad loc.* in *Texts and Studies* 8. 3. 76. Kittel in *T.W.z.N.T.* s.v. κατοπτρίζεσθαι quotes *Leg. Alleg.* 3. 33 (101, M. 1. 107) for the meaning "sees as in a mirror", but see p. 121, n. 4.

to transform him into the resemblance of the divine nature or imprint the likeness of God upon the soul.[1]

This discussion of the nature of the Christian ministry, which had passed into a discussion of the whole Christian life, had brought Paul to a point at which he could vindicate himself from the charges of his opponents (4. 1 *seqq.*). It was absurd to suppose that one who had such a ministry committed to him should be guilty of treachery or of concealing some part of the truth.[2] He was only concerned to manifest the truth; the only element of concealment or "veiling" in the matter was to be found among unbelievers, whose hearts had been veiled by the god of this aeon[3] so that they could not gaze on the light of the Gospel of the glory of Christ, who was the image of God. It was God who said "Light shall shine out of darkness" and thereby brought into being Jesus, the precosmic light and the Wisdom of God;[4] it was a continuation of that first illumination that He should still shine in the hearts of His ministers, in order that the light of the glory of God in the face of Christ might be made to shine in the hearts of mankind. The conception of the teacher as the torch, from which the divine flame was passed on to the hearts of others, was a commonplace; it was in virtue of this thought that Paul could interpolate into his argument the statement that it was not himself that he preached, but Jesus Christ; Paul was merely the servant of the Corinthians, whom he served for the sake of Jesus,[5] handing on to them the light which he had himself received.

Thus the original light created by God in the beginning had been equated not with the Torah, the mere reflection of the light, which had been vouchsafed to Moses, but with the true knowledge of God revealed in the person of Jesus, who, as the divine Wisdom, was Himself that primal light. The relation of Jesus to God was left entirely undefined, for Jewish speculation was quite content to

[1] The myth in the *Poimandres*, *Corp. Herm.* 1. 14 (Scott 120), expresses the thought from the opposite point of view; the nature of man is due to the union of the celestial Man with his reflection in matter. Cf. p. 224.

[2] ἐγκακοῦμεν in 4. 1 = behave treacherously (Polybius 4. 19. 10). Presumably the charge was that he sought to commend himself by not imposing the observance of the Law on Gentile converts, though he really knew that they were bound to observe it.

[3] Cf. above, p. 93.

[4] Cf. above, pp. 45, 68; Philo, *De Somn.* 1. 13 (75, M. 1. 632); *De Migr. Abr.* 8 (40, M. 1. 442), where wisdom survives as the archetype of light, i.e. Philo is working on older material.

[5] V. 5 would be clearer if it followed v. 6. The god of this world prevents the light from shining in men's hearts, as God intends that it should shine through the agency of His servants, who merely pass on the light which they have received. For the flame and torch cf. Philo, *De Gigant.* 6 (25, M. 1. 266).

describe God Himself in terms of light, taken over by the later prophets from the religion of Persia.[1] The glory of radiance which was the pictorial imagery commonly used for describing the divine nature might therefore be applied equally well to God Himself or to Jesus as the Wisdom of God.[2] The object of the argument was to prove that Jesus, not the Torah, was the true revelation of the divine glory and the divine light;[3] the relation of Jesus to the Creator and the creation did not need precise definition as long as the whole matter was left on the homiletic plane.

Up to this point Paul had been concerned to prove the superiority of the Gospel to the Torah and so of his own ministry, which rejected the Torah, to that of his opponents, who sought to retain it, while at the same time proving that he was not guilty of "self-commendation" in making such a claim. He proceeded from this to his next purpose. His opponents, as orthodox Jewish Christians, were presumably wedded to the apocalyptic tradition in which the Gospel had been set. Experience had shown that it was vital to abandon the eschatological emphasis if the substance of the Jewish belief in eternal life, which was essential to Christianity, was to be maintained. Yet he was compelled to do so without affording his Jewish opponents an opening for accusing him of perverting the word of God. His approach to the subject was a natural continuation of his argument from the light of the Gospel; but it led on to a line of argument which was familiar to Hellenistic Judaism, and had probably begun to influence the teaching of the Pharisees.

The light of the knowledge of God was already equated in Paul's

[1] This influence appears to have made itself felt in such passages as Is. 45. 7 or the apocalypse of Is. 51. 4 *seqq.* Meyer, *Urspr. u. Anf.* 2. 95, puts the influence later, but it is difficult to see how the influence of Iranian religion in these passages can be denied, unless it is denied that there is any such influence anywhere.

[2] For God as light in Philo cf. *Quod Deus Imm.* 12 (58, M. 1. 281); *De Praem. et Poen.* 7 (45, M. 2. 415) and *passim.* Philo is quite indiscriminate in regard to the relation of God or the Logos to the original light. There is equal indifference in the Hermetica, e.g. *Poimandres,* 5a *seqq.* (Scott 116), where a φωτεινὸς λόγος comes forth from the light which is Mind (Scott's emendation here is quite unjustified). Cf. 3. 1b (Scott 146) for light proceeding from God at the beginning; for the probability of Jewish influence cf. Dodd, *The Bible and the Greeks* 210 *seqq.*

[3] For the Shekinah as a blaze of light on O.T. grounds, cf. *Judaism* 1. 435. Kittel in *T.W.z.N.T.* 2. 255 rightly points out that while the idea may have been derived from contact with Persia, the source of the N.T. language is simply the O.T. Δόξα only appears to be used of the glory of God once in Philo (*De Spec. Legg.* 1 (*De Mon.*), 6 (45, M. 2. 218)), where the usage is imposed by Exod. 33. 18; here the glory of God is equated to His "powers". Elsewhere it is used of "belief" (so in *De Virt.* (*De Fort.*) 7 (35, M. 2. 381)) in a good sense (Cohn-Wendland's index wrongly notes this passage as meaning "glory"), or the depreciatory sense of "opinion" as in the Platonic tradition, or of human reputation.

argument with Jesus as the cosmic Wisdom. Yet again it was the divine *afflatus* of the Spirit, with its unspecified relation to the highest element of the soul of man. It was an easy matter to equate the light of the knowledge of God, as revealed in Jesus, or the Spirit, as given to the Christian or at least to the fully developed Christian, with that divine element which, in accordance with the tradition of popular philosophy, was imprisoned in the worthless and burdensome vessel of the material body. It was thus (4. 7 *seqq.*) the light carried in an earthen vessel, the essential nature of man, which might hope in the end to obtain deliverance from the vessel in which it was enclosed,[1] the living corpse which was its tomb.[2] The soul particularly felt the burden of the corpse which it must carry as it approached perfection;[3] the commonplace was adapted to the ministry of the Apostle and to the general conception of the Christian life as a death to the old life and the rising to the new in baptism. What the minister of Christ carried with him was not simply the corpse of the material body, but a body in which the dying of Jesus was continually being re-enacted; for him the Christian life was not simply a death with Jesus and a rising to a new life, but a continual dying, as a result of which the new life was continually being made available for his hearers. He was animated by that same spirit of faith in which Jesus had been ready to fulfil the prophecy of the Psalmist, speaking in spite of the opposition of men;[4] for he knew that God, who had raised up Jesus, would also raise up both himself and his hearers and bring them into His presence, where all would be united in offering their praise and thanksgivings to His glory.[5]

Paul thus brought (4. 16 *seqq.*) the life and labours of the Apostles into line with the sufferings of the Saints of the old covenant. Con-

[1] Cf. Servius on *Aen.* 6. 724; the mind, like the light in a lantern, is freed from stains contracted by association with the body as soon as it departs from the body. For the correspondence between the Torah as the lamp of God and the soul as the lamp of man cf. *Exod. R.* 36. 3. The "vessel" here may be suggested by the method of carrying a lamp in Judg. 7. 16, a method described as still in use in the East by Burney, *The Book of Judges, ad loc.* The body as the ἀγγεῖον of the soul appears in Philo, *De Post. Cain.* 47 (163, M. 1. 257) and *passim*; cf. Cicero, *Tusc. Disp.* 1. 22. 52: *vas animi*. In the system of Heracleon, as described by Epiphanius, *Panar. Haer.* 36. 3, the initiate describes himself as a σκεῦος ἔντιμον on passing through the sphere of the demiurge; but it is only after this that the "inner man" lays aside the "bond and the angel (ἄγγελον (Oehler): should this be ἀγγεῖον?), that is the soul". The Mandean use of the "vessel" (cf. *G.R.* 326, Lidzb. 332. 21) may be derived from Hellenistic commonplace. For the language of 4. 8 cf. Epict. *Diss.* 1. 25. 28.

[2] Cf. Philo, *Leg. Alleg.* 1. 33 (108, M. 1. 65).

[3] Philo, *Leg. Alleg.* 3. 23 (74, M. 1. 101).

[4] Ps. 116. 10 (=LXX, Ps. 115. 1). The allusion is to the whole Psalm, which is traditionally interpreted of the death of the Saints; cf. *Midr. Teh.* on the Psalm; Orig. *In Ev. Matt.* 16. 6; *Sel. in Ps. ad loc.*; *Exh. ad Mart.* 28; Tert. *adv. Marc.* 4. 39.

[5] Ps. 116. 17 *seqq.*

sequently he did not yield to cowardice; he was content that his "outer man" should be destroyed by this gradual martyrdom in which he shared the death of Jesus, for the more the outer man was destroyed, the more the new "inner man" was formed in him.[1] His present light afflictions were transmuting the burden of the earthly body into an eternal burden of glory, a phrase suggested by an atrocious Hebrew pun which may have been a commonplace of the rabbinical schools in discussing the glory of the martyrs.[2] He looked not on the temporal world that could be seen with the eyes of the body, but on the eternal and invisible.[3]

Up to this point Paul had ostensibly written of the Apostles, as sharing in the dying and resurrection of Jesus, not of all converts as such. But Judaism regarded the sufferings of the martyr not merely as accomplishing his transformation from the mortal to immortality;[4] they were also a manifestation of the truth of the Torah to the nation as a whole.[5] Further, they were available for the redemption of the whole nation.[6] Much more were the sufferings of Jesus, as manifested in His Apostles, a means of transforming not only themselves but their converts from mortality to immortality. Paul passed over these steps in the argument, merely using the term "we know"[7] (5. 1 *seqq.*) as a means of passing from the position of certain privileged souls to the position of all Christians as such. With the single phrase he proceeded to develop a substitution of an accepted Hellenistic view of the life to come for the eschatology of Jewish Christianity.

The earthen vessel which contained the treasure of the knowledge of God was explicitly equated with the body as the house or tabernacle[8]

[1] The "inner man" comes from Plato (*Rep.* 589a) through the commonplace of Hellenistic theology; cf. Philo, *Quod Det. Pot. Ins.* 8 (23, M. 1. 196); *Quod Omn. Prob. Lib.* 17 (111, M. 2. 462). With an elaborate mystification it appears in *Corp. Herm.* 13. 3 (Scott 240).

[2] The weight of the body as the burden which it has to bear is a commonplace of the contrast between body and soul; cf. Jos. *B.J.* 7. 8. 7 (346), Wisd. 9. 15; with a pseudo-scientific colouring in *Corp. Herm.* 10. 13 (Scott 196), Sext. Emp. *adv. Math.* 7. 290. The "weight of glory" is a pun on כבד (so Strachan rightly in Moffatt's *Commentary*, *ad loc.*).

[3] Another commonplace, cf. Philo, *De Mund. Op.* 2 (12, M. 1. 3), and again with a pseudo-scientific explanation, *Corp. Herm.* 6. 4b (Scott 168); the eye can only see "images", therefore it cannot see God or the good. "Images" here are interpreted as phantoms, but properly in this connection mean the "images" projected from the object which impinge on the eye and produce sight (*Placita* 4. 13. 1, *Dox. Gr.* 403).

[4] 4 Macc. 9. 22, and see below, p. 142.

[5] 4 Macc. 16. 16.

[6] *Judaism* 1. 547 *seqq.*

[7] Rom. 2. 2, 3. 19; ironically in 1 Cor. 8. 1 and 4.

[8] Philo, *Quod Omn. Prob. Lib. loc. cit.* n. 1 above, where the "true man" (the "inner man" of this passage) is the unseen mind, which has to carry about the perceptible form as its house; *Quod Deus Imm.* 32 (150, M. 1. 295), the body is the house or tomb, or whatever else it may be called, of the soul. For the "tabernacle"

of the soul, the garment which it was anxious to cast aside,[1] the burden from which it longed to be delivered.[2] Paul was too good a Jew and too poor a Hellenist to describe the soul as being delivered from the clothing of the body so that it might ascend to heaven naked. The Jews had an intense dislike of nakedness, which made it seem improper for a man even to pray in private until he had clothed himself.[3] Consequently he adopted the conception that the soul did not simply lay aside the body, but put on a new and glorious one, the eternal habitation prepared for the soul in its true home in heaven. The language was drawn from the conventional Jewish picture of the righteous soul raised to heaven as a radiant and glorious body. The origin of that belief was the Chaldean conception of the divine monarch translated to the stars at death,[4] but it had long since been acclimatised in Judaism; Paul treated it as entirely equivalent to the thought of the heavenly counterpart of the soul, which awaited it in heaven; the conception properly belonged to Zoroastrianism, but had been adopted by Judaism in the form of a celestial robe awaiting the righteous;[5] Paul transformed it into a dwelling in order to make a suitable antithesis to the earthly habitation of the body. But the thought of the "garment" remained in the somewhat grotesque language in which he described the dwelling as something to be "put on" as a robe; in imaginative language the glorified state of the righteous was more naturally pictured as a "robe" of celestial glory than as a

cf. 2 Pet. 1. 13; Wisd. 9. 15; Timaeus Locrus 100a. According to Taylor's commentary on the *Timaeus* σκῆνος is a Pythagorean term (660, 661). It appears in *Corp. Herm.* 13. 15 (Scott 248). Philo does not use it, presumably because he avoids using the word in a bad sense, when it has also to be used of the idealised tabernacle of the Pentateuch. For "house" cf. Seneca, *Ep.* 7. 3 (65). 21.

[1] *Corp. Herm.* 7. 2b (Scott 172). Cf. the treatment of Nadab and Abihu in Philo (see above, p. 104). The command to bury them in their coats is interpreted to mean that they have left the body behind.

[2] In *Leg. Alleg.* 3. 22 (69, M. 1. 100) Philo describes Er (meaning skin with an obvious reference to the coats of Adam and Eve) as the "burden of skin", which is also a corpse (cf. above, p. 83, for this passage).

[3] Mishnah, *Berakhoth* 3. 5 (Danby 4). Philo is sufficiently Hellenised to have no such objection, e.g. *De Virt.* (*De Human.*), 4 (76, M. 2. 388); here the body of Moses is stripped off him like a shell that has grown about the soul, which is thus left naked. The thought of the soul as being stripped naked and set free to ascend to heaven is common in Philo.

[4] Cf. p. 30.

[5] For the celestial robes cf. p. 127 and Str.-B. on Mt. 17. 2 and this passage; *Od. Sol.* 7. 6, 11. 9 and 20. 7. For the *fravashi* or celestial counterpart of the soul see Lommel, *Die Rel. Zarath.* 152 and Moulton, *Early Zoroastrianism* 254 *seqq.* The celestial original, which is also the counterpart of the soul, appears as a garment in the Hymn of the Soul in the *Acts of Thomas* 108. 9, 110. 46 and 112. 76 (*Apocr. N.T.* 411). In the last passage the soul beholds itself in the garment "as it had been in a mirror". It seems natural to see here a conflation of the thought of the *fravashi* as the "true self" with the Hellenistic view of the mind as a mirror in which man sees God, because he sees the divine element in himself (p. 132).

house; moreover, the practice of Hellenistic mysteries had accustomed the world to the thought of a change of garments as a symbol of the change of the spiritual status of the initiate. It was therefore easy and natural to describe the inward and spiritual change in terms of the outward and visible symbol of the change of garments. The thought was at least as naturally at home in Christianity as in any other religion, since the practice of adult baptism by immersion involved a literal "putting-off" of the garments as a preliminary to the laying aside of the old evil and material nature, and a subsequent "putting-on" of garments, whether the same or new, simultaneously with the assumption of the new Christian nature.[1] The practice of wearing special robes for religious purposes was common in ancient religions, including those of Syria,[2] and formed part of the mysteries of Isis.[3] The similarity of the later practice of clothing the Christian neophyte in a baptismal robe to that of the mysteries was sufficiently obvious to allow later Christian writers to compare Christian baptism to initiation into the mysteries, when the latter were no longer serious rivals of the Church.[4] Some years before this Epistle Paul had been able to assume that the conception of baptism as the "putting-off" of the old sin and the "putting-on" of Christ was so familiar in circles which were largely influenced by the Jewish tradition that he could describe baptism as the "putting-on" of Christ without any further explanation.[5] The whole use of metaphors of clothing was so familiar in the conventional language of Judaism that it could be adapted without any thought of its origin; and the need of "putting-off" the robe of the material body and "putting-on" a new one was a commonplace in Jewish writers. The Christian emphasis on baptism with its inevitable "putting-on" and "putting-off" of garments naturally gave a fresh reality to the language; later the metaphor was carried over into the ritual practice of the Church.

[1] The practice of clothing the neophyte in a special baptismal robe cannot be established as a certainty before the fourth century A.D. (see De Puniet in *Dict. d'Arch. Chrét.* 1. 2. 3118 *seqq.*, where patristic references are given). To the early language of baptism as putting on a new robe given there may be added the *Odes of Solomon* quoted above. For pagan usage cf. Diog. Laert. 8. 33, Herodian, *Vita Gallieni* 8.

[2] Lagrange, *Ét. Rel. sém.* 148. Cumont, *Fouilles de Doura-Europos* 61 *seqq.*

[3] Apuleius, *Metam.* 11. 24. 804.

[4] Cf. the interesting extract from Athanasius, *Vita Antonii* 14, quoted in *Conversion* 278. For such assimilation cf. *Clem. Recog.* 6. 15, where Clement's baptism is followed by *cumque...feriati laeti egissemus*; for such a celebration cf. Apuleius, *Metam.* 11. 24. 806.

[5] Gal. 3. 27 implies either that Paul's Jewish opponents will see nothing objectionable in the language or else that he is so familiar with language of this kind that he uses it without realising the possibility of such objections from those who are less Hellenistic in their outlook than himself.

Thus it was an easy matter for Paul to adopt the language of "putting-on" a new robe to express the change of the soul at death into a state of glory. The change may have been rendered easier by the fact that Hellenistic theology had already conflated this idea of the robe with that of the soul as an element of the divine fire to which it returned at death except in so far as it had achieved immortality.[1] The strict Stoic view had indeed been so far forgotten that the character of the soul as fire could be divorced from the thought of its necessary reabsorption in that element at stated periods, and used as an argument in favour of its inherent immortality.[2] Judaism was ready to adopt any of these conceptions and to conflate them as it thought fit; it could not indeed adopt the belief that the soul became a star or that it was translated to the sun, but it could use language which approximated to such beliefs, and was ultimately derived from them.[3]

Thus up to this point Paul had followed a recognisable convention of the Hellenistic synagogue in his description of the immortality which the soul would enjoy in its future state of radiant glory, and the arguments by which he had supported it were a Christian version of the traditional arguments of Judaism, with the substitution of Jesus as the living Lord, whose life and death were re-enacted in His Apostles, for the Saints of the Old Testament. Naturally (5. 5 *seqq.*) the transformation of the soul into its state of glory was the work of God; its full accomplishment in the future was guaranteed to the Christian by his present possession of a preliminary instalment of the Spirit of God. The possession of that instalment was a fact of Christian experience; the Christian was aware of a deliverance which was the work of the Spirit, and yet was conscious that his present state was only a partial realisation of the full deliverance that awaited him hereafter. But its

[1] *Corp. Herm.* 10. 18 (Scott 198); the soul exchanges its coat of earth for its proper coat of fire; here the conflation of Iranian and Stoic ideas may be later than Paul, but shows the ease with which the conflation suggested itself.

[2] Cf. above, p. 125. For a combination of the immortality of the soul with its nature as fire cf. Cicero, *Tusc. Disp.* 1. 17. 40. In Philo, *De Mut. Nom.* 33 (180, M. 1. 605), διάνοια, in virtue of its inherent nature as fire, can rise to the aether and the sphere of the fixed stars and enter the world of ideas. This is during life, but these ascents to heaven are an anticipation of the fate of the soul or mind at death. The thought is identical with Cicero, *loc. cit.*; both probably go back to Posidonius.

[3] 1 Cor. 15. 40 may in the last resort go back to that belief; cf. Philo, *De Somn.* 1. 22 (137, M. 1. 641), where the number of souls is equal to that of the stars, a belief presumably drawn from Posidonius on the *Timaeus* (41 d); Plato's language could be adapted to astrology, if it was not drawn from it; cf. p. 73, n. 6. In *De Vit. Moys.* 2 (3), 39 (288, M. 2. 179) Moses is changed at death from a duad into a monad and becomes νοῦς ἡλιοειδέστατος, a phrase which suggests the influence of solar religion (cf. p. 31, n. 2).

relevance to Paul's argument at this point lay in the fact that the divine *afflatus* of Hellenistic belief could itself be regarded as "life" and "light"; consequently the Spirit as given to man could be equated with the light of the knowledge of God and with the risen life of Jesus, and again the heavenly dwelling of glory prepared for the soul could be regarded as the transformation of it into "light and life" by the work of the Spirit.[1] Although the ordinary Hellenistic writer would more naturally have described the change as the work of "mind", he would not have found the term "spirit" particularly unusual; the Jewish Hellenist would have regarded it as natural, in view of the conventional equation of the element of "mind" or "spirit" with the prophetic spirit of the Old Testament. The innovation lay not in the language or thought but in the reality which the conception of the Spirit had derived from the burning enthusiasm of the primitive Christian community.

By a further adoption of Hellenistic ideas Paul described the present state of the Christian life as one in which the soul was an exile from its true home in heaven; it was content to wait until it should be restored. It is possible that the language was already little more than a convention of homiletic rhetoric, which had forgotten that the only real reason why the soul was an exile in this life was that it, or the highest part of it, was of divine origin and, although a celestial being, imprisoned in the material world.[2]

There was indeed one essential difference between the Jewish conception, at any rate in its Pauline form, and the Hellenistic. The

[1] Jno. I. 4; Philo, *De Mund. Op.* 8 (30, M. I. 6); *Corp. Herm.* I (*Poimandres*), 17 and 21 (Scott 122 and 126), 13. 9 and 18 (Scott 246 and 252). In the last passage "life and light" in man praise "life and light", i.e. God. Cf. also Philo, *Quod Omn. Prob. Lib.* I (5, M. 2. 446). The terms are drawn from a common stock of Hellenistic religion, which would seem to have drawn "life" from the Semitic thought of life as the specific attribute of the dying and rising god, properly the vegetation-god (Baudissin, *Adonis und Esmun* 403 *seqq.*), and "light" from Zoroastrianism. But Judaism had adopted them long before the close of the O.T. canon. In any case the terms are such as would naturally commend themselves to any religion which looked for personal salvation through knowledge of or union with God, to whom the terms are obviously appropriate.

[2] The thought appears frequently in Philo, normally because the soul or mind of the righteous is an exile from its πατρίς in heaven. Cf. *De Conf. Ling.* 17 (77, M. I. 416); *Q.R.D.H.* 55 (274, M. I. 512). Cf. also *Q.R.D.H.* 16 (82, M. I. 484), where ἀποδημία occurs. But it shows signs of becoming a commonplace in him as in *De Agric.* 14 (65, M. I. 310). The original thought has entirely vanished in Heb. II. 13 *seqq.* In *Corp. Herm.* I (*Poimandres*), 21 (Scott, 126) the power of the soul to enter into life and light depends on its recognition of its nature as light and life, which are also soul and mind, in spite of the fact that "mind" is a divine power coming to the righteous (cf. above, p. 75). The writer of *Poimandres* is as confused as Paul, without the excuse that he has to accommodate himself to a revealed religion.

latter tended to confine immortality in its proper sense to the best and noblest of mankind.[1] Judaism had originally reserved immortality for the saints and heroes of the nation; and the tendency of Jewish writers of the Dispersion to borrow the language of Greek thinkers leaves it obscure whether they believe in the immortality of the soul as such, or only in the immortality of some special souls; their choice of language is dictated by the source which they happen to follow.[2] Paul left no such uncertainty. He was ready to abandon the apocalyptic tradition in favour of the ascent of the soul or spirit of man to the firmament which was the abode of God, and its transmutation into a radiant state of glory by the work of the Spirit; he was not prepared to abandon the eternal responsibility of man for his deeds. His discussion of the destiny of the soul of man ended with the statement that all must stand before the judgment seat of Christ (5. 10), a phrase borrowed from the traditional picture of the final judgment of mankind. This judgment, as in the book of Wisdom, retained a formal position in the scheme of things, though it had ceased to possess any real significance when the thought of the gradual transformation of the soul from the material to the spiritual during life, and the completion of the process at death, had been substituted for the final assize at the end of the world-process. Paul was at one with Judaism and the first generation of Christian writers in being indifferent to consistency in regard to matters as uncertain as the details of the life of the world to come.[3] He had succeeded in meeting the objection of the Corinthians to the Jewish scheme of eschatology by substituting for the final judgment of all men the transformation of the soul or spirit of man into a state of radiant glory beginning in this life but awaiting its completion in

[1] Cf. pp. 73 *seqq.* In *Corp. Herm.* 1 (*Poimandres*), 19 (Scott 124) the soul forfeits immortality by refusing knowledge.

[2] Meyer, *Urspr. u. Anf.* 2. 302; the language of Philo, *Quod Omn. Prob. Lib.* 18 (117, M. 2. 463); *Leg. ad Gaium* 16 (117, M. 2. 562) may imply a belief that martyrdom secures immortality. The book of Wisdom preserves a general judgment in 3. 7, which probably represents the writer's real view; 1. 12 *seqq.*, 2. 24, 4. 15 *seqq.* leave it hard to say whether he believes in anything but the immortality of the righteous. Philo treats the soul as immortal in the passages quoted p. 140, n. 2: in *De Mund. Op.* 46 (135, M. 1. 32) man, in virtue of the divine element in him, is capable of immortality. In *De Mut. Nom.* 38 (210, M. 1. 610) the prayer of Deut. 33. 6 that Reuben may live cannot be a prayer for his incorruption and immortality, for this is impossible for man. But the allusions to Moses (above, pp. 137, n. 3 and 139, n. 2) make it clear that he believes in the immortality of some peculiarly righteous souls, and probably includes all pious Israelites. He incorporates others so freely that it is hard to say more; in *De Somn.* 1. 23 (151, M. 1. 643) he retains Hades for the wicked and Olympian and heavenly rewards for the righteous, but this is a description of their present life.

[3] Cf. the inconsistency of Jno. 5. 28 with the general scheme of the fourth Gospel (e.g. 3. 16 *seqq.*).

heaven.[1] Henceforward apocalyptic was to be relegated, so far as Pauline Christianity was concerned, to an entirely secondary position; it was only the Jewish tradition that preserved it as an element of Christianity which found its way into the Creeds.[2]

The nature of the passage raises an interesting probability. Paul was writing to conciliate Hellenistic Christians who rejected the idea of a bodily resurrection at the second coming, and his method was to substitute the immortality of the soul, with the second coming left as a possibility, suggested though not necessarily implied by his reference to the judgment-seat of Christ. Yet he was writing with Jewish opponents in view who would be swift to seize on any opening for accusing him of unorthodoxy. His argument seems to reflect a Jewish justification of the resurrection of the dead or the immortality of the soul, beliefs which from the Jewish point of view did not need to be distinguished. If the martyr, who in the earthen vessel of his body was afflicted for the sake of the Torah, the lamp and treasure of Israel, was by his sufferings a testimony to all the nation, to save it no less than himself,[3] how could any Israelite refuse to share in the light affliction, which brought so great a weight of glory? And if the martyr were so transformed, it must follow that the same transformation awaited all righteous Israelites, while on the other hand there would be a fearful judgment on the sinners of Israel and the Gentiles. Such a scheme, whether in the form of homiletic tradition or a written document, seems to be the foundation of Paul's argument from the sufferings of the Apostles to the immortality of the soul and his abrupt transition from one to the other; the substitution of the risen life of Jesus for the Torah as the centre of the scheme is of course his

[1] The beginning of the transformation during the earthly life in 2 Cor. 4. 16 is a striking instance of Paul's method of adapting current ideas to his purpose. We have (*a*) the "mind" as the inner man, (*b*) the thought of true life as being death to the present world and life to a better one (going back to Plato and Heraclitus) and (*c*) the thought of the martyr as being "transformed into immortality". In Paul the true "inner man" in virtue of his affinity to Jesus gradually "dies" to this world and in doing so re-enacts the death of Jesus. Through this process of dying he is renewed daily. The association of the labours of the Apostle with the death of Jesus on the Cross has given an entirely new life to the commonplaces of philosophy and the rather stilted glorification of the martyr. Paul is not likely to have read 4 Maccabees, and is probably drawing on traditional material; see next page, n. 2.

[2] The second coming survives in Phil. 1. 6 and 10, and 2. 16; cf. 4. 5. But Philippians represents the older Pauline point of view. 1. 23 represents the later development. In Col. 3. 4 we have a formal appearance of Christ with His Saints, but the whole emphasis is on the new life, which is of immortal quality and a present fact. Phil. 3. 20 combines the two views in a manner which shows how little Paul is concerned to be consistent in such matters.

[3] Cf. pp. 135 *seqq.* Cf. Prov. 6. 23, 8. 19, *Mekilta*, Tr. *Beshallah* 1. 65 (ed. Lauterbach, 1. 174).

own, as is the enthusiasm which distinguishes his writings from the stilted pedantry of most Jewish excursions into Hellenistic ideas.[1] It may also explain the large number of words and phrases which occur in this section and nowhere else in Pauline literature.[2] It seems probable that Paul was employing a traditional argument, which would be recognised as entirely orthodox from the point of view of rabbinical learning, in which he had a solid advantage over his Jewish-Christian opponents.

From his excursion into Hellenistic eschatology Paul returned to defend himself (5. 11 *seqq.*). He was concerned with the judgment of God, but he trusted that he had cleared himself in the judgment of his readers. His object was not to commend himself, but to give the Corinthians a chance of boasting that in their Apostle they had one who was of a higher authority than those who relied on external qualifications. He had been described as mad, but he was only mad in his enthusiasm for the service of God; in his dealings with the Corinthians he had acted with absolute sanity. In all his actions he was constrained by the love of Christ. Since He had died for all, all had shared in His death; and He had died for all in order that all might live not for themselves but for Him who had died and risen for them. In consequence of this the ordinary standards of human qualifications had ceased to be of importance; even personal acquaintance with the Lord in His human life (5. 16) had ceased to be of decisive value.[3] All that mattered was to be in Christ, and so to be a new creation in that new age, in which the old had come to an end and all things were made new. This was a bold statement of the doctrine of the "new age" inaugurated by Jesus; the importance of it at this point lay in

[1] Wisd. 1–11. 4 is an honourable exception.

[2] The argument from *ἅπαξ λεγόμενα* is hazardous as a test of authenticity, but less so as a test of the possibility of the use of sources. In this section the phrase "weight of glory" must be drawn from a Hebrew original, even if the original be found in Paul's own Hebrew thought. The words *πρόσκαιρα*, *οἰκητήριον*, *σκῆνος*, *ἐνδημεῖν* and *ἐκδημεῖν* appear only here in Paul. The same applies to the double compound *ἐπενδύσασθαι*, but this cannot be pressed. Of the words which can be pressed, the first is only found in 4 Maccabees; *σκῆνος* once in Wisdom; *ἐνδημεῖν* and *ἐκδημεῖν* do not appear in the LXX. They thus do not belong to the Greek translation of the Hebrew Bible with which Paul would naturally be familiar. Nor is it easy to parallel Paul's reference to Ps. 116. 10 in 4. 13, where the reference is to the whole of the rest of the Psalm, the reader being left to complete the passage for himself in accordance with common rabbinical usage. It seems probable that we have here a rabbinical exposition of immortality current in Hellenistic circles before the time of Paul's mission to the Gentiles.

[3] It is clear from 11. 22 and 12. 1 that Paul could not claim to have "seen the Lord", except in visions. His claim to be an Apostle on the strength of having seen the Lord in 1 Cor. 9. 1 does not distinguish between "seeing the Lord" in the flesh and in visions; it would seem that his opponents had fixed on the language of the last passage to discredit his authority.

the charge of innovation brought against Paul by his opponents, not without a considerable measure of justice; Paul defended his innovations by an appeal to that teaching as to the "new age" which had proved attractive to some of the Corinthians.[1] Yet Paul was prepared to justify his doctrine by an appeal to approved rabbinical methods, If orthodox Jewish teachers held that God could be reconciled to man by the sacrifices of the old covenant, it was obviously far truer to hold that He had reconciled man to Himself through Christ, and that Paul's preaching was the announcement of this reconciliation. That reconciliation could be summed up by saying that God was in Christ as the divine Wisdom in whom God dwelt, and whom He filled, reconciling the world to Himself by a free act of forgiveness, the announcement of which He had entrusted to the Apostle. So Paul as Christ's ambassador, through whom God appealed to man, called on them to accept the offer of reconciliation. It was not the Day of Atonement, recently past,[2] which brought the forgiveness that amounted to a new creation or the beginning of the new age.[3] The scapegoat could not bear away the sins which were transferred to it, while it remained innocent itself.[4] The true bearing of sin was to be found in Christ, whom God had made to be sin, in order that those who accepted reconciliation to God through Him might be raised to the righteousness of God through the atonement effected by the death

[1] Cf. above, p. 126.

[2] "The fast" of the Day of Atonement marked the end of the safe season for sailing (Acts 27. 9; cf. Ramsay in Hastings' *D.B.*, Art. "Roads and Travel in N.T.", extra vol. p. 376). Paul left Troas when he failed to find Titus there, and travelled overland to meet him (2 Cor. 2. 13). This means that Titus was too late to reach Troas by sea, and would necessarily travel overland, and that Paul on the other hand could not risk sailing to Athens to meet him. Paul must have left Troas, in spite of the "open door", when he realised that Titus had missed the last boat and would have to come through Macedonia. Presumably this letter was written soon after.

[3] *Judaism* 1. 533; cf. Str.-B. on Jno. 3. 3; for forgiveness as a "new creation" cf. also on 2 Cor. 5. 17. The Day of Atonement (Tishri 10) fell soon after the New Year for the starting of the Jubilees and for the judgment of mankind (Mishnah, *Rosh-ha-Shanah* 1. 1, Danby 188). It seems that there is some evidence that the New Year had at one time begun with the Day of Atonement, not with Tishri 1 (Driver and White in Hastings' *D.B.*, Art. "Atonement, Day of", 1. 199). It was held by some that Tishri 10 was the day of Creation (*Judaism* 2. 64; cf. the quotation from the Liturgy to that effect). Philo has little to say of the Day of Atonement and makes creation begin with the vernal equinox and the Passover (cf. above, p. 30). Paul, having been educated at Jerusalem, would attach more importance to the Day of Atonement than Philo, since the solemnities of the day were primarily concerned with the Temple. Naturally Christianity was more concerned to read its teaching into the cult of Judaism during this period when the breach between the two was not complete. For the call of Abraham as a "new creation" cf. *Gen. R.* 39. 11.

[4] *Judaism* 1. 464 and 498; cf. Heb. 9. 7 and Orig. *In Ev. Jo.* 28. 14, where this passage is explained as meaning that Jesus became the *περικάθαρμα* of the world, though Origen does not notice the scapegoat typology.

of Jesus. As the herald of such a message Paul was content to bear anything that might befall him. The misrepresentations of his opponents were merely one of the incidental sufferings that must be expected by those who were privileged to be the ambassadors of Jesus.

The remainder of the Epistle was devoted to Paul's personal relations to his converts and to the preparations for the collection for the Saints. He had asserted his claim to interpret the Gospel as a new revelation from God to man, which could not be confined to the beliefs and outlook of the primitive communities of Palestine. Paul himself was far too good a Jew and too thoroughly trained in the highest ethics of Judaism to realise the perils that might arise from his repudiation of a knowledge of Christ after the flesh as a decisive factor in the teaching of the Gospel.

CHAPTER VII

HERESY AND ORTHODOXY

IN the Roman and Corinthian Epistles Paul had been perfectly content with expositions of doctrine of a homiletic type. Judaism had never felt the need of drawing up a dogmatic statement of its beliefs, which were sufficiently safeguarded by the Torah and the cultus and liturgy of Judaism. Anything that glorified the one true God and expressed the supreme authority of His one revelation of Himself was to be welcomed. Hellenistic Judaism had been entirely ready to adopt any philosophical speculation that might serve this end; Paul had been quite ready to follow the general practice.

But orthodox Judaism could only maintain its orthodoxy by an observance of the Torah which constituted a barrier against close social intercourse with the surrounding world. There was always a temptation to abandon its literal sense in favour of a "spiritual" observance which would impose no restraint on social conduct and would deliver the pious Jew from the necessity of believing the more improbable stories of the Old Testament.[1] The wealthy and influential Jew was tempted to accept so much of the external practice of the cultus of the Emperor as might be regarded as no more than an external expression of loyalty, to which no serious religious importance could be attached. In Phrygia such lapses from strict orthodoxy are known from the inscriptions; the Jews of these regions were largely descended from colonists established in the cities of Asia early in the Seleucid era before the reforms of Ezra had taken full effect.[2] In this region the wife of a ruler of the synagogue appears as a High Priestess of the imperial cult and as ἀγωνοθέτις, an office scarcely compatible with a strictly Jewish attitude to idolatry; it is possible that other members of this Jewish family held equally ambiguous positions.[3] The Talmud records the fact that the luxuries of Phrygia separated the Jews of that region from their brethren,[4] a statement which suggests rather a worldly wisdom, avoiding too much stiffness in refusing to

[1] Cf. above, p. 62.

[2] For the Seleucid colonies in Asia cf. Schürer, *G.J.V.* 3. 12 *seqq.*

[3] Julia Severa, wife of G. Tyrrhonius Cladus; see Ramsay, *Cities and Bishoprics of Phrygia*, Inscrr. 550, 559 and pp. 674 *seqq.* Some of Ramsay's identifications are distinctly temerarious. For Gentile games as idolatrous cf. Mishnah, *Abodah Zarah* I. 7 (Danby 438), and I Macc. I. 14.

[4] Neubauer, *Géogr. du Talmud* 315.

share the public life of the Gentiles, than a serious adoption of heathen religion. Elsewhere we find a considerable resemblance between Jewish and Gentile practice in regard to the manumission of slaves, a fictitious gift to the synagogue taking the place of a gift to the Temple; in one case we have a suspicious mixture of language, but it is uncertain whether we have Jewish adoption of a heathen cult or a heathen approximation to Jewish language, which may be due to chance or to the influence of the language of the Greek Bible on loosely attached adherents of the synagogue.[1] Yet again we find pictorial representations on Jewish monuments, which show that Judaism of the first century A.D. was not entirely dominated by the rabbinical tradition; but the full ascendancy of that tradition was not established until after the end of that century, and the Mishnah is silent as to the extent to which pictorial representations are permissible; in no case do the pictures appear to show more than a willingness to adopt conventional *motifs* from pagan art; we do not find the God of Israel represented in a pictorial form, nor does He appear to be in any way identified or amalgamated with any of the deities of the Hellenistic pantheon.[2]

On the other hand there was, as has been noticed, a tendency to

[1] The evidence here is derived from the inscriptions of the Bosporus (texts in *The Beginnings of Christianity* 5. 90 *seqq.*). Two allude to the synagogue of the Jews but show no trace of syncretism. The third begins with a dedication to *θεῷ ὑψίστῳ παντοκράτορι* and ends with a reference to Zeus, Earth and Sun; the fourth opens in the same way but has no mention of heathen deities: the end of the text however is missing; the fifth and sixth reveal a body of *εἰσποιητοὶ ἀδελφοί* who reverence the most High God, with no heathen features. Thus only the third reveals any syncretism; and this only if *θεῷ ὑψίστῳ παντοκράτορι* is necessarily Jewish. There is ample evidence that the title of *ὕψιστος* is not necessarily Jewish (Roberts, Skeat and Nock, "The Gild of Zeus Hypsistos", *Harvard Theol. Rev.* 29. 1. 39 *seqq.* (Jan. 1936)). *παντοκράτωρ* appears to be uncommon in texts which are not under Jewish influence, while *εὐλογητός* "has no chance of being Greek" (*ib.* 65). It must, however, be noted that we have an inscription of Palmyra about A.D. 150 containing the words לבריך שמא, which is not Jewish (*Rép. d'Épigr. Sém.* 4. 2143, and cf. Cook, *Rel. Anc. Pal.* 216). Judaism was not the only Semitic religion which was affecting the Hellenistic world. A further influence was that of magic, with its fondness for phrases from the LXX, as in *Papp. Mag. Gr.* 4. 967 (*παντοκράτωρ*), 998 (*εὐλογητός*). Jewish language need not imply the presence of Jewish religion. It is indeed possible that here we have an isolated community of a syncretistic type; but it must be noted that we have only one clear case of syncretism, and this only if the assumption that *παντοκράτωρ* and *εὐλογητός* are Jewish is correct. Professor Nock in a private letter suggests that in any case the form of manumission need mean no more than D.M. in Jewish epitaphs.

[2] Cook, *Rel. Anc. Pal.* 210 *seqq.*; Mishnah, *Abodah Zarah* 4. 5 (Danby 442); cf. Elmslie's note *ad loc.* (*Texts and Studies* 8. 2), and the excursus, p. 74. The opposition at Jerusalem described by Josephus appears to represent a determination to suspect idolatry in an unpopular ruler rather than an entire abhorrence of sculptured figures as such (*Antt.* 17. 6. 2 (151); *B.J.* 1. 33. 2 (650) for Herod's eagle, where the fact that it was on the Temple may have been the real gravamen; *Antt.* 18. 3. 1 (55); *B.J.* 2. 9. 2 (169) for the Roman standards).

adapt Judaism to the speculations by means of which popular theology sought to accommodate a theoretical monotheism with the conventional pantheon of Hellenistic religion. The one God in the firmament remained the supreme source and centre of divinity, but His reason was diffused through the various elements of the cosmos; in particular it was manifested in the movements of the celestial bodies. It was easy for Judaism to adapt itself to this outlook by seeing in the divine Wisdom, or in the "powers" of God, the activity of the one God in the realm of matter. The procedure avoided the awkward anthropomorphisms of the Old Testament, and brought Judaism into line with popular thought.[1] These activities might again be ascribed to the angels, who could again be identified with the heavenly bodies or alternatively represented as a hierarchy of good, opposed to the planets as a hierarchy of evil; the result was something dangerously near to the popular theology of the age, and the tendency to syncretism in this direction has left its traces on the artistic monuments, in which Judaism makes use of types closely resembling those of the pagan world.[2]

In another direction already noticed Judaism was in contact with Gentile religion. The claim that the God of Israel was above all gods was one which no practitioner of magic could afford to ignore; it was possible that the claim might be true. Jewish Gnosticism, of the kind outlined above, would seem to have declined into magic, though it is difficult to be certain of the extent to which it had declined in this way at the period of the Pauline missions. But the boundary between religion and magic is never easy to fix; in particular astrology stood in an ambiguous position on the borders of religion, magic and science. Paul himself had been in contact with the Ephesian practitioners of the art, who were presumably drawn from the synagogue, but had left it in favour of Christianity as a more potent system of magic, whose efficacy was vindicated by its results.[3]

[1] Cf. pp. 44 *seqq*.

[2] Cf. the Jewish coffin with pictures of the infant Bacchus and the four seasons (i.e. the deified aeon), found at Shiloh and dating from the Antonine age, described by Reitzenstein, *Hell. Myst. Rel.* 147, cf. plates I and II.

[3] Acts 19. 11–20, where St Luke's source seems to have associated Paul's remarkable cures with the interest of the magical world. It is unfortunate that he is here following a secondary and inferior source and that the text of 14 is in considerable confusion. For the whole passage cf. notes in *The Beginnings of Christianity* 4. 239 *seqq*., especially Burkitt's explanation of Sceva as a "rascally Levantine" who knew that "the High Priest of the Jews alone knew the name of God". Even the 50,000 drachmae, however exaggerated, are in some touch with reality (as are the figures of 2. 41 and 4. 4 as compared with the fantastic figures usually given by Josephus). Cf. p. 43.

The synagogues of Phrygia,[1] with a tendency to laxity in other directions, would be particularly disposed to come into contact with the types of speculation which were coming into vogue in the Hellenistic world and were beginning to have a certain influence on orthodox Judaism. Where Judaism was already unorthodox it would naturally be disposed to admit such speculations to a degree which the stricter synagogues would at once reject. We have no account of the mission of Epaphras to Colossae; but it appears that after the lapse of some years from Paul's mission to Ephesus, apparently after his arrival in Rome,[2] Colossae was the scene of an attempt to fit the Gospel into the fashionable scheme of Hellenistic religion, as interpreted by circles which had a definitely Jewish character.

From the point of view of the exponents of this scheme Paul was perfectly right in proclaiming Jesus as a being of the cosmic order who had brought to mankind "the remission of sins". The desire for liberation from sin and initiation into the mysteries of the divine nature as the means of obtaining it were conceptions which would appear natural and normal in such circles.[3] Baptism was obviously a suitable form of lustration for the laying aside of the sins of the past.[4] But the convert must not be content to stop short at conversion; there were higher mysteries to attain and higher realms to conquer. Baptism was merely a first step; from it he must go forward "increasing and bearing fruit".[5] Full redemption could not be a mere forgive-

[1] Phrygia was a peculiarly favourable soil for enthusiastic religions (*Rel. Or.* 47; Rohde, *Psyche* 257), but there is no evidence that the Church at Colossae was particularly addicted to such outbursts. The speculations which Paul condemns are common property of the age.

[2] Col. 4. 10 implies a reconciliation with Mark, which can hardly have taken place except at Rome. Cf. below, p. 178.

[3] Cf. *Corp. Herm.* I (*Poimandres*), 27 *seqq.*, 7. I *seqq.*; see *Conversion* 179 *seqq.*

[4] Cf. *Rel. Or.* 35, and for "cleansing" in Philo see above, p. 30. The conception of such a cleansing as a "new birth" or regeneration appears in Judaism (cf. Köhler, *Jewish Encyclopedia*, Art. "Birth, The New"), but there is no evidence that it was current in the N.T. period; Jno. 3. 3 suggests that it made its way from Hellenistic religion into Christianity before it gained a similar acceptance in Judaism to meet the same need of accommodation to popular views.

[5] The phrase *καρποφορεῖν* (-*εῖσθαι*) *καὶ αὐξάνεσθαι* appears in Col. 1. 6 and 10 and nowhere else in Paul. In 1. 6 it is brought in very awkwardly (note the repeated *καθώς*), apparently to show that the true "bearing of fruit" is to be seen in the extensive increase of the Gospel in the world as well as its intensive increase within the individual character. But the phrase is a regular Gnostic catchword; advance in knowledge appears as a "bearing of fruit" in Ir. *Haer.* 1. 1. 3, 4. 4, 18. 1, 21. 5; cf. 13. 7 for a parody of Gnostic usage by Irenaeus. The phrase may be derived from the parable of the sower (Mk. 4. 8 and parallels). But it does not follow that the phrase was so derived from Paul; it would seem that his opponents either invented the phrase or borrowed it from the parable, and used it for their purpose. It is interesting that Luke modifies the parable by making all the seed on good ground bear a hundredfold, not "some thirty, some sixty and some a hundredfold", and omits *αὐξανόμενα*

ness which left man free from sin, but otherwise where he was before;[1] it must be a gradual attainment to perfection which was only possible for those who had achieved the full knowledge of God.

This knowledge, however, was not as in the tradition of classical philosophy a knowledge of the nature of God, the divine origin of the soul, the true nature and end of man and the distinction of virtue and vice. It dealt with the method by which the nature of the one invisible God had expanded itself by "increasing and bearing fruit" in the creation of a spiritual realm of being, some part of which had been subordinated by the sin of man to the planets who ruled the material world. A man must understand these mysteries and the hierarchy of powers which ruled the destinies of the world, and the means by which he must liberate himself from their authority, if he was to achieve full redemption and ascend to his true home in the firmament of heaven. The orders of angels and archangels, with which Judaism was familiar, were pressed into service in order to provide assistants for the deliverance of man; the rebel angels were identified with the celestial rulers of the conventional scheme of astrology in accordance with the current Jewish view.[2] But instead of being confined to their orthodox rôle of obedient ministers of God or rebels doomed to eternal punishment in a cosmos divided according to the simple Pauline antithesis of the realm of light, where Jesus was King, and the realm of darkness opposed to Him,[3] they became the more or less independent rulers of

(8. 8 and 15); note that they bear fruit "in patience", cf. Col. 1. 11. The parable is used in a Gnostic sense by the Naassenes, Hipp. *El.* 5. 8 (114). Luke has also modified the parable of the five, three and one talents into one of ten pounds. (For the identity of the parable of the pounds in Lk. 19. 12 *seqq.* with the talents of Mt. 25. 14 *seqq.* cf. Creed, *The Gospel according to St Luke*, *ad loc.*) He thus avoids countenancing the three types of mankind of Gnosticism in both parables.

[1] Col. 1. 14. From 1. 9 and 10 it seems that ἐπίγνωσις was the catchword of Paul's opponents as against Gnosis; the term appears to be drawn from popular philosophy, cf. *Voc. Gr. N.T.* s.v. For the conception of redemption implied cf. below, p. 158.

[2] For "thrones, lordships, rules and dominations" as titles of Jewish angels cf. Str.-B. on Eph. 1. 21; for angelic rulers of the nations cf. p. 100. It is of course possible that the words are due to Paul himself (cf. "rules" in an astrological setting in Rom. 8. 38). In Philo the planets appear as "rulers", e.g. *De Spec. Legg.* 1 (*De Mon.*), 1 (13, M. 2. 213). For similar terms in an astrological sense in post-Christian Gnosticism cf. Behm in *T.W.z.N.T.* 2. 569. Here, however, we are dealing with language coloured by the N.T.

[3] The antithesis of Col. 1. 12–14 suggests Iranian influences, but the contrast goes back to the O.T. (cf. above, p. 134). It is a commonplace in Philo, e.g. *De Mund. Op.* 9 (33, M. 1. 7), where the retreat of the rival darkness before the newly created νοητὸν φῶς is striking, and may be due to contact with Zoroastrianism. In the tract *De Spec. Legg.* 4 (*De Just.*), 4 (166, M. 2. 363), 7 (187, M. 2. 367) and 14 (231, M. 2. 373) we have a standing equation of light with the virtue of equality as manifested in the cosmos and of darkness with inequality; thus light represents order, darkness chaos; in the last passage we have an allusion to a "source of

the higher regions of the heavens. Jesus was apparently a messenger sent from God, with a considerable measure of authority; it would be natural in this type of theology to suppose that He could deliver men from the sphere of the lower air and Satan and raise them to the moon where eternity begins;[1] but beyond that there were realms which could only be passed by those who had access to knowledge which He had not revealed, and powers which mere initiation into Him in the Church could not convey. He might well be the Messiah of Judaism, and possibly the "spirit" of God which had been manifested in Adam and had appeared to the patriarchs.[2] Paul's own distinction between "psychic" and "spiritual" Christians recognised the actual inequality of spiritual attainments among Christians, which was too patent to be ignored, while his theology, presupposing as it did a sudden conversion, which carried with it righteousness, provided no real explanation of the possibility of spiritual progress or the means of making it. His opponents in maintaining that there were higher stages to be achieved could trade on a real weakness in Pauline theology. It appears from Paul's reply that his opponents did not regard Jesus as a mere prophet of the human order,[3] nor do they seem to have claimed to be His equals after the manner of several of the earlier heresiarchs.[4] On the other hand they do not appear to have allowed to Jesus that prominence in the scheme of redemption by which the Gnostics from the time of Cerinthus and Satornilus endeavoured to preserve, at least in theory, the position held by Jesus in the teaching of the Church.[5] It seems that they allowed Him an important position in the

darkness" as opposed to the νοητὸς ἥλιος. Possibly here we have Iranian influences; but they may have come through the Jewish devil. They have been attached to a panegyric on equality from a "Pythagorean" source (cf. p. 39). In *De Somn.* 1. 13 (75, M. 1. 632) God Himself is light or rather older than light and superior to it, as its source. This may reflect Iranian influences. (Dodd, *The First Epistle of John and the Fourth Gospel*, Bulletin of John Rylands Library, 21. 1. 23 (April 1937), derives it from current Hellenistic thought as an amalgam of Platonism and Zoroastrianism. But it must be remembered that light as a symbol of all goodness is natural and would never have excited suspicion in Philo if it had not been for the use made of the conception by Valentinus and Mani.)

[1] So Heracleon *ap.* Orig. *In Ev. Jo.* 2. 8 limits His creation to the material.

[2] For this Ebionite view cf. Epiph. *Panar.* 30. 3. The Peratae (Hipp. *El.* 5. 16. 131), whose O.T. symbolism suggests a system of some antiquity, place both the God of salvation and the gods of destruction outside the realm of becoming; the system implied in Colossians might have regarded Jesus as delivering from the material, but leaving other gods of destruction to be faced.

[3] The Ebionites in Ir. *Haer.* 1. 26. 2 make Him a mere man; cf. Epiph. *Panar.* 30. 14 and 18.

[4] Simon Magus (Ir. *Haer.* 1. 23. 1) and Menander (*ib.* 5) did so, as did Dositheus according to Origen, who however appears to confuse Dositheus and Simon (see *c. Cels.* 1. 57 and 6. 11).

[5] Ir. *Haer.* 1. 24. 2, 26. 1.

scheme of redemption, but held that there were higher stages to be attained in the knowledge of the one true God.

Nor were Paul's opponents without an impressive argument. Obviously Jesus had in fact been unable to deliver Himself from the power of the planets to determine His fate, and He was equally unable to deliver His messengers. Paul's persecutions were proof that he had no power to overcome the hostility of the lords of the heavenly spheres; it would seem that both he and Jesus only offered a partial and preliminary salvation, which must be completed by a knowledge of those higher forms which a more fully developed system was in a position to offer. Those who knew only the forms of deliverance revealed by Jesus and taught by Paul would continue to be liable to the persecutions which they had suffered.[1]

The methods by which this salvation was to be attained were part of the common stock of the religion of the time. There were mysteries, in which secret wisdom was revealed, and philosophy to expound the esoteric meaning of external rites.[2] Through these the adept learnt to control the "elements" which rule the world and attain to the utmost "fullness" of which he was capable; baptism was a beginning, but other measures of "fulfilment" or completion were needed.[3] Possibly it was urged that baptism was no better than circumcision; both availed for a preliminary putting off of the body and the planets which

[1] The Crucifixion was more easily explained on these lines than on those of 1 Cor. 2. 8 and Col. 2. 14, even when the conception was reinforced by the thought of a reconciliation through blood, drawn from Jewish sacrificial ideas (Col. 1. 20, cf. above, p. 144). The language of Colossians is not primarily an assertion of the reality of the death of Jesus on the Cross, but an attempt to explain why a being of so high an order as Jesus could and must suffer death. The normal Hellenistic view was docetic: He did not really suffer (Ir. *Haer.* 1. 24. 4 (Basilides), 26. 1 (Cerinthus); cf. *Acts of John* 98 (*Apocr. N.T.* 254); Clem. Alex. *Exc. ex Theod.* 1. 2 (ed. Casey 5 and see Casey's note *ad loc.*) and 62. 2 (Casey 584)). (In this passage the prophecy "a bone of him shall not be broken" (Exod. 12. 46) as applied to the soul of Jesus implies that the writer knows enough Hebrew to regard עצם as meaning either "bone" or "self". It is interesting to find this knowledge of Hebrew in the Gnostic tradition.) Col. 1. 24 carries on the thought. Paul's sufferings have been treated, like those of Jesus, as a proof of his inferiority. Normally divine protection should deliver the adept from persecution; cf. *Papp. Mag. Gr.* 1. 197 *seqq.*, 4. 2163 *seqq.*, 13. 289 (the "Eighth Book of Moses"; the prayer is addressed to Christ, as creator of necessity, for deliverance from prison). For Gnostic views cf. Ir. *Haer.* 1. 13. 6 (Mărcus), 24. 6 (Basilides; cf. Clem. Alex. *Strom.* 4. 12. 81 (599 P) for his view that a Christian could only suffer persecution for past sins), 25. 2 (Carpocrates). 23. 3 and 5 may imply that Simon and Menander held similar views. Cf. the escape of Apollonius of Tyana from Domitian (*Vit.* 8. 8 *seqq.*; cf. 8. 3 for the prohibition of "books" and amulets in trials before the Emperor), and the heathen question "Where is their God?" in the Letter of the Churches of *Vienne and Lyons* 60 (Eus. *H.E.* 5. 1 (210)). Porphyry *ap.* Eus. *Pr. Ev.* 3. 4. 3 describes popular religion as a search for deliverers from fate; cf. Celsus *ap.* Orig. *c. Cels.* 1. 66.

[2] Col. 2. 3 and 8, and see below, p. 170.

[3] Col. 2. 10.

ruled it, but neither could do more.[1] A system based on or similar to the practice of Judaism was advocated as the preliminary means of delivering man from the power of the planets;[2] in particular fasts were advocated as a means of preparation for initiations, which were to be accompanied by visible revelations of the higher orders of cosmic powers which completed the work of redemption begun by Jesus. It is probably safe to assume that abstinence from sexual intercourse was also required; Paul does not allude to it specifically, but such abstinence was a normal preparation in the Gentile world for initiations, revelations and the successful performance of magical rites; since it was also a normal accompaniment of Jewish fasts, it would naturally suggest itself to the exponents of such a system.[3] Fasting was represented not simply as a means for subduing the power of the flesh over the spirit,[4] a view which Paul was prepared to recognise as possessing at any rate a measure of justification. It was intended as a preparation for

[1] The reference to circumcision, Col. 2. 11, appears to be forced on Paul, yet he is not concerned to argue that it is not "necessary to salvation". It is possible that his opponents had already abandoned it, and retained only the proselyte's bath. For circumcision as the cleansing of the soul in traditional Jewish exegesis cf. Philo, *De Somn.* 2. 4 (25, M. 1. 662)—one of Philo's rare allusions to the subject.

[2] Col. 2. 16 and 20 *seqq.* Jewish practice naturally had many parallels in Gentile religion; cf. those recorded by Alexander Polyhistor *ap.* Diog. Laert. 8. 33, which may show Orphic influence; if Orphic sects were influential at the period, they may have affected Paul's opponents. For Orphic practice cf. *Orpheus* 196. For the resemblance of Pythagoras and Moses cf. Clem. Alex. *Strom.* 2. 18. 92 (477 P). For fasts of idolaters and Magi who serve demons cf. *ib.* 3. 6. 48 (533 P). For Gnostic practice cf. Ir. *Haer.* 1. 24. 2; see also *Corp. Herm.* Ascl. 3. 41b (Scott 376); Porphyry *ap.* Eus. *Pr. Ev.* 5. 10. 1. If the reading θέλων ἐν ταπεινοφροσύνῃ in Col. 2. 18 and the translation "take pleasure in condemning you in respect of fasting" be correct (so Dibelius in *H.H.z.N.T. ad loc.*), we have a reference to fasting in preparation for visions. For this sense of the word cf. Hermas, *Vis.* 3. 10. 6; *Sim.* 5. 3. 7. The word is a literal translation of the Hebrew *Ta'anith*; Paul normally prefers νηστεία (2 Cor. 6. 5 and 11. 27). It is likely that Paul borrowed the word from the vocabulary of his opponents, who would naturally emphasise the spiritual significance of the practice. Cf. Philo, *De Post. Cain.* 13 (48, M. 1. 234), with reference to the account of the Day of Atonement in Lev. 23. 27, where the fast is a "humbling of your souls" (cf. Is. 58. 3). For Jewish fasting in preparation for visions cf. Dan. 10. 3; 2 Bar. 5. 7; 4 Esdr. 5. 13. For Hellenistic usage cf. Plut. *De Gen. Socr.* 20, 588d; Philostr. *Vit. Apoll. Tyan.* 2. 37; *Conversion* 108 and Reitzenstein, *Hell. Myst. Rel.* 131; Apul. *Metam.* 11. 23. 803. According to Orig. *c. Cels.* 3. 36 inquirers in Egyptian temples were liable to be examined on their observance of the prescribed rules of abstinence, etc.

[3] For continence as a preparation for initiation cf. *Conversion* 72 (Dionysus), Plut. *De Is. et Os.* 2. 351f, and the magical papyri, *passim*; in 13. 5 (the Eighth Book of Moses) a period of forty-one days is demanded. For an ethical interpretation of the requirement in Roman religion, cf. Cicero, *De Legg.* 2. 10. 24; for Jewish fasts as involving continence, Mishnah, *Ta'anith* 1. 6, *Yoma* 8. 1 (Danby 195 and 171).

[4] *De Spec. Legg.* 4 (*De Conc.*), 4 (101, M. 2. 352); Nock, "Vision of Mandulis-Aion", *Harvard Theol. Rev.* 27. 1. 63 and 73; Clem. Alex. *Exc. ex Theod.* 73. 1 (Casey 640) ascribes the power of the adversaries to the body, as is inevitable in Gnosticism.

the visions which were part of the system; fasting as a preparation for visions could claim venerable Jewish authority and was a prominent feature in the literature of apocalyptic Judaism, no less than in the general tradition of Hellenistic religion. In such visions the neophyte was privileged to behold the angels who were to conduct him through the spheres of the rulers, and was initiated into full union with God or assured of such union in the life to come.[1] There is no evidence to show whether the "angels" were regarded as angels in the conventional Jewish sense or as the "powers" or names of God in which His activity in the cosmos was manifested; either system would formally preserve its continuity with Jewish monotheism.[2]

An account of this teaching reached Paul from his friends at Colossae, and this report, whether written or oral, underlies Paul's letter in reply, and explains its apparent lack of order. We may reconstruct it thus: "They tell us that we must learn to grow in 'wisdom and knowledge', thus 'increasing and bearing fruit'. Only so shall we gain the power and strength we need to attain to our full portion in the light. In Jesus we have forgiveness, but not full redemption, which is reserved for those who know how to triumph over the rulers of the higher spheres of the cosmos; Jesus was inferior to them, as is shown by the fact that they were able to cause Him to be crucified and are able to persecute Paul now. To attain to 'the fullness of wisdom' we must know the 'hidden mysteries' revealed by 'philosophy', which bring us to that 'completion' to which baptism is a preliminary stage, as circumcision was under the old covenant (and perhaps still is). It confers the first measure of the new life; but we must attain to its fullness by a complete putting off of the material. This can only be achieved by the observance of those sacred seasons

[1] The insistence on the fact that Jesus is the head and on the Christian's present union with Him is a reply to those who offer other means of ascending to heaven. For such ascents cf. p. 101. Here we seem to have an ascent in the form of a mystery which is a guarantee of immortality, as in the "Mithras-Liturgy" of *Papp. Mag. Gr.* 4. 485 *seqq.* In the Isis-mysteries (Apul. *Metam.* 11. 23. 804) this is replaced by a descent through the underworld. The angels are not the hostile rulers of the planets as in *Papp. Mag. Gr.* 4. 557 (here they are "gods"); nor does Paul object that they are being worshipped. They seem to be the "angels of the right" who protect the soul in its ascent against the hostile "powers of the left". Cf. Clem. Alex. *Exc. ex Theod.* 73. 1 (Casey 640); *Acts of John* 114 (*Apocr. N.T.* 269); Orig. *c. Cels.* 6. 27 (angels of light opposed to archontic angels) and the homily of Macarius of Egypt, quoted by James in *The Testament of Abraham* (*Texts and Studies* 2. 2. 19).

[2] Cf. pp. 46 *seqq.* In Philo we have the Logos subdivided into seven forms; in Orig. *c. Cels.* 6. 31 seven planetary spheres each described by one of the names of God. In the magical papyri the names of God and the archangels are used indiscriminately (*Papp. Mag. Gr.* 3. 146 *seqq.*, 210 *seqq.* and *passim*). In the Ophite system of Origen the rulers, though described by the names of God, are hostile; this represents the later Gnostic tradition.

and those ritual abstinences from food and material pleasures which will enable us to be initiated successfully into the higher orders of truth, where angels will reveal to us the secrets by which we can pass safely from the material world to the heights of heaven. When we have done this, we shall be fully equipped with the fivefold spiritual equipment, which must replace the five senses through which we live in the material world."[1]

The whole system is a relatively simple type of Gnosis of the earlier type before Valentinus had introduced the complication which was bound to result from the attempt at a complete duplication of things celestial and things terrestrial. The heavenly and Christian ogdoad, i.e. the Christian Trinity, expanded into a counterpart of the Stoic division of the soul into eight parts, and set above the real planets, identified with the Jewish hebdomad, the celestial fall of Sophia-Achamoth and the transformation of the orthodox symbolism of the Cross, as the boundary between good and evil or heaven and earth, into a celestial barrier preserving the pleroma of heaven from contact with the material world, appear to be Valentinus' contribution to Gnosticism.[2] His scheme duplicates the commonplaces of Hellenistic

[1] Reitzenstein (*Hell. Myst. Rel.* 265 and *Erl.-Myst.* 161, n. 2) derives the scheme of pentads, which are also units in Col. 3. 5, 8 and 12, from Iranian and Indian religion; so Prajapati is made up of five mortal and five immortal parts. The grouping into pentads figures largely in Manicheanism; cf. *Acts of Thomas* 27 (*Apocr. N.T.* 376 and Burkitt's note *ad loc.*); Burkitt, *Religion of the Manichees* 19, 24 and 107, and Polotsky in *P.R.E.* Supp. 6. 249, who finds in Mani borrowings from Paul (*ib.* 251). It seems probable that Paul himself is borrowing from his opponents' language, since the scheme of pentads does not appear elsewhere in his writings. But the convention of groups of five which make up a single whole is so widespread that it has lost any connection with possible Iranian origins, cf. Cicero, *Acad. Post.* 1. 10. 42 (probably a purely fortuitous case), and a whole mass of pentadic mysticism in Plut. *De Def. Orac.* 36, 429d; *De Ei ap. Delph.* 7 *seqq.*, 387e. In Col. 3. 14 the good pentad has a Pythagorean colouring, for friendship is the σύνδεσμος of all the virtues in this system (cf. *Voc. Gr. N.T.* s.v.). Naturally the five senses would lead to the use of such groupings, which in later Christian literature are made still more popular by the pentads of the Gospel tradition; in *Epist. Apost.* 5 (*Apocr. N.T.* 487) the five loaves of Mk. 6. 38 represent the "Lord of the Christians", the conventional Trinity being expanded by the addition of the Church and the forgiveness of sins. Cf. *ib.* 42 for the five wise virgins as the supernatural virtues, the five foolish being natural virtues which "slumber" in the careless. The parable was a favourite one in Gnostic circles (Tert. *De Anim.* 18, and cf. Clem. Alex. *Strom.* 7. 12. 72 (875 P)). The grouping by pentads was also natural in view of the five books of Moses making up the one Torah; in Orig. *c. Cels.* 6. 31 the soul claims to pass the sphere of Sabaoth, because his law has been conquered by a more powerful pentad, whose nature is not specified. For the pentad in place of the Trinity cf. Aphraates, *Dem.* 23. 60 (*Patr. Syr.* 2. 123). Paul's source is his opponents' language, while their source is the pentadic convention in popular theology.

[2] For Horos, the boundary, who is also the Cross in Ir. *Haer.* 1. 2. 2 and 4 and 3. 1, cf. the liturgy of Hippolytus, 1. 4. 8 (*The Apostolic Tradition*, ed. Easton, 36), and that of *Testamentum Domini* (ed. Rahmanni, p. 41, l. 27). Irenaeus himself (*Haer.* 5. 17. 4) sees in the Cross a manifestation of the "length, height, depth and breadth",

religion of the type preserved in Philo and the Hermetic literature and forces them into the Christian scheme by means of a Philonic interpretation of the New Testament, as in the case of his elaborate explanation of the "perfect fruit" of the *pleroma*, Jesus; He is simply introduced as an explanation of Col. 2. 9.

Valentinus, however, was only complicating a scheme which was originally simple and had the comparatively reasonable purpose of adapting Christianity to astrology. But naturally Paul could make no compromise with it. He was quite prepared to recognise the power of the rulers of the planets. But his whole system was based on the belief that Jesus was the full revelation of God's purpose; he was not for a moment prepared to admit the existence of other powers of redemption or other methods of attaining to God than those provided by the worship of the Church. Consequently his answer to the report of the new teaching was a direct and emphatic negative (Col. 1. 1–15). The initial thanksgiving and prayer contained potentially the whole of his answer. Paul thanked God for the faith, love and hope of his readers, which made them a striking example of that "increase and bearing of fruit" which was being manifested by the Gospel throughout the world, as it had been manifested in them from the time of the first mission of Epaphras. He prayed, with language which would be bombastic if it were not a parody of his opponents' phrases, that they

and quotes "one of the elders" for the outstretched hands as a symbol of the drawing together of the two peoples. The "stretching out of the hands" of Moses in Exod. 17. 11 and of God in Is. 65. 2 typifies the Cross in *Ep. Barn.* 12. 2; cf. *Didache* 16. 6. In the interpretation of the Targum on Gen. 8. 1 ascribed to Hippolytus (ed. Bonwetsch and Achelis 2. 91), the ark travels to the four quarters of the world and then returns to the East. Cf. also Origen's exegesis of Eph. 3. 18, *In Gen. Hom.* 2. 5. The symbolism is explained by Firmicus Maternus, *De Err. Prof. Rel.* 21. 4 and 27. 3; the upright beam keeps heaven and earth in place, while the two arms touch the East and raise up the West; here again we have the allusion to Moses holding up his hands against Amalek. Justin Martyr, *Apol.* 1. 55 (90b), reads a grotesque Cross-symbolism into the whole of nature, including the Stoic commonplace of the erect position of man as against the beasts; he does not here read it into the celestial regions, but this would be out of place in a tract addressed to the heathen; for the O.T. symbolism cf. *Dial. c. Tryph.* 90 *seqq.* (317c), where the arms of Moses, the serpent in the wilderness and the horns of the unicorns from Deut. 33. 17 are pressed into service. For less orthodox specimens cf. *Acts of John* 99 (*Apocr. N.T.* 255); *Acts of Andrew, Martyrdom* 1. 14 (*ib.* 359). The Cross as the means of establishing order in the chaos of the material world has been transferred in Hippolytus and *Test. Dom.* to Sheol: in itself it appears to be an adaptation of Christianity to the common *motif* of the divine redeemer, as in Hipp. *El.* 5. 8 (111), where the Naassenes interpret Attis' name Papas as meaning παῦε, παῦε, applied to the disorder of the world. The Cross as a principle of order in chaos appears to have been accepted by the old-fashioned Roman orthodoxy of about A.D. 200, represented by the liturgy of the *Apostolic Tradition.* It would scarcely have been so accepted if it had not been orthodox before Valentinus; for his views see further Clem. Alex. *Exc. ex Theod.* 22. 4 (Casey 244) and 42. 1 (*ib.* 406).

might be filled with the knowledge of the will of God in every form of wisdom and spiritual understanding, so that they might walk worthily of the Lord to please Him in all things, "bearing fruit" in all good works and "increasing" in the knowledge of God. Thus their own "fruitbearing and increase", as the counterpart of the general "fruitbearing and increase" of the triumphant march of the Gospel through the world, would manifest the true version of that correspondence between the inward "fruitbearing and increase" of the Gnostic and the "fruitbearing and increase" manifested within the nature of God, which was a central feature in the system of Paul's rivals. They would thus be strengthened with all power, in virtue of the might of the glory of God, to show forth all endurance and longsuffering; for suffering, it was implied, was a mark of the glory of God, not of lack of support in the heavenly places. Thus their life would be one of continuous thanksgiving to the Father, who had given them a share of His own "sufficiency"[1] to enable them to attain already to the inheritance of the Saints in the light, and had saved them from the realm of darkness by transferring them to the kingdom of the son of His love, the human Jesus, whom Paul had preached to them.[2] The words were an allusion to the voice at the Baptism which had identified Jesus with the promised Messiah of Ps. 2. 7, and to His proclamation of the kingdom of God, a phrase from the terminology of the Gospels which had been relegated to the background on account of the dangers attaching to its indiscriminate use in the Hellenistic world. By implication the phrase restated the whole of the traditional message

[1] Cf. above, p. 131. There may be an allusion to some use of the name "Shaddai" in the sense of ὁ ἱκανός here; the verb is rare, but its use may be merely an unconscious reminiscence; καλέσαντι is an obvious attempt to emend the text.

[2] "Son of His love" only appears here and in the Ephesian continuator (Eph. 1. 6) in Pauline writings. In the Synoptists it appears in Mk. 1. 11, 9. 7 and by implication in 12. 6 and the parallel accounts. The first incident was of vital importance; cf. Justin Martyr, *Dial. c. Tryph.* 49 (268a) and 88 (315b), which prove at length that Elijah had appeared as the forerunner of Jesus in the person of the Baptist. Justin records the blazing forth of fire in Jordan at the time, a feature which appears in the Gospel of the Ebionites (*Apocr. N.T.* 9). The importance of the Baptism appears from Ign. *ad Eph.* 18. 2 and *ad Smyrn.* 1. 1; it would seem that it came near to inclusion in the Creed; cf. Dodd, *The Apostolic Preaching* 107. Later mythology represented the Baptism as the bringing of the oil from the Tree of Life for the anointing of Adam, *Vit. Ad. et Ev.* 36. 1, for the Jewish form; for its application to the Baptism of Jesus cf. *Acta Pilati* (Latin A and Greek 3 (19); *Apocr. N.T.* 127); it appears from Ign. *ad Eph.* 17. 1 that He was Himself anointed with it. A heretical version of the story is known to Celsus, though curiously enough it is unknown to Origen (*c. Cels.* 6. 27). The story of the Baptist's recognition of Jesus had the further advantage that it could be adapted to the distinction of the "voice" and the "word" of popular philosophy; cf. Ign. *ad Rom.* 2. 1; Orig. *In Ev. Jo.* 2. 26, and the distinction of ἠχώ and φθόγγος in the Gnostic cosmogony of *Papp. Mag. Gr.* 13. 546. But this is post-Pauline, since Paul does not use the term Logos of Jesus.

of the earthly ministry of Jesus and was thus an emphatic reminder of the historical character of the Gospel and the position of Jesus in it as against attempts to belittle His place in the scheme of redemption; the call for thanksgiving, though the thought of thanksgiving as the natural response to a divine revelation bringing salvation was a commonplace of Hellenistic religion, was essentially part of the Jewish-Christian religious life, with its use of the Psalter and prayers of thanksgiving, coloured by the intense spiritual fervour of the early disciples.[1] Even the contrast between the portion of the Saints in light and the power of darkness, however strongly coloured by the language derived by Judaism from its contact with Zoroastrianism, was drawn from the language of the Old Testament and strictly in keeping with its tradition.[2] The opening section of the letter concluded with an emphatic statement of the completeness of the redemption wrought by Jesus as the Messiah; the forgiveness of sins which resulted from conversion was the whole of redemption. Paul made no attempt to harmonise the statement with his recognition elsewhere that the work of redemption needed completion and that the gift of the Holy Spirit was only a preliminary instalment of the final state of glory into which man was to be transformed: the admission might have been used by his opponents as a dangerous handle for their doctrine that the redemption obtained in Jesus was only a preliminary step, which had to be completed by the full knowledge of the other powers, through whose realms the soul must pass.[3]

[1] *εὐχαριστεῖν* appears not very frequently in the Greek books of the O.T., as against the *εὐλογεῖν* and *ἐξομολογεῖσθαι* of the LXX translators. In Philo the word is frequent, with a tendency to be associated with liturgical reference to hymns, sacrifices, etc. (whether literal or allegorical), as against *εὐλογεῖν*; *ἐξομολογεῖσθαι* is comparatively rare. (For the ritual associations of the word see the references in Cohn-Wendland, index.) Here Paul's thought is coloured by the parallel with the deliverance from Egypt, which is especially connected with *εὐχαριστία* (Philo, *De Agric.* 17 (80, M. 1. 312); *De Migr. Abr.* 5 (25, M. 1. 440)). In the Synoptic Gospels the word is used only in the eucharistic or quasi-eucharistic sense except by Luke, who allows it to appear in 17. 16 and 18. 11 (both peculiar to himself) without noticing the Hellenistic colouring. It may be noted that in the Logion 10. 21 (=Mt. 11. 25) the ultra-Hebraic form *ἐξομολογεῖσθαι* (=ידה) appears. Norden, *Agnostos Theos* 284, has to assume the influence of the LXX use here and in Ecclus. 51. 1 *seqq.* in tracing the Logion to Hellenistic Gnosis. It is curious that the thanksgivings after revelation in the Hermetica (see p. 176) are always *εὐλογίαι*. In Aquila's version *εὐχαριστεῖν* appears nine times with a tendency to association with ritual and liturgical thanksgiving.

[2] "Realm of darkness" may be drawn from the opposition; there appear to be no rabbinical parallels, and the material world as "darkness" is common in Gnosticism (e.g. Ir. *Haer.* 1. 30. 1 *seqq.*). But the phrase might easily occur independently; cf. p. 150. The phrase here seems to have made its way into Lk. 22. 53 from Pauline usage. (Creed, *ad loc.*, regards it as having a Johannine ring; but the Pauline parallel here is closer, and the "hour" is the converse of that of Rom. 13. 11.)

[3] Col. 1. 14 replies to views similar to those of Marcus in Ir. *Haer.* 1. 21. 2;

The reason (1. 15 *seqq.*) for the fullness of the redemption wrought by Jesus lay in the fact that He was nothing less than the divine Wisdom. It was perfectly true that the one true God, the God of Israel, was invisible, and that no words could exaggerate His infinite greatness.[1] But He had seen fit to reveal Himself by making His image, the Wisdom created from the beginning, visible to mankind in the person of Jesus.[2] That the divine Wisdom was the "image" of God was part of the regular Jewish-Hellenistic tradition; the divine Wisdom was also the first-born of all creation,[3] the divine pattern of the world in which all things were potentially present before they were created in a material form.[4] It was an advantage of this conception that the Wisdom of God or the ideal cosmos was also the "beloved" of God, and thus could be clearly identified with the historical Jesus, of whom God had testified that He was His "beloved Son". The coincidence of the Messianic and cosmogonic titles could not have been more appropriate to Paul's argument. It followed from the position of Jesus as the divine pattern, in whom all things whether seen or unseen were potentially present from the beginning, that even

but it was essential to any system of Gnosticism that it should claim to offer a fuller redemption than that obtained merely by baptism. The references to ἐπίγνωσις imply that the fuller redemption offered was described by this term.

[1] For Ἰαώ as ἀόρατος cf. p. 44. The term is only applied to God here in the Pauline writings apart from the imitation in 1 Tim. 1. 17. It is associated with the tendencies to unorthodox speculation noted above, *loc. cit.* (For the possibility that it represents contact with the deified Helios-Aion derived by Hellenistic speculation from Zoroastrian sources, cf. Peterson, Εἷς Θεός 241 *seqq.* and 267.) It seems likely that it represents a deliberate adoption by Paul of a phrase of his opponents' use of the terminology of Jewish Gnosticism.

[2] Cf. pp. 65 *seqq.* Paul perhaps intends the phrase εἰκὼν ἀοράτου to represent the fact that Jesus is not merely an "image" as is the conventional Wisdom, but a visibly manifested image. Of course the Wisdom or Logos could not be manifested any more than God Himself; but since Jesus had been made visible, the general conventions of the Jewish figure of Wisdom had to be changed to meet the facts of the case. εἰκών, πρωτότοκος and ἀρχή may all come from Paul's opponents, cf. p. 49.

[3] This is a commonplace of the Hellenistic synagogue. Wisdom was present with God before the creation and therefore could be the living and divine pattern of the *Timaeus*. For the Logos as the ideal world, the oldest and first-born son of God, see Philo, *De Conf. Ling.* 14 (63, M. 1. 414); the cosmos is the one and beloved son in *De Ebr.* 8 (30, M. 1. 361), and the younger in *Quod Deus Imm.* 6 (32, M. 1. 277). In *De Agric.* 12 (51, M. 1. 308), "The Lord is my shepherd" in Ps. 23. 1 refers to the cosmos, whose elements and natural phenomena, including the heavenly bodies, are guided by God as a flock, over which He has set His "ὀρθὸς λόγος", who is also His first-born son. The reference to the Psalm suggests a non-Philonic source. The confusion of thought reflects the obscurity of the *Timaeus*, which is also the source of the "only-begotten" (31 b and 92 c). For the addition of "beloved" to "only-begotten" cf. Plut. *De Def. Orac.* 23. 423 a.

[4] *Timaeus* 30 c; Philo, *De Mund. Op.* 4 (17, M. 1. 4); the plan was present in God and transferred by Him to the intellectual world. For all things as present in the Creator cf. *Corp. Herm.* Ascl. 1. 2 (Scott 288).

the unseen rulers of the planetary spheres were inferior to Him in the scale of being.[1] For whatever their character as thrones, lordships, rules and authorities might be, they were created by Him; the divine pattern of the cosmos was also the agent of God in creation.[2] It was a simple matter to add that, as the Messiah, Jesus was the end to which all things were created, for in current Stoic speculation Zeus, as the one divine power manifested in the cosmos, was the beginning, the sustaining force and the end of the recurring world-ages, which made up the eternal circle of revolving time; Jesus, as the Messiah, was not the end of one such age in a recurring system, but the end of the present age, as the close of history, and therefore the object which all creation had in view.[3] Rabbinical speculation was quite ready to adopt such conceptions of God as first and last, and it was a matter of course to apply them to Jesus as the climax of creation.[4] He was before all things, and therefore the best of all things,[5] and it was through Him that all things came into and remained in being.[6]

Yet again He was the head of the body. The Church, the purely human society of Rom. 12. 5 and 1 Cor. 12. 12, was thus raised to the cosmic order, so that the position of Jesus in relation to the lords of the planets might be the same as His relation to mankind; whatever the position of such beings might be as regards the rest of the universe, they were still subordinate to Jesus, for He was the head of all existing things and all were merely members of the Church of which He was the head, deriving from Him their salvation, just as in the first instance

[1] Cf. above, p. 51 *seqq.*

[2] For the divine pattern as the agent of creation cf. Philo, *De Mund. Op.* 6 (24, M. 1. 5).

[3] It was an old saying in the time of Plato (*Laws* 715 e) that God was the beginning and end and middle of all things; the thought could be read into the hymn of the priestesses of Dodona (Pausanias 10. 12. 10); but though this hymn appears to be accepted as genuine by Cook (*Zeus* 2. 350) of Zan, the Illyrian Zeus, and by Frazer (*Pausanias' Description of Greece*, *ad loc.*), its appearance in a list of famous prophetesses, including the Jewish Sibyl, suggests that it is derived from a tract on prophecy of the later Stoic type; hence it may be doubted whether the hymn really taught that Zeus was and is and shall be; later Stoics could read almost anything they wished into religious practices of antiquity. For the commonplace cf. Pacuvius *ap.* Cicero, *De Div.* 1. 57. 131 and the "Orphic" verses of Aristobulus *ap.* Eus. *Pr. Ev.* 13. 12. 9 and of Porphyry, *ib.* 3. 9. 2; also Plut. *De Ei ap. Delph.* 20, 393 a. The view is implied in the correspondence of the end to the beginning in Philo, *De Mund. Op.* 27 (82, M. 1. 19): Jos. *c. Ap.* 2. 22. 190 quotes Plato. There is no need to find Indian and Mandean parallels (Reitzenstein, *Erl.-Myst.* 242).

[4] *Gen. R.* 81. 2, where אמת (truth) is the "seal" of God as the beginning, middle and end of all things; cf. Rev. 1. 8 and *Midr. Teh.* on Ps. 72. 1 (Buber, p. 324, l. 9).

[5] Cf. pp. 94 and 112.

[6] For συνέστηκεν cf. Philo, *De Migr. Abr.* 1 (6, M. 1. 437) and *Q.R.D.H.* 57 (280, M. 1. 513), where the genesis of all things "consists" through the planets and the Stoic commonplace *artifici sensu universa constare*, *Clem. Recog.* 8. 28. The phrase has found its way into *Papp. Mag. Gr.* 4. 1769.

they derived from Him their existence. The Church as a body, of which the individuals were members, was derived from the Stoic commonplace of the state as a body in which each member had his part to play; in this form Paul had already worked out the parallelism in the same way in which it is worked out in the later rabbinical literature, no less than in the classical writers.[1] Naturally it was also a commonplace of Hellenistic Judaism; the Stoic commonplace was the more easily adapted in view of the metaphors from the body found in such passages as Deut. 28. 13.[2] But the political developments of the Hellenistic age had changed the conception of the state from a body in which each member played its part into a body in which the head was the all-important matter; it is likely enough that the transition was accomplished in Alexandria in favour of the Ptolemies before it became a convenient method of flattering the Roman Emperors; it is possible that the headship descended from the wise man of the Stoics[3] to the more or less deified ruler and from him to the High Priest at Jerusalem.[4] The transference of the conception of the "headship" of the state to the "headship" of the cosmos was an easy matter for Paul, since the cosmic headship of the Lord was a headship not so much over the planets as over the living beings who ruled them; but in any case the transference was already a commonplace of popular theology. On the one hand the firmament or the sun was the "head" of the universe in Oriental religion;[5] on the other the cosmos was animated by a divine mind, which also was concentrated in the firmament; thus the cosmos was a "body" and the divine mind either

[1] For the elaborate Stoic simile cf. Seneca, *De Ira* 2. 31. 7; Zeno *ap.* Maximus, *Florilegium* 6 (v. Arn. 1. 56. 236); Livy 2. 32; Dion. Halic. *Antt. Rom.* 3. 11 and 6. 86. For rabbinical usage cf. Str.-B. on 1 Cor. 12. 12 and 26.

[2] Philo, *De Spec. Legg.* 3. 23 (131, M. 2. 321); cf. *De Virt.* 12 (103, M. 2. 392); for the association of the conception with Deut. 28. 13 cf. *De Praem. et Poen.* 20 (125, M. 2. 428).

[3] In Philo, *De Praem. et Poen.* 19 (114, M. 2. 426), the good man or nation dominates the surroundings for their own good, as the head does the body; in *De Vit. Moys.* 2. 5 (30, M. 2. 139) Ptolemy is the "head" of kings, as is the dominant principle (mind) in a living creature. Here the mind has replaced the head, as it does in Seneca (see n. 3 next page). It is safe to assume that this correspondence represents the Alexandrine tradition (?Posidonius).

[4] For the High Priest cf. reference to Philo, *De Spec. Legg.*, in n. 2.

[5] Manetho *ap.* Diod. Sic. 1. 11. 6; cf. Peterson, Εἷς Θεός 262. In Philo, *De Somn.* 1. 22 (144 *seqq.*, M. 1. 642), Jacob's ladder represents the macrocosm where heaven is the head and earth the base, and also man, the microcosm, where mind is the heavenly and sense the earthy element; Philo's exegesis is really pointless, since he cannot equate heaven with God as his source did. The conception may go back to Iranian sources (Reitzenstein, *Hell. Myst. Rel.* 224), but it has become a commonplace. The extent to which this theme has become generally current appears in *De Vit. Cont.* 10 (78, M. 2. 483), where the O.T. is the "body" of Scripture, and the hidden meaning is the "unseen soul" as in a living creature.

its "head" or the spirit which animated it.[1] This conception was popular in the Stoic-Orphic tradition which was generally accepted in Hellenistic-Jewish circles;[2] the extent to which the two ideas were conflated appears from the fact that they are treated as identical by Seneca.[3] It is an interesting irony of history that the *ex officio* High Priest, who was probably Caiaphas,[4] and the Emperor Nero are the rivals of Jesus for the "headship" of the "body" in the literature of the first century A.D.

It is of course possible that the thought of a cosmic Church originated with Paul's opponents. It could easily originate in Jewish circles, as is evident from the fact that the angels appear as the "upper" and Israel as the "lower" family of God,[5] a correspondence which seems to represent the influence of the conventional fondness for finding heavenly counterparts of earthly things on orthodox Judaism. In any case the thought would naturally suggest itself to the teachers whom Paul is answering, if they were sufficiently interested in the Church or the "congregation of Israel" to feel the need of a heavenly counterpart for those institutions. The allusion to the Church provided Paul with a suitable transition from the cosmic to the historical; the position of Jesus as first in the order of creation corresponded to His position as "the beginning" in the order of resurrection.[6] The argument from such a parallel was calculated to be eminently convincing to Hellenistic readers;[7] Paul was not concerned to prove the fact of the resurrection of Jesus, which would seem to have been admitted by his opponents: they presumably regarded it as true, but only interpreted it to mean that He had achieved for Himself and His followers a preliminary

[1] Verg. *Aen.* 6. 727; the thought goes back to *Timaeus* 30b.

[2] Cf. pp. 36 *seqq.*

[3] Seneca, *De Clem.* 2. 2. 1, represents Nero as the head from which the body derives its health; but *ib.* 1. 5. 1: *tu animus reipublicae tuae es, illa corpus tuum.* For the universe as a *corpus* of which we are members cf. *Ep.* 14. 4 (92), 30.

[4] There is no means for dating Philo's works, but it is reasonably probable that most of them were written between A.D. 18 and 36.

[5] Cf. Str.-B. on Mt. 16. 19 (p. 744c) and Eph. 3. 14; see also 4. 1117. Orig. *In Num. Hom.* 3. 3 treats the Church of the first-born of Heb. 12. 23 as an angelic Church, but in *c. Cels.* 6. 35 the Gnostic conception of a heavenly Church of which the Church on earth is an emanation is heretical; for the Gnostic view cf. Clem. Alex. *Exc. ex Theod.* 41. 2 (Casey 396).

[6] Paul appears to have transferred the title of Wisdom as "the beginning" of Gen. 1. 1 to the historical Jesus as "the beginning" in the order of resurrection. For the Logos as "the beginning" cf. Philo, *De Mund. Op.* 7 (26, M. 1. 5); the title appears in the seven titles of the Logos (p. 49); cf. *Kerygma Petri ap.* Clem. Alex. *Strom.* 6. 7. 58 (769 P) and the speculations of Orig. *In Ev. Jo.* 1. 22.

[7] *Conversion* 251. For such correspondences in philosophy cf. Plut. *De Def. Orac.* 34. 428e; in an entirely different sphere cf. the elaborate parallel between John the Baptist and Jesus in Hippolytus, *De Antichristo* 44 *seqq.*; for an abbreviated version see Orig. *In Ev. Jo.* 2. 30.

deliverance from sin and the material world, which needed further completion both in His own case and in that of His disciples. Their view could easily be read into the view implied in 1 Cor. 15. 45, where Paul had only been concerned with the position of Jesus in eschatology, and therefore had only proved that the resurrection of Jesus had restored man to that spiritual condition which he had possessed before the fall of Adam; it did not necessarily follow that Adam had been perfect and without need of "completion" before his fall.

The supremacy of Jesus was due to His character as the divine Wisdom in whom the whole "fullness" (*pleroma*) of the godhead dwelt (1. 19 *seqq.*). It was again a general conception of the age that the whole cosmos was completely "full"; there was no vacuum in it.[1] But the material world was always giving out and taking in; fullness was properly a quality that belonged to God alone.[2] His fullness pervaded the whole cosmos in the form of reason, the divine element present in the material world, and present in every part of it.[3] But with the later Stoic distinction between God as the divine element concentrated in the firmament and God as the divine element permeating the material, it became necessary to distinguish between God in His own nature and God as filling the world, God in his latter character being identified with the deities of the pantheon. Thus the cosmos could itself be regarded as eternal and divine, in so far as it was the embodiment of the divine reason; it could also be regarded as the dwelling-place of gods and men and the various things created for their benefit.[4] In this sense the cosmos was the *pleroma* of gods and men: the sphere which they filled completely.[5] More commonly the cosmos was a "system" (σύστημα) of Gods and men;[6] this phrase, however, was impossible for Jews or Christians, and even the description of the cosmos as a "system" of God and mankind implied a parity in degree between God and man, which was impossible for either. But it remained true for Jewish thought that God filled the world; the

[1] *Placita* 1. 18 (*Dox. Gr.* 316); Ar. Did. *Epit.* 29. 1 (*ib.* 464); Cicero, *De Nat. Deor.* 2. 13. 37; Plut. *De Def. Orac.* 25, 424a.

[2] Macrob. *In Somn. Scip.* 1. 5. 3.

[3] Diog. Laert. 7. 138; Seneca, *De Benef.* 4. 8. 2; *Corp. Herm.* 11 (1), 4b (Scott 208), 12 (2), 15b (Scott 232); Ascl. 3. 17a (Scott 316).

[4] Ar. Did. *Epit.* 29. 3 (*Dox. Gr.* 464). Cf. Timaeus Locrus, *De Anima Mundi* 105a.

[5] Cf. Achilles' summary of the teaching of Diodorus of Alexandria in Diels' introduction to *Dox. Gr.* 20; according to Diels Diodorus' system was based on that of Posidonius as given in Diog. Laert. 7. 138. It is therefore possible that the use of *pleroma* in this sense goes back to Posidonius.

[6] So Posidonius *ap.* Diog. Laert. 7. 138; Chrysippus *ap.* Ar. Did. *Epit.* 31 (*Dox. Gr.* 465), and commonly. In Epict. *Diss.* 1. 9. 4 we have a σύστημα ἐξ ἀνθρωπῶν καὶ θεοῦ.

conception was found in the Bible,[1] and could be used to explain one of its difficult passages. "The place" which Jacob "met" was interpreted to mean that God Himself was "the place" which he "met" (Gen. 28. 11). For God was Himself "the place" in which all things existed, since He filled all things completely with His own "sufficiency".[2] The curious language of Genesis, according to which the patriarch "met a place", suggested the term "the Place" as a name of God to rabbinical Judaism; in Hellenistic Judaism it was combined with the thought of Him as "filling the world".[3] With the growth of the figure of Wisdom in Jewish speculation it was natural to regard the Wisdom or Spirit of God as that which filled the world.[4] But that Wisdom again was itself "filled" by God, since it was only a periphrasis for God as "filling" the universe and could not be regarded as seriously different from Him without introducing a plurality into the divine nature or a secondary order of divinity.[5] Thus Wisdom was the house of God, just as the cosmos itself was the house of God or the gods in pagan thought.[6] Again, the analogy of macrocosm and microcosm could be used to show that the soul of man was the house of God and that it must be "filled" with God or the virtues; the thought was naturally valuable for homiletic purposes and could be used with edifying effect.[7]

Thus the whole *pleroma* of the godhead dwelt in Jesus as the divine

[1] Is. 6. 3, Jer. 23. 24, Ps. 72. 19, etc.

[2] Philo, *Leg. Alleg.* 1. 14 (44, M. 1. 52); *De Somn.* 1. 11 (62, M. 1. 630). In both places the thought of God as "the place" is combined with the thought of His sufficiency, for which see above, p. 131; *Leg. Alleg.* 3. 2 (4, M. 1. 88).

[3] The usage of "the Place" as a periphrasis for the name of God appears to be derived from this passage; its curious language is preserved in LXX.

[4] Wisd. 8. 1; Philo, *De Plant.* 2 (9, M. 1. 331), with an obvious affinity to Cicero, *De Nat. Deor.* 2. 45. 115, of "nature", i.e. the nature, fate, reason or Zeus of Stoicism. Cf. also Wisd. 1. 7.

[5] For God as filling the Logos cf. Philo, *De Somn.* 1, quoted above, n. 2, and for the "spirit" of God *De Gigant.* 6 (27, M. 1. 266). Cf. also the "second god" in *Corp. Herm.* Ascl. 1. 8 (Scott 300).

[6] *De Migr. Abr.* 1 (4 *seqq.*, M. 1. 437); cf. *De Aet. Mund.* 21 (112, M. 2. 509), where, if the tract is Philonic or Jewish, the "gods" have been allowed to pass the reviser.

[7] Cf. the conventional exegesis of Lev. 26. 12 in Philo, *De Somn.* 1. 23 (148, M. 1. 643) and 2. 37 (248, M. 1. 691), and 2 Cor. 6. 16. The thought is a commonplace in Philo. For the soul as a *pleroma* of the virtues cf. Philo, *De Spec. Legg.* 1 (*De Sacr.*), 3 (272, M. 2. 253), where God prefers the soul as a *pleroma* of virtue to sacrifices, and *De Praem. et Poen.* 11 (65, M. 2. 418), where the twelve sons of Jacob represent the perfect number produced by the perfect soul, to correspond to the signs of the zodiac. The passages suggest that the word is taken from Alexandrine Pythagoreanism; elsewhere Philo uses it literally except *Quod Omn. Prob. Lib.* 7 (41, M. 2. 451), where it is in a colourless Stoic setting, and *De Abr.* 46 (268, M. 2. 39) (of faith as the fulfilment of hope). In Heracleon *ap.* Orig. *In Ev. Jo.* 13. 11 the celestial counterpart of the spirit sunk in the material is its *pleroma*, apparently a conflation of the *fravashi* with the Pauline *pleroma* dwelling in Jesus.

Wisdom and therefore His sacrificial death upon the Cross was able to effect a complete reconciliation of all things in the universe. In so far as there were powers in the world which were hostile to man, they needed, no less than man, to be reconciled to God. But Jesus, in virtue of His supremacy in the whole sphere of creation and resurrection, could extend His work of reconciliation to the whole universe, not merely to the sublunar sphere, or whatever other lower stage His opponents may have assigned to the efficacy of His work. The conception was not Paul's own, but forced upon him by the arguments of his opponents. Even in orthodox Judaism the cosmic symbolism of the High Priest's robe showed that part of his function was to make propitiation not only for all the races of mankind but also for the cosmos; for his robe symbolised the elements of earth, air, fire and water.[1] It was easy and natural to combine the planets with the elements in this type of symbolism, especially in its less orthodox forms. From Paul's point of view the extension of it to the heavens presented no difficulty for it was possible that the heavenly beings themselves had been imprisoned in the material world as the result of Adam's sin, and needed, like man, to be delivered from that punishment.[2] Of this cosmic redemption the Colossians were themselves an instance;[3] they, like the heavenly rulers, were once alienated by sin, but had now been reconciled to God to be presented to Him in that state of perfect holiness, which would leave no adversary any opening for accusing them.[4] Holiness, accompanied by steadfastness in the faith and perseverance in the hope of eternal life, as revealed in the Gospel, was the means for conquering all the powers of evil, both for the Colossians

[1] Philo, *De Spec. Legg.* 1 (*De Sacerd.*), 6 (97, M. 2. 227). It is not far from this to the planets as the angels who rule the nations as rulers of the material world; it is possible that Philo has inserted an orthodox form of a more temerarious speculation. For the sacrifices of the Temple as offered for all nations cf. *Judaism* 2. 43.

[2] Ign. *ad Smyrn.* 6. 1 may be simply a correct interpretation of this passage, or may reflect independent speculations. Ignatius is a better astrologer than Paul; cf. *ad Trall.* 5. 2. Cf. also Orig. *In Lev. Hom.* 1. 3, where we have speculations as to the sprinkling of the heavenly altar with the blood of Jesus and the "church of the firstborn" as an angelic Church, and *In Ev. Jo.* 13. 58 for the possibility of repentance for the "archons".

[3] The redemption of the heavenly bodies on the one hand and the Colossians on the other is perhaps contrasted to the parallel drawn by the opponents between the "bearing fruit and increase" of the heavenly powers, and the "bearing fruit and increase" of the individual Gnostic.

[4] ἀνεγκλήτους may be intended in its strict sense of "free from accusation". If so, it is a direct assertion that holiness is the only key by which man can pass through the spheres of the rulers; for Gnostic methods of doing so cf. Ir. *Haer.* 1. 21. 5 and the Gnostic literature *passim.* But in 1 Cor. 1. 8 the word scarcely means more than "irreproachable" in its conventional English sense; cf. *Voc. Gr. N.T.* s.v.

and for every other creature under the heaven. To all such creatures the Gospel had been preached, and of that Gospel Paul was a minister. The implication of the allusion to "faith" and "hope" was that it was through them, not through admission to higher forms of secret knowledge, that the Christian could attain to heaven; heaven, which in v. 16 had included all the spheres of being above the moon, was here (v. 23) used of the firmament, as the abode of God and the future abode of the righteous.[1]

Paul therefore (1. 24 *seqq.*) was not ashamed of the sufferings which he had to endure on behalf of his converts; rather he rejoiced in them. Jesus had reconciled man to God in His fleshly body through death; but this work of reconciliation had to be completed by the sufferings of His ministers on behalf of the Church, which was now the "body" of Christ, in which He, through His servants, must continue to suffer until the whole quantity of suffering needed for the redemption of the world was completed. Here again Paul was adapting Christianity to the accepted outlook of the age. It was a dogma of conventional theology that the quantity of matter in the cosmos was definitely fixed; Plato himself had said so.[2] Since matter was the cause of evil, it followed that the quantity of evil was also fixed.[3] The duration of the period from one world-conflagration to the next was a fixed number of years determined by the stars. The number of souls was fixed, for it corresponded to the number of the stars.[4] In Judaism this view found a ready welcome, especially in the sphere of eschatology; apart from the numerical schemes for determining the total duration of the world, the coming of the Messiah and the end of the world-process, it might be held that the duration of history depended on the divine decree that a fixed number of souls should be created and a fixed number saved.[5] Among such quantities Scripture included the sins of the Amorites, whose fulfilment up to the predestined limit had determined the date at which the chosen people could enter the land of Israel; the passage

[1] "Heaven" is always ambiguous where astrology is not taken seriously; here the point is that the rulers of the heavens have heard the Gospel, no less than the Colossians; Paul is superior even to the "rulers" in so far as he is a minister of the Gospel.

[2] *Timaeus* 33a; how the statement is to be reconciled with 49a is a matter which does not concern the Hellenistic period, which preferred the simple view; cf. Philo *ap.* Eus. *Pr. Ev.* 7. 21. 1; Plut. *De Is. et Os.* 56, 374b.

[3] Celsus *ap.* Orig. *c. Cels.* 4. 62.

[4] Cf. above, p. 139, and cf. Gregory of Nyssa 1. 205d for a *pleroma* of souls. So Orig. *De Princ.* 2. 9. 1; the number of souls and the quantity of matter are fixed in due proportion.

[5] 2 Bar. 23. 4 and 4 Esdr. 4. 36; cf. Box's note on the latter passage in *Ap. and Ps.* Rev. 7. 4, *Clem. Recog.* 3. 26.

possessed a certain importance since it allowed incautious speculators to find in it an excuse for believing that Moses had taught belief in fate on the lines of Hellenistic thought.[1] Another fixed quantity was the sufferings of the Saints; and their sufferings might be part of a still larger mass of suffering, the rest of which was to be borne by the Messiah.[2]

Thus Paul's sufferings were part of the divine dispensation, not a proof of his inferiority to his rivals, or evidence that he was only the minister of an inferior order of redemption.[3] In them he was fulfilling the divine purpose, a mystery hitherto concealed from all eternity.[4] But God had now revealed to the Saints the full riches of its glory, that to Gentiles, no less than to Jews (it was here in particular that Paul was a minister of the "mystery"), was offered that power of union with the indwelling Christ, which constituted man's hope of glory. It was for no less a hope than this that he laboured through the power of Christ working in him, to train all men in all wisdom so that he might present them to God, made perfect in Christ (as against some supposedly "higher" form of perfection). No labours were too great for him to endure on behalf of the Churches which he had never seen in the flesh, in order that he might build up in them the character of love, which was the only means by which the Christian could attain to that complete wealth of the fullness of wisdom which would enable him to understand the mystery of God, namely Christ, in whom were all the hidden treasures of wisdom and knowledge. The language again was coloured by a rhetoric which reflected the style of Paul's opponents; it was forced upon him by the singular poverty of Christianity in respect of the complicated mysteries of theosophical knowledge which had a potent appeal to the Hellenistic world. Paul had to present Christianity in the light of a supreme cosmic revelation, without sacrificing its essential insistence on love as the one thing needed.

[1] Gen. 15. 16; cf. above, p. 100.

[2] Cf. *Midr. Sam.* 19. 1. 51 a, quoted by Str.-B. on Mt. 8. 17 (1. 481 *ad fin.*) (the authority quoted is R. Acha (*c.* A.D. 320), but the view of a fixed quantity of the sufferings of the Saints appears in Rev. 6. 11); it is interesting that the conception is associated with Is. 53. 5, in view of the fondness of the Church for that prophecy. Paul may have arrived at the conception of the fixed quantity of the sufferings of the Saints independently, but it is quite possible that he was using traditional Jewish material. Rabbinical exegesis may have avoided it during the height of the controversies with the Church.

[3] Cf. above, p. 152.

[4] For "mystery" see below, Note V. It is possible that the "aeons" are to be regarded as personal and borrowed from the language of the opposition, but the purely temporal sense is perfectly satisfactory.

Since all the hidden mysteries of God were to be found in Jesus as the Christ (2. 2 *seqq.*),[1] the Colossians must not allow themselves to be led astray by strange teachers, however persuasive they might be; although Paul was unable to be present with them in the flesh, he was with them in the spirit, contemplating the steadfastness of their faith, the only real ground for congratulation (there was by implication no cause for pride or for congratulation in progress in "knowledge"). They had received the knowledge of Christ Jesus as Lord, the essential Christian Gospel; they must stand fast in Him in accordance with the faith which they were taught, and abound in thanksgiving for so great a revelation and so great a deliverance. They must not allow themselves to be carried away captive by philosophy and deceit and the tradition of men (as opposed to the "tradition" of Christ Jesus as Lord) into following the "elements" of the world rather than Christ;[2] for the "elements" which ruled the material world, whatever their power might be, were nothing as compared with the fullness of the godhead which dwelt in Jesus in visible bodily form.[3]

Since the *pleroma* of the godhead was in Jesus, it followed that the Christian attained to his fullness by being "in Him"; the phrase was a conflation of the normal Pauline usage of being "in Christ" and the thought that as God "fills" His Wisdom, so His Wisdom fills the soul of the righteous, which is thus brought to the "fullness" of its being.[4] There was no room left for any further progress; for Jesus was the head of all the rulers and authorities; consequently they were inferior to Him, and any power which they might possess was derived from Him. The convert therefore could stand in no need of any further initiation. Under the old covenant circumcision had symbolised the putting off of the material body, though it could not actually effect it.[5]

[1] "Christ" in 2. 2 and 1. 24 has almost its correct sense of Messiah; elsewhere, as usually in Paul, it is simply a name for Jesus which carries no particular implications.

[2] For the "elements" cf. above, p. 108.

[3] σωματικῶς is not a reply to a docetic view of the humanity of Jesus, since there is no sign that the Colossian teachers took a docetic view; Docetism exaggerated His divine nature, whereas they seem to have depreciated it. It seems to be a summary reply to the argument that Jesus could not have been divine, for He had a real body and was really crucified, which is impossible for a divine being. Paul, however, may be simply asserting that although Jesus as the divine Wisdom is ἀσώματος, yet He could assume and has assumed a real body. For the Logos as ἀσώματος cf. Philo, *Q. D. Imm.* 18 (83, M. 1. 285); and *De Conf. Ling.* 14 (62, M. 1. 414).

[4] For Wisdom as filling the soul cf. Philo, *De Post. Cain.* 41 (136, M. 1. 251), cf. 39 (132). Dibelius, *H.z.N.T. ad loc.*, suggests that πεπληρωμένοι is drawn from the language of the opposition.

[5] Cf. pp. 30 and 153. It is conceivable that Paul's opponents retained baptism as the equivalent of the proselyte's bath, and described some other initiatory rite of admission to a higher degree as a "spiritual circumcision" (cf. Orig. *c. Cels.* 6. 35

But baptism was the true circumcision, a divine and not a human ordinance; in baptism the Christian put off the fleshly body in virtue of a circumcision of which Christ was the minister; in baptism he shared in the burial of Jesus and, through faith in the power of God who raised Jesus from the dead, rose himself to a new life,[1] in which he was no longer subject to the old conditions of the material world.

The Gentile convert (2. 13 *seqq.*) thus received a completely new life when he was raised with Jesus, for his previous condition was simply one of death, in which he had not even circumcision to reveal to him the sins which the Law made known, though it gave no power to overcome them.[2] The Jew was in a different position, since there stood against him the bond of the written ordinances of the Law.[3] These bound him to avoid sin by obedience to the letter, so long as he remained in the material world. Since, however, the Law gave him no power to obey, and therefore no deliverance from the dominion of the material world and the powers that ruled it, the Jew too was hopelessly indebted; he too needed that free gift of grace by which God had cancelled the written bond that subjected him to slavery; Christ had taken it out of the way and nailed it to the Cross.[4] He had descended secretly through the spheres of the rulers, and assumed a body that was subject to them in so far as it was of a material character, but exempt from them in so far as He was free from sin; thus Jesus reversed the fall of Adam, who was by nature free from the rulers but subjected himself to them by sinning. Having thus allowed Himself to be subject to them, Jesus had on the Cross put aside His material body, nailing it to the Cross and allowing them to claim it as their own. By

where the association of a "heavenly Church" and a "true circumcision" appears to be drawn from a fairly early Gnostic tradition, which may however have been drawn from Colossians).

[1] For these conceptions in contemporary religion cf. *Rel. Or.* 64. The symbolism here is drawn from the Exodus-symbolism of Judaism, cf. pp. 28 *seqq.* The point of contact lies in the common conception of the age that religion and religious rites are a means of obtaining "salvation".

[2] καὶ ὑμᾶς is addressed to Gentile converts as opposed to Jews. For once Paul gives a fairly clear explanation of the relative position of Jews and Gentiles; the Gentile is "dead", the Jew merely "in bondage".

[3] Cf. above, p. 109. For sin as a debt, which God registers against man, cf. Str.-B. on this passage; Paul adapts this view to his belief that the Torah revealed sin but gave man no power to overcome it.

[4] The subject changes from God to Jesus at the beginning of v. 14; Lightfoot, *ad loc.*, is certainly right against Dibelius in understanding ἐν αὐτῷ at the end of v. 15 as "in it", i.e. in the Cross. The meaning of the passage depends on Christ having "put off" the material body at His death; the middle ἀπεκδυσάμενος could not be used of God "putting off" the rulers in Christ. In Orig. *c. Cels.* 2. 64 the body of Jesus which had "put off the rulers" was invisible to all but the disciples; this (cf. 3. 42) is a fair statement of Paul's thought that Jesus at death "put off" the material.

this compensation He satisfied their claims over man; He proceeded to put them to open shame[1] by triumphing over them in His resurrection from the dead; in virtue of this triumph the claims of the rulers against mankind, whether Jew or Gentile, were henceforth cancelled. The argument depended for its validity on the belief that Adam's fall carried with it subjection to the rulers of the material world, while the death of Jesus carried with it deliverance. Jesus thus assumes the place of the divine element of "mind" in popular gnosis; "mind", which was one of the conceptions which went to make up the Jewish figure of the divine Wisdom, was subject to fate in virtue of its assumption of a psychic and material character borrowed from the planets, but was able to deliver itself if it recognised its character as mind, and by knowledge or by suitable rites obtained the power to rise again to its celestial home. It is not, however, clear how far Paul was simply adapting this conception or how far he was influenced by his opponents' use of a myth intended to explain the method of subjection and the means of deliverance. In any case the "mythology" here is of secondary importance. His exposition of the method by which Jesus conquered the powers of the material spheres is simply his conception of the Cross as the reversal of Adam's fall into sin and death and the material world; it represents the Christian experience of "salvation" fitted into a setting, taken over from his opponents, in which Jesus delivers man once and for all, instead of merely initiating a system from which man can go forward to full "redemption".[2]

It followed from the argument (Col. 2. 16 *seqq.*) that the Colossians must not allow themselves to be impressed by the assumed superiority of those who sought to impose on them a system of ordinances, of rules as to eating and drinking and the observance of special days as sacred. Under the old covenant such observances were a shadow of things to come; in Jesus the reality had appeared. Nor must they let themselves be impressed by those who sought to impose on them higher standards of special fasts, enjoined as a means of propitiating the angels, whose appearances to them in vision would mark the stages of their progress to higher things.[3] Those who claimed such special

[1] The "open triumph" is contrasted with the secret descent through the spheres of the rulers; there is possibly also an allusion to secret rites practised by the opposition. For *παρρησία* of a public ceremony as opposed to a mystery cf. Heb. 10. 19; Philo, *De Spec. Legg.* 1 (*De Sacr.*), 12 (321, M. 2. 260); *Ep. ad Diogn.* 11. 2. For *ἐδειγμάτισεν* cf. *παρεδειγμάτισεν*, Polyb. 2. 60. 7, 27. 1. 5, and for the rabbinical use of פרדיגמטא see references *ap.* Krauss, *Lehnwörter in Talmud.*

[2] See Note III.

[3] In v. 18 read *θέλων ἐν ταπεινοφροσύνῃ...ἃ ἑόρακεν ἐμβατεύων*, where *ταπεινοφροσύνῃ* refers to special fasts; cf. above, p. 153. For *ἐμβατεύων* cf. Dibelius, *ad loc.*,

prerogatives were merely inflated with that vanity which came from the "mind of the flesh"; this implied that their claim to a fuller possession of "mind" or "spirit" was the direct opposite of the truth; they were more than ever plunged into the material world. Access to the heavens was only to be obtained by union with Christ, who, as head of the Church and the cosmos, provided to everything in it that life which enabled it to grow with a divine increase. The Colossians having already died with Christ to the material world had no need to observe ordinances as if they still lived in the world. All the taboos of Judaism, as preserved in the system of the opposition, came to an end in the moment when they were practised, since they represented the commandments and teachings of men. Such practices might have some rational justification as a form of voluntary piety and humility, produced by mortifying the body in which the Christian was for the time being still forced to dwell, but not as practices which were valued because they gratified the vanity of those who practised them.[1] The death of the Christian to this world prevented him from attaching

and Preisker in *T.W.z.N.T.* s.v. The latter points out the difficulty of supposing a formal initiation in a temple, which the word implies in its technical sense of a formal entry into a temple after initiation, since Paul would deal otherwise with definite participation in heathen rites. He suggests the meaning "enquiring fully into" in the sense of trying to elaborate a doctrinal interpretation of such visions, comparing 2 Macc. 2. 30 and Philo, *De Plant.* 19 (80, M. 1. 341). But in the former passage the sense is rather "covering the ground". In the latter Cohn-Wendland read ἐμβαθύνοντες, which is a regular cliché in this connection, cf. *De Mund. Op.* 25 (77, M. 1. 18), and almost certainly right. The papyri use the word frequently of "entering into possession of" as in Josh. 19. 49 (cf. *Voc. Gr. N.T.* s.v.). Such a progressive entering into possession might suggest the use of the term for a progress in a series of initiations into higher mysteries, similar to that described by Apuleius; the convert would be told that he must "enter into" or "take possession of" a new stage in his spiritual growth (note the reference to "increase" of the true kind in v. 19, perhaps in contrast to the spurious kind involved in the initiations, cf. above, p. 149).

[1] The passage 2. 20–23 is comparatively easy when it is remembered that Paul has to face the fact that the Christian although already "in heaven" is none the less in the body. He does not mean to deny that the mortifying of the body may have some value as a means of liberating the soul from its power (1 Cor. 9. 26 *seqq.*, where the "enslaving" of the body is the opposite of the normal state in which the spirit is "enslaved"). But he does not value such means and the word ἐθελοθρησκία looks like a sarcastic borrowing from his opponents' language. On the other hand they have no rational justification if they are used for the gratifying of vanity or as a means for inducing visions which convey a sense of spiritual pride; if so regarded, they are not a means for destroying the influence of the body over the soul, but a positive means of gratifying the flesh and increasing its influence. (For the inclusion of such attitudes of mind under the flesh cf. Gal. 5. 20.) The grammatical confusion would be avoided if the clause οὐκ ἐν τιμῇ κ.τ.λ. had been replaced by one beginning μωρία δέ ἐστιν or some similar phrase. But this would involve too definite a sanction of such practices and Paul is not willing to make quite so large a concession. In itself the phrase λόγον ἔχειν may mean either "to possess a reasonable justification" or "to have a pretence of justification". Here as often Paul is handicapped by the difficulty of admitting any value in external practices without appearing to justify the claims of his opponents.

more than the most trivial and temporary value to such things, even if they possessed any value at all. For he had not only died with Christ; he had also risen with Him. He must therefore seek the things which were above, where Christ was seated at the right hand of God; he must let his mind be occupied with things which were in heaven, not with things which were on earth. The Colossians had died and their true life was one which was hidden with Christ in God; when Christ, who was the Christian's true life, should appear, they too would be manifested with Him in glory. The passage was a remarkable conflation of the Hellenistic thought of the true life as an incorruptible heavenly life in which the body had already been put to death[1] with the pictorial eschatology of Judaism. The Jewish tradition was still too strong to be eliminated completely, but it could be relegated to a parenthetical clause.

At the same time the thought of the true life enabled Paul to pass to the thought of the true "mortification" (3. 5 *seqq.*). His opponents had justified their system as a means of mortifying the five senses which made up the earthly body;[2] Paul replied with a demand for a complete and immediate mortification of the earthly "members". It was a commonplace that the body was the source of evil; it must be put to death not merely in the form of the flagrant vices of impurity, lust[3] (or desire as the source of evil) and covetousness,[4] the desire of unjust acquisition, which in a widespread Stoic convention was re-

[1] The thought in Philo is normally associated with the more grotesque problems of O.T. exegesis, such as Nadab and Abihu (cf. p. 104) and leprosy (cf. p. 198). Cf. Clem. Alex. *Strom.* 5. 14. 106 (712 P), where the command to watch is interpreted as meaning to learn to live and separate the soul from the body, an interesting attempt to allegorise the apocalyptic element in the N.T.

[2] The duplication of the pentads of vice is peculiar; it seems that Paul, having set down the first, thinks it well to go on from vices in which his readers had once walked (v. 7), which are largely sins of action, to the second list, mainly consisting of sins of speech.

[3] The Chester-Beatty codex here has simply *ἐπιθυμία* for *ἐπιθυμία κακή*. H. C. Hoskier in *J.T.S.* 38. 150, pp. 158 *seqq.* sees a parallel with Indian religion; but *ἐπιθυμία* has already appeared as a summary of the Law in Rom. 7. 7, the last commandment of the decalogue being put for the whole, presumably in order to find in it the commonplace of the evil of desire as such. Cf. Philo, *Leg. Alleg.* 3. 38 (115, M. 1. 110), going back to the ordinary Platonic physiology of *Timaeus* 70e *seqq.*, and *De Decal.* 28 (142, M. 2. 204); note especially the closing section 153. See also Diog. Laert. 7. 113; *Corp. Herm.* 1 (*Poimandres*), 23 (Scott 126). Paul's source is, if *ἐπιθυμία* be correct, the commonplace of Stoicism, as read into the Decalogue, rather than the Brahmins, unless it is supposed that they were the ultimate source of Zeno's teaching.

[4] For *πλεονεξία* as a source of all evils cf. Diod. Sic. 21. 1. 4 (Exc. Hoeschl. p. 480) and 21. 10 (as *ἡ τοῦ πλείονος ἐπιθυμία*) and *passim.* For the end of it as the source of evil in the new golden age, cf. Philo, *De Vit. Moys.* 2 (3), 22 (186, M. 2. 163). For avarice in the narrower sense of the word as spiritual idolatry cf. Philo, *De Spec. Legg.* 1 (*De Mon.*), 2 (23, M. 2. 214), where however *φιλαργυρία* is used; *Test. Jud.* 19. 1.

garded as the main source of human evils: as such it was equated by Judaism with the idolatry of the Old Testament, in order to find a value and meaning for the warnings of Scripture on the subject, idolatry in the literal sense being regarded as out of the question for a Jew or a proselyte.[1] It must also be mortified from all sins against charity. Against two pentads of vice, making up the "old man", Paul set the "putting-on" of the "new man" by the Christian through the knowledge of God which conformed him to the image of the Creator.

The "new man" was possibly drawn with the scheme of pentads from the language of Paul's opponents. In itself it expressed very adequately the experience of conversion; Paul was conscious of a change which could be described as the substitution of a "new man" for the old.[2] It was associated with the conception of the new age, and the new race of men which was to appear with it. But already Gnostic speculations had associated the language with the highest type of mankind, the true Gnostic who enjoyed the vision of God;[3] such men were the true "new race" from heaven; and Judaism had boldly identified the "new race" of those who "saw God" with Israel, who enjoyed that vision in virtue of the Torah, and whose very name showed that they enjoyed the vision of the one true God.[4] The thought of the "new man" produced by the vision of God would seem to have been drawn ultimately from the conception of the identification of the votary with the deity in Egyptian and Eastern religion.[5] But it had passed thence into theology on the one hand[6] and magic on the other.[7]

[1] For the metaphor of "putting-on" Christ at baptism cf. above, pp. 137 *seqq*. For "putting-on" in rabbinical Judaism cf. *Gen. R.* 49. 2: the "men" of Gen. 18. 16 "put on" angels at 19. 1 when the Shekinah has left them.

[2] For the new age cf. above, pp. 92 *seqq*. The new age is characterised by a new race from heaven (Verg. *Ecl.* 4. 7), without prejudice to the poet's chance of living in it (*ib.* 53).

[3] In Philo, *De Abr.* 12 (56 *seqq*., M. 2. 9), Israel as the new race represents the third stage in a scheme of world-ages, the first two beginning with Adam and Noah. This entirely artificial introduction of a scheme of world-ages, in which the new race consists of those who see God because He draws them up to Himself, suggests that Philo is aware of a scheme in which the Zoroastrian system of three stages of redemption (p. 21) was adapted to justify the belief that those who possessed a higher degree of knowledge were the true Israel. Here again it is possible that Philo has preserved in a harmless form a less orthodox speculation. Cf. the Israel-Uriel speculation (p. 49): the association of Israel as against Abraham with the beginning of the "new race" is perhaps significant.

[4] Philo, *Q.R.D.H.* 56 (278 *seqq*., M. 1. 513).

[5] For a full treatment of the subject cf. Kirk, *The Vision of God* 23 *seqq*.

[6] So in the "conversion" of *Corp. Herm.* 13. 8b *seqq*. (Scott 244): the "new man" as such does not appear except in Scott's ingenious conjecture in 11a: the transformation into *νοερὰ γένεσις* is however the same thought.

[7] So in *Papp. Mag. Gr.* 7. 561, 8. 2 *seqq*. the god is to enter into the soul of the worker of the spell and transform him to his own likeness; this seems to represent religion which has decayed into magic.

It may have been assisted by the thought that the latest saviour of the world was a "new Heracles" or whatever other deity he might consider himself to represent.[1] But it was also associated with the thought of Judaism that God created man anew by His forgiveness;[2] the thought itself may have been derived from Hellenistic religion but had acclimatised itself in the religious life of Israel, which could easily adopt the outlook of the age and express it in terms of a "new man", who was implanted by God in the soul in virtue of the prophetic promise of a "new Torah" and a "new heart".[3]

Thus Paul was following an existing convention of popular theology when he described the ethical growth which must result from conversion as the "putting-on" of a "new man". He was equally following those conventions when he described (3. 10) that renewal as leading to a knowledge in virtue of which the Christian would conform to the image of the Creator. It was a commonplace of the age that knowledge implied a "likeness" between the knower and the thing known: thus in astrological physics man could only know the secrets of the universe because all the elements of it entered into his composition, and the thought harmonised well with the Stoic analogy of macrocosm and microcosm.[4] Again, mystical theology held that only "life and light" could enter into "life and light".[5] The belief might again be stated in the form of an axiom of metaphysics; "only the like can know the like" sounded reasonable and convincing, so long as its meaning was left unexplored.[6] But the language could be used to express the ethical truth that the knowledge of God was only possible in so far as man resembled Him in holiness, and it was in this sense that Paul used it.[7] The "image of the Creator" was the pattern after which the new man must be formed and also the means by which the new man, so formed, was made capable of the knowledge of God. That

[1] For the conception cf. above, pp. 20 and 74. The subject has become a standing joke in Philo, *Leg. ad Gaium* 12 (89, M. 2. 558) and 13 (97).

[2] Cf. above, p. 144. So far as I can see the language of the "new man" in this connection is Jewish, though it is drawn from a Judaism which is entirely Hellenistic in its general outlook.

[3] Jer. 31. 31 *seqq.*; Ezek. 11. 19, 36. 25 *seqq.*; cf. p. 130.

[4] Firm. Mat. *Math.* 3, *Proem.* 3; Manilius, *Astron.* 4. 893; Philo, *De Mund. Op.* 51 (146 *seqq.*, M. 1. 35); Hipparchus *ap.* Pliny, *N.H.* 2. 24. 95; *Corp. Herm.* Exc. 2a, 2 (Scott 382).

[5] Cf. above, p. 140.

[6] Philo, *De Gigant.* 2 (9, M. 1. 263); there are souls in the air, but they can only be known by Mind, in order that the like may be known by the like; cf. *Corp. Herm.* 5. 2 (Scott 158). In *Q.D.P.I.* 45 (164, M. 1. 222) we get the final futility that that which is found must be found either by the like in virtue of its likeness or by the unlike in virtue of its contrast. The classical expression is Posidonius *ap.* Sext. Emp. *adv. Math.* 7. 93, following Philolaus.

[7] 1 Jno. 3. 2; *Corp. Herm.* 4. 9 (Scott 154), Exc. 6. 18 (Scott 418). Naturally the mystical and ethical shade into one another.

image was of course Jesus the divine Wisdom, not a divine element present in some particular class of men in spite of the fall of Adam and constituting them the "new race". Those who were really in the image of the Creator were in the image of Jesus, in whom all distinctions of race or class had been done away;[1] for Christ was all things and present in all men. The diversities of mankind might indeed be due to the fall;[2] but the original unity was restored to all those who were in Christ; it was not a special prerogative of a chosen few who possessed some higher knowledge of God. For those who were in Him there was no difference of Greek or Jew,[3] of cultured barbarian or pure savage[4] (the distinction between two classes of barbarians may allude to some claim on the part of Paul's opponents that their system contained the truth not only of Judaism but of the ancient wisdom of the barbarians; the claim was certainly true in so far as it attempted to substitute for the main Christian tradition a system dominated by the Oriental influences at work in Hellenistic religion). Christ was all things and present in all men, so that in Him the ancient unity of mankind was restored. Here again Paul used a rhetorical

[1] 3. 11 appears to be entirely irrelevant and its introduction here may be due to the association of it with the thought of "putting-on Christ" at baptism, as in Gal. 3. 27. So Dibelius, *ad loc.*, perhaps rightly. The thought may have been taken over from the preaching of the synagogue; cf. *Seder Eliahu Rabba*, quoted by Dibelius. But the element of "mind" as a divine emanation in man is the image of God and the source of the kinship of all men in spite of their diversities (Philo, *De Mund. Op.* 51 (145 *seqq.*, M. 1. 35); cf. Seneca, *Ep.* 4. 2 (31), 11). Yet again it is the element which enables man to ascend to heaven (*De Mund. Op.* 16 (70, M. 1. 16); cf. Seneca, *N.Q. Prol.* 12). The element of "mind" or "spirit" is in the Gnostic-Hermetic tradition the prerogative of a special class. Consequently it is possible that Paul's language here is not irrelevant but a claim that the reversal of the fall and the restoration of unity are not the prerogative of a special class, who have somehow preserved the divine spark in spite of the fall, but of all who are "in Christ". It must be admitted that this is only a conjecture.

[2] For the fall of Adam as producing the diversity of mankind cf. the fable that men and beasts understood one another's language before the fall (p. 80) and Orig. *De Princ.* 1. 6. 2, and Plutarch's account of the Zoroastrian belief that men will have one πολιτεία and one speech at the end of all things (*De Is. et Os.* 47, 370b).

[3] "Greek" for "Gentile" may reflect a Greek version of the Morning Benedictions which seem to be the source of Paul's language (*Authorized Jewish Prayerbook* 5 *seqq.*).

[4] The distinction between barbarian and Scythian seems to imply some such conception. For the wisdom of the barbarians cf. Philo, *Quod Omn. Prob. Lib.* 11 (74, M. 2. 456) and 14 (94, M. 2. 460); cf. also p. 206; Jos. *c. Ap.* 1. 2 (6 *seqq.*), where Josephus avoids the word "barbarians", substituting "Egyptians and Babylonians" as recognised instances of non-Hellenic learning; Clem. Alex. *Strom.* 1. 14. 59 *seqq.* (350 P) for the barbarians as the inventors of all culture, following Tatian, *Or. adv. Gr.* 1. 3, or employing the same source, which may well have been a Jewish *apologia* against the Greeks; it must be remembered that the Jews were "barbarians". For Scythians as a type of the wildest savagery cf. Jos. *c. Ap.* 2. 37 (269); Philo, *Leg. ad Gaium* 2 (10, M. 2. 547); Cicero, *De Nat. Deor.* 2. 34. 88; Seneca, *De Ira* 2. 15. 1; Orig. *c. Cels.* 1. 1.

phrase which formally applied better to the divine Mind or reason of Stoicism, which was potentially all things, as working itself out in the cosmos and present in them, than to the historical Jesus, but was admirably suited to express Paul's consciousness that in Him was to be found the answer to all the problems of the universe.[1]

Thus the Christian's task (3. 12 *seqq.*) was to put on the nature that suited those whom God had chosen, the various forms of charity united by charity itself. The list was artificially arranged to form a group of five corresponding to the pentads of Paul's opponents, but roughly covering the account of charity in 1 Cor. 13. 4–7; Paul made no real attempt to provide an exhaustive list of the various forms of Christian virtue. The effect of putting on the new man would be to produce in the hearts of the readers the domination of peace, which was the purpose to which they were called in the one body of Christ; they must always be thankful for such a privilege. The word of Christ[2] must dwell in them abundantly, expressing itself in wisdom, which would enable them to teach and advise one another, and in the outpouring of psalms and hymns and spiritual songs, which would express the inward thanksgiving of their hearts. All their actions would be done in the name of the Lord Jesus and would express their offering of thanks to the Father through Him. The whole passage reflected the spiritual enthusiasm of the primitive Christian community, though there was no mention of the outpourings of incoherent glossolalies. But while the description of the Christian attitude was entirely Pauline, the mention of the duty of enthusiastic thanksgiving at this point reflected the methods of propaganda favoured by Hellenistic religion, and was very probably suggested to Paul by his opponents' claim that the revelation of the true knowledge must express itself in a spontaneous outburst of thanksgiving.[3] It was only right that the Christian revelation of the true cosmogony should end with a call to such an outburst.

[1] Cf. p. 128.

[2] The "word of Christ" seems to be a conflation of the Gospel expressing itself in utterance as in 1 Cor. 12. 8 with the thought of Christ as dwelling in the Christian.

[3] There is no apparent relevance in the passage 3. 15 *seqq.* But the Hermetic tradition represents spontaneous thanksgiving as the result of a revelation (*Corp. Herm.* 1 (*Poimandres*), 31 (Scott 130), 5. 10b (Scott 164), 13. 17 (Scott 250), Ascl. 3. 41b (Scott 374). For this conventional form cf. Norden, *Agnostos Theos* 295 *seqq.*, who finds the same form in the concluding chapters of Romans (11. 25 *seqq.*). The thanksgiving there, as in Colossians, leads on to moral exhortation. The same convention may underlie such a passage as Philo, *De Migr. Abr.* 5 (25, M. 1. 440). But the convention has become so commonplace that its origin has been lost; it is merely a regular form of exposition, in which revelation or teaching leads to thanksgiving, which must express itself in a life of suitable conduct. Cf. Epict. *Diss.* 1. 16. 6 *seqq.*

Thus it is possible that the sequence of revelation and thanksgiving was derived from a current literary convention; this sequence again was expected to lead on to an exhortation to a life of virtue in accordance with the revelation given. On the other hand there were philosophers who held that the function of philosophy was not to reveal the mysteries of the universe, but to advise mankind as to their conduct in the relations of domestic life.[1] Paul himself may have felt no little sympathy with this point of view, for him the position of Jesus as the centre of the life of the cosmos was not a matter of philosophy but an obvious and indisputable fact. The short and pedestrian summary of domestic duties which he appended to his exhortation to thanksgiving (3. 18 *seqq.*) stood in marked contrast to the exalted style of the earlier part of the letter and was intended to contrast the simplicity of the practice of the Christian life with the "mysteries" on which it might depend; for the Christian life was more important than all mysteries. Only in dealing with the duties of slaves did he expand his treatment beyond the briefest injunctions; the normal type of such exhortations would hardly envisage a philosophical slave. There were, however, many slaves among the primitive Churches, and the abandonment of the apocalyptic message that the time was short made it necessary to find some other grounds for comforting the depressed classes. A general upheaval of the slave-world as a result of the Gospel was not to be thought of; but the recent affair of Onesimus had shown that the problem of the Christian slave demanded serious consideration. Paul's message to them was expanded in order to give some measure of consolation to those who needed something more than a mere injunction to good conduct.[2] The rest of the Epistle was occupied with personal messages.

Such was Paul's reply to the first serious aberration from the received tradition of the Church. The danger which he was called to

[1] Seneca, *Ep.* 15. 2 (94). 1: *Eam partem philosophiae quae...marito suadet quomodo se gerat adversus uxorem, patri quomodo educet liberos, domino quomodo servos regat, quidam solam receperunt.* For the regular forms of moral exhortation of this type cf. Dibelius in *H.z.N.T. ad loc.* The baldness and brevity of the injunctions seems explicable only on the grounds suggested in the text. It may be contrasted with more exalted language used by his opponents to the effect that a correct cosmogony was a necessary basis for true virtue, cf. Chrysippus *ap.* Plut. *De Stoic. Rep.* 9. 1035 C.

[2] This would seem to be the explanation of the greater length with which the duties of slaves are set out and the typically Pauline association of them with the ultimate principles of Christianity. The Ephesian continuator does not realise the model on which Paul is working and expands the short list into a general homily on Christian duties, extending to forms of vice which the philosopher would hardly regard as possible for his hearers (Eph. 4. 25 *seqq.*; a philosopher would hardly warn his readers not to steal).

meet was one which threatened the whole structure of Christianity, for it involved the replacement of Jesus by personifications of the powers or names of God, identified with or set above the lords of the planets, as man's only hope of escaping from the fate to which astrology condemned him.[1] The system would have resulted in the conflation of Christianity with its heathen and Jewish competitors, in a form which substituted the knowledge of such secrets [combined in a few rare souls with the mystical contemplation of God, in the majority with a cult of visions artificially induced, and regarded as the end of religion], for the Gospel of the love of God and man, achieved by personal union with the historical Jesus accepted as the risen Lord of the Church. In meeting the danger Paul had been compelled to make a profound and far-reaching change in his method of presenting the Gospel. In his earlier letters he had substituted cosmogony for apocalyptic as a means of converting the Gentile world. The change meant nothing to him, for he was not concerned with philosophy, and any system of thought and language that expressed the position of Jesus as the Lord was equally acceptable. But the effect of the Colossian controversy, whether Paul realised it or not, was to substitute philosophy for homiletic as the basis of Christian preaching. The divine Wisdom, the pattern and agent of creation and the divine Mind permeating the cosmos, was identified with Jesus not as a matter of midrashic exposition which could be used and thrown aside, but as an eternal truth in the realm of metaphysics; for only so could the supremacy of Jesus be asserted as against such potent beings as the rulers of the stars in their courses. It is probable that Paul was entirely unaware that his letter would produce this effect: whether he realised it or not, he had committed the Church to the theology of Nicaea.

[1] The best product of this type of Gnosis is represented by the Hermetica, the worst by the magical papyri. The ease with which such systems could be merged in one another appears from a comparison of the closely related systems of Valentinus and Marcus, as described by Irenaeus.

CHAPTER VIII

THE PAULINE EPILOGUE

COLOSSIANS marks the completion of Paul's theology. One other genuine letter remains, the Epistle to the Philippians. This letter appears to have been written from Rome, when he was faced with the prospect of death. It has been suggested in recent years that the letter may have been written from a captivity at Ephesus.[1] It cannot be denied that Paul was imprisoned on various occasions which are not mentioned in the Acts. But it must be remembered that Acts makes no pretence of narrating Paul's adventures between his first departure from the Syrian Antioch to Tarsus and his visit to Jerusalem during the famine; we know that he returned to Antioch to help Barnabas, and proceeded to Jerusalem, and we also know that this information covers a period of nine years.[2] Consequently the discrepancy between the account of Paul's adventures in Acts and his own narrative in 2 Cor. 11. 23 *seqq.* cannot be urged to prove that he may have been imprisoned during his stay at Ephesus, any more than the silence of Acts can be used to prove the contrary. On the other hand the hypothesis involves a more than doubtful interpretation of Paul's allusion to the πραιτώριον (Phil. 1. 13); traditionally it has been held that this refers to the praetorian guard.[3] It has been maintained that it can refer to the official residence of any provincial governor; but there is a remarkable lack of evidence for this in the case of the senatorial provinces, including Asia.[4] Further, it involves the view that "Caesar's household" in 4. 22 refers not to

[1] For a statement of the argument on the other side cf. Duncan, *St Paul's Ephesian Ministry*. Michael in Moffatt's commentary xii *seqq.* gives both sides.

[2] Cf. *Jerusalem* 179.

[3] Lightfoot, *The Epistle to the Philippians* 99 *seqq.*

[4] Mommsen, *Hermes* XXXV, 1900, 437 *seqq.*, inclines to this view. But apart from a general reference to official residences of travelling judges in Julian, the authorities he quotes are inscriptions from imperial provinces and Tac. *Ann.* 3. 33. The last passage, however, seems highly doubtful; the complaint is made that if a magistrate takes his wife to his province *duorum egressus coli, duo esse praetoria*; the speaker who makes the complaint is considering both classes of province, as the reference to the interference of women in military matters shows. The sense is at least as good if it means "There are two general headquarters" as if it means "There are two Government Houses". The references in Moulton and Milligan, *Voc. Gr. N.T.* s.v., come from Egypt, as is natural, except for the inscription *Sylloge* 932 (=880), 63, which comes from Thrace, an imperial province. It does not appear that there is evidence for *praetoria* in the senatorial provinces; Michael *loc. cit.* suggests a detachment of praetorian guards at Ephesus; but could they be "the whole" πραιτώριον?

the imperial household in Rome but to the staff which managed the imperial estates and revenues in Ephesus and Asia. It cannot be said that this interpretation is impossible in itself; but it involves the supposition that Paul had friends both in the proconsular staff and in the imperial. Considering the friction which normally prevailed between the two sides of the administration the supposition is highly improbable, especially when it is remembered that the Pauline mission at its Ephesian period was only just making itself felt outside the synagogue. Finally it is very difficult to interpret "the beginning of the Gospel" as referring to the period only three years before Paul's mission at Ephesus, when the Philippians appear to have sent some financial help to Paul at Corinth or Athens; it suggests a period some long time ago, since Paul is now able, in retrospect, to see that his first visit to Macedonia was in some sense a new departure, which marked a first step in his progress towards Rome. It seems hardly likely that he would have written "the beginning of the Gospel" unless he was looking back on a longer period than the interval between Philippi and Ephesus both in space and time.[1]

Consequently the traditional dating of Philippians from Rome appears to be far more natural than the attempt to predate it to an otherwise unrecorded imprisonment at Ephesus. In itself the letter contains no further development of Paul's theology; the much discussed passage, 2. 5 *seqq.*, cannot be pressed to mean that Jesus was God in the sense of Nicene theology, just as it cannot mean less than that He was the pre-existing pattern and agent of creation, the Wisdom of the Old Testament and Paul's Epistle to the Colossians. The incompatibility of the figure of Wisdom with the historical Jesus remains; Paul was entirely indifferent to the need of philosophical consistency as against the recognition of Jesus as the centre of the universe and its history. In the same way he combines the Jewish thought of the "day of Christ", implying a catastrophic second coming of the Lord, with the Hellenistic thought that the Christian is already living in heaven and is "with Christ" at his death.[2] It would seem

[1] I cannot help feeling that the attempt to date Philippians from Ephesus is due to a desire to vindicate the authenticity of the Pastoral Epistles or some fragments of them. I see nothing in favour of the view that the personal fragments are genuine insertions into otherwise spurious compilations; in particular 2 Tim. 4. 9 *seqq.* is condemned by the phrase ἐπουράνιος βασιλεία (v. 18), which is the language of a conventional piety which has forgotten that apocalyptic and astrology are different.

[2] Cf. p. 141. The language of 3. 20 is a remarkable conflation, since the Hellenistic thought of the soul's true home in heaven (p. 140; Str.-B. give no real rabbinical parallels) is immediately combined with the hope of a second coming. Here, as elsewhere, Paul was perfectly prepared to use any conceptions which enabled him to express what he regarded as the essential truth.

that the Christians at Philippi were quite content with the earlier form in which he had preached the Gospel, and Paul uses either his earlier or later methods of expressing his message with complete certainty that they will not be misunderstood in the most faithful of all his Churches, even if there is a certain tendency to quarrelling among some of its leading members. As an expression of Paul's personality with its glowing love for his converts the letter is the most attractive of all his writings. His last word from prison is "Rejoice in the Lord"; there we may leave him.

Of the greatness of his achievement there can be no doubt. In one sense he had turned Christianity into a mystery-religion, for he had not hesitated to express it in terms of that Hellenistic cosmogony which was the general form in which the cults of his time were adjusting themselves to the needs of the age. But the essential difference remained that for him, in spite of the incautious outburst of 2 Cor. 5. 16, Jesus, as the risen Lord of the Church, remained the concrete figure of the Gospels; however much the Jewish Christians may have quarrelled with his attitude to the Torah, there is no scrap of evidence to hint that they disagreed with his conception of the person of the Lord; both to Paul and his Jewish-Christian opponents Jesus was the centre of their life and their religion. The essential difference between Pauline Christianity and Hellenistic religion remains: Pauline Christianity is a religion which centres on the historical Jesus expressed in terms of popular theology; the central figures of Hellenistic cults, where they rise above the level of heathen religion, dissolve into vague abstractions symbolising a deity projected into the cosmos from the mind of man.

His transformation of Christianity from a system of Jewish apocalyptic, with a purely local and temporary appeal, into a religion of salvation by faith in the historical Jesus as the first-born of all creation was essential if Christianity was to survive and to conquer the world. Whether he was right or wrong in his faith that Jesus was the author of creation and the meaning of history is a matter which the study of Christian origins cannot fail to raise; it cannot within its own limits provide the answer.

CHAPTER IX

THE EPHESIAN CONTINUATOR

IT is scarcely possible to maintain the view that the Epistle to the Ephesians is a genuine Pauline document. The difference between the long sentences and involved clauses of Ephesians and Paul's ordinary style might conceivably be explained by the theory that it represents a set piece of doctrinal exposition,[1] not a document written in the heat of controversy.[2] This, however, fails to account for the obscurity of the letter. Paul might well have thought it desirable to expound his theology in the form of a general exposition. Elsewhere, however, although his language may be obscure, his general purpose is clear. Here the language is clear but the occasion and purpose are at first sight a mystery. Moreover, the leading ideas of other Epistles reappear in Ephesians not because they are relevant to the theme, but as if they were part of a system which has to be expounded as something given; the mere fact of their irrelevance is not a sufficient reason for omitting them.[3]

There is a further difficulty in regard to the historical situation. Judaism and judaising Christianity are no longer serious rivals to the Church. It is possible that this complete separation of Church and synagogue was achieved in Paul's lifetime in some of the Churches of his foundation; it is highly doubtful whether he would have realised it so completely as to confine his allusions to that controversy to the parenthesis of 2. 5 and its resumption in 2. 8. It is still more difficult to explain the allusions to idolatry. In the genuine Pauline letters it is

[1] So Armitage Robinson, *The Epistle to the Ephesians*, intr. p. 12, where however the extraordinary difference of style is not noted.

[2] Rom. 1. 18 is somewhat similar. Paul's *apologia* to his own people is set out in long sentences. But compare the opening words with ἀποκεῖται γὰρ παρὰ θεῶν μῆνις in Pap. Par. 63 col. IX (*UPZ* 144. 47), a school-copy of a pattern essay (*ib.* p. 622). It seems that the whole passage is a deliberate imitation of a conventional style, leading to the dramatic turning of the tables on Judaism in 2. 1, where three brief clauses demolish the elaborate structure of the previous chapter.

[3] Note the insertion of "By grace are ye saved" in 2. 5 and the expansion of the thought in v. 8. The whole thought belongs to the Jewish-Christian controversy, not to the theme of the Christian "ascent to heaven". There is a certain parallel in 1 Cor. 15. 56, where the reference to the Law is quite irrelevant. Here, however, there is a clear association with the thought of sin and death, which forms the theme of Rom. 7, a theme which was still fresh in Paul's mind, and no expansion of the associated thought as here. But it is typical of a continuator to feel that grace and works must be dragged in at all costs.

assumed that there is no danger that the Christian will relapse into idolatry; no doubt the assumption was justified by the large number of Jews, proselytes and adherents of the synagogue to be found in the earliest communities. In Rom. 1. 18 *seqq.* the conventional Jewish argument against idolatry is turned into an attack on Judaism. In 1 Cor. 8. 5 and 10. 14 there is no question of the readers lapsing into idolatry; the danger is that they may seem to countenance it, or that they may bring themselves into the power of the demons who lurk behind the idols of the heathen by an undue self-confidence. In Col. 3. 5 idolatry is explained to be the same as covetousness in accordance with the Jewish-Hellenistic convention. In Ephesians, however, we have two warnings against idolatry. The first of these (4. 17 *seqq.*) is a variation on the conventional Jewish argument based on Rom. 1. 21 *seqq.*, of which it is a recapitulation. But the second (5. 5 *seqq.*), while introduced by the conventional equation of covetousness with idolatry found in Col. 3. 5, abandons the thought of covetousness in favour of an apparently serious warning against the belief that it is possible to combine Christianity with secret heathen rites. The warning (5. 6–14) is noticeably lacking in the reminiscences of Pauline writing which are found elsewhere in the Epistle; it would seem that the writer thinks it necessary, as Paul did not, to warn his readers against the danger of syncretising Christianity with pagan cults and has to rely on himself for this passage for lack of a Pauline model.

Yet another objection is the word "mystery" in 5. 32. The term is employed of a natural action which is to the initiate a symbol of a spiritual truth. It is drawn from the theology of "mystery" cults. These were compelled to expound the rites, which were the essential feature of their systems, in terms of the popular philosophy and theology of the age. Thus the "mystery" ceased to be the actual rite, and became the spiritual meaning which its exponents imported from that theology in order to justify the crude and primitive practices of barbarous religion, in this case the "sacred marriage".[1] Paul, however, does not use the term in this sense; he uses it in its strictly Palestinian-Jewish sense of a divine secret, hitherto concealed but now revealed, or else revealed to Israel but concealed from the rest of mankind;

[1] For the universality of the practice of reading a mystic symbolism into cult-practice at this period cf. Orig. *c. Cels.* 1. 12. The use of the term "mystery" in this sense goes back to Plato, *Theaet.* 156a; *Rep.* 378a; cf. Varro *ap.* Aug. *De Civ. Dei* 7. 5, where those *qui adissent mysteria* recognise the soul of the world and its parts in the images of the gods. Properly the "mystery" is not the theology, which is common property, but the rite, which may not be divulged to the uninitiated.

nowhere else does he use it in its secondary Hellenistic sense of a rite with a "mystical" meaning. It cannot of course be denied that he might have used the term here in a different sense from that in which he uses it elsewhere; but the variation in meaning is suspicious.[1]

Other objections sometimes raised are less serious. In particular the change from the "body of Christ" as a cosmic entity in Col. 1. 18 and 2. 19 to the Church on earth in Eph. 1. 22 *seqq.* and 4. 16 involves no real difficulty.[2] The cosmic Church was forced on Paul by his opponents; his own interest lay entirely in the Church on earth. If there were spiritual beings in the higher spheres, they too needed redemption in Christ, if they were to be saved from the material state into which they had fallen. Paul probably believed that they existed, but his arguments cannot be pressed even to prove that he believed in them, still less to prove that he regarded them with any serious interest.

On the whole, however, the difficulties seem fatal to the tradition of Pauline authorship. This must not be taken as depreciating the value of the letter. The writer combines a real measure of originality with a deep understanding of Paulinism and a thorough loyalty to it; he has no ulterior motive of the kind usually found in pseudepigraphic writings. The best explanation of the Epistle seems to be that it is intended as an introduction to the genuine Pauline letters; it is possible that the writer is their first collector. His object is to make them known to the Church as a statement of Paul's message; his further object is to warn his readers against disunity and a general lowering of the Christian standard. His understanding of Paulinism is remarkably clear; and his familiarity with Jewish methods of expounding the Scriptures and traditional Jewish explanations of them[3] suggests that he may have been one of Paul's personal companions; the general Hellenistic outlook makes it unlikely, though not impossible, that he had a personal knowledge of the rabbinical exegesis of Palestinian Judaism.[4]

[1] See Note IV. He uses μεμύημαι in Phil. 4. 12, but the religious meaning of the word there has almost entirely vanished.

[2] As urged by Bousset, *Kyrios Christos* 286, followed by Dibelius in *H.z.N.T.* on the latter passage.

[3] Cf. p. 195.

[4] The solution put forward above is that of Goodspeed in *The Meaning of Ephesians*. His statement of the difficulties of accepting its authenticity and his suggested solution appear entirely convincing. I am not clear that it is necessary to suppose, as he does, that the author wrote after the publication of Luke-Acts or that Luke-Acts is as late as he holds. But his general view of the author's intention and the occasion of writing appears to offer a convincing solution both of the authorship of the Epistle and of its great value and importance as a statement of Paulinism. A full discussion of the difficulties of the traditional authorship is given by Goodspeed, *op. cit.*; the foregoing summary is largely based on his statement of the problem and that of Dibelius in *H.z.N.T.*

Thus Ephesians, like the Pastorals, is a product of a time when the veneration attached to Apostolic authorship made it necessary to borrow a name in order to give sanction to documents, whose purpose was to expound the Christian message in a manner suited to the changing conditions of the Church, but before there was a canon of the New Testament to which it would be sacrilege to make any addition. The difference between Ephesians and the Pastorals is that the author of the former really understands the meaning of Paulinism and is only concerned to expound it; the writers of the Pastorals are concerned to supply Paulinism with a system of regulation and discipline for the life of the Church. It was an obvious weakness of Paulinism as expounded by Paul that it made no such provision. Paul could hardly have admitted its necessity without offering an opening to those who held that the element of regulation would be best supplied by commanding the Gentiles to observe the Torah, while in his own lifetime he was able to substitute a personal autocracy for a system of regulation. The result is that Ephesians is an accurate exposition of Paulinism; the Pastorals are concerned to accommodate Paulinism to the practical needs of the Church after Paul's death.[1]

The Epistle opens with a thanksgiving after the Pauline fashion, but the thanksgiving is unrelated to any particular circumstances. It is simply a statement of the combination of cosmogony and eschatology at which Paul had arrived in Colossians. God has elected the Christian (I. 3 *seqq.*) from before the foundation of the world for adoption through Jesus Christ for the praise of the glory of that grace which He bestowed on him in the Beloved, in whom we have received redemption, that is the forgiveness of sins. (Col. I. 12 *seqq.* adapted to the general Pauline insistence on grace; the point of Paul's identification of redemption with forgiveness has been lost.) Through the abundance of this grace the Christian has received wisdom (I. 8 is modelled on the pleonasm of Col. I. 9 without the excuse that it is a counterblast to the rhetoric of Gnosticism) to understand the mystery of God's purpose in summing up in Christ all things, whether in heaven or on earth, when the duly appointed time is fulfilled (Gal. 4. 4). For in Christ the Jew received that portion, to which he had been foreordained by God's purpose in virtue of the hope in the Messiah that was given him (here "Christ" has its proper sense), while the Gentile

[1] Cf. Scott in Moffatt's *Commentary* on the Pastoral Epistles, intr. pp. xxiv *seqq.*, perhaps with an insufficient recognition of the necessity of providing Paulinism with a system of regulation to replace Paul's personal influence.

by believing in the Gospel obtained a preliminary sealing with the Holy Spirit of promise (2 Cor. 1. 22); that preliminary gift was a pledge both to Jews and Gentiles that they would one day receive the full inheritance (Rom. 8. 23). The term ἀνακεφαλαιώσασθαι was admirably chosen to cover the position of the divine pattern in whom all things were potentially created (Col. 1. 16), the beginning of the new age and presumably the end of all things,[1] though the abandonment of eschatology in this Epistle goes even further than in the later Pauline writings. The allusion to "sealing" was drawn from Pauline usage, though it seems likely that the writer is aware of the transference of the metaphor from circumcision to baptism as a more or less technical term.[2]

The prayer which follows (1. 15 *seqq.*) is only a prayer in form, just as the thanksgiving is not really a thanksgiving but a general doctrinal exposition. The prayer asks that the readers may receive a spirit of wisdom and revelation which will enlighten the eyes of their hearts (the reverse of 2 Cor. 4. 4), so that they may understand the full meaning of the Christian hope, the glory that awaits them and the power with which God works towards those who believe (Col. 1. 5, 27 and 11). The great manifestation of that power was the raising up of Christ from the dead and His exaltation to heaven above all the powers of the lower spheres of the heavens and every name that can be named both in the present age and in that which is to come. (Vv. 20–22 conflate Phil. 2. 9, where Jesus has already been exalted to heaven, with a formal tribute to eschatology in the allusion to some possible further triumph in a future age drawn from 1 Cor. 15. 24 *seqq.*) This supremacy of Jesus in the cosmos carries with it supremacy in the Church, the body which He continually fills with Himself just as He is Himself continually being filled with God; the double conception of the Wisdom-Logos as filling the Church and being filled Himself is a consistent application of the commonplace which underlies Col. 1. 18 and 2. 9;[3] if the writer was a member of the Pauline circle he would no doubt be familiar with a full exposition of the double

[1] Cf. συγκεφαλαιώσασθαι...οἰκειώσαντες τὴν ἀρχὴν τῷ τέλει, Polyb. 39. 19. 3.

[2] In Rom. 4. 11 the rabbinical usage of "sealing" for circumcision is implied; for this cf. Sanday and Headlam, *ad loc.* Since baptism is the true circumcision (Col. 2. 11), it follows that it is a "seal", which marks the person sealed as belonging to God, though the term is obviously less suitable for baptism than for circumcision. Anrich, *Das antike Mysterienwesen*, 120, is probably right in holding that the term is drawn from Jewish usage; though the conception of the believer as the property of his god is natural to the Hellenistic outlook, it is of Semitic origin.

[3] Cf. p. 164. The sense of v. 23 is "that which is filled by Him who is always being filled".

aspect of the "filling" of the Wisdom of God. If not, he is merely interpreting those passages in the light of the ordinary convention of Hellenistic thought. The cosmic aspect of the *pleroma* has been allowed to drop out of sight; the writer correctly interprets Paul as being entirely concerned with the Church on earth as the sphere of redemption and "filling" with the spirit of Jesus.

In this *pleroma* "life" is given to the Gentiles, who were in the past subject to the "aeon of this world",[1] the ruler of the lower air, and of the spirit that works in the children of disobedience. The traditional Satan of Judaism was thus recognised as lord of the sublunar sphere, the only place left to him if the planetary spheres possessed their own lords of evil; Paul had not been sufficiently concerned with the working out of a consistent scheme to relate the Jewish to the Hellenistic view; the writer of Ephesians shows more concern for a harmonious system.[2] The Jews too had been subject to the desires of the flesh and the natural mind, and were like the rest of mankind children of wrath (a summary of Rom. 7). But God in the riches of His mercy had raised them to a new life with Christ and established them with Him[3] in the celestial sphere of the firmament in Christ (Col. 3. 1–4), as a standing proof to the future ages of the world of the abundant riches of the grace of God.[4] They must always remember that they are saved by grace through

[1] The sense is easier if the "aeon" is a personal being. Sasse in *T.W.z.N.T.* accepts the personal sense here alone in the N.T.; Dibelius, *H.z.N.T.* s.v., understands a personal "aeon" in the Iranian sense. The writer probably had some vague knowledge of personal "aeons" and used the "aeon of this world" as equated with the "ruler of the realm of the air" as a periphrasis for the "god of this world" in his model (2 Cor. 4. 4); naturally the original phrase was too startling to be reproduced.

[2] The only early Jewish parallels for Satan as lord of the lower air seem to be *Test. Benj.* 3. 4, where however Charles rejects ἀερίου, and 2 En. 29. 5, where Satan after his fall flies below the moon; but the date of 2 Enoch is uncertain. In the normal Hellenistic tradition the thicker air below the moon (Cicero, *Tusc. Disp.* 1. 18. 43; Servius, *ad Aen.* 6. 640) is subject to chance, fate and evil (cf. *Placita* 2. 4. 12 (*Dox. Gr.* 332) (the view ascribed to Aristotle) and Epiph. *adv. Haer.* 3. 8 (*ib.* 590) (to Pythagoras)). Thus it was suitable for the lower orders of δαιμόνια of the "Pythagorean" tradition, and it appears in this light in Philo, *De Spec. Legg.* 1 (*De Mon.*), 1 (13, M. 2. 213); cf. *Corp. Herm.* Exc. 24. 1 (Scott 496). Normally, however, Philo remembers to revise his sources so as to eliminate the inferiority of the lower air as an abode of spiritual beings; for the lower air is the sphere of action of the angels of Jewish convention (*De Conf. Ling.* 34 (174. 1, M. 1. 431)). In *De Gigant.* 4 (17, M. 1. 265) he logically commits himself to evil angels in the lower air, but proceeds to explain them away as wicked men.

[3] The language goes beyond Paul; the nearest parallels appear to be the frankly astrological glorification of the mother of the Maccabean martyrs and her sons in 4 Macc. 17. 5 and the curious attack on the deification of alien rulers in Philo, *De Execr.* 6 (152, M. 1. 433), where the foreigner receives a "firm position" in heaven. The passage is a paraphrase of Deut. 28. 43, but the protest against the deification of an alien ruler seems to be drawn from an Egyptian hatred of foreign kings (cf. p. 12).

[4] The aeons properly imply a number of future world-ages, but probably simply reflect the Hebrew usage, as employed by Paul in such passages as Rom. 11. 36.

faith; the gift comes from God, not from themselves, lest any man should boast. For all Christians are of God's making, having been created anew in Christ Jesus to perform those good works which God had prepared for them to walk in. The systematiser of Paulinism could hardly ignore the controversy with Judaism over faith, works and grace; as a preliminary to an appeal to the reader to live that life of good works which was the inevitable result of his translation to heaven, it was perhaps as apposite as it could be, in view of the fact that Paul's teaching on the subject had been entirely concerned with the controversy over the relation of the Gentile Christian to the Torah, a controversy which by this time had ceased to have any real significance. It is typical of the writer that he should try to make Paul's teaching on the subject consistent; Paul himself had been quite content to combine the statement that the Christian had died to sin (Rom. 6. 2) or had risen with Christ (Col. 3. 1) and therefore presumably could have no desire to sin, with peremptory injunctions to abandon what *ex hypothesi* he could not desire. At the same time the attempted harmonisation served as a means of alluding to the problem of predestination which was a standing puzzle of popular philosophy no less than of Judaism and Pauline Christianity.[1]

Thus the Gentiles (2. 11 *seqq.*) must remember that they were once without hope in the world, despised by the so-called but really spurious circumcision (Col. 2.11). They were aliens from the commonwealth of Israel,[2] to whom alone the Messianic promises had been given (the term "Christ" is again used in its strict Messianic sense). The outward symbol of their alienation was the Torah, which professed to serve as a barrier against sin,[3] but actually failed to do so and only served to foster enmity as between Jew and Gentile. This barrier had been done away in Christ, who had through His flesh abolished the old law of external ordinances (Col. 2. 14) and united both Jew and Gentile into one new man, making peace and reconciling both in one body to God through the Cross. He had thus slain the enmity which existed on the one hand between Jew and Gentile, on the other hand between God and man, preaching peace both to those who were far removed from God and those who were already near Him, but still

[1] *Placita* 1. 27. 5 (*Dox. Gr.* 322); Hipp. *El.* 1. 19. 19 (*ib.* 569); 4 Esdr. 7. 132 *seqq.*; Jos. *B.J.* 2. 8. 14 (162).

[2] Cf. Philo, *De Spec. Legg.* 1 (*De Mon.*), 7 (51 *seqq.*, M. 2. 219). The thought is a revision of the popular language of the proselytising synagogues of the Dispersion.

[3] *Letter of Aristeas* 139 and 142; 3 Macc. 3. 4 and 7. Note the recognition in the latter passage that the Torah is a cause of anti-Semitism. There may be an allusion to the barrier excluding Gentiles from the inner Courts of the Temple (Armitage Robinson, *ad loc.*), but there is no need to find any such reference.

separated; for through Jesus both Jew and Gentile had free access to the Father in one Spirit (Rom. 5. 2). The obscurity of the passage is due to the writer's attempt to fit the thought of the reconciliation of Jew and Gentile into the language in which Paul expounded the reconciliation of man and the celestial powers to God through the death of Jesus on the Cross (Col. 1. 20 and 2. 14). The parenthetic allusion to the difference between Jew and Gentile in Col. 2. 13 has here become the writer's primary concern. Gentiles are no longer aliens or at best mere πάροικοι, who can claim only limited rights; they are fellow-citizens of the Saints and members of the household of God, possessing those privileges which the synagogues of the Dispersion offered to the proselyte.[1] The allusion to the household of God is employed to introduce the Church as the Temple of the living God (1 Cor. 3. 11 *seqq.*); the Christian is built into that Temple of which the Apostles and prophets are the foundation and Jesus the head corner-stone, an interesting allusion to the historical tradition of the teaching of Jesus (Mk. 12. 10 seems a more probable source than a direct use of Ps. 118. 22). The headship of Jesus in the building offers an opportunity of introducing the Pauline doctrine of His headship of the body as the source of its growth (Col. 2. 19);[2] the writer disregards the difficulty involved in the thought of a building which "grows" after the final stone has been set in its place.

The writer reverts to the prayer-form at 3. 1. Paul is the prisoner of Jesus Christ on behalf of the Gentiles; the fact is a claim to veneration, not a difficulty to be explained as in Col. 1. 24. In other words the Church has already faced the issue of persecution and decided it successfully; the Jewish view of martyrdom as a title to glory has within the Church prevailed over the Hellenistic. His ministry[3]

[1] Philo, *De Cher.* 34 (120, M. 1. 160–1), expresses the same thought in the form that as against one another all men have equal rights as natives of the cosmos, though as against God all men are at best πάροικοι, while the wicked are exiles. Citizenship was a standing cause of friction between Jews and Gentiles; the exemption of Jews in the Hellenistic world was a serious grievance (cf. Schürer, *G.J.V.* 3. 121 *seqq.*; Meyer, *Urspr. u. Anf.* 3. 124 *seqq.*); in Palestine the alien had no theoretical right to exist, since he could not rent a house or field (Mishnah, *Abodah Zarah* 1. 8, Danby 438); the friction at Caesarea was one of the causes of the rebellion (*B.J.* 2. 13. 7 (266)). Naturally the standing difficulty of the position of the resident alien in the ancient city-state was complicated when the religion of the state claimed to be the only true one.

[2] The author of 1 Pet. 2. 4 seems to have felt the difficulty and avoided it by the introduction of a "living" stone from Is. 28. 16, interpreted as referring to Jesus. The same difficulty is reflected in the various renderings of the passage recorded by Armitage Robinson, *ad loc.* For the meaning of "corner-stone" cf. Jeremias in *T.W.z.N.T.* s.v. γωνία.

[3] "If ye have heard" is dramatically appropriate; there will not have been any readers of the Epistle who have not heard, but Paul is represented as introducing himself to a new circle of readers.

(3. 2 *seqq.*) is the revelation of the great mystery hidden from all ages, but now revealed to the Church not merely on earth but in heaven, the mystery of the fellowship of Gentiles with Jews in the promises made through Jesus in the Gospel. To Paul, though the least of all the Saints, has been given the privilege of making manifest the mystery that has hitherto been hidden from all ages in God the Creator of the universe. This is the "mystery" (3. 9 *seqq.*) to which the writer has been working. Paul had been content to describe the Incarnation as a "mystery" in the Jewish sense of a secret hitherto hidden but now revealed; in the same way the present blindness of the Jews was a "mystery" whose meaning would be revealed at some future date in their conversion (Rom. 11. 25). The Pauline language was necessary as an explanation of the transfer to the Church of the promises made to Israel; it was adequate for circles which were largely concerned with the relation of Jews and Gentiles. But Ephesians was written for Hellenistic readers who were not seriously concerned with that problem, but wanted a "mystery" which would explain the Gospel and the practice of the Church in terms of the ascent of the soul to heaven. The writer has conflated Paul's two independent themes, the equality of Jew and Gentile and the soul's ascent to heaven as a result of the resurrection of Jesus and His position in cosmogony, and made one "mystery" of a more Hellenistic type; the position of the Jews in relation to the Gentiles is not really the centre of the mystery, which is concerned with the ascent of the Church to heaven and its consequent triumph over the powers that rule the heavenly spheres. For even the rulers and powers learn from the Church, as it passes through their spheres, the manifold wisdom of God, His purpose concealed from all eternity (Col. 1. 25 *seqq.*). In an astrologically conceived universe the worshipper has to pass those spheres if he is to ascend to heaven; here the Church as a body takes the place of the individual. The writer has thus established Christianity as a "mystery" as against other "mysteries" which threatened to prove more attractive. The union of the Church with Christ enables it to have free access to God in spite of all opponents, just as knowledge of the celestial origin of the soul and its relation to the supreme godhead, coupled with the necessary formulae of religion or magic, enabled the Gnostic to triumph over all the attempts of the planets to confine him within the limits of fate and the material world, and to ascend to God. It seems that the rulers are not regarded as capable of redemption (Rom. 8. 38 as against Col. 1. 20); they are passive spectators of an ascent which they cannot impede. The Church as a corporate body has grown in importance. The ascent

of the Church as against that of individuals seems to have no parallel; the congregation of Israel does not ascend in spite of the planets, though Judaism is familiar with ascents of the patriarchs and Moses to the heavenly spheres to intercede on behalf of Israel, and with the disapproval of the angels of the action of God in permitting Moses to ascend to heaven to receive the Torah.[1] The motive of the change is to emphasise the element of mystery and so to provide the Church with a more adequate counter-attraction to the mysteries of Gnosticism; it must be recognised that Christianity was poorly provided in this respect.

With such a task laid on him the writer prays that he may not play the coward in face of the afflictions which he must endure on behalf of his readers (2 Cor. 4. 16, Col. 1. 24); his sufferings are their glory. He prays (3. 14 *seqq.*) to the Father, from whom every family in heaven and earth is named (apparently the angels of midrashic Judaism, not the rulers and powers in the heavenly places; the point of the reference to them here is that the growth of the Church, God's family on earth, is to the advantage of the angelic family in heaven), that God will so strengthen his readers in accordance with the riches of His glory (the rhetoric of Colossians) in the inner man (2 Cor. 4. 16) that Christ may be able to dwell in their hearts by faith (the commonplace of 2 Cor. 6. 16),[2] and that they may be so rooted and grounded in love (Col. 2. 7) that they may be able to "comprehend" with all their fellow-saints the full dimensions of the love of God.[3] The writer's faithfulness to his model is responsible for the addition to the normal three dimensions of Greek geometry, length, breadth and height (or depth), of a fourth of depth (or height).[4] His reason for the insertion was that he found both "height" and "depth" in Rom. 8. 39 and did not understand their meaning; after all the Pauline circle was not really interested in astrology; Paul had used it and then let it drop after the

[1] Cf. p. 195. The Church here takes the place of the congregation of Israel in a heightened form; the idea of a "Church" seems alien to Hellenistic mysteries, cf. *Conversion* 135: "The supposed or desired piety of the world is no more than an aggregate of individual pieties."

[2] Cf. above, p. 163.

[3] Apparently the author meant originally to say "the length etc. of the love of Christ", but inserted *γνῶναι...γνώσεως* in order to avoid the appearance of saying that it is really possible to understand the fullness of the love of Christ. Possibly the mention of *βάθος* associated itself with Rom. 11. 33 and so introduced the new thought at the expense of the grammar.

[4] For the normal "dimensions" of length, breadth and height cf. *Placita* 1. 12. 1. (*Dox. Gr.* 310); Ar. Did. *Epit.* 19 (*ib.* 457); Philo, *D.C.E.R.* 26 (147, M. 1. 540); Cicero, *De Nat. Deor.* 1. 20. 54. Cf. also Sext. Emp. *Pyrr. Hyp.* 2. 30 for the argument that you cannot *καταλαμβάνειν* a three-dimensional object as against the Stoic *καταληπτικὴ φαντασία*.

normal habit of midrashic exposition. The writer found it in his original and it suited well with his taste for a lofty style of writing; consequently he has inserted it here. He is not to be blamed if his "fourth dimension" proved an irresistible attraction to the compilers of magical literature as providing for a fuller control of the spirits by their masters.[1]

Paul had written (Phil. 3. 12) of "grasping" God as God had already grasped him, in language in which the thought of laying hold on God was coloured by the thought of "grasping" the goal in a race (1 Cor. 9. 24). The writer of Ephesians seems to have missed that colouring and treated the language of Philippians as if it meant "comprehending" God with the understanding in the sense of "knowing" Him as in 1 Cor. 13. 12. The change of meaning was natural, for the difficulty of finding God, of which Plato had written in the *Timaeus* (28c), was one of the most hackneyed quotations of Hellenistic literature,[2] especially in Jewish literature, which used the quotation to prove the need of a special divine revelation, such as it alone possessed; the quotation usually appeared in the form that God was ἀκατάληπτος.[3] Another tradition of Judaism, however, held that man could "comprehend" or lay hold of God, at any rate if God took the first step and laid hold of him.[4] In the present passage the rhetorical dimensions suggested the vastness of the love of God; it can indeed be "comprehended", yet it passes knowledge (Rom. 11. 33, 1 Cor. 2. 9). At the same time the thought may have been coloured by the common belief that the "mind" can ascend to heaven and "comprehend" its dimensions or

[1] *Papp. Mag. Gr.* 4. 970, where the god (Iao with a strongly Jewish colouring, as the god of fire and the unseen creator of light) is summoned to appear in fire, so that the light may become breadth, depth, length, height and brightness for the god to show himself. Reitzenstein (*Poimandres* 25) regards the magical formula as the source of this passage. But there is no reason for such a fourth dimension in magic. On the other hand, if once suggested by the text of Eph. 3. 18 (or by its quotation in a Christian sermon), it would commend itself to magic, which cannot afford to ignore any possibility of evasion. Peterson (Εἷς Θεός 250) associates the four dimensions with the deified aeon as a heavenly cube; but a cube is not four-dimensional in Greek mathematics, except in those of Pythagoras, where the unit is the point, the duad the straight line, so that a solid cube is represented by four (the τετρακτύς of Pythagoreanism). There is no suggestion of this here.

[2] Cf. the doxographic collection embodied by Cicero, *De Nat. Deor.* The quotation occurs in the form that he cannot be named (1. 12. 30); cf. Jos. *c. Ap.* 2. 31 (224); Clem. Alex. *Strom.* 5. 12. 78 (692 P), and the doxographic collection in Minucius Felix, *Octavius* 19. 14.

[3] Philo, *De Post. Cain.* 5 (15, M. 1. 229); it is a great gain καταλαβεῖν ὅτι ἀκατάληπτος ὁ θεός; cf. *De Spec. Legg.* 1 (*De Mon.*), 4 (32) and 5 (36) (M. 2. 216–17) and *passim* and the doxographic collection in Hipp. *El.* 1. 19. 3 (*Dox. Gr.* 567).

[4] Philo, *De Abr.* 24 (122, M. 2. 19); *De Post. Cain.* 48 (167, M. 1. 258); cf. *De Plant.* 15 (64, M. 1. 339), where the mind ignores "becoming" and knows only τὸ ἀγένητον, to whom it approaches and by whom it is received (προσείληπται).

the variation of the theme in the form that the full "comprehension" of the cosmos carries with it the "comprehension" of God.[1]

In any case the love of Christ cannot be fully understood; it surpasses knowledge and is better than Gnosis.[2] It is the only power which will bring the readers to a completeness in which they can contain all the fullness of God (Col. 2. 9). The transition from Christ dwelling in the heart to the "comprehension" [with a suggestion of occupying], the full dimensions of the divine nature, and back to the thought of being filled with a divine *pleroma*, would be abrupt if the passage were not largely a cento of Pauline phrases and if the transition from the language of the soul's ascent to God to that of God's descent to the soul were not a common feature of popular theology.[3]

The writer has thus established the plain Pauline system of the love of God as manifested in Jesus as the supreme mystery and the highest Gnosis. To God, who can perform all this, all glory is to be given both in the Church on earth and in Christ Jesus in heaven; the conjunction of the Church and Christ Jesus here is intended to express the "mystery" already established. The praise of the Church on earth is offered to God in heaven in the person of Jesus, who is the head of the Church, and the means by which the Church is able to ascend to heaven to offer its praises. The doxology marks the end of the "mystery" and leads on to an appeal for the preservation by means of love of the unity of the one body (4. 1 *seqq.*). The humility which is the essence of Christian love must make Christians anxious to preserve the unity of the spirit in the "bond" of peace (Col. 3. 14). Only so will the one spirit within the one body enable them to attain to the one hope of their calling. That unity is based on the unity of the Lord, of the faith of the Church and of the baptism by which they enter it. Paul had argued in Colossians from the unity of mankind in Christ to the need for charity; the writer appeals for charity as a means for preserving the unity of the Church. Sects, it would seem, are multiplying, in a manner unknown in Paul's lifetime. The writer has no Pauline model to follow, but the language of 1 Cor. 8. 6–7 has suggested the adoption of the widespread literary convention of Hellenistic-

[1] So Dibelius, perhaps rightly, in *H.z.N.T. ad loc.*, though, if so, τί is a grammatical outrage; and the expression is rather a hackneyed commonplace of popular theology than a piece of mystical Gnosis. To *Corp. Herm.* 10. 25 (Scott 204), which he quotes, may be added Philo, *De Somn.* 1. 32 (186, M. 1. 649); *Q.R.D.H.* 23 (111, M. 1. 488); *Q.D.P.I.* 24 (89 *seqq.*, M. 1. 208), where the mind "contains the cosmos in virtue of the fact that it is a fragment of the divine nature". Cf. also *Corp. Herm.* 4. 5 (Scott 152).

[2] Dibelius rightly, *ad loc.*

[3] *Leg. Alleg.* 1. 13 (38, M. 1. 51), and cf. p. 192, n. 4. In its simplest form the thought is simply that of Jas. 4. 8.

Jewish literature, which saw in the unity of Torah, people and Temple a symbol of the unity of God.[1] The writer expands this theme; the unity of the Church in outward form, inward spirit and future hope, corresponding to the unity of Lord, faith and baptism, is a manifestation of the one true God who is supreme above all things, present throughout the cosmos and in all men (an independent use of the commonplace which lies behind Col. 1. 16). This universal divine presence (4. 7 *seqq.*) manifests itself in the grace that is given to every man according to the measure of the gift of Christ (Rom. 12. 3). This is the meaning of the prophecy of the sending of the Holy Spirit in the words: "Ascending up on high he captured a captivity, he gave gifts unto men." The argument implies that it is impossible to refer the words of Ps. 68. 19 to Moses in accordance with the usual rabbinical tradition. The word "ascended" must mean that whatever "went up" had on some previous occasion "come down".[2] The argument

[1] 2 Bar. 48. 24; Jos. *c. Ap.* 2. 23 (193); *Antt.* 4. 8. 5 (201); Philo, *De Spec. Legg.* 1 (*De Templo*), 1 (67, M. 2. 223); *ib.* (*De Sacr.*) 11 (317, M. 2. 259); *ib.* 4 (*De Just.*), 3 (159, M. 2. 362); *De Virt.* (*De Fort.*), 7 (35, M. 2. 381); Ps.-Sophocles *ap.* Ps.-Just. *Coh. ad Gent.* 18 (17e) = Clem. Alex. *Strom.* 5. 14. 113 (717 P), where it is ascribed to (Pseudo)-Hecataeus, a Jewish forgery earlier than Josephus (*Antt.* 1. 7. 2 (159); *Or. Sib.* Fr. 1. 7 (*Ap. and Ps.* 2. 377)). It appears in an independent version in Orig. *c. Cels.* 5. 44 from a Jewish source (note the reference to the one High Priest and the one Altar). Peterson, Εἶς Θεός 255, notes numerous Christian variations but fails to recognise the frequency of the theme in Jewish writings, not exclusively Hellenistic (note 2 Bar. above, but Hellenistic influence is possible here). The origin of the form is clearly based on Pseudo-Hecataeus, who associates the line from Pseudo-Sophocles (εἶς ταῖς ἀληθείαισιν εἶς ἐστιν θεός) closely with the fragment of Aeschylus, Ζεύς ἐστιν αἰθήρ Ζεὺς δὲ γῆ Ζεὺς δ' οὐρανὸς κ.τ.λ. The Jewish-Christian usage would seem to be derived from the Jewish attempt to read monotheism into the literature of Greece in the first century B.C. (It should be noticed that the alleged quotation from Xenophanes of Colophon in Clem. Alex. *loc. cit.* 109 (714 P) is probably from a similar source. Up to the end of 107 he has been quoting Aristobulus, see Eus. *Pr. Ev.* 13. 12. 19; it is probable that the passages which intervene are borrowed from a similar Jewish compilation.) The liturgical expression of the unity of God in the Shema and the emphasis laid on it in the missionary propaganda of Judaism would naturally enhance the popularity of the argument and the form in which it finds regular expression. (Peterson, *op. cit.* 241, may be right in supposing that the "Orphic" line in Ps.-Just. *Coh. ad Gent.* 15 (16a), εἶς Ζεὺς εἶς Ἀίδης εἶς Ἥλιος εἶς Διόνυσος κ.τ.λ., is inspired by Iranian theology; but its appearance in Pseudo-Justin is simply due to the willingness of this type of propaganda to use any superficially plausible argument to prove that Gentile theology really leads to monotheism. Its absence from the earlier collections suggests that it only came into circulation after their compilation.) In all these cases we have the use of a current literary convention possibly originating outside the synagogue, but taken over by it in the interests of Judaism and then becoming a Jewish and later a Christian convention. For such use of current phrases cf. Meyer, *Urspr. u. Anf.* 3. 378.

[2] Seneca, *N.Q.* 6. 16. 1 *seqq.*; *Corp. Herm.* Exc. 26. 12 (Scott 522), both going back to the same theory of universal "ebb and flow" which appears in Strabo 1. 3. 8 (53) and so presumably to Posidonius; cf. Orig. *De Orat. Lib.* 23, where the Logos empties Himself to descend to us and returns (παλινδρομεῖ) to His own *pleroma*, leading us, who, as we follow, are "filled" and freed from "emptiness"; this is the anabasis of Mind.

was one which was perfectly legitimate on the principles of rabbinical exegesis. But it appears to have been drawn from Hellenistic conceptions, in which everything, including the souls of men, was in a continual state of ascending and descending between earth and heaven; the heavenly bodies were nourished by an element of "spirit" which they drew from earth and returned to it again. Here the argument proves that the reference is not to the supposed "ascent" of Moses to receive the Torah.[1] The Psalm, traditionally associated with the day of Pentecost, is referred not to the supposed association of that day with the giving of the Torah, but to the descent of the Holy Spirit on the Church on the first Pentecost after the resurrection of Jesus.[2] It was of course necessary that Jesus should descend from heaven to the earth below and then return to heaven in order that He might fulfil His appointed function of filling all parts of the universe.[3]

From this midrashic parenthesis the writer returns at 4. 11 *seqq.* to the theme of the unity of the Church. The gifts that Jesus bestows on the Church are varied in accordance with the needs of the body of

[1] The text of Ephesians follows the Targum in reading "he gave" for "he received" of Heb. and LXX. The Targum interprets Ps. 68. 19 of Moses going up to heaven to receive the Torah. For rabbinical interpretations to the same effect, reading "he received" but applying it to Moses' receiving of the Torah, cf. Str.-B. on this passage.

[2] For Pentecost as the feast of the Torah in rabbinical tradition cf. p. 57. Ps. 68 is one of the Psalms of Pentecost in the Jewish Liturgy and its use is implied in Acts, where the language of 2. 33 reflects the Targum on Ps. 68. 34, "He with His word (Memra) gave with His voice the spirit of prophecy to the prophets". The rather unorthodox theology, according to which Jesus, at His Ascension, received the Holy Spirit from the Father and gave it to the Church on earth, underlies both Acts and Ephesians. It is scarcely likely that the writer of the latter would have borrowed such an unorthodox piece of exegesis; it looks more like an independent use of a midrashic exegesis of the Psalm, going back to the period when the association of the Holy Ghost with the day of Pentecost was first coming into general currency in Christian circles. It survives in Justin Martyr, *Dial. c. Tryph.* 87 (315a), where the gifts of prophecy are withdrawn from the Jews and rest on Jesus at the Incarnation, but are returned by Him as gifts to the Church after the Incarnation; cf. Orig. *In Ev. Jo.* 6. 37.

[3] V. 9 may simply mean "the lower parts of the earth", which is more consistent with the cosmography of the writer, who regards the lower air as the abode of Satan. But the writer may be following Phil. 2. 10, and have introduced a reference to Sheol for the sake of rhetorical completeness without regard for 2. 2. Armitage Robinson, *ad loc.*, accepts the reference to Sheol, which is supported by the use of the thought of "ascent" and "descent" in Philo, *Q.R.D.H.* 9 (45, M. 1. 479); the divine life never descends, the lowest never ascends but lurks in the recesses of Hades, while the ordinary mixed life of man sometimes goes "up" and sometimes "down". Here we have an independent use of the same Hellenistic convention of "ebb and flow" in this sense which described the material life in terms of "Hades", in which Philo certainly does not believe. Philo here seems to be applying to the "ascent to heaven" in this life an account of the state of the soul after death, similar to that of Plut. *De Ser. Num. Vind.* 23 (564a); but Philo's source seems to have retained a subterranean Hades for the thoroughly wicked, perhaps only as a literary convention.

Christ. (1 Cor. 12. 28; the expansion of "teachers" into "evangelists, pastors and teachers" perhaps represents the necessity of recognising the "evangelists" of 2 Cor. 8. 18, understood in this sense, whether rightly or wrongly (and Acts 21. 8 if known to the writer), and also the more developed Christianity of the later years of the first century A.D., when there were settled Churches which needed "pastors" rather than missionaries and teachers.) These ministries, each with its proper degree of authority, are all needed, in order to build up the body of Christ into that unity of faith and knowledge in which it is a full-grown man, whose adult state enables him to contain the whole pleroma of Christ. The full-grown man, who leads on to the warning that the individual Christians must not behave like children, is based on 1 Cor. 14. 20, expressed in the terminology of the Church as the body of Christ; the comparison of the Church to the perfect man rather than to the body is drawn from Hellenistic commonplaces comparing the state to a single person.[1] Thus the development of each individual Christian will enable the whole body to grow into that perfection in which each member has attained to the measure of full growth in which he can manifest the distinctively Christian character of love.[2]

The thought of the perfect man leads (4. 17 *seqq.*) to a warning against idolatry, based on Rom. 1. 21 *seqq.*, though missing its point, the condemnation of Judaism, as being itself guilty of sinning no less than the Gentiles, in language drawn from its own conventional condemnation of Gentile idolatry. The warning against idolatry and the vices to which it leads, including sexual immorality and avarice, enables the writer to pass on to the theme of the new man, who is created after the image of God. If the readers have really learned the truth as it is in Jesus, they will know that they must abandon the sins of the old life and put on the new (Col. 3. 5 is thus attached to the section on idolatry in Romans). The new man is naturally associated with the next main section of the Epistle, the lengthy homily on Christian duties of 4. 25 *seqq.* The author did not appreciate the purpose of the passage on the duty of thanksgiving for the revelation of the "mystery" in Col. 3. 15b, while he had already anticipated the exhortation to love. Consequently he proceeds immediately to his

[1] Polybius 6. 1. 6; cf. the cosmos as τελεώτατος ἄνθρωπος in Philo, *De Migr. Abr.* 39 (220, M. 1. 471). For ἡλικία cf. Schneider in *T.W.z.N.T.* s.v. The association of the word with τέλειος in Philo, *De Abr.* 32 (168, M. 2. 25) and *In Flacc.* 3 (15, M. 2. 519), seems decisive in favour of the sense of "age" rather than "capacity to contain" here; in Philo the sense of age appears to be universal.

[2] Col. 2. 19, possibly with a colouring drawn from the commonplace of the Hellenistic synagogues as preserved in Philo; see the references on p. 161, n. 2.

homily describing in detail the character of the "new man" (Col. 3. 18 *seqq.*), expanding the very terse admonition of Paul in regard to the home life of the Christian into a complete list of moral duties. The list is based on pagan philosophical convention; but the low moral standard implied suggests that the usage of the synagogue is his immediate source.[1] But at 5. 5 the conventional list of warnings brings the writer to immorality and avarice, which he had already associated in accordance with his Pauline model in 4. 19. Here he suddenly digresses from his general list of sins to a further warning against the danger of deception by vain words; the readers must not allow themselves to be led astray into any dealings with the unfruitful works of darkness. The warning is formally far less impressive than the solemn protestation which introduced the denunciation of idolatry in 4. 17. But that denunciation was a Jewish convention adapted from a Pauline model which had to be included; there is no real reason to suppose that the original author was really concerned with the danger of relapsing into heathenism. Here, however, the writer deserts Paul, in order to introduce a warning (5. 6 *seqq.*) against "darkness". They were once darkness themselves, but now they are light in the Lord. They must therefore walk as children of the light, bringing forth the fruits of holiness. They must test all their actions by the pleasure of the Lord and have no share in the barren works of darkness. Rather must they convict these of their sinfulness. The sins of those who seek to deceive them are too shameful to mention, but if convicted by the light they will be exposed; for that which is exposed to the light becomes light itself; as "it" says, "Awake, O sleeper, and rise from the dead, and Christ will illuminate thee".

This is an entirely different matter from the conventional warning against idolatry of 4. 17. It is aimed at religions which practise their rites in secret, thereby proving that they are too shameful to be performed in the open. The argument was a popular one as against mystery religions, destined later to be used against Christianity.[2] But it can hardly be doubted that the writer is in deadly earnest. His distinction of good and evil as light and darkness is derived from the common Jewish-Hellenistic convention and immediately from Paul (Rom. 13. 12, Col. 1. 12–13), but in a quite different application.[3] As children of the light the readers have light in themselves, which

[1] Cf. Dibelius on Col. 3. 18 *seqq.*

[2] Cf. *Jerusalem* 120, n. 35.

[3] The "fruit of the light" appears to come from Hosea 10. 12. Here as elsewhere Iranian influences may have affected the language of the O.T.

enables them to turn into light the darkness of those who practise such secret mysteries.

The reason for this really is the presence in them of Christ, who as the divine Wisdom is essentially light in accordance with the general convention of Alexandrine exegesis which equates Wisdom with the first-created *νοητὸν φῶς*. This Wisdom can be identified equally with Jesus Himself, with the divine element of Mind pervading the universe and especially the mind of man, or with the human conscience (which is in some sense akin to the divine). Thus the hymn which the writer quotes in v. 14 can be applied either to Christ as enlightening the soul of the believer (its proper sense), or to the divine element of mind as expelling darkness from his soul,[1] or to the believer as exposing and so turning to light the darkness in which the hideous secret rites of the would-be deceivers are carried on. The fragment itself presents a well-known problem. It is written in the Orphic-Hermetic style of missionary literature,[2] but this style is fairly common in Hellenistic-Jewish writings. It is introduced by the formula "as it says", which in Paul, as in rabbinical literature, implies Scriptural authority; but the phrase is not Scriptural, nor, in Paul's lifetime, could it have been possible to suppose that so distinctively Christian a saying came from the literature of the O.T.[3] The fragment appears to come from a Christian source, perhaps a liturgical hymn current in the primitive community,[4]

[1] The thought of "conviction" by light appears in *Quod Deus sit Imm.* 26 *seqq.* (123 *seqq.*, M. 1. 291) in a long exegesis of the law of leprosy (Lev. 13. 14 *seqq.*). The living flesh reveals leprosy just as conscience reveals sin. In 135 the priest (who is the Logos in 134) if absent from the soul leaves it clean, for there is none to reveal its guilt (Lev. 14. 36). It is when the true priest ἔλεγχος enters, like a ray of pure light, that he reveals the impious thoughts stored up in the soul, and is able to have them removed and to cleanse it. The allusion to 1 Kings 17. 10 in 136 suggests that we are dealing here with traditional matter incorporated by Philo. Cf. also *De Spec. Legg.* 4 (*De Judice*), 2 (60, M. 2. 345) for light as illuminating and convicting all things, and *De Post. Cain.* 16 (58, M. 1. 236) for mind as the sun which if it fails to rise leaves the microcosm in darkness. The thought is sufficiently commonplace for ordinary wisdom to be *νοητὸν φῶς* in *Quod Omn. Prob. Lib.* 1 (5, M. 2. 446). For truth as light illuminating the conscience cf. *De Jos.* 14 (68, M. 2. 51).

[2] Cf. p. 38 for this style of addressing an audience.

[3] Paul might, like the rabbis on rare occasions, have quoted as Scripture something that was only part of the oral tradition of Judaism (cf. Str.-B. on Rom. 12. 14 and 1 Tim. 2. 8). But he could not have supposed that this fragment came from any O.T source, since the whole conception of the Messiah as raising the dead to life or rousing sinners to repentance is outside the range of the O.T. But if Ephesians is not genuine the difficulty does not arise, since the writer might easily confuse Christian liturgical writings with the O.T. or accept in good faith a Christian interpolation.

[4] Cf. Severian, quoted by Armitage Robinson, *ad loc.* Dibelius, *ad loc.*, rightly doubts the Iranian origin, in view of the frequency of the whole thought of religion as illumination, and suggests a baptismal hymn. For the patristic conjectures cf. Schürer, *G.J.V.* 3. 365.

incorporated into some fairly popular apocryphal document, or inserted into the canonical text of the O.T.[1]

The whole warning is important as evidence of the existence of sects which practised secret rites of such a character that they can, rightly or wrongly, be accused of the vilest secret vices, although they cannot be accused simply of idolatry. They are similar to those attacked by Paul in Colossians; yet they are known to the writer independently, since the whole passage is of his own construction and not in any sense a reproduction of the Pauline condemnation; the whole emphasis is on their secrecy, which may be implied in the Pauline allusions to "mysteries" and "initiations", but does not figure prominently in his condemnation.[2] It appears that sects of a more or less Christian kind are a serious danger, known to the writer independently of the Pauline tradition, and that they make a parade of secrecy which enables him to attack them on the usual lines of the writers of the age; we have no evidence as to the extent to which his charge was justified, in view of the prevalence of such accusations, but his warning shows that there is a danger of syncretism in the Church.

In view of the dangers that surround them (5. 15 *seqq.*) Christians have no time to waste.[3] The days are "evil", and they must devote all their time to understanding the will of the Lord (Rom. 12. 2). It is worth noticing that the days are no longer short, as was the "time" of 1 Cor. 7. 29, although their "shortness" would have offered a better reason for "buying up the time" (Col. 4. 5) than the fact that they are evil; eschatology is less real than it used to be, and asceticism is replacing it.[4]

The drunkenness of the world must be replaced by spiritual

[1] The fragment is ascribed by Hippolytus to Isaiah (Schürer, *loc. cit.*); a Christian hymn might have been inserted into a Christian version of an apocryphal writing ascribed to Isaiah, or have been inserted into the canonical text. It is doubtful if the writer would have quoted in this way from anything but what he supposed to be Scripture. Christian interpolations into the O.T. are old enough for Justin to accuse the Jews of having suppressed them (*Dial. c. Tryph.* 72, 297 d).

[2] For the extent to which secrecy as to the rite and teaching, whether of Christianity or the mysteries, was a fiction cf. *Conversion* 214 *seqq.* The Gnostics seem to have insisted more thoroughly; cf. Tert. *adv. Valent.* 1 and Ir. *Haer.* 1. 24. 6 (Basilides). The same accusation is made against Simon (23. 4), who is decidedly nearer to magic, in which secrecy is common, e.g. *Papp. Mag. Gr.* 4. 851 and 1873.

[3] For the thought cf. Philo, *De Vit. Cont.* 2 (16 *seqq.*, M. 2. 474), for worldly cares as a waste of time for those devoted to religion (dressed up here as "philosophy"). The Pauline phrase (Col. 4. 5) is from Dan. 2. 8.

[4] The whole passage has a close resemblance to *Test. Napht.* 2. 9 *seqq.*, which Charles accepts as genuine. But a comparison of 2. 10 with 1 Cor. 12. 17 and 2 Cor. 6. 14 (note also Beliar in *Napht.* 3. 1 and 2 Cor. 6. 16), 3. 1 with Eph. 5. 5–6 and 17, and 3. 2 with Rom. 1. 23 suggests that the rather pointless panegyric on "orderliness" is simply a cento of N.T. passages and a Christian interpolation.

enthusiasm; the synagogues of the Dispersion were familiar with an enthusiastic type of religion which might easily be mistaken for drunkenness, and the worship of primitive Christianity was still more liable to such suspicions;[1] the thought of 1 Cor. 14. 23 and Acts 2. 13 reappears with an entirely new implication, which suggests that the general level of the average convert is lower than in the Pauline period. The danger of enthusiasm of this kind provides an opportunity for incorporating a revision of Paul's exhortation to thankfulness from Col. 3. 16 with an added emphasis on order and subjection in worship; the transition to this theme enables him to return to the main line of thought in Colossians. At 5. 22 he proceeds to his treatment of marriage; thus Paul's brief moral homily is fitted into his larger scheme with a corresponding expansion, based on an appeal to theological principles. The relation of Jesus to the Church is suggested by the relation of God to the restored Jerusalem (Is. 62. 5 *seqq.*), as applied in rabbinical exegesis to the relation of God to the congregation of Israel;[2] it is expounded in terms drawn from Jewish bridal custom.[3] This again leads to the thought that the union of a man to his wife makes them one flesh; thus a man's care for his wife must be as great as his care for his own body, which in Stoic commonplace was inevitably the first concern of man.[4]

This union of man and wife (5. 29) was itself nothing less than a symbol of the love of Christ for the Church. Just as a man leaves father and mother to cleave to his wife, so did Christ leave His Father and His home in heaven to join Himself to His new body the Church, a great mystery.[5] The writer here has followed the general practice

[1] It is possible that the substitution of drunkenness for madness reveals a knowledge of Acts 2. 13, but it is also possible that both passages reproduce a common argument against Christianity. For "enthusiasm" in Judaism cf. Philo, *De Ebr.* 36 (146 *seqq.*, M. 1. 380), where the story of Hannah is explained as referring to the effect of grace (Hannah = grace). It is surprising to find this type of enthusiasm in Judaism; but it must be remembered that Judaism outside Palestine was a religion which made converts, and this type of enthusiasm goes with conversion.

[2] Cf. Str.-B. on Rev. 19. 7.

[3] Cf. Str.-B. on Mt. 9. 15 (vol. 1, pp. 505c and 506).

[4] Polybius 5. 104. 5; Seneca, *Ep.* 2. 2 (14). 1; Aulus Gellius, *Noct. Att.* 12. 5; Plut. *De Stoic. Rep.* 12, 1038b.

[5] Cf. p. 183, and for the myth of the descent of the redeemer in general Note IV. For this myth in terms of a "mystical marriage" cf. *Corp. Herm.* 1 (*Poimandres*), 14 (Scott 120), and see p. 85 for other instances. The thought of Jesus as the husband of the Church and the reference to Gen. 2. 24 may be inspired by the Pauline association of Jesus with Adam, though this is not necessary. There is an obvious resemblance between this passage and *Corp. Herm.* Ascl. 3. 21 (Scott 332), where however the "mystical marriage" has been changed to the parallel conception of a bisexual creator. It is possible that the Hermetic writer is dependent on Ephesians; but it is possible that both are drawing on a common tradition. For the passage as meaning that Jesus "left" His Father cf. Orig. *In Ev. Matt.* 14. 17.

of contemporary religion in equating the central figure of any given cult with the divine reason emanating from the supreme deity and entering into the cosmos to establish order and harmony in the chaos of matter. The recognition of this was the secret of salvation, which was obtained by the knowledge of the divine origin of the soul as a spark or fragment of the divine nature immersed in the material. Here the union is not that of a divine being with the material, and the consequent possibility of salvation by Gnosis, but the union of the historical Jesus with the Church as a community whose members are redeemed by faith. But the language implies that the writer has the theme of the mystical marriage in mind; the passage depends for its point on the correspondence between the action of Jesus in leaving His Father for the sake of the Church and of a man in leaving his father for the sake of his wife. But such "marriages" were not merely a commonplace of the religion of the age, in which they often figured as the central feature of a new cult.[1] They were also a commonplace of philosophy in view of the predilection of the Stoic tradition for reading its system into the loves of the gods in classical mythology.[2] Judaism was quite prepared to follow suit; the words of Genesis were commonly employed to expound the most frigid allegories of conventional philosophy. Thus the author was merely applying to the relation of Jesus to the Church a commonplace of popular theology, whose ultimate association with the mythology of some of the cults of the Hellenistic age had long since been forgotten.[3] Jesus here as elsewhere assumes the character of the divine nature immanent in the cosmos, while the place of the element of mind which He delivers is taken by the Church.

This summary is followed by a final appeal for perseverance (6. 10 *seqq.*). The armour of righteousness of 1 Thess. 5. 8 is fitted into the world-view of Rom. 8. 38. The conflation of the two Pauline themes enables the writer to produce a vigorous and dramatic answer to the fatalist outlook on life which was common in ancient religion. In an age familiar with mercenary armies it was natural to regard the

[1] The most obvious instance is Alexander of Abonouteichos (Lucian, *Alexander* 38). But the theme appears in Simon of Samaria (Ir. *Haer.* 1. 23. 2 *seqq.*) in its crudest form as it does in Marcus (*ib.* 1. 13. 3 and 5).

[2] Cf. the "natural theology" of Chrysippus, Cicero, *De Nat. Deor.* 2. 26. 66, Sext. Emp. *adv. Math.* 9.5, *De Civ. Dei* 4. 10 and the predilection for "mystical marriages" among the Naassenes, Hipp. *El.* 5. 7 (98); cf. *Clem. Recog.* 9. 3 for an orthodox instance.

[3] Philo, *Leg. Alleg.* 2. 14 (49, M. 1. 75), where the passage is referred to mind, when it deserts God, its Father, and Wisdom, its Mother, and cleaves to sense, and *De Gigant.* 15 (65, M. 1. 272), of "children of earth" who desert the better and go over to the worse; here the passage has lost all association with any thought of marriage and has been interwoven with a Stoic-Orphic allegory (cf. p. 75).

service of one of the new gods as a warfare on earth under the orders of a divine commander. Hence the old myths of the armour of the gods, which had passed into the Old Testament tradition of Judaism, received a new life and meaning in the Hellenistic age.[1] But it was not only the votaries of the various religions which offered salvation who claimed to be the soldiers of their deity.[2] The philosophy of Stoicism could offer no better prospect to man than to be a good soldier obeying the commands of fate.[3] The phrase was a commonplace which had passed into the liturgical religion of the age, from which it has found its way into the fragments of such cult-forms as were later incorporated into the literature of magic.[4] The Christian is not in this position. He has at his disposal the armour of God, which will enable him to fight with the certainty of victory not against flesh and blood, but against Satan himself, the lord of those celestial spheres which are under the control of the cosmocrators who rule the present age of darkness.[5]

Thus the armour, while in itself going back to Pauline language and so to Is. 59. 17, with a possible extension from Wisd. 5. 17 *seqq.*,[6] is drawn from a widely diffused convention of the time. But while it is placed in an astrological setting in which it appears with some frequency, it is used with a deliberate change of meaning; the duty of the Christian is not to resign himself to the decrees of fate like a good soldier obeying his commander, but to fight against the rulers who ordain them with the panoply which will enable him to conquer the temptations which beset him.[7] The "sword" as the word of God is

[1] For the line of development cf. Dibelius in *H.z.N.T. ad loc.*

[2] Dibelius, *loc. cit.*, gives a collection of parallels from the mystery-religions.

[3] Seneca, *Ep.* 18. 4 (107). 9, regards it as man's privilege to be a soldier of Jupiter (=fate); in *Catal. Codd. Astrol.* 5. 2 (Kroll 30. 10) it is the lot of man to which the astrologer resigns himself. In Seneca, *Ep.* 20. 3 (120). 12, the good man is *civis universi et miles.*

[4] *Papp. Mag. Gr.* 4. 193, 211 and 17b. 22; both passages are drawn from sources which were once religion rather than magic.

[5] "Cosmocrators" is an astrological term, cf. *Test. Sal.* quoted by Dibelius on Col. 2. 8; cf. πρυτάνεις τοῦ κόσμου, Wisd. 13. 2, Cumont, *Fouilles de Doura-Europos* 103 and 129. It is commonly applied to human world-rulers by Jewish writers (Krauss, *Lehnwörter* 2. 502). But the distinction between more or less deified human world-emperors and the planets which rule the fate of a world-empire is easily passed. The reading ὑπουρανίοις in this verse seems to reflect an attempt to fit the "rulers" into the lower air or to extend the dominion of the "prince of the power of the air" up to the firmament, in order to make the rulers subject to him.

[6] Cf. Holmes in *Ap. and Ps.* 1. 527; but the picture may be due to independent variations on the same convention.

[7] The soul which obeys the commands of the rational element in it is able to receive God into itself, and is free from the demons subject to the planets and so from fate; the demons control only the body and the irrational soul (*Corp. Herm.* 16. 16 (Scott 270)).

drawn immediately from Is. 49. 2 and 11. 4; Judaism was accustomed to interpret the swords of the O.T. as a symbol of the Torah.[1] The symbolism of the word as the sword was a standing convention of Judaism, whatever its ultimate origin may have been.[2]

With this armour to defend them (6. 18 *seqq.*) the readers are to persevere in prayer for all the Saints and for Paul himself that he may not fail to preach the Gospel with due courage as an "ambassador in bonds" (Col. 4. 2 *seqq.*, but the thought of courage from Phil. 1. 14). This furnishes a suitable conclusion to the writer's introduction to Paulinism; the allusion to Tychicus may be a thinly veiled statement of the author's identity. In any case his work is an impressive exposition of the later Pauline theology. Although however he adheres closely to Pauline thought and language, he is by no means a mere imitator; he understands his subject, and where he has no model to guide him he shows himself capable of vigorous and original insight and clear expression. At times he comes nearer to the beliefs and language of Hellenistic religion than Paul, but without in any way compromising his fidelity to the main stream of Christian tradition. His letter, though not the work of Paul, is entirely worthy of the place it has always held in Christian theology and devotion by the side of the letters of his master.

[1] Str.-B. *ad loc.* and on Heb. 4. 12.

[2] Apart from Isaiah the convention seems to be implied in Hosea 6. 5. It appears in Philo, *De Cher.* 9 (28, M. 1. 144); cf. *Leg. Alleg.* 3. 8 (26, M. 1. 92). In the N.T. apart from Heb. 4. 12 it is common in the Apocalypse (Rev. 1. 16, 2. 16, 19. 15). It may be derived from the slaying of the wicked "with the breath of his lips"; cf. p. 16. But there seems no obvious reason for the change of the fairly obvious breath into the rather grotesque imagery of a sword. In *Papp. Mag. Gr.* 4. 1717 an incantation is described as "the sword of Dardanus". The actual "sword" (l. 1814) is the formula, "One is Thuriel, Michael, Gabriel, Uriel, Misael, Irrael, Istrael". Dardanus is a peculiar figure. A set of writings said to have been discovered by Democritus in the tomb of Dardanus (Pliny, *N.H.* 30. 2. 9) were the foundation of alchemy (cf. Riess in *E.R.E.* 1. 288b). According to Dion. Halic. 1. 61 Dardanus survived a great flood in Arcadia; he thus could claim to be a kind of Noah, and Noah at the instruction of the angels wrote down a book of "medicines" after the Flood (Jubilees 10. 10 *seqq.*). On the other hand one of the wise sons of Mahol in 1 Kings 4. 31 appears as Darda, which Josephus (*Antt.* 8. 2. 5 (43)) gives as Dardanus. Pliny's list of magicians puts Moses and Jannes immediately after Dardanus. This probably comes from an Alexandrine source; Jewish magic would naturally identify Dardanus and Noah as predecessors of Moses. Darda could also be interpreted as "generation of Wisdom" (Dor Da) and taken as the generation which received the Torah (Ginsberg, *Legends of the Jews* 3. 79, 4. 130 and 6. 283). The "sword" of Dardanus seems to be an account of the Logos as a word composed of seven archangels; the doubling of Irrael and Istrael shows that it has passed through Gentile hands; an archangel (? Raphael) has been lost and replaced by the meaningless doublet).

NOTE I

GREEK WRITERS AND PERSIAN RELIGION

The most striking feature of classical Greek literature in its treatment of the religion of Persia is its lack of interest. Herodotus, who gives half a book to the religion of Egypt, only gives four chapters to that of Persia, and includes one bad blunder in his account.[1] Xenophon, in spite of his interest in Cyrus, tells us little; we read of a cult of Ahura-Mazda, Mithras and Anahita.[2] He suggests that Cyrus was fairly impartial in worshipping the gods of other nations; the O.T. supports this and suggests that Xenophon had access to a well-informed source. This general indifference is continued in the later historians. Diodorus Siculus, though he describes Alexander's conquest of Persia, tells us nothing of Persian religion, except that Zoroaster claimed that his laws were revealed to him by the ἀγαθὸς δαίμων, that the Persians worship Artemis (Anahita), and that they extinguish the sacred fire when the king dies.[4] There is scarcely any system of religion and mythology which he treats so cavalierly. Strabo is still more remarkable; he was a native of Amasea in Pontus, a member of the priestly family of Comana, and his family had served Mithridates Eupator till they found it wiser to go over to Rome.[5] He must have had ample opportunities for learning the faith and practice of Magian religion. He had at his disposal the works of Posidonius and the numerous other authorities whom he quotes. Yet his account of Persian religion proper consists simply in a repetition of Herodotus with a correction of his error as to the identity of Mithras and Anahita, and an account of the fire-cultus.[6] He describes the Asiatic cultus of Anahita as Persian,[7] which it certainly was not in the proper sense.

The *Persica* of Dinon in three volumes may have given an account of Persian religion; if so, it was not regarded as interesting enough to be copied; all that remains of his information is that the Persians use the *baresman*, that they regard fire and water as the only true images of the gods, and that they sacrifice in the open air.[8] He may have related more; but he may have given as little information as Herodotus himself.

The most important evidence is that of Plutarch, who knows of the two "Gods" of Zoroastrianism and the six Amhaspands together with numerous

[1] Herodotus 1. 131–133 and 140. For a discussion of his evidence cf. Moulton, *Early Zoroastrianism* 36 and *passim*; Meyer, *Gesch. des Alterthums* 3. 1. 122. Whether his account represents a decadent Zoroastrianism or primitive Iranian nature-worship need not concern us.

[2] *Cyropaedia* 7. 5. 22, 53, 57.

[3] *Ib.* 3. 3. 21 *seqq.*

[4] 1. 94. 2, 5. 77. 8 and 17. 114. 4. Either Ctesias said little about Persian religion, or Diodorus and the Greeks in general did not regard his information as worth repeating.

[5] Strabo 10. 4. 10 (477), 12. 3. 15 (547), and 33 (557).

[6] *Ib.* 15. 3. 13 (732) and 15 (733). For the latter passage cf. Pausanias, *Descr. Gr.* 5. 27. 5. The Magus seems to have found Pausanias somewhat gullible.

[7] Strabo 12. 3. 37 (559).

[8] Cf. the fragments *ap.* Müller, *Fr. Hist. Gr.* 2. 90. 8 *seqq.*

astrological accretions; he makes the unorthodox statement that Mithras is the mediator between Ahura-Mazda and Ahriman.[1] According to his authority there was coming a time when Ahriman would bring an age of tribulation on the earth, after which he was to be destroyed; the earth will then become flat, and men will live happily with one method of life and government and one language. Clearly the Iranian religion has been revised in a thoroughly Hellenistic sense. Plutarch proceeds to quote Theopompus to the effect that each of the two Gods will rule and be ruled in turn for 3000 years, after which there will be 3000 years of conflict. At the end Hades (Ahriman) will perish and the golden age be established. The God who has devised this rests at present in a slumber whose duration is for a God no more than that of an ordinary man. To this account of the evidence of Theopompus may be added the statement of Diogenes Laertius, to the effect that according to the "Magians" all men will come to life, return and be immortal.[2] Aeneas Gazaeus also says that according to Theopompus Zoroaster believed in a resurrection of the dead.[3]

Theopompus, as quoted by Plutarch, seems to show a knowledge of the Zarvanite heresy, which sought to get behind the dualism of Zoroaster to the one supreme deity of "Unending Time".[4] Plutarch's other source is Mithraic and therefore Zarvanite (*Rel. Or.* 139). Normally the dualism of Zoroaster would discredit him in the eyes of the Greek world, even though Plato in his old age had inclined to an ultimate dualism, perhaps under the influence of the Persian tradition.[5] The heretical system, to which Theopompus appears to allude, was certainly known to Eudemus of Rhodes about 300 B.C.,[6] unless Damascius has made a mistake; but in general the Greeks only know of Zoroastrianism as a dualist system, which was to be rejected for that reason; after all, an ultimate dualism is a counsel of despair, and the Greeks did not as a rule accept counsels of despair. Aristotle and his school took some interest in Persian thought;[7] but again it is not clear that they went beyond a knowledge of its ultimate dualism. It is perhaps not without significance that the only two philosophers credited with a close knowledge of the Magi and their religion were Democritus and Pyrrho.[8]

[1] *De Is. et Os.* 46 *seqq.* 369e. This represents Mithraism adapted to the normal Hellenistic view of the divine principle in the material world, cf. p. 46.

[2] I. 9.

[3] *Theophr. P. G.* 85. 996a: ἔσται ποτὲ χρόνος ἐν ᾧ πάντων νεκρῶν ἀνάστασις ἔσται. This would be important if it really meant that Theopompus described Zoroaster as believing in the ἀνάστασις νεκρῶν. But Aeneas is probably using Christianised language.

[4] For a discussion of the question of whether this refers to the Zarvanite heresy or not cf. Lommel, *Die Religion Zarathustras* 139. For the heresy cf. Irvin Blue in *Anglo-Iranian Studies* (Kegan Paul and Trubner, 1925) 61 *seqq.*

[5] *Laws* 896e; Meyer, *Urspr. u. Anf.* 3. 651, accepts the Zoroastrian influence: but Plato seems to stand alone.

[6] Quoted by Damascius, *Dub. et Sol.* ed. Ruelle, 125 *bis*, I. 322.

[7] Diog. Laert. I. 8; cf. Nock in *Beginnings of Christianity* 5. 166. The work referred to entitled Μαγικός may have shown closer knowledge. The other authorities quoted by Diogenes, Hermippus and Eudoxus merely confirm Aristotle and Theopompus. Aristotle denied that the Persians practised magic.

[8] Diog. Laert. 9. 34 and 61.

Occasionally the later Pythagoreans appear to have appealed to Zoroaster in support of their belief that the unit is the ultimate good and the duad the ultimate evil.[1] Later writers were prepared to appeal to him in support of their theology, as Plutarch does in the interests of Egyptian religion,[2] and Clement of Alexandria in the interests of the Christian devil.[3]

But between the writers of the fourth century and those of the beginning of the Christian era there is little or no evidence of independent interest in Persian religion in spite of the conquests of Alexander. The old views are repeated, the only new point being the tendency to associate "magians" with magic, in spite of Aristotle's assertion that they did not practise it. Possibly this was due to the tendency of Persian colonies in Asia, isolated from the main stream of national religion, to adopt various elements from the religions of their surroundings, and to the tendency of practitioners of magic to claim the prestige of the ancient religion of the East for their practices. They were sufficiently successful to lead Pliny to regard magic as the invention of Zoroaster,[4] imported to Greece by Hostanes, a companion of Xerxes in the invasion of Greece. Thus we have two distinct traditions, one that the Magians practise magic, marriage with their mothers and other horrid rites[5]; the other that they are a race of wise men, who will not allow any man to become king of the Persians until he has learnt all the wisdom of the Magians.[6] Zoroaster as a magician and the father of astrology reappears in the *Clementine Homilies*,[7] where Nimrod, known to the Greeks as Zoroaster, destroys the ὁμόνοια that had existed under Noah by compelling the star that now governs the world to give him the kingdom; the star could not resist him, but avenged itself by pouring out the fire of its kingdom on the magician. The reputation of Zoroaster as a magician goes back to Dinon,[8] and is conflated with Nimrod's reputation in that line in Jewish literature.[9] The story explains the Persian worship of fire; it seems to retain a memory of Zoroastrian dualism; it has introduced from popular philosophy the Hellenistic ideal of ὁμόνοια and an explanation of the origin of astrology from popular magic.[10] The manner of his death suggests the king who is destroyed by a thunderbolt (Salmoneus of Elis and the variously

[1] Diodorus of Eretria and Aristoxenus the musician *ap.* Hipp. *El.* 1. 2 (7).

[2] *Loc. cit.*

[3] *Strom.* 5. 14. 92 (701 P). With the question of the extent to which it is just to describe Zoroastrianism as dualistic we are not concerned; cf. West, *Pahlavi Texts*, p. lxviii; Moulton, *Early Zoroastrianism* 125.

[4] *N.H.* 30. 2. 3 *seqq.*, where Pliny does not realise that he is identical with "Zaratus the Mede". For the explanation suggested above see Nock, *loc. cit.*

[5] Diog. Laert. 1. 7; Philo, *De Spec. Legg.* 3. 3 (13 *seqq.*, M. 2. 301); from the *Magica* of Xanthus (Clem. Alex. *Strom.* 3. 2. 11 (515 P)).

[6] Philo, *op. cit.* 18 (100, M. 2. 316); Cicero, *De Div.* 1. 41. 90. The two passages in Philo are significant of his methods of compilation; he betrays no sense of inconsistency at incorporating two entirely different accounts within a few pages of one another. The second passage, as the parallel with Cicero shows, is drawn from a defence of divination (treated by Philo here as mystical contemplation); it may be drawn from Posidonius' defence of divination.

[7] *Clem. Hom.* 9. 4 *seqq.*

[8] Diog. Laert. 1. 8: "ustra" = camel, but is taken to mean ἄστρον.

[9] The apocryphal view that Abraham invented astrology and saw through it, but was persecuted by Nimrod for his belief in the one true God, is implied as early as Philo, *De Gigant.* 14 (62, M. 1. 272).

[10] Hipp. *El.* 4. 37 (73) describes the method for causing the moon or a star to appear in the roof of the magician's house.

named Roman king), who derives from the lightning magic of Etruria and the East (or the royal rainmaker).[1] The possession of world-empire rests on the possession of the sacred fire which is continued from the ashes of Nimrod, presumably a reference to the fire of Vesta and the Roman legend of the destruction of the king by a thunderbolt. Syncretism could hardly go further.

The inconsistency of the two Zoroaster traditions has led to one curious conception, which is preserved by Clement of Alexandria; according to Democritus on the *Sacred Writings of Babylon*[2] Pythagoras learnt the magic of Zoroaster the Persian magus; but Alexander[3] relates that Pythagoras was the pupil of Zaratus the Assyrian, who is sometimes wrongly identified with Ezekiel. The latter statement is Clement's own; it is significant, as showing that the interpretation of the "Chapter of the Chariot" (Ezek. 1) is identified with the fourfold Aion of Hellenistic-Oriental speculation,[4] which is ascribed to Zoroaster. Clement agrees with Pliny[5] in distinguishing Zoroaster from Zaratus.

The whole attitude of educated Greek thought to Iranian religion betrays a striking lack of interest as compared with the interest taken in the religion of Egypt. It would seem that the reason is the difficulty of reading Greek mythology into it, except for purely superficial identifications of the Zeus-Ahura-Mazda type, and the incompatibility of dualism and a general resurrection and a final judgment of the world at the end of time with the whole Greek outlook. Even where there was some willingness to syncretise Iranian ideas it was necessary to remodel them, as when Nigidius Figulus interprets the final triumph of Ahura-Mazda as a kingdom of Apollo (i.e. the sun as in the Aion-speculations of the period) with the Stoic ἐκπύρωσις.[6] There is indeed a striking change in the dramas of Seneca, which apparently under Iranian influences actually envisage a real end of the world: but Seneca himself, as his prose-writings show, only looks forward to a Stoic ἀποκατάστασις.[7] Seneca's language is striking because it stands by itself, as against the world-ages which go back to Heraclitus. It is of course possible that Heraclitus drew his system of world-ages and conflagrations from this source; but it seems doubtful whether the evidence for his contact with the Magi is very serious.[8]

[1] Warde Fowler, *Religious Experience of the Roman People* 52, as against Frazer, *The Golden Bough, The Magic Art* 2. 180 *seqq.*

[2] Diog. Laert. 9. 49. Clement (*Strom.* 1. 15. 69 *seqq.* (356 P)) calls them "ethical writings". [3] Polyhistor, περὶ πυθαγορικῶν συμβολῶν.

[4] For the fourfold Aion and the "Chapter of the Chariot" cf. Peterson, Εἷς Θεός 250. For the dangerous qualities of the chapter see Mishnah, *Meg.* 4. 10 (Danby 207) and *Hag.* 2. 1 (*ib.* 213). Cf. pp. 53 *seqq.* [5] See p. 206, n. 4.

[6] *Ap.* Servius on *Ecl.* 4. 10; for the sun as equated to the Aion in "solar syncretism" cf. Peterson, *op. cit.* 243.

[7] For Seneca's dramatic writings with their apparent acceptance of a real "end of the world" cf. Kroll, *Gott u. Hölle* 418 *seqq.* The transformation of Pluto into a figure of the Satan-Ahriman type is particularly significant. For Seneca's real belief, as expressed in prose, cf. *Ad Marc. de Cons.* 26. 6; *Ep.* 1. 9. 16.

[8] According to Clem. Alex. *Protrepticus* 2. 22 (19 P) Heraclitus denounces the Magians and others who practise secret rites and mysteries with a fire that awaits them after death. In *Strom.* 5. 1. 9 (649 P) Clement ascribes this to his knowledge of barbarian philosophy: but I doubt if he is a very reliable authority. Naturally Heraclitus knew of Magi: anyone at Ephesus in 500 B.C. did. The threat of "fire" may be Clement's Christian interpretation of Heraclitus.

NOTE II

JEWISH INFLUENCES ON MAGICAL LITERATURE

Apart from the omission of the God of Abraham, Isaac and Jacob,[1] a formula of Jewish exorcism of the orthodox *kerygmatic* type appears to survive in the collection of recipes in the Paris magical papyrus; except for its conflation with an extremely crude formula by one who had heard of Christianity, but only as a variation of Judaism, it appears to represent a duplication of the same theme, the greatness of the God of Israel in creation, and His mighty works in bringing His people through the waters.[2] The reference to Christianity suggests a date before the close of the first century A.D. or very early in the second; a later date is scarcely compatible with such ignorance of the precise relation of Jesus to Judaism and of His place in Christian theology. The Empire could afford to persecute Christianity, but magic cannot afford to be slovenly or inaccurate in its designation of spiritual beings. The reference to the Temple at Jerusalem shows that this part of the formula goes back to the time when the Temple was standing (Deissman, *Licht. v. Ost.*[1] 181 *seqq.*).

It would appear that the mystery of the name of God, the exalted language of the Bible, and the success of the Jewish practice of exorcism, which was largely due to these advantages, won for it a high esteem in the practice of Hellenistic magic. Judaism itself was largely influenced by a demonology which inevitably involved a belief in the efficacy of magic; and while magic was repudiated there was a considerable measure of disagreement as to

[1] For the God of Abraham, Isaac and Jacob cf. Justin Martyr, *Dial. c. Tryph.* 85 (311 b); Origen, *c. Cels.* 1. 22 *seqq.*, 4. 33 and 34, 5. 45. [For his belief that the names will not work if translated cf. *Corp. Herm.* 16. 1 b *seqq.* (Scott 262).] In 4. 34 he notes the prevalence of forms describing the drowning of the Egyptians in the Red Sea. For Jewish acquaintance with the belief that demons cannot cross running water cf. Talmud, *Sanh.* 67 b and the sixth-century charm (Christian) banishing a demon across the Jordan which he cannot cross again (*Dict. d'Arch. Chrét.* 1. 1804). Is the unexpected Jewish-Christian insertion in *Papp. Mag. Gr.* 12. 174 in a spell for escaping from prison due to the obvious capacity of the Christian God for delivering His servants from prison?

[2] *Papp. Mag. Gr.* 4. 3009 *seqq.* Ll. 3009–3017 might come from any source; they may be herbs of Solomon. Ll. 3017–3032 may belong to the same; they come from a source which is neither Jewish nor Christian (Nock, *Gnomon* 12. 11. 607 compares the sons of Sceva in Acts 19. 14). The same hand may have changed the "Perizzites" of Gen. 15. 20 into "Pharisees" (3044). A knowledge of "Jesus the god of the Hebrews" might include a knowledge of the Pharisees as the villains of the Gospel narrative. The rest consists of a series of formulae, which appear to have been originally independent spells for different types of demoniac possession as ascribed to different types of demons. I have discussed the document at length in *Harvard Theological Review*, July 1938 and attempted to analyse the various formulae. For Dieterich's view (*Abraxas* 143) that the "pure men" of l. 3085 are Essenes there seems no reason; the reference is to the ritual purity which forms a large element in Judaism, conventionally identified with ethical holiness. For the date and meaning of the papyri in general cf. Nock in *Journal of Egyptian Archaeology* 15. 3 and 4. 219 *seqq.* (1929).

what was magic in a bad sense and what was legitimate medicine.[1] Moreover, there were elements in Jewish religious practice which looked to the outsider extremely like ordinary magic, such as the ritual of the ashes of the Red Heifer,[2] or the wearing of phylacteries; these resembled amulets of the ordinary type, though Judaism naturally distinguished them from those amulets against demons, whose legitimacy it recognised, even to the extent of allowing those of proved efficacy to be worn on the sabbath.[3] Phylacteries appear to be derived not from magic but from the literal interpretation of Deut. 6. 8;[4] but to the heathen, and to the less educated Jew, they would often appear to be amulets of magical potency rather than continual reminders of the Israelites' duty towards God; the literal interpretation of Deuteronomy by the rabbis seems to have been due to the necessity of finding an orthodox substitute for heathen amulets.[5] The same applies to the *mezuzoth* on the doorposts, which appear as a protection against demons in the religion of Babylon.[6]

For the use of the *kerygma*-form in Jewish exorcism it is interesting to compare Justin Martyr, *Dial. c. Tryph.* 85 (311 b), where the summary of the Creed is clearly quoted from a form of exorcism; cf. Orig. *c. Cels.* 1. 6, where the name of Jesus and "the histories concerning Him" drive out demons; the reference might be to a liturgical pericope from the Gospels (cf. *Papp. Mag. Gr.* Vol. 2. pp. 191 (P. 4), 207 (P. 18), 210 (O. 3)). But these are much later, while in *c. Cels.* 3. 24 Origen writes "the history" in the singular; it is far more likely that a summary of the *kerygma* is meant; summaries of this kind in a credal form appear to have been replaced later by passages of peculiar potency, such as the cosmogony of the prologue to the Fourth Gospel (*Papp. Mag. Gr.* Vol. 2. p. 192 (P. 5b)), or by false analogy the opening words of all the Gospels (*ib.* p. 207 (P. 19)).

The papyri offer abundant confirmation of the Christian allusions to magical practice. Thus the devils who tremble (Jas. 2. 19; Str.-B. give no parallels) appear in the Jewish exorcism already noted (l. 3017) and in the same papyrus, l. 359, in a passage inspired by the LXX. Origen's complaint that Christians use Jewish adjurations is abundantly confirmed by such

[1] Cf. Mishnah, *Berakhoth* 5. 5 (Danby 6) = *Papp. Mag. Gr.* 4. 132, for saliva in the mouth as an omen in prayer and magic respectively. Cf. Mishnah, *Shabb.* 6. 10 (Danby 106), where R. Meir regards it as legitimate to carry a nail from the gallows of a dead man on the sabbath for medical purposes when visiting a sick man; but the sages forbid it as following the ways of the Amorites. For the demonology of Judaism cf. Str.-B. 4. 1. 530 *seqq.* (excursus on demonology), which shows a combination of primitive folklore and borrowings from alien sources.

[2] Cf. Str.-B. *loc. cit.* for the dialogue between R. Jochanan b. Zakkai and a heathen, where the Red Heifer is explained as magic. When the heathen has gone his disciples ask whether he really regards it as magic. He replies that of course he does not; it is a commandment of God and therefore to be obeyed. In other words it is exactly similar to magic in practice, but differs in virtue of the intention of obedience to a command which cannot be understood.

[3] Mishnah, *Shabb.* 6. 2 (Danby 105). Rashi, *ad loc.*, notes the use on such amulets of Exod. 15. 26, promising that if the Israelites are faithful, God will not bring on them the plagues of Egypt; this may be a reminiscence of the *kerygmatic* exorcism.

[4] Cf. Kennedy *ap.* Hastings' *D.B.* 3. 869, Art. "Phylacteries". The refusal of the Sadducees and the ordinary Jew of the *am-ha-'arez* to wear them seems conclusive.

[5] 2 Macc. 12. 40.

[6] Jastrow, *Die Rel. Bab. u. Ass.* 1. 286.

documents as P. 2a (*Papp. Mag. Gr.* Vol. 2. p. 190), where the "strength of our God has prevailed and the Lord stands at the door and allowed not the destroyer to enter. Abraham dwells here. Blood of Christ put an end to evil", or the remarkable conflation of the pericope describing the giving of the Lord's Prayer, obviously a potent passage, with an exorcism of Solomon (*ib.* p. 206 (P. 17)). There seems little doubt that we have here attempts to make the best of both religions as late as the fifth or sixth century A.D. Further instances of this confirmation may be found in Origen; cf. *c. Cels.* 2. 34 for the opening of prison (*Papp. Mag. Gr.* 1. 101), also the interesting Christian insertion into an otherwise heathen context (*ib.* 13. 289); in *c. Cels.* 1. 68 he describes the calling up of the souls of heroes (*ib.* 4. 1390 *seqq.*) and the practice of providing splendid banquets through a Paredros; cf. *Papp. Mag. Gr.* 1. 103 *seqq.* This Paredros will carry you through the air (l. 120), as did Simon Magus' demon, until faced by the more potent magic of St Peter [*Acts of Peter* 32 (*Apocr. N.T.* 332); in the later *Acts of Peter and Paul* 77 (ed. Lipsius) Peter adjures the demon by the God who created all things and by Jesus Christ whom He raised from the dead, which shows the survival of the *kerygmatic* form]; for the danger of precipitation cf. 4. 2505 *seqq.* It is interesting that the demon will not provide either fish or pork; the combination shows that we have Egyptian not Jewish prohibitions. Cf. Tatian, *Or. adv. Gr.* 17. 77 and 80, for the value of herbs and relics of those who have died a violent death; 19. 87 for erotic charms; and Ir. *Haer.* 2. 32. 3 for *pueri investes.* These are all part of the regular stock-in-trade of the papyri. The extravagant claims of Simon Magus in *Clem. Recog.* 2. 9 suggest a lack of contact with regular practice.

For later Christian forms cf. *Dict. d'Arch. Chrét.* 5. 966; the Paris papyrus contains one interesting specimen (4. 1227 *seqq.*), in which the God of Abraham, Isaac and Jacob is addressed together with Jesus Christ and the Holy Ghost; the allusion to being "among the seven and in the seven" raises suspicions as to the orthodoxy of the present form, but it may well go back to an original which combined ante-Nicene orthodoxy with the advantage of the names of the Patriarchs.

There is a further question as to the extent to which Jewish Gnosticism, of the type which is presupposed in the Colossian heresy, may have influenced Gentile magic. Philo appears to be aware of a sevenfold division of the Logos, representing seven stages of the action of God, the seven days of creation and (presumably) corresponding to the seven planets (pp. 45 *seqq.*). We meet with a "sword of Dardanus" which consists of seven archangels in a state of some confusion (p. 203); the equation of "sword" and "word" is an established convention of Judaism. Here there seems a possibility of a direct connection between Jewish Gnosticism and magic, which renders it probable that in other cases where the connection is not so clear we are dealing with a legacy of unorthodox Judaism to magic, not simply with a borrowing of Jewish elements in heathen magic or purely Jewish magical practice. Cf. for instance *Papp. Mag. Gr.* 3. 145, where Adam (as the "original man"?) conjures the sun by a ninefold use of the names of God and the angels; for nine here cf. p. 31; in the same papyrus (but a different spell) 570 *seqq.* a god addressed as Iao is also "begotten in every man", i.e. originally the divine element of mind; at 591 *seqq.* the spell incorporates the prayer of *Corp. Herm.* Ascl. 41b (Scott 374), which is fairly clear evidence that we have here a link with Hermetic Gnosis. In Pap. 351 *seqq.* we have a set of seven adjurations by seven rulers sitting in the various heavens, including Raphael; the whole document has a strong Jewish colouring, and though late in date (fifth century A.D.) probably carries on an older tradition. In the earliest papyrus (no. 16), dating from the first century A.D., there is a ninefold adjuration of the demon of the dead by various names; one is by the heart of the son of Cronos, others by Adonai Sabaoth, Abaoth and Adonai;[1] here we seem to have an indication that syncretism had gone to considerable lengths by the time that the New Testament was written, since the "heart of the son of Cronos"[2] has the appearance of being an alien intruder into a Jewish compilation. If we may assume that the ninefold adjuration represents an adjuration by the firmament, the seven planetary spheres and the earth, Adonai Sabaoth is in the right place for Saturn and the heart of the son of Cronos for Jupiter.

It may be added that the title of "Eighth Book of Moses" attached to the Gnostic cosmogony of Pap. 13 suggests that Moses was regarded as a suitable author of such a work, i.e. that he was not merely known as the author of the orthodox story of creation, but of a more attractive and mysterious one. But this supposition is by no means necessary; the cosmogony in question does not appear to be particularly Jewish.

In any case the magical papyri preserve only fragments of a decayed form of Jewish Gnosticism. Their chief importance seems to lie in the fact that they show a contact between Judaism and the Hellenistic world which is quite different from that which we learn from more orthodox literature. For the understanding of Pauline theology they contribute very little, but they enable us to understand the early appearance and the wide influence of Gnosticism. Gnosticism and magic appear to represent the higher and the lower aspects of a view of the world and its problems which was characteristic of the age; in the earliest Gnostics the line between the two can hardly be drawn.[3]

[1] For a later (third century A.D.) adjuration of a sevenfold type with mixed "Orphic" and Jewish influences cf. Pap. Berol. 1 Parthey, 305 *ap.* Kern, *Orph. Fragm.* p. 312: Origen, *c. Cels.* 5. 9, derives the alleged worship of angels by unorthodox Jews from magic. Note his allusion to their appearances, and cf. col. 2. 18.

[2] Is this a mistake for "grandson" and an allusion to the legend of the heart of Dionysus, the only part which was not swallowed by the Titans (*Orpheus* 82)? We know that Judaism in Alexandria was interested in "Orpheus" from the time of Aristobulus, and it is just conceivable that this fragment of Orphic mythology, with the blunder substituting Cronos for Zeus as the father of Dionysus, should have been made in Jewish circles; the heart of Zeus is meaningless.

[3] Nock (*loc. cit.* 232) sees an essential difference of tone between Gnosticism and magic. I agree entirely in the case of such men as Valentinus; but Simon, Menander and Cerinthus seem to come much nearer both to magic and to the magical papyri.

NOTE III

THE MANDEANS

The Mandean system of redemption, whatever its origins may have been, bears every mark of being an attempt to introduce the common presuppositions of Hellenistic religion into an existing system of cultus, whose central feature was the frequent practice of baptism by immersion as a means of obtaining communion with the divine world and ensuring a free passage to the Mandean heaven. The attempt to read into it a pre-Christian system of Gnosis from which Christianity has derived those features which resemble Mandean tenets appears to be quite untenable in view of the examination of the documents by Pallis in *Mandaean Studies*, and more especially in view of Burkitt's demonstration in *J.T.S.* 29. 115. 225 *seqq.* that its use of Jewish names presupposes a knowledge of the Peshitta version of the Bible. The substitution of a journey through the various planetary spheres for a journey to the underworld (Pallis, *op. cit.* 22) represents a stage through which all Hellenistic religion was passing; Christianity seems to have reverted to the traditional Jewish view of Sheol in opposition to Gnosticism, thus abandoning the view implied in Colossians and Ephesians that the soul of the Christian ascends to heaven, while the planets are unable to prevent it; the Mandean system provides suitable passports for such a passage (*G.R.* 362 *seqq.*, Lidzb. 383. 25 *seqq.* and *passim*). The attitude to the celestial bodies is rightly described by Pallis as showing the hostility of the Gnostics (as also of Paul and rabbinical Judaism) to the general Hellenistic belief in a fate determined by the stars; like Christianity and Judaism, Mandeism offered a deliverance from the stars and therefore was not concerned to describe them correctly. Later the Mandeans (no less than Christians and Jews) were quite prepared to practise astrology (Brandt, *Die Mandäische Religion* 116). The fact that the female demon Ruha is mother of the seven planets in her character of Venus, while she is also "the spirit" and in anti-Christian polemic the Holy Spirit, is suggestive; Astarte has seven daughters in Sanchuniathon *ap.* Philo of Byblus *ap.* Eus. *Pr. Ev.* I. 10. 18. This suggests a system in which a goddess was identified with the divine spirit pervading the material—as is Isis in Plut. *De Is. et Os.* 53, 372e—here the planetary spheres; this explains the character of Venus as "spirit" and her consequent equation with the third person of the Christian Trinity; for the equation of Astarte with Isis cf. above, p. 61. [Naturally Ruha might be derived from Ishtar in Babylonia no less than from her Syrian form of Astarte.] Pallis (*op. cit.* 55) derives the seven children of Ruha from the Persian view of the planets; but the "seven", i.e. the seven planets, and the "five", i.e. the seven planets minus the sun and moon, were liable to confusion in Hellenistic religion; the ultimate origin may be Persian, but the immediate source need not be.

Yet another approximation to the Hellenistic world-view appears in the Mandean system of world-ages. Here we have four ages, the first ending in a destruction of all mankind by the sword, the second by fire, and the third by water, this destruction being equated with Noah's flood. Pallis points out the affinities with Zoroastrianism (*op. cit.* 60). But their details, especially the ridiculous end of the first with a destruction by the sword, leaving only two alive, have no particular Iranian affinities; they become explicable when it is remembered that the destructions by fire and water are Hellenistic commonplaces, while it is also an accepted view that the end must correspond to the beginning. Now the end of the world-age is to be ushered in by "wars and rumours of wars" not only in Judaism and Christianity but in the general literature of the first century B.C. It would seem that the end of a first world-age by the sword has been imported (*G.R.* 26, Lidzb. 27. 19) to provide an initial destruction by the sword to correspond to the last; it remains open to question whether the source is Christian or Hellenistic and whether we have here a genuine echo of the wars which preceded the establishment of the Roman Empire (or the wars which culminated in the downfall of the Jewish state) or a doctrine borrowed from Christian-Jewish apocalyptic at the time of the Mohammedan conquest (cf. *G.R.* 231, Lidzb. 232. 24 *seqq.*).

Both the date and place at which Mandeism arose can only be settled by those who are able to form a judgment on the linguistic problems involved. If the Mandean veneration for "Jordan" is an original part of the system, and if it refers to the actual river and is not a generic name for rivers as such, their origin must be sought for in the neighbourhood of Palestine. (So Lidzbarski, *Johannesbuch der Mandäer*, xix; but Brandt, *Die Mand. Rel.* 66, regards it as a name for rivers as such, while Pallis, *Mandaean Studies* 24, holds that "Jordan" as a name has replaced an earlier generic phrase, "living waters", under the influence of the late introduction of the figure of the Baptist to provide Mandeism with a suitable figure of a prophetic founder in order to secure Mohammedan toleration; the figure of the Baptist was according to him derived from Christianity.)

On the other hand, even if it were possible to demonstrate that the Mandean system has early affinities with Judaism, it would by no means follow that they exercised any serious influence either on Judaism or Christianity. On the showing of the Mandean documents themselves the revelation of the true religion in the present (and last) world-age is the work of "Enos-Uthra", who appears on earth shortly after the crucifixion of Jesus and the destruction of Jerusalem (*G.R.* 29 *seqq.* and 56 *seqq.*, Lidzb. 29. 28 *seqq.* and 50. 14 *seqq.*). Enos elsewhere abandons the world after the coming of Mohammed; up to this time he has remained in it unseen (*G.R.* 302, Lidzb. 300. 9). The sentence is a pathetic surrender of any claim that Mandeism could still hope even in name to be a world-religion; henceforth it is the religion of a "remnant". Now it is highly doubtful if these passages retain any ancient tradition, and it is clear that the "history" of the appearance of "Enos-Uthra" in connection with the fall of Jerusalem as it stands contains much that is derived from the O.T. as learned through Christian sources. But it is perhaps worth noting that the conception of a historical founder who remains in the world suggests the first century A.D. Origen (*In Ev. Jo.* 13.27) records that similar beliefs were entertained as to Dositheus; Simon and Menander seem to have claimed to be Messiahs:

the intensification of Mk. 13. 21 in Mt. 24. 23 is suggestive. It must remain an open question whether the character of "Enos-Uthra" and Dositheus is drawn from Mt. 28. 20 or whether that verse represents a statement of the Christian belief in the Holy Ghost in language reflecting a similar point of view.

A further suggestion of early elements in Mandeism might be found in the figures who retain the Hebrew name of God. Josamin (according to Lidzb. *Johannesbuch*, p. xxiii) replaces Baal-Samin, the well-known Syrian figure. He appears as the ruler of the firmament of heaven, and has a place to correspond to it; for he sometimes appears as good, or at any rate capable of repentance, sometimes as evil. This seems a natural position for a god of the firmament, since the development of Gnosticism would naturally degrade the "God of heaven", as the God of the Jews was commonly regarded in the Hellenistic age (cf. p. 67), to the rank of a demiurge and then to that of an even lower being. On the other hand Jorabba, another form of the god of the Jews, is always evil; yet Jochabad, Jochasar and Jozataq are good. The confusion is in any case difficult to explain. But it seems conceivable that a Syrian sect which lived on the upper reaches of the Jordan and suffered forcible conversion to Judaism under Aristobulus I might have been left with the name of its "Lord of the heaven" in the judaised form. (For Aristobulus cf. Jos. *Antt.* 13. 11. 3 (318).) An Iturean or Galilean tribe in this region might also be sufficiently exposed to oppression from centres of Syrian religion to reply by making the Syrian goddess the mother of the stars and the queen of the powers of evil; Judaism had to transform the Isis-Astarte of that region into the divine Wisdom. On the other hand, it is not easy to see why so hospitable a religion as Mandeism should have objected to adopting her, even if it had not already worshipped her; it is conceivable that she was first degraded to this position by Jewish conquerors and left there by the first introduction of a "Gnostic" reformation. (For Ruha cf. p. 212: it is difficult to explain her position as "spirit", Venus and queen of the planets unless she was the divine element in the material world in her own religion.)

There is a further difficulty in so far as the figures of Adam, Eve, Abel and Seth remain; while Adam and Eve are the first parents of mankind, Abel (Hibil) and Seth (Sitil) are beneficent beings of a supernatural order; this might be due to the fact that "Enos-Uthra", whose title suggests the enigmatic and quasi-Messianic titles which are familiar in Judaism and are reflected in Jesus' use of the title "Son of Man", might have thought it well, in describing himself as "Enos" the true man (cf. Philo, *Quod Det. Pot. Ins.* 38 (138, M. 1. 218)), who is also of the supernatural order, to leave the position of Seth his father undisturbed. It must always be remembered that he is a purely hypothetical figure; but such a reformer would naturally degrade the God of the Jews to the position of a thoroughly evil demiurge, while he might leave the "God of heaven" in spite of his identity with the God of the Jews in an intermediate position, introducing above him purely celestial beings, superior even to the vault of heaven itself. It seems that he degraded Jorabba below the firmament, making him a purely evil power; the other forms Jochabad, Jochasar and Jozataq survived as powers of good because their names were associated with deities of the Syrian pantheon

(Lidzb. *Johannesbuch*, p. xxv): Judaism when dominant may have tolerated the titles as "attributes" of God, so that the names survived as names of deities in Mandean polytheism and its Gnostic "reformation": if so, it was forgotten that 'Jo" was the God of the Jews except in the form "Jorabba". This would also explain the appearance of "Ptahil" as the creator of the material universe; Lidzbarski identifies him with the Egyptian creator Phthah (*ib.* xxvii), and Pallis (*op. cit.* 203) regards him as an ancient Mandean figure. If he is indeed the Egyptian creator, it is difficult to see how he can have reached the Mandeans unless it was in a period when Egyptian influence was still predominant in Northern Palestine in an unhellenised form; the Ptolemaic Empire might have introduced Serapis and Isis but not the Memphite creator; in this case we should have to see in Ptahil a survival of the era when the cedars of Lebanon were being felled for the Egyptian navy, i.e. some time before the conquest of Egypt by the Persian Empire. Phthah, however, had a certain vogue in magic: possibly this explains his appearance as the demiurge.[1] In the system as it appears in the texts Ptahil has become a kind of duplicate of his father Abathur, regarded by Pallis (*loc. cit.*) as ancient, by Lidzbarski (*op. cit.* p. xxix) as a Persian figure (this is denied by Pallis, *op. cit.* 114). In the existing system Ptahil and Abathur are responsible for a defective creation of a Gnostic type (cf. p. 224). Pallis holds (*op. cit.* 191) that the original Mandean cosmogony was a creation by powers of evil, but here he is considering the original Gnostic cosmogony; there must have been an earlier creation, and if Ptahil was originally Phthah, it was presumably a good one. As it stands Mandeism has certainly adopted the conventions of the Hellenistic age in regard to the evil of matter, and the division of labour between Abathur and his son or reflection Ptahil enables the pair to do the work of Sophia-Achamoth in the system of Valentinus. The original position of Abathur as against Josamin is completely undiscoverable.

On these lines it would be fairly simple to explain the two conceptions of the highest powers. We have the great Mana, who was originally in the "Fruit" (possibly a variation of the Orphic cosmic egg), from whom proceed innumerable "fruits" and "shekinas", and among these appear the "first life" and the "second life" (*G.R.* 68, Lidzb. 65. 25 *seqq.*). Brandt (*op. cit.* 24 *seqq.*) regards these as remnants of Mandean polytheism, but this seems entirely mistaken; the character of the great Mana and the two lives are completely colourless, and the second life is sometimes an entirely superior being (there is sometimes even a third, *G.R.* 196, Lidzb. 196. 11), while at others he is dangerously compromised with the work of creation (*G.R.* 70,

[1] Curiously enough Phthah appears twice in the magical names of the Jewish exorcism of "Pibeches" discussed in Note II (*Papp. Mag. Gr.* 4. 3013 and 3015). As the Jewish creator had to be definitely evil, another deity had to be introduced as a demiurge of an intermediate type; it may be that Phthah was known in this way. A similar contact may explain the fact that the Hebrew tongue ascends to heaven when the world is destroyed (*G.R.* 307, Lidzb. 306. 28). At first sight this seems inexplicable; but the magical prestige of Hebrew (cf. p. 42) may have led to its inclusion as one of the eternal elements in the cosmos by a writer who did not even know that Hebrew was the language of the Jews. Possibly the fact that the name of God is not uttered in Jerusalem (*G.R.* 329, Lidzb. 338. 14) comes from a similar source.

Lidzb. 66. 27), and at others he is Josamin (*G.R.* 295, Lidzb. 291. 21 *seqq.*), whose sons are responsible for this blunder; while in 360 (Lidzb. 381. 21) the world was created by the second. This confusion becomes intelligible in the light of the ordinary Gnostic convention of an ultimate "Abyss" or unknowable deity with various "emanations" who somehow unite him to the material world; here it is perfectly possible to see the supreme God, the visible pattern or Logos of the system taken over from Posidonius, with a third emanation (the "second life") to enhance the gulf between the supreme being and the created world; but this being had at an earlier stage been regarded as creator of matter and so identified with Josamin, the firmament of heaven. Such an origin would also explain the Mandean fondness for describing "deficiency" as a mark of the material world; it has been seen above (p. 166) that Hellenistic thought demands that there should be a *pleroma* in all things. So the conception of the world as being entirely "birth" (*Qolasta* 23, Lidzb. *Mand. Lit.* 36. 4) seems to reflect the Hellenistic tendency to confuse "birth" and "becoming".[1]

On the assumption of this hypothesis it might be possible to explain the beggar Ado, described by Theodore bar Konai as the founder of the Mandeans, whose doctrine is borrowed from various sources, including the Manichees (Burkitt, *op. cit.* 231). Theodore's only error would be that Ado was not the founder, but the reformer who substituted the "king of Light" for the "Great Mana" and the "Lives". This view finds some slight support in Theodore's statement that the Mandeans are Dositheans, which is certainly untrue, but might preserve a knowledge of a founder of Mandeism who shared Dositheus' quality of being in the world till the end of time. It may safely be assumed that the "king of Light" is Manichean (Brandt, 198 *seqq.*; Burkitt, *loc. cit.*). A course of events such as that suggested above would explain the leading features of the Mandean view of the soul, which is an independent "soul" yet possesses some affinity with the original divine element implanted in the original Adam, who was created by lower beings, yet unable to stand upright until a spark of divine life was placed in him by Hibil (*G.R.* 159, Lidzb. 168. 10; cf. Ir. *Haer.* I. 24. 1 (Satornilus) and 30. 6, "the Gnostics"). As Adam includes all mankind, this explains the nature of the individual soul as a divine spark, which none the less retains its individuality to all eternity; in other words, the usual Hellenistic inconsistency remains, for the soul, if it is simply a divine spark, ought to be reabsorbed into the divine, not simply reascend to a realm of light. In the same way the double character of the Mandean redeemer, Manda d'Haije, as conqueror of the abyss and the personified "knowledge of life" which brings salvation to the soul of the individual by conveying it through the spheres of the hostile planets (*G.L.* 24, Lidzb. 441. 35 and *passim*), is a characteristic feature of Hellenistic religion of the *Poimandres* type. It would also explain the resemblance between the imagery of the New Testament and the Mandeans; for both are concerned either with the common concepts of Hellenistic religion, such as life and light, or with the normal features of Palestinian life, vines, seed and sheep, or of the

[1] For the two meanings cf. Philo, *Quod Deus sit Imm.* 25 (119, M. I. 290) and Prestige, *God in Patristic Thought* 52 *seqq.* But the use of "birth" suggests a late and distant connection, which interpreted "becoming" as meaning "birth".

needs of life in general, such as houses and clothing: pearls are for both a type of precious stones in general. But the features are far too general to make it necessary to assume a common Palestinian origin. Similarly, the presence of very striking resemblances between the accounts of the descent of the Mandean redeemer through the spheres and the Christian descent into Hades proves nothing beyond the fact that both draw on a common stock of literary convention describing a descent of a divine being into hell. The Mandean redeemer in the extant literature generally descends through the planets to the sphere of earth, as Jesus does in the more Hellenistic elements of the Pauline writings. But the Mandean redeemer's descent is a revised form of a descent into hell, suited to the normal world-view of the Hellenistic age, while it would seem that the Mandean religion at one time believed in a genuine descent (Kroll, *Gott u. Hölle* 281 *seqq.*). In any case the similarities are due to a common convention going back to a remote past and naturally reproduce similar features (Kroll, *op. cit.* 297).

Even if this purely speculative reconstruction were true, it would not prove that Mandeism exercised any influence on Judaism or Christianity, but rather the reverse, since "Enos-Uthra" would belong to a class of Gnostic "saviours" who appear in Palestine as competitors not of the historical Jesus but of the early Church (cf. above, p. 213); it would seem that the success of Christianity suggested the new character. It also involves one very serious difficulty. It seems agreed that the Mandeans migrated to their present dwelling-place from a region of "Jordans", i.e. a region in which it was natural to see in fresh and rapid streams (or in the Jordan) a manifestation of the divine beings who lived in mountains in the North. The location in Northern Galilee or Ituraea is therefore possible. But if "Enos-Uthra" conceals a historical founder, it would seem that there was a migration of the Mandeans from their original home to Southern Mesopotamia at a time when the religion had reached a form which can still be found in their literature. This presents a serious difficulty: there is no allusion to such a migration in the texts: their silence would be intelligible if the practice of baptism, as a cult-survival, was all that remained of the Mandean religion in its pre-Gnostic stage; it might also be possible to see in the hostility to Jorabba and Ruha the remains of a hostility to Judaea and Syria, which dated from a period before such a migration. If the Gnostic influence only made itself felt in Mesopotamia, it might have obliterated the historical "Exodus". Otherwise its absence from the texts is very difficult. An "Exodus" after Mandeism reached its present form could scarcely fail to leave its mark on the literature; such incidents are more likely to be invented than to be forgotten.

In any case the possible course of events outlined above is no more than a speculation. Attempts to explain the origin of Mandeism and its relations to Christianity must be governed by the consideration pointed out by Burkitt (*op. cit.* 234) with regard to the common astrological pre-suppositions of all Gnosticism, to which he might have added the common presuppositions as to the nature of the soul and the essentially fluid character of all "Gnostic systems". It remains possible that he is entirely right in ascribing its origin to contact between a primitive cult and the Eastern systems of Gnosticism of which Bardaisan is a representative. In any case it is dangerous to suppose that all influences must or can be traced to one period of contact. Any race living between the Euphrates and the Mediterranean was exposed to contact with Zoroastrianism, Judaism, Hellenistic thought and Syrian paganism at any period after the conquests of Alexander, and from at least A.D. 200 with Christianity, whether orthodox or Gnostic. (Cf. Harnack, *Mission u. Aufbreitung* 440.) In this melting-pot of cultures the conception of a gradual evolution from polytheism to monotheism, from myth to philosophy, from magic to mystery and from ritual to ethics, leading to the substitution of ethical conduct for the outward observance of religious rites, except in so far as religion decays under the influence of sacerdotalism, does not apply, any more than it applies to Western European religion after the date of August 4, 1914.

Note. The *Mandaeans of Iraq and Iran* by E. S. Drower (Clarendon Press, 1937) is invaluable as a description of the peculiar ritual and liturgical practices of the Mandeans. It is perhaps to be regretted that the author has ventured into the study of their origins. The fact that they eat a ritual meal every year in memory of the Egyptians drowned in the Red Sea while pursuing Israel during the Exodus (pp. 10 and 89) may "come from a Jewish source", but it cannot be used to suggest that "that part of the Israelites who were taken captive by Sargon were in truth settled near the Caspian" (the supposed home of the Mandeans); the Israelites taken captive by Sargon can hardly be supposed to have heard of the story of the drowning of the Egyptians. But it is not unnatural that an experience of forcible conversion to Judaism should lead to sympathy with the drowned Egyptians, which any reader of the *Mekilta* is bound to feel. In the same way the legend of the Exodus on p. 266 is an obvious conflation of the anti-Semitic propaganda of Manetho and Apion with the Jewish legends in which Abraham appears as the destroyer of the idols of Babylon.

In general it may be said that while the liturgical practice of the Mandeans reveals obvious affinities with primitive nature-religion, it is by no means clear how far these affinities are due to primitive practice which has survived from the beginning, or how far they represent a reversion to a lower stage of religion during the centuries of decadence and assimilation to neighbouring religions. The principles of Life and Light, with their very slight personification, cannot be taken (as on p. xxi) to represent a primitive form of religion which has been preserved at a pre-mythological stage, in view of the armies of mythological figures who still retain a shadowy existence in literature and cult; they clearly represent a Gnosticising attempt to replace mythology by allegory. The "beings" treated as demons and evil in the Mandean scriptures who reappear "in magic rolls as beneficent beings" (note that John the Baptist does not appear) are significant; the opposition of the classical literature to magic (as to astrology) has failed to resist the popular demand for such protection, much as astrology found its way into orthodox Christian circles (even high ecclesiastical circles) in spite of the opposition of classical Christian theology.

Such statements as those that "the *haoma*" as used at weddings is "an intensified fertility symbol; it is possible that the wine at the Cana marriage-feast (John 2. 3–10) had a similar ritual meaning" (p. 72); "this sign [of the Cross] was not at first associated even by the Christians with the instrument of Christ's passion but was a 'life' or 'sun' symbol" (p. 107); or the comparison of the removal of the seal from the mud on the Mandean grave on the third day with the breaking of the seal on the tomb of Jesus on the morning of the Resurrection (p. 201), suggest a failure to avoid the more obvious pitfalls of comparative religion; this is combined with the further statement (p. 203) that the journey of the soul through the *mataratha* in forty-five days, or in the case of the perfect soul forty, "recalls the Ascension of Jesus on the fortieth day. Forty is used generally as the Semitic equivalent of many and would therefore not be significant were it not for the parallel of the resurrection on the third day and the removal of the seal". But forty days is a common period in the O.T.; if there is any connection, it would seem that the Mandean forty days are due to the necessity of proving that Jesus was no better than the best Mandeans.

It is a pity that so valuable a book should attempt to deal with the resemblances between Christianity and the Mandeans on the basis of *The Golden Bough*. It is conceivable that it would be difficult to reconstruct the theology of St Thomas Aquinas from an observation of the cult-practices of the remoter Roman Catholic communities of South America.

NOTE IV

THE DESCENT OF THE REDEEMER

The "myth" of a divine being who descends into hell and returns in triumph appears to go back to Babylonian religion; possibly it is derived from the character of Marduk (originally Tammuz) as a vegetation god (Kroll, *Gott u. Hölle* 239).[1] The same *motif* appears in Egypt as a descent of the sun-god into the darkness of the underworld (*ib.* 185 *seqq.*). The dualistic world-view characteristic of Iranian-Chaldean religion, which influenced the general Hellenistic outlook in which Christianity grew up, substituted for the descent of the saviour-god into the lower world his descent through the spheres of the planets into the material cosmos.

The mere descent of a divine figure through the planets into the lower world does not prove any immediate connection with the myth, nor do the literary conventions associated with it; these conventions, such as the bursting of the gates of brass and the bars of iron, the bringing of light into the realm of darkness through a shattering of the earth, the panic of the rulers of the realms of the dead and the like, are to be found in literature which was quite unacquainted with the source from which they were drawn. In Pauline literature there is an obvious instance of this in 1 Cor. 15. 55, where the triumph over death suggests an acquaintance with the triumph over a personified figure of death which is a regular feature of the conventional account; but the acquaintance with it must go back behind Is. 25. 8 and Hos. 13. 14, from which the passage is compiled. Similarly, the breaking of the gates of brass and the bars of iron in Is. 45. 2 seems to show the language of this myth; but in Col. 2. 3 the "hidden treasures" which in Isaiah belong to the "darkness", and are the spoils to be taken from Hades, have become treasures of wisdom hidden in Christ.

At the risk of some repetition of points already noticed, it is perhaps worth analysing the passages in the Pauline writings which have been held to indicate Paul's knowledge either of the "descent" of a divine redeemer or of some of the features commonly associated with it.

(1) 1 Cor. 2. 8. That the "rulers" crucified Jesus because they did not know who He was suggests the motive of the redeemer who passes through the various doors of the planetary spheres unrecognised.[2] This is very commonly found in the Mandean and Gnostic literature, but, except on the

[1] Kroll's exhaustive study is marked by a restraint in finding parallels and in drawing inferences which it would be an impertinence to praise; a shorter study of the subject appears in Clemen, *Religionsgeschichtliche Erklärung des N.T.* 89 *seqq.*

[2] Clemen, *op. cit.*, holds that the same thought is implied in Col. 2. 15 *seqq.*, but this seems quite uncertain. He compares *Asc. Is.* 9. 13 *seqq.*, which dates from the second century A.D., but may incorporate older material; but the Pauline explanation was obviously a natural way out of the difficulty involved in the crucifixion of Jesus by the "rulers" on earth. If they could crucify Him on earth, where His death could effect the redemption of man, their prisoner, why had they not opposed Him on His descent and so prevented Him from delivering mankind? The motive of the failure to recognise Him appears in Ign. *ad Eph.* 19. 1; *Epist. Apost.* 13 (*Apocr. N.T.* 489).

assumption of the priority of the Mandean writings, pre-Christian parallels do not seem to be found. (Dibelius, *Geisterwelt im Glaube des Paulus* 88 *seqq.*, and Bousset, *Hauptprobleme der Gnose* 242, assert a pre-Christian source, but adduce only post-Christian or Mandean parallels.) It must, however, be noticed that in this passage Paul is not concerned to argue that Jesus came down from heaven through the planetary spheres; this was obviously necessary if He was to come to earth from heaven. He is concerned to prove the foolishness of the so-called wisdom of this world as against the Wisdom of God; his crowning proof is that the "rulers" themselves, i.e. the angelic powers, identified on the one hand with the angels who rule the nations and on the other with the planets, did not understand God's purpose, which is known to every Christian, and therefore crucified the Lord of glory. But this is simply a transfer to the angelic rulers of the ignorance of the rulers of the Jews in Acts 3. 17; some such explanation of the conduct of the rulers of the Jews was necessary as long as there was any hope of avoiding a final breach with the synagogue, and as long as the Church hoped to live on friendly terms with the authorities of the Roman Empire; and it was a mere commonplace of contemporary thought that things on earth were counterparts of things in heaven. Thus the ignorance of the rulers is naturally explicable from the given facts of the situation in which Paul is writing.

(2) In Colossians Paul is to a large extent concerned to prove that, even if the arguments of his opponents are true, the supremacy of Jesus remains unaffected. Hence it is not always easy to distinguish his own beliefs from those which he is prepared to accept for the sake of argument. None the less his own world-view, as appears from Rom. 8. 20, is very similar in so far as God is in heaven, separated from the earth by the spheres of hostile planets. This view was certainly drawn from the conflation of dualism with astrology, which in various forms was the generally accepted view of the age.[1] But there is no suggestion here that Jesus burst through the bars of the planetary spheres or that He conquered the rulers by force. That He acquired either a material or a psychic nature from the planets, as He descended through their spheres, was part of the general convention (pp. 103 and 108). That He should have laid it aside on the Cross and not during His ascension through the planetary spheres shows a lack of serious interest in the whole scheme, though a similar levity is easily paralleled in the literature of the time.[2] The reconciliation effected by the Cross seems to have no place in the myth, while it figures largely in Col. 1. 20 and 2. 13 *seqq.* Here too Paul does not try to be consistent; in Rom. 8. 38 the rulers remain hostile; for the reconciliation of the rulers cf. Ign. *ad Smyrn.* 6. 1, perhaps representing an independent tradition, and Orig. *In Ev. Jo.* 1. 15; contrast *Od. Sol.* 5. 4; *Acts of Thomas* 156 (*Apocr. N.T.* 432); *Acts of John* 114

[1] Cf. Kroll, *op. cit.* 268 and 365.

[2] So Verg. *Aen.* 6. 730 describes a purification in Hades which is really that which takes place in the lower air (cf. Servius, *ad loc.*), as it does in Seneca, *Ad Marc. de Cons.* 25; Plut. *De Ser. Num. Vind.* 23 *seqq.*, 563e. For purification in the moon and in the planets cf. pp. 31 and 103. In Eph. 2. 2 Satan is in the lower air, but in 6. 12 the Christian wrestles with the planets. Origen, in *De Princ.* 2. 11. 6, speculates on a celestial purgatory which appears in full in Clem. Alex. *Strom.* 4. 18. 116 *seqq.* (616 P).

(*ib*. 269). The reconciliation of man is effected by the surrender to the rulers of the material body, which is all that they can claim; this thought seems to transfer to the rulers the "ransom" by which Jesus delivered mankind from the duty of obedience to the Torah by assuming the "curse" of a material body to which alone the Torah applied. There is no question of a recipient of the "ransom"; it would be as absurd to ask who received the "ransom" of Gal. 3. 13 as to ask who received the "ransom" of Ethiopia, Egypt and Saba in Is. 43. 3. The language of "ransom" without any specified recipient is common in the second Isaiah; cf. also Philo in such passages as *De Conf. Ling*. 20 (93, M. 1. 419); in Paul it may go back to the logion of Mk. 10. 45, where again there is no thought of the recipient.[1] On the other hand in Colossians Paul uses language as to the "laying aside" of the material which closely resembles that used in the *Hymn of the Soul* (*Acts of Thomas* 108, *Apocr. N.T.* 412 *seqq*.) and the Manichean and Mandean literature, as well as in the *Odes of Solomon* (cf. Reitzenstein, *Erl.-Myst*. 84 *seqq*.). But here we are in a region of Hellenistic commonplace, and the "putting-on" of the flesh by Jesus at His descent from heaven to earth plays no part in Paul's treatment of the subject. In any case, if treated seriously, the "putting-off" should have taken place during the ascent to heaven.[2]

(3) In Phil. 2. 10 we have an allusion to "things under the earth" which might allude to a conquest of hell, but seems only to reflect the conventional division of the universe into heaven, earth and the lower regions; the development of a system of monotheism, in which the supreme God was in heaven, carried with it the supremacy of that God over the lower regions (cf. Peterson, *Εἶς Θεός* 259, n. 2 and 262). This was a matter of common form.

(4) In Rom. 10. 6 we have a commonplace of Jewish-Hellenistic exegesis of the O.T. applied to the impossibility of going up to heaven to bring Christ down or of going down to hell to bring Him up from the dead (cf. p. 102). Here, however, there is no allusion to the myth of a descent into hell in any recognisable form; it is merely a way of pointing out that Christianity is a very simple thing. Since Jesus had risen from the dead and since union with Him by faith was a simple matter, there was no need to attempt the impossible. Naturally Paul would have supposed that Jesus, if He had not risen from the dead, would have remained in Sheol, if he was addressing Jewish circles, as in Romans.

(5) The rest of the N.T. suggests a knowledge of the myth in such passages as Mt. 27. 52 (cf. Kroll, *op. cit*. 6), possibly Heb. 2. 14, which may, however, be Jewish commonplace, Rev. 1. 18, and apparently 1 Pet. 3. 18 *seqq*. This passage however presents a peculiar difficulty. The generation of the Flood belongs to a separate world-age, and the preaching of the Gospel to them may represent a special concession to those who had no chance to hear the message preached at the end of the present. Moreover, Jesus preached it to them "in the spirit". 1 Cor. 5. 3 and Col. 2. 5 suggest that

[1] Cf. Rawlinson, *The Gospel according to St Mark*, *ad loc*. and above, p. 109.

[2] Cf. p. 138. Kroll, *op. cit*. 209, connects the laying aside of garments at each gate in the descent to the underworld in Babylonian religion with the Gnostic belief that the soul puts on garments as it descends into the material and puts them off as it ascends, but the symbolic use of garments is Hellenistic religion.

this is contrasted with a presence, such as is normally assumed in Christian stories of the descent into Hades. I cannot help suspecting that the writer is substituting a modified version of the descent for that normally current, in which there really was a bodily descent, though naturally orthodox theology could not say so.[1]

(6) Superficially, however, the most remarkable resemblance appears in Eph. 4. 9. Here we have an "ascent" to heaven, following a "descent" to the "lower parts of the earth", in which Jesus goes up on high and "leads captivity captive". But here again the resemblance vanishes on closer inspection. Possibly the "lower parts of the earth" are intended to mean Sheol, though the writer of Ephesians in 6. 12 transfers the struggle between the Christian and the powers of evil to the planetary spheres; but the emphasis is not on the descent, but the ascent, in virtue of which Jesus is able to "fill all things", i.e. to make His work effective not only on earth (and in any lower spheres which there may happen to be) but in heaven itself. As a result of His ascent to heaven (an "ascent" which implies a previous "descent" (see p. 194)), He has been able to win the prize of victory which rabbinical Judaism wrongly supposed had been won by Moses, when he ascended from earth to heaven and brought back the Torah. The error of Judaism appears from the fact that Moses could not properly be said to have "ascended", for he had not "descended" first; hence, too, the promised "gifts" were not the Torah, but the Holy Spirit, the prize which Jesus had won at His ascent and now gives as His gifts to men, i.e. the gifts of Apostleship and the other qualities needed for the work of the ministry. It is conceivable that the rabbinical accounts of the ascent of Moses to receive the Torah have been coloured by the myth, in so far as they represent the angels as being opposed to the giving of the Torah to Moses; it is again conceivable that the language of Ps. 68. 18 depicts the triumph of the Jewish king in language drawn from the mythology of the Babylonian redeemer, but there seems no reason for this, since the Psalm seems a straightforward account of a triumphal procession. The writer of Ephesians has produced a passage which superficially resembles the myth, but depends for its whole point on its reference to the entirely different rabbinical conception. The remarkable similarity of such lines as Seneca, *Hercules Furens* 423, seems to depend simply on a common conception of the structure of the cosmos.

Naturally the myth of the descent into hell when transferred to the descent of a divine being into the world of the material produces language similar to that of Paul when he describes the descent of Jesus as the divine

[1] The development of the myth is traced by Kroll. It is clear that it appears in a fully developed form in the Apostolic Canons (cf. Kroll, *op. cit.* 17), but it does not appear in the credal form of exorcism in Justin Martyr, *Dial. c. Tryph.* 85, 311 b (for this form cf. p. 209); it seems that Justin does not know of a descent into Hades, though he is acquainted with such mythical accretions as the cave of the nativity at Bethlehem (*ib.* 78, 304 a) and the light at the baptism of Jesus in Jordan (*ib.* 88, 315 d). One is tempted to suspect that the story made its way from popular religion into liturgical Christianity with the help of the isolated allusions in Scripture which sanctioned or seemed to sanction it. (Kroll, *op. cit.* p. 128, assumes that Justin's allusions to exorcism imply a knowledge of the descent and that he is evidence for its currency in his time. But Justin says nothing to imply it.)

Wisdom into the material world which is subject to the celestial powers. Both the Pauline and the parallel myths are attempts to fit a given story into a setting which was the received theology of the Hellenistic age. That theology held that there was a divine element permeating the whole cosmos, which in man took the special form of an element of "mind" or "spirit" which was also an independent personal being or δαιμόνιον. The establishment of this view seems to have been the work of Posidonius (cf. p. 72), but it was really a necessity of Stoic logic; if there was a divine element in man, it must either be present in all men, merely as part of their nature, in which case there was no reason for being virtuous, or it must be present in such a way that man could make it the dominating element in his personality, if he chose to do so. I suspect Posidonius of having been inconsistent in his utterances on the point.

This element had somehow been imprisoned in the material which was the source of evil. Moreover, being in the lowest stage of the cosmos, earth, it was subject to the stars, as being "below" them. It had evidently fallen into the material world in some unexplained manner; the popular myth of an "original" man who had somehow fallen in this way was one such explanation. If it was to return to its home in heaven, whether by virtue, Gnosis or magic, it had somehow to "ascend" through the spheres of the planets, which intervened; if they were regarded as hostile and as determining man's fate, which was the normal view, some means had to be found for overcoming them. The normal means was a recognition of the divine origin of the element of mind, if the scheme was considered from the point of view of philosophy; if it was regarded from the point of view of religion, it was natural to identify the divine element in man, which explained his origin and enabled him to attain to deliverance, with the hero of the votary's particular cult (cf. pp. 100 *seqq.*).

This is precisely the element that is the common property of the mystery-cults and of all other religions which retained any vitality. It was the underlying assumption of all intelligent religion; if you were not an Epicurean and took any interest in theology instead of conforming without asking for explanations, your religion was almost invariably a myth, which explained how the divine element in man had come to be imprisoned in the realm of the material (cf. Orig. *c. Cels.* I. 20).[1] The doctrine appears in the *Poimandres* in the form of an adaptation of the story of Narcissus, or the Pythagorean tabu (on looking at one's own reflection), which has found its way into the Mandean system,[2] where a spiritual "first man" of a

[1] Although Celsus is described as an Epicurean by Origen (I. 8), he often uses purely Hermetic language; he agrees that the word is the son of God (2. 31), but it is a "pure and holy" word (cf. *Corp. Herm.* I (*Poimandres*), 5a (Scott I. 116), which shows that we are dealing not with the supposed Jewish opponent, but with Celsus himself), cf. 6. 41 and *Corp. Herm.* 16. 16 (Scott 270), 7. 36 and 45 and *Corp. Herm.* 6. 4b (Scott 168), and 7 (Scott 170). There is of course no need to suppose a direct connection; the views are mere commonplaces of the age.

[2] *Corp. Herm.* I (*Poimandres*), 14 (Scott 120). The resemblance to the Mandean myth (*G.R.* 168, Lidzb. 173. 38 *seqq.*) is obvious, but it is by no means clear which is the original or whether both are derived from Narcissus; on the other hand, the exegesis of the mirror of Dionysus by neo-Platonists (Kern, *Orph. Fr.* 209; according to *Orpheus* 123 this is the only point in the Orphic system which Plotinus deigns to

divine origin falls into matter, while "mind" remains a celestial being, which visits the righteous and enables them to escape from fate and the material; mind is on the way to becoming a personified cult-hero. Once "mind" was recognised as a special manifestation of the divine power immanent in the cosmos, the normal Stoic allegory could be made into a myth of the deliverance of "mind" from matter. Among the figures who appear in this capacity are Osiris and Isis in Plut. *De Is. et Os.*[1] Here Osiris is the pure principle of deity and Isis the divine element fighting against evil in the material world, whereas in Apuleius, *Metam.* 11. 23. 804 *seqq.* (where the interest is entirely religious, not theological), Lucius traverses the lower regions with Osiris in order to enter into the full protection of Isis; here the goddess is clearly the more important figure. For Mithras as the "world-soul" and a possible allusion to a solar cult with a similar interpretation as early as Philo cf. p. 46; for Attis, Sallustius, *Concerning the Gods and the Universe* 4 (ed. Nock 9); for Apollo and Dionysus Plut. *De Ei ap. Delph.* 9. 388 e, cf. *Orpheus* 255; for the Cabeiri in Varro cf. above, p. 86; for Zeus and Hera, Celsus *ap.* Orig. *c. Cels.* 6. 42. The last three represent the ordinary allegory: for Heracles as "mind" at the end of a comprehensive allegory of pagan religion, cf. Clem. *Hom.* 6. 16, and the Naassene system as described by Hippolytus 5. 8 (107 *seqq.*); in spite of Hippolytus' confusions or those of his source we have the spiritual man in heaven, actual humanity below and a power which raises man from earth to heaven; it appears from the text of the hymn (*ib.* 10) that this is Jesus as the second mind, who pities the soul imprisoned in matter, lamenting its sufferings in language which seems to be drawn from the account of Adam at the gate of Hades in *Test. Abr.* 11 (ed. James, *Texts and Studies* 2. 2. 89 and 112).

Naturally Paul tends to approach the language of mythological attempts to fit the divine element in the cosmos into the figures of contemporary religion, since he is concerned to expound the historical figure of Jesus in terms of the earlier tradition by which Alexandrine Judaism had attempted to read that divine element, as the Wisdom of God, into the cosmogony of Genesis. His lack of consistency is due to the intractability of the material. Hence his inconsistency in regard to the relation of Jesus to the element of "mind" or "spirit" in man on the one hand and to the Spirit of God as manifested in the prophets and the Church on the other. The casual

notice) shows how obvious the allegory was; it must be remembered that the reflection in a mirror is produced by an "emanation", cf. p. 71; it is never a "mere" reflection. It is of course possible that the original story originated in the superstition that to see one's face in the water in a dream is an omen of death (Artemidorus, *Oneirocritica* 2. 7. 88); and it is one of the Pythagorean tabus that one must not look at one's face in a river (*Pythagorica Symbola ap.* Mullach, *Fr. Phil. Gr.* 510. 24). Originally we may have a widespread superstition about reflections [cf. Frazer, *The Golden Bough* 1. 292 *seqq.* (ed. 1900)]. But the Pythagorean connection suggests Posidonius as the source of the Hermetica and probably of the Mandeans.

[1] Cf. p. 68. For Isis here cf. Ruha in the Mandean system as the "spirit" who is also the Syrian goddess (Lidzbarski, *Ginza*, intr. p. xi); the identification of the goddess with the spirit seems to reflect the normal Hellenistic tradition. Lucian and Apuleius do not mention such speculations; but they are concerned with cult not theology. Ruha is also Venus (*G.R.* 27, Lidzb. 28, 27), just as Isis can also be the moon. Cf. also p. 61.

identification of "the Lord" and "the Spirit" in 2 Cor. 3. 17 never leads him to identify Jesus with the "spirit" of man nor with the Spirit as given to man. Nor again does he ever identify the spirit of man with the Spirit of God, as Origen does in some of his more incautious speculations (e.g. *In Matt. Comm. Ser.* 57), and as the orthodox Syrian writers normally do (Tatian, *Or. ad Gr.* 13. 62 and 15. 69, where man consists of soul and body; he lost the spirit at his fall into the present earth, but retained an ἔναυσμα of it (cf. Basilides *ap.* Hipp. *El.* 7. 22 (233)), which enabled him to seek God and so to fall into idolatry. Now, however, the Spirit of God is willing to dwell in man, who otherwise is no better than the beasts except that he can speak.) Cf. also the Syrian *Apocalypse of Paul* 14 (*Apocr. N.T.* 531), the Zadokite Fragments 7. 12 and 8. 20 (*Ap. and Ps.* 811 and 815).

NOTE V

PAUL AND "MYSTERIES"

μυστήριον transliterated into Hebrew became מִסְטָרִין. The change of the hard T (Teth) into the soft T (Tau) gave מִסְתְּרִין, "hidden things" or "secrets" [Bibl. מִסְתָּרִים, from the common root סתר (to hide)]. While the LXX translators of the Hebrew Canon do not use the word, it occurs eight times in Daniel, as the equivalent of רזא (of the dream of Nebuchadnezzar and its interpretation by Daniel); in the O.T. apocrypha 13 times. Of these Tobit 12. 7 and 11 contrast the "secret" of a king which must be kept hidden with the works of God which it is glorious to reveal; cf. Judith 2. 2 of the secret counsels of Nebuchadnezzar. In Wisd. 14. 15 and 23 it is used in its proper sense of "mystery-cults". This appears to be its only Biblical use in its proper sense, but the earlier part of the book of Wisdom (8. 4) uses the term *μύστις* of Wisdom. Wisd. 2. 22 and 6. 22 use it in a similar atmosphere, for the "mysteries" of the origin of Wisdom have a manifest resemblance not to any particular mystery-cult, but to the esoteric doctrines which these cults were supposed to symbolise. Thus here it has an apocalyptic sense with Alexandrine modification. Ecclus. 3. 18 uses the word of divine secrets. In Ecclus. 22. 22 and 27. 16 it is simply used of human secrets, as *ib.* 17 and 21, in Prov. 11. 13 (Symm.) and Prov. 20. 19 (Theod.). In Job 15. 8 (Symm., Theod.) and Ps. 25. 14 (Theod., Quint.) it is used of divine secrets. In 2 Macc. 13. 21 it is used of betraying a secret to the enemy.

Thus it is hardly correct to say (Armitage Robinson, *Ephesians* 234) that the word was a natural one to use, and that it is but sparingly used of divine secrets, since we have eight such usages in Daniel, two in Wisdom and one in Ecclesiasticus, and four usages of important royal or military secrets. These, with two cases in Wisdom where it is used in its proper classical sense, leave only four instances in one section of Ecclesiasticus of its use as an ordinary secret, together with two instances in other Greek versions (against two of the secrets of God). Is. 24. 16 in Q defies interpretation ("my mystery is mine" for רָזִי לִי (A.V. "leanness"); here we have a borrowing from Daniel LXX). The usage suggests rather a tendency for the word to decline from the sense of divine secrets into that of human ones.

The rabbinical usage shows a quite clear tendency to confuse the two words and to employ them indifferently with reference:

(1) To divine secrets, revealed to man or particular men in the past, or to Israel as a whole, or alternatively to things to be revealed hereafter by God. Thus *Pesikta Rabathi* 5 (ed. Friedmann, 14b) of the Oral Law revealed to Israel, not to the Christians; so in *Gen. R.* 50. 9, 78. 2, 98. 2, 3, Num. Rabba 20. 2; here the Greek form (Teth) replaces the Hebrew: cf. Targ. Ps.-Jon. Deut. 29. 5, where Kohut *Arukh* 5, f. 198 notes that the spelling with Tau shows that the Greek and Hebrew words were identified. For a Messianic "mystery" cf. *Cant. R.* on 2. 7.

(2) The word is used in the Hellenistic sense in *Lev. Rab.* 32. 4 probably of the "mystery" of the name of God and *Exod. R.* 19. 6 of the Passover; another nation shall not know its "mysteries". These are two of Philo's stock usages for depicting Judaism as the true "mystery-religion", cf. above, pp. 28 and 40. In *Tanhuma* (Stettin) לך לך 30. 19 the "secret" is circumcision (here סוד) in a sense between (1) and (2).

(3) Apparently the use with the simple meaning of "secret" is found with reasonable frequency.

The Pauline usage is quite constant, apart from Eph. 5. 32, for which cf. p. 183: this Epistle is not written by Paul. The other uses of the term in his writings (not including the Pastorals) all fall under the first of the rabbinical usages of a divine revelation, usually of the revelation of God made in Christ (e.g. 1 Cor. 2. 1 (v.l. *μαρτυρίου*) and 7, 4. 1, 13. 2, 14. 2 and Rom. 16. 25). In Rom. 11. 25 the "mystery" that some of Israel have been blinded till the Gentiles are brought in is very like the converse quoted above that the Oral Law is a "mystery" only revealed to Israel.

There is a deliberate contrast of Jewish and Greek usage in Col. 2. 2. The hidden treasures of wisdom and knowledge in Christ are the hidden treasures of Is. 45. 3, which in LXX are *θησαυροὶ ἀπόκρυφοι* and in the Hebrew are מסתרים. Paul has simply applied the ordinary rabbinical conflation of the two words in order to prove from Isaiah that all the "mysteries" of God are in Christ, and consequently that "mysteries" of the type advocated by his opponents can have no place in the Christian revelation. In his other uses of the word he follows the first of the three rabbinical usages noticed above. Some such conception was necessary for Judaism or Christianity, since both assumed a progressive revelation by the one God of perfect goodness of a full and complete religion. It followed as a corollary that He must in the past have kept some parts of the truth secret from all mankind, or from all but a few favoured individuals, for some good reason of His own. This was particularly necessary for Pauline Christianity, which had to explain both the promulgation of the Torah and its abolition. Clearly God had possessed secrets, which He had now revealed, or would reveal at some future date.

The same meaning appears in 1 En. 8. 3 (Syncellus' text) and 9. 6. In 2 Thess. 2. 7 there is a slight variation from the normal sense, in so far as the "mystery" is in a transitional state, partly revealed and partly hidden. As the "mystery" appears to have been Caligula's attempt to set up his statue in the Temple, and as his plan had been made known but not fulfilled, it was in the curious status of a half-revealed "mystery". In *Papp. Mag. Gr.* 5. 109, where the form is Jewish (cf. Norden, *Agnostos Theos* 187), though the content is heathen, we find a quite rabbinical use of the word: *ἐγώ εἰμι Μωϋσῆς ὁ προφήτης σου ᾧ παρέδωκας τὰ μυστήρια τὰ συντελούμενα Ἰστραήλ*. Here the phrase is exactly analogous to the first usage noticed above and to the Pauline. Probably the presumably heathen author had heard Jews describing the Torah as a "mystery".

INDICES

I. GREEK AND LATIN WRITERS

II. INSCRIPTIONS

III. PAPYRI

(See also *Papyri Magicae Graecae*, *Ægyptus*)

IV. JEWISH[1]

[1] References to the Pseudepigrapha of the O.T. are given from Charles' *Apocrypha and Pseudepigrapha*.

V. OLD TESTAMENT

VI. NEW TESTAMENT

VII. CHRISTIAN LITERATURE

[1] References to M. R. James, *The Apocryphal N.T.*, except where otherwise stated.

VIII. MANDEAN SCRIPTURES

(Tr. Lidzbarski: references in brackets to page and line of his translation)

IX. MODERN WRITERS, INCLUDING PERIODICALS, ETC.

X. NAMES AND SUBJECTS

[Names marked with * are also referred to in the indices of authors]